C. H. Hutchinson
COMPILER

THE CHRONICLES OF MIDDLETOWN

CONTAINING

A COMPILATION OF FACTS, BIOGRAPHICAL SKETCHES, REMINISCENCES, ANECDOTES, ETC.

CONNECTED WITH

THE HISTORY OF ONE OF THE OLDEST TOWNS IN

PENNSYLVANIA

C. H. Hutchinson

HERITAGE BOOKS
2012

HERITAGE BOOKS
AN IMPRINT OF HERITAGE BOOKS, INC.

Books, CDs, and more—Worldwide

For our listing of thousands of titles see our website
at
www.HeritageBooks.com

A Facsimile Reprint
Published 2012 by
HERITAGE BOOKS, INC.
Publishing Division
100 Railroad Ave. #104
Westminster, Maryland 21157

Copyright © 1906 C. H. Hutchinson

— Publisher's Notice —
In reprints such as this, it is often not possible to remove blemishes from the original. We feel the contents of this book warrant its reissue despite these blemishes and hope you will agree and read it with pleasure.

International Standard Book Numbers
Paperbound: 978-0-7884-3252-1
Clothbound: 978-0-7884-9254-9

An Open Letter to Mr. C. H. Hutchinson from Rev. George Whitman.

Buffalo, N. Y., *Oct. 18, 1904.*

My Dear Sir: Through the kindness of good friends in dear old Middletown, I have been permitted to read the articles published by you in the Journal, entitled "Chronicles of Middletown." To say that I have been interested, is to state very mildly the feeling of happiness that I have experienced, in common with many others of the readers of the Journal. We all owe you a debt of gratitude for your labor in searching out the old records, that will be but incompletely paid by the purchase of your forthcoming book. Human nature is sometimes slow in expressing its appreciation, and on this account I am all the more anxious to assure you of our gratitude for the good work you have done, and will continue to do. My residence in Middletown run from 1846 to 1862, and thus the most impressible years of my life were spent in association with Middletown people. A person remembers the associates and scenes of youth long after he has forgotten those encountered in after years. During the early days of the War of the Rebellion, I was the only newsboy in the town, and was the first to carry papers from house to house, and to sell them on the streets; and in this way I came to know more than half the people in the town. I flatter myself that people liked to see me, in those days, not that they cared much for me, but they were anxious to get the papers, filled as they always were with news of the great war. If suggestions are in order, I should advise that your "Chronicles" include a history of the newspapers of the town.

Many people await with eagerness the issue of your book, and every Middletowner of the past or present, ought to assist in making it a paying enterprise to the energetic and scholarly editor and publisher.

Gratefully yours,

Geo. Whitman.

INDEX.

Chapter.		Page.
I.	William Penn proposes to locate a city here,	9
II.	Indian tribe located here. Scotch Irish settle, and build churches,	11
III.	History of an old trading post,	12
IV.	Churches established by the Presbyterians nearly two hundred years ago,	14
V.	Swiss and German immigrants come here,	22
VI.	Copy of deed from sons of William Penn to John Fisher, in 1747, for site of town,	24
VII.	Settlement of Middletown. Town laid out,	27
VIII.	Indian depredations in vicinity. A parallel. Rewards for Indian scalps. Paxton boys organized. Indian massacres,	31
IX.	Sketch of Col. James Burd,	37
X.	Building of old Lutheran Church in 1767,	41
XI.	Title deed to Royalton by Thomas and John Penn,	45
XII.	Protest of Middletown settlers in 1774, against aggressions of British government. Names of volunteers in Revolutionary army,	48
XIII.	A shelter for Wyoming Valley fugitives from Indian massacre in 1778. Tax lists of 1778 and 1782,	53
XIV.	Oath of Allegiance. Northern boundary line supplies, etc. Navigation of Susquehanna. Slaves held here,	59
XV.	Sketch of George Frey and his mill. Litigation over. Stubbs' Furnaces,	63
XVI.	History of Union Canal. William Penn's proposals for a water-way,	67
XVII.	Turnpike. Main street. Conestoga Wagons,	69
XVIII.	Whiskey Insurrection. Major George Fisher,	71
XIX.	Town over a century ago. Taverns. John Penn stops here,	77
XX.	Biography of George Fisher, founder of Portsmouth,	80
XXI.	Proposed location of U. S. Capital. Address to President Adams. His reply. Middletown advertisements. Prices current in 1800. Procession and services on death of Washington. Wages,	87

Chapter.		Page.
XXII.	Portsmouth, founding of. Lots offered for sale. Navigation of Susquehanna Rafts. Boats. Lumber traffic, etc.,	93
XXIII.	Fairs in Middletown Swatara Bank. Middletown as it was over a century ago,	96
XXIV.	Looking backward continued. Post Office. Doctors. School teachers, etc.,	98
XXV.	Looking backward continued. Charlie Ross,	103
XXVI.	Looking backward continued,	107
XXVII.	Frey's Will. History of Emaus Orphan House. Litigation over. Scholars in 1841-47,	113
XXVIII.	Pennsylvania Canal. Breakwater. Mount Joy Railroad. First locomotive (The "John Bull"). The Pennsylvania Railroad,	124
XXIX.	The Mud Pike. The Middletown Furnace. The Slab Mill. The Lath Mill. The Furnace Saw Mill. The Feeder-dam,	127
XXX.	Middletown advertisements in 1802. Coal-oil. Fourth of July celebration,	130
XXXI.	Lafayette here. Advertisements a century ago. Yearly market. First Steamboat Line,	133
XXXII.	Turnpikes laid out. Cameron Furnace. Cameron Grist Mill. Arnold ferry-house,	135
XXXIII.	History of Methodist Episcopal Church and Sunday Schools,	139
XXXIV.	History of Bethel Church and Sunday School; list of scholars in,	144
XXXV.	Soldiers in War of 1812. Incorporation of Borough. Mexican War Volunteers,	148
XXXVI.	Middletown proposed as County-seat,	151
XXXVII.	History of St. Mary's Catholic Church,	154
XXXVIII.	Petition for road from Pineford to Harris' Ferry in 1745. Middletown Militia Companies,	157
XXXIX.	History of United Brethren Church. The Aymish. The Dunkards. The Mennonites,	160
XL.	History of St. Michael's Protestant Episcopal Church. Old Saw-Mills,	164
XLI.	Burgesses and Councilmen of Borough,	166
XLII.	Water-right from Frey's Mill-race,	170
XLIII.	Citizens' Meeting at opening of Civil War, 1861. Extracts from Dauphin Journal,	172
XLIV.	Fire Companies,	178
XLV.	War Record of Company G, Thirty-fifth Regiment, Pennsylvania Volunteers. Roll of Company,	182

Index. vii

Chapter.		Page.
XLVI.	Middletown Volunteers in Eighty-seventh Regiment, Pennsylvania Volunteers; in Ninety-second Regiment, Ninth Cavalry,	196
XLVII.	Middletown Volunteers in Ninety-third Regiment, Pennsylvania Volunteers,	207
XLVIII.	Middletown Volunteers in Thirty-sixth Regiment, in Company G, Forty-first Regiment, Twelfth Reserve,	212
XLIX.	Middletown Volunteers in Forty-third Regiment, First Artillery,	215
L.	Middletown Volunteers in Eightieth Regiment, Seventh Cavalry. In Eighty-third Regiment. In One Hundred and First Regiment. In One Hundred and Thirteenth Regiment, Twelfth Cavalry. In One Hundred and Seventeenth Regiment, Thirteenth Cavalry,	218
LI.	Middletown Volunteers in Company H, One Hundred and Twenty-seventh Regiment,	222
LII.	Middletown Volunteers in One Hundred and Eighty-seventh Regiment. In One Hundred and Ninetieth Regiment. In One Hundred and Ninety-first Regiment. In Company C, One Hundred and Ninety-second Regiment. In One Hundred and Ninety-fourth Regiment. In Two Hundredth Regiment. In Two Hundred and First Regiment,	229
LIII.	Middletown Volunteers in Twenty-second United States Colored Regiment (Company G, Fifth Massachusetts Cavalry),	238
LIV.	Middletown Volunteers in other Regiments. In Quartermaster's Department, U. S. A.,	240
LV.	Roll of Militia Companies in 1862 (Guards, Cavalry),	243
LVI.	Roll of Militia Companies in 1863. (Three Companies),	247
LVII.	Secret Orders organized in Middletown,	250
LVIII.	Musical Organizations in town. G. A. R. Post,	257
LVIX.	Middletown Cemetery. Banks. Newspapers,	261
LX.	Biographical Sketch of Col. James Young,	264

OLD MIDDLETOWN

In the year 1690 William Penn published in London, England, the following, which I give in its entirety, as it is of special interest to the citizens of Middletown:

SOME PROPOSALS FOR A SECOND SETTLEMENT IN THE PROVINCE OF PENNSYLVANIA.

"Whereas, I did, about nine years past, propound the selling of several parts or shares of land, upon that side of the Province of Pennsylvania next Delaware river, and setting out of a place upon it for the building of a city, by the name of Philadelphia; and that divers persons closed with those proposals, who, by their ingenuity, industry and charge, have advanced that city, from a wood, to a good forwardness of building (there being above one thousand houses finished in it) and that the several plantations and towns begun upon the land, bought by those first undertakers, are also in a prosperous way of improvement and enlargement (insomuch as last year ten sail ships were freighted there, with the growth of the province, for Barbadoes, Jamaica, &c., besides what came directly for this kingdom). It is now my purpose to make another settlement upon the river Susquehannagh, that runs into the bay of Chesapeake, and bears about fifty miles west from the river Delaware, as appears by the common maps of the English Dominion in America. There I design to lay out a plan for the building of another city, in the most convenient place for communication with the former plantations on the East; which by land is as good as done already, a way being laid out between the two rivers very exactly and conveniently, at least three years ago; and which will not be hard to do by water, by the benefit of the river Scoulkill; for a Branch of that river (the Tulpehocken) lies near a branch that runs into Susquehannagh river (the Swatara)* and is the Common Course of the Indians with their Skins and Furrs into our Parts, and to the Provinces of East and West Jersey, and New York, from the West and Northwest part of the continent from whence they bring them. "And I do also intend that every one who shall be a Purchaser in this proposed settlement, shall have a proportionable Lot in the City to build a House or Houses upon; which Town-Ground, and the Shares of Land that shall be bought of me, shall be delivered clear of all Indian Pretensions; for it has been my way from the first to purchase their title from them, and so settle with their consent.

---

*The distance between the two creeks (connected by the Union canal in 1827) is about six miles.

The Shares I dispose of, containe each Three Thousand Acres for £100 and for the greater or lesser quantities after that rate: The acre of that Province is according to the Statute of the 33rd of Edw. I. And no acknowledgment or Quit Rent chall be paid by the Purchasers till five years after a settlement be made upon their Lands, and that only according to the quantity of acres so taken up and seated, and not otherwise; and only then to pay but one shilling for every hundred acres forever. And further I do promise to agree with every Purchaser that shall be willing to treat with me between this and next spring, upon all such reasonable conditions as shall be thought necessary for their accommodation, intending, if God please to return with what speed I can, and my family with me, in order to our future Residence.

"To conclude, that which particularly recommends this Settlement, is the known goodness of the soyll and cituation of the Land, which is high and not mountainous; also the Pleasantness, and Largeness of the River, being clear and not rapid, and broader than the Thames at London bridge, many miles above the Place intended for this Settlement; and runs (as we are told by the Indians) quite through the Province, into which many fair rivers empty themselves. The sorts of Timber that grow there are chiefly oak, ash, chestnut, walnut, cedar and poplar. The native Fruits are papaws, grapes, mulberries, chestnuts, and several sorts of walnuts. There are likewise great quantities of Deer, and especially Elks, which are much bigger than our common Red Deer, and use that River in Herds. And Fish there is of divers sorts, and very large and good, and in great plenty.

"If any Persons please to apply themselves to me by letter in relation to this affair, they may direct them to Robert Ness, Scrivener in Lumber street in London for Philip Ford, and suitable answers will be returned by the first opportunity.

"But that which recommends both this Settlement in particular, and the Provinces in general, is a late Pattent obtained by divers Eminent Lords and Gentlemen for that Land that lies north of Pennsylvania up to the 46th degree and a half, because their Traffic and Intercourse will be chiefly through Pennsylvania, which lies between that Province and the Sea. We have also the comfort of being the Centre of all the English colonies upon the Continent of America, as they lie from the North East parts of New England to the most Southerly parts of Carolina, being above 1000 miles upon the Coast.

There are also Instructions printed for information of such as intend to go, or send servants, or families thither, which way they may proceed with most ease and advantage, both here and there, in reference to Passage, Goods, Utensils, Buildings, Husbandry, Stock, Subsistence, Traffick, &c., being the effect of their expence and experience that have seen the Fruit of their Labors.

"WM. PENN."

II.

In 1676 the remnant of the Susquehannas, a once powerful Indian nation, worn out by long contests with the Iroquois, and decimated by pestilence, finally disappeared.

In 1678 the Shawanese, a southern tribe, by permission of the Six Nations and of the proprietary Government of Pennsylvania removed from Carolina and planted themselves on the Susquehanna. At that time "so desolate was the wilderness that a vagabond tribe could wander undisturbed from the Cumberland river to the Alabama; from the headwaters of the Santee to the Susquehanna." The Conoys or Ganawese, the Nanticokes from Maryland, and the Conestogas all located in this vicinity, that is from Pequea creek to the Conodoguinet.

There was an Indian town at Dekanoagh (about the site of Bainbridge), near the mouth of Conoy creek, and another near the mouth of the Swadahara. (Swatara.) This latter creek seems to have been a favorite one with the Indians. In the meadow immediately north of the bridge where the old turnpike, the king's highway, crosses it, flint arrow and spear heads, and stone axes used to be frequently picked up.

In 1701, at a council held in Philadelphia, "on the 22nd of 2nd month," the "Susquehannagh" Indians made a treaty with Wm. Penn. Among the chiefs present was Weewhinjough, chief of the (Conoy) Ganawese.

In 1705, James Logan, with several others, visited the Ganawese settled some miles above Conescoga, at a place called Conojaghera, above the fort, to learn the news among them, give them advice, and exchange presents.

July 22nd, 1707, Governor Evans laid before the Council an account of his journey among the Susquehanna Indians. He speaks of "Dekanoagah about nine miles distant from Pequehan." Here the Governor was present at a meeting of Shaois, Senequois, and Canoise Indians, and the Nanticoke Indians from seven towns.

At that time this part of the State was much more densely wooded than the eastern; in this immediate vicinity was the belt of pine that gave its name to the ford which now the turnpike bridge spans, and from which the first settlers of Middletown drew their supplies of building material. Tradition says that in the neighborhood of the present centre square stood the Indian town marked on old maps as Swahadowri.

The first white men who visited these parts were probably French Indian traders, who came down from Canada near the close of the seventeenth century, as the colonial records allude to them in the beginning of 1700.

The English and Irish were probably the first settlers here; there is no record fixing the exact date of their coming, but it must have been early in the century, for in 1720 they were numerous enough to erect churches.*

These Irish, better known as the "Scotch-Irish," were descendants of those Scotch Presbyterians, who, to avoid the persecutions of the Episcopal church, had fled to the north of Ireland about the sixteenth century; and who, becoming dissatisfied there, and hearing of the religious toleration guaranteed by Penn, sought a home in this country.

They were soon followed (about 1740) by the Dutch, (so-called in all the colonial documents) who were no more Dutch than their predecessors were Irish, but came from the upper parts of Germany.

The first of this nationality who settled here also fled from religious persecutions. They were Moravians (Mennonites), Dunkards, Schwenckfelders, Lutherans, German Reformed, etc.

About 1720 commenced a traffic which continued until nearly the close of the century. Agents called Newlanders were sent to Germany by prominent firms of Philadelphia, to entice emigrants to Pennsylvania by false representations; the offer of lands, free transportation, &c. They were brought over by the ship load, were known as "Redemptioners," and, upon arrival, put up at auction, and knocked down to the highest bidder, for a three years' term, in payment of their passage.

A class of speculators called "Soul-Drivers" soon arose, who bought them up in lots of fifty or more, and driving them through the country, disposed of them to the farmers. (For the heirs of one of those purchased in Middletown, who afterwards married, moved away and was lost track of, a considerable property is waiting.)

The traffic in white slaves paid better than that in black. In many instances they were treated worse, and when their time had nearly expired, being accused of some misdemeanor, were sentenced by complaisant justices to a further period of servitude. The trade was brisk for awhile, and there were few householders who did not own one or more; it finally died out about 1785 or '90.

III.

In this connection it might be as well to state that Susquehanna is derived from an Indian name, Sa-os-qua-ha-na-unk, meaning "long crooked river." Swatara is likewise purely aboriginal. Heckwelder supposes it to be a corruption of the Delaware name Sa-hadow-a into some other tribal dialect. In the early surveys it is written Swa-hatowra, later Swatorah, finally it became Swatara. Swa-ha-dow-ry, meaning, "where we feed on eels." Peter Bazillion and Martin Chartier, French Indian traders, were at the mouth of the Swatara previous to 1704. Later, Gordon Howard opened a trading post here. We have no data as to when he first came, but in 1718 he was "at the mouth of Swatara, in Conestoga township, Chester county," and he was one or

*See later article on the Presbyterian Church.

The Presbyterian Church.

First United Brethren Church.

CHRONICLES OF MIDDLETOWN. 13

two seasons here with his son and his partner, James McFarland, in 1719-20.*

Of the many who traverse South Union street, between the subway and the (now filled in) outlet lock, few can have failed to notice the quaint building that stands, isolated, on the eastern side of the thoroughfare. Its weather-beaten appearance, old-fashioned dormer windows and general look of age, point it out as a relic of the past. And that old house has a history. Sixty years ago it was known as the "Ferry house," and this was one of the two points where travelers by the river road were ferried across the Swatara. But it has an earlier and more romantic record. It was a stockaded and garrisoned frontier post in the earlier part of the eighteenth century. Afterwards, during the Revolution, some of the Hessian prisoners captured at Trenton, were quartered here. To old inhabitants, some of whom have recently been gathered to their fathers, it was known as the "Barracks." It is probable that several superstructures have been erected upon its venerable stone walls. Their record is lost. The accumulations of soil, deposited there during the digging of the Union Canal, the basin, and by the river, have gradually encroached on and hidden them, until, on three sides, they are but a foot or two above the surface, while the fourth is entirely removed. The old loop-holes which pierced them, about a foot square in the inside, and sloping to three inches in width by a foot long on the outside, have been bricked up, but seventeen years ago some of them were as intact as when the pioneers fashioned them, and to the student of history they told the story of our forefathers. Later constructions have materially changed the appearance of the vicinage, but one can yet see in what an admirably defensive position, against savage attacks, it was located. What tales could those old walls tell of wild carousal and wilder forray—of savage feasts and dances—of battles and skirmishes—of besiegers and besieged. The dust of assailants and assailed have long since commingled—the frontier, which it once aided in defending, has disappeared. Where the war whoop once rang, is heard the whistle of the locomotive and fields of grain wave over leagues of ground, which, when this redoubt was erected, were covered by virgin forest. The historian has hitherto, failed to mention this post, and its only record is tradition.†

---

*He married Rachel, daughter of Robert McFarland, who lived on Little Chickies creek, near Mount Joy. In 1722, Howard resided about a mile east of Springville, and owned several hundred acres of land. Was County Commissioner in 1729, 1730, 1731. The family was a very prominent one, none of whom have descendants residing in this vicinity.

†In the possession of Dr. D. W. C. Laverty, is an extensive collection, consisting of at least a thousand Indian relics, all (with one exception) gathered in Middletown, and its immediate neighborhood.

NOTE.—Since article No. 4 was written the walls of the "Old Ferry House" have been repaired, and the loop-holes formed therein for defensive purposes, filled up. They were originally probably ten in number—three on the north and south sides, respectively, and two each on the east and west ends of the building. They were about five feet above the ground; 12x3 inches on the outside of the walls and 12x12 inches on the inside.

There must have been settlements here then, for in an account of a "treaty held at Conestogue" in 1721, published by the Proprietary Government, it is stated that the "village of Conestogue (Lancaster), lies about 70 miles distance (from Philadelphia), almost directly west of the city; and the land thereabout being exceedingly rich, it is now surrounded with divers fine plantations or farms, where they raise quantities of wheat, flax and hemp, without the help of any dung." This is a very good evidence that the emigrants had made improvements of the best character some years before 1721. As the country was "very heavily wooded" much labor and time must have been expended to present "fine plantations," and it is certain that they extended further west than the present city of Lancaster.

Another proof that these settlements were of importance is, that as early as 1720, preparations had been made by the Presbyterians to erect places of worship. The population was so numerous that a demand for a State road was made in 1731. One was finally located in 1736, from Lancaster, via the Swatara, to Shippensburg, connecting with the one between Lancaster and Philadelphia.

May 10th, 1729, Lancaster county was erected. June 9th, of the same year, it was divided into townships. Of these "Derry township, beginning at the mouth of Conewago, thence up Sasquehannah to the mouth of Swataaro, thence up Swataaro to the mouth of Quetepehello, thence south on a direct line to Conewago, and down the same to the place of beginning." "Peshtank—beginning at the mouth of Swataaro, thence up the river to Kehtohtoning mill above Peter Allen's, thence eastward by the south side of said mill to the meridian of Quetopohello mouth, thence on a south course to the mouth of the same at Swataaro, and down Swataaro to the place of beginning." Are now both in Dauphin county.

IV.

Presbyterian Church.

Within a radius of eight miles around Middletown, are the sites and remains of three churches; all organized at least forty years prior to the Revolution, and around whose crumbling and fast disappearing ruins cluster many memories of the past. In this locality the Scotch-Irish settled; and when the log cabin was built, and a few acres of forest cleared, those rigid Presbyterians erected their temples of worship, and thus arose the churches of Derry, Paxton and Conewago.

They were earnest people, those early settlers of Middletown; they kept Sunday as a holy day, and although not possessing the austerity of the Puritans, but on the contrary, jovial, generous, and hospitable; yet retained enough of the old Scotch leaven, to make them observe it with a strictness, which perhaps, in these later days of latitudinarianism, materialism and infidelity, it were well to emulate. Then the horse, the ox, the man servant, and the maid servant, must rest from all unnecessary labor, and church be visited at least once a day. Long rides or walks eight miles in one direction, to Derry; eight in another, to Paxton; or four in another, to Conewago, no matter for ice, sleet, hail or rain; the drifted snow or the bottomless mud; the heat of midsummer, or the cold of winter—the stern frontiersman would have deemed his chances of Heaven lessened, had he omitted this sacred duty. So with musket loaded, and bullet pouch and powder horn well filled, he set forth, either on horseback, with wife on pillion behind him, or on foot, with the whole family trudging beside. At each clearing others joined, and they traveled on together; for the wild beast and wilder Indian lurked near, and the churchyard sometimes claimed precedence of the church.

Derry Church—This congregation was organized in 1719, and in 1720 the house of worship was erected. The land, forty acres, was deeded by William and Thomas Penn several years later. The building was constructed of oak logs two feet thick, which were covered with hemlock boards on the outside. The pews and floors were of yellow pine, cherry and oak. The pulpit was low and narrow, crescent shaped, and entered by narrow steps from the east side. Above it, on the south side, was a large window which contained thirty-eight panes, made of glass of different sizes; the sash was made of lead, and was brought from England. Pegs were stuck in the wall inside, for the men to hang their muskets and when in 1883 it became necessary to take the decaying building down, many a bullet was found imbedded in the oak logs. The first services we have any record of were held in April, 1724. The congregation was addressed by Revs. Geo. Gillespie, David Evans and Robert Cross. Among the members present at that time were: Rowland Chambers, Thomas and William Clarke, James Galbraith, Patrick and Robert Campbell, John Mitchell, William McBey, James Quigley, William Hay, Robert Moody, Malcolm Kerr, Thomas and Hugh Black, James Harris, William McCord, Morgan Jones, David McClure, James McFarlane, Alexander Hutchinson, John and Benjamin Boyd, James Hamilton, John McCosh and sister.

The old stone step at the main entrance was greatly worn by the feet of the thousands who had passed over it. In the graveyard adjoining, the sandstone tombstones have so crumbled away, that many of the inscriptions cannot be read. The oldest decipherable is of 1734. Rev. William Bertram, and Rev. John Roan, were both buried here, the former in 1746, the latter in 1775.

Paxton Church was organized at an early period, at least prior to 1725, and Rev. James Anderson, of Donegal, preached there one-fifth of his time until 1729. In 1732, Rev. William Bertram was minister of this, as well as Derry church; he was paid about £60, "half in money, the other half in hemp, linen, yarn, or linen cloth, at market price."

Rev. John Elder, a graduate of Edinburgh University, succeeded him in 1738.

Mr. Elder, who was also a colonel in the Provincial service, used to take his musket with him into the pulpit. On one occasion the Indians surrounded the meeting house while he was preaching, but having counted the guns, retired without making an attack. At another time they arrived by mistake on Monday instead of Sunday, and after waiting several days, were discovered, and left by way of Indiantown Gap, murdering a number of persons on the Swatara, and carrying off several prisoners.

The custom of seating women at the inner end of the pews exclusively, is said to have originated in these times, when the frontiersman was required to be ready to spring to the doors, gun in hand, at the first note of alarm.

There were three entrances to the church; the pulpit used to stand in the middle of the house, fronting the southern entrance; it was afterwards built against the north wall, high above the heads of the worshippers. One aisle ran from east to west, and another from the southern door to the pulpit. The pews were not uniform, each being built by the family occupying it. Two large ten-plate stoves were in the long aisle, the smoke from which ascended by pipes to the loft, and found its way out through a hole in the roof.

Southeast of the church is the burial ground, surrounded by a substantial stone wall. Here rest the Elders, Espys, Sturgeons, McClures, Maclays, Rutherfords, Simpsons, Harrises, Grays, Gilmores, and generations of the English and Scotch-Irish settlers, who once inhabited this section of the country, and to whom Middletown was the business, political and social centre. Here also lie the remains of Gen. James Cronch and Gen. Michael Simpson, Revolutionary heroes. Men are here entombed who fought at Quebec, and all through the War of Independence.

Conewago Church—This church was located about four miles from Middletown near where the village of Gainsburg (laid out in 1812), now stands. There is no account of its erection, but in 1741, Rev. Samuel Black was their regular preacher, indicating that a church had been built previous to that time. This structure had probably fallen to decay, for another was erected, the only record of which, that has come down to us, is that its builder was killed by falling from its roof in 1745, and was buried in the graveyard attached. It could have had but a transitory existence, for in the recollection of old Presbyterians, still living, their parents and grandparents went to Derry and Paxton. The land connected with this church is contiguous to, or rather enclosed by, a tract of over two hundred acres, which James Clark held by a warrant from the Land Office, dated August 1, 1743. It was afterwards patented to Robert Spear in 1785. The following memorandum, accompanying a draft, will explain itself:

"Resurveyed for Robert Spear, August 18th, 1785, the above tract of

Ann Street M. E. Church.

land, containing two hundred and two acres and five-eighths and allowances, situate in Derry township, Dauphin county, late Lancaster, by warrant granted to James Clark, 28th of July, 1743.
(Signed) "BERTRAM GALBRAITH.
"N. B.—The above square piece of nineteen by twenty perches is a Presbyterian meeting house and burying grounds.
"To John Lukens, S. G.
"Returned into the Land Office the third November, 1785, for John Lukens, Esq., S. G.
"EDWARD LYNCH."
This tract of land afterwards passed, successively, through the hands of Robert Coleman, Robert Dempsey, John Conrad, John Fisher, George Hess and Abraham Rutt, to John Olwine.

So this church lot is in the midst of a farm, repeatedly sold and transferred. The title, however, to the old graveyard, is by law vested in the Presbytery of Carlisle, who should take charge of it, and have it properly enclosed. What has been supposed to have been a church foundation, is a dilapidated wall inclosing a burial place.

We have thus given a brief history of three churches, each of which numbered among their communicants, and were partly supported by the early inhabitants of Middletown.

Pastors and people are all gone, but in the well filled graveyards close by, rest the ancestors of many families whose names have since become well known throughout our country. The Harrisons, the McLeans, the Forsters, the Ramseys, the Dixons, the Allens, the Fergusons, the Stewarts, the Polks, the Calhounes, the Hamptons, the Wilsons, the Pettigrews, and a host of others—pioneers in Western Pennsylvania, in Virginia, the Carolinas, Georgia, Ohio, Kentucky, Missouri, California, and elsewhere. The lands they once settled, know them no more, and only in the musty records of the past, in ruined walls and moss-covered tombstones, can the historian find traces of the departed glories of Derry, Paxton and Conewago.*

These churches were then considered at a reasonable distance from, and sufficient for the wants of the inhabitants of Middletown. Services were, however, frequently held in the German Lutheran church by Presbyterian preachers, among whom were Revs. N. R. Snowden and James R. Sharon. There must have been some organization among the members here, however, for the old Presbyterian graveyard on High street, consists of two lots, numbered 94 and 95; and Lot No. 95 in the plan of the town still extant, is marked "Burying-ground;" and in his list of ground rents due from lots in the town, opposite the number 95 is the following entry: "*Granted by George Frey in 1773. N. B., inquire whether for a church-yard or burying-ground.*" Colonel James Burd and his wife were buried here, the latter in 1785, and the former

---

*Since the matter contained in this chapter was written, (January, 1887) Paxton church has been remodeled, and a modern edifice erected.—C. H. H.

in 1793. Lot No. 94, is marked as owned by Swineford, and no ground-rent due from it. The title of the church comes through Swineford. The brief of title is as follows: Thomas and Richard Penn to John Fisher, February 14th, 1747; January 17th, 1759, John Fisher and Grace his wife, to George Fisher; March 1st, 1761, George Fisher and Hannah his wife to Joseph Greenwood; October 27th, 1766, Joseph Greenwood and Mary his wife to Thomas Carmicle; July 29th, 1770, Thomas Carmicle and wife to Albright Swineford; December 2nd, 1795, Albright Swineford to J. Russel; June 7th, 1802, J. Russel and Frances his wife to John McCammon, William Crabb and Edward Crouch, "Trustees of the English Presbyterian Congregation or Society of Middletown," for five shillings.

The Burds, McClures, Kirkpatricks, and McClanegans were among the first Presbyterian families who settled about here, and had large tracts of land. In the early part of the present century the Crabbs, McCammons, Crouches, Jordans, and Elders, took their places, and later, the McKibbens, McNairs, and Kendigs.

We have no data, however, respecting any church organization prior to 1850. The records are lost, having probably been among the private papers of some one of the original members, who are all dead.

April 10th, 1850, the Presbytery in session at Carlisle appointed a committee to visit Middletown, and confer with the Presbyterians there as to the practicability of building a church. At a meeting in June following, of the Presbytery, the committee reported favorably. On October 29th, the Presbytery met here, when a petition signed by Daniel Kendig, Sarah Kendig, Robert F. Snoddy, Edward Burgett, Dr. B. J. Wiestling, Matilda Wiestling, Sara Allen, Mary E. Wilt, and David Thompson was presented, asking for the organization of a church here. The elders then elected were Dr. B. J. Wiestling, Daniel Kendig, and Edward Burgett. Thus was organized the first regular congregation since the original one had expired half a century before. Supply preaching was had in the brick church on Water street ("Christ church").

April 8th, 1851, Rev. John Cross was authorized to solicit funds for erecting a church edifice; on June 10th he was called as pastor and installed June 23rd. Mr. Cross died suddenly, August 22nd, at Dickinson, Cumberland county, while raising money to build the church, and his remains were brought to Dr. B. J. Wiestling's house, from which the burial took place.

On March 31st, 1852, C. W. King conveyed to Daniel Kendig, lots Nos. 63 and 64, upon which to erect the church. On August 24th, 1854, Mr. Kendig conveyed the same to Dr. B. J. Wiestling, Davis Thompson, Dr. J. C. Whitehill, C. H. Roe, George Crist, Jeremiah Rohrer and D. E. Martin, in trust for the church and congregation. A building was immediately erected. It was a neat brick edifice; with a basement for Sunday school and lecture room. Its builders were Messrs. Leedom and Fisher. August 28th, 1858, the congregation was incorporated. In 1860 an act was passed by the Legislature, and ap-

CHRONICLES OF MIDDLETOWN. 19

proved by Governor Wm. F. Packer, March 31, authorizing the congregation to sell the old graveyard on High street. In March, 1864, the trustees purchased of Dr. Mercer Brown, a piece of ground in Lower Swatara township, adjoining Middletown, of 77 4-10 perches, on which they erected a parsonage.

In 1852 the Rev. O. O. McLean became pastor, and continued to April, 1854. In October, 1855, Rev. John W. White was called, and remained until the spring of 1858. His successor was Rev. T. K. Davis, from March, 1858, until May 4th, 1863, when Rev. C. Ferriday became pastor. (During his absence, from ill health, Rev. H. T. Lee, of Philadelphia, preached.) Mr. Ferriday's continued sickness compelled him to resign, and January 25th, 1865, Rev. H. L. Rex was called. He was installed June 6th, 1865, and remained until May, 1874. In January, 1875, Rev. Daniel McAfee became pastor, and resigned in January, 1876. For some time Rev. A. D. Mitchell supplied the pulpit, but being appointed post-chaplain in the United States army, Rev. Robert P. Gibson acted as pastor until April 14th, 1878, when Rev. D. C. Meeker was called; he declined, and on May 20th, Rev. Malachi C. Bailey became pastor. He resigned in 1880, and his successor was Rev. William G. McDonald, who took charge November 1st, 1881, and resigned April 10th, 1884. He was succeeded by the Rev. John Groff, the present pastor.

In 1889 the church building needing repairs, it was decided to erect a new edifice. The last service in the old church was in June, 1889.

The new building, which is in the Gothic style of architecture, is built of brownstone. Cost, $20,000. Was dedicated in October, 1890. A pipe organ was installed in 1895. The church is a handsome edifice with several memorial windows contributed by the Camerons, Kendigs and others. Has a seating capacity of 500.

The Sunday school connected with the church was organized in the latter part of the year 1851, in the basement of "Christ Church." (In which building the congregation then worshipped.) In the summer of 1852 it was moved to the Emaus Institute (then at the junction of Union and Spring streets), and in November of the same year, on the completion of the church, to the room it at present occupies, in the basement of that building.

The records of the school are incomplete, many of them having been lost. There have been but three superintendents since its organization, viz: Daniel Kendig, Benjamin Kendig and John W. Rewalt, the latter being the present incumbent. The superintendent of the infant school is Miss Annie E. Kendig.

When George Fisher planned Middletown, he seems to have intended to aid and encourage the establishment of churches of all denominations, as, in laying out the town, ground was appropriated for sects which at the time had no existence in the place; as, for instance, to the Moravian

20 CHRONICLES OF MIDDLETOWN.

and Episcopal churches. The Moravian lot adjoined those of the Presbyterians. They afterwards sold it, and it came into the possession of George Smuller.

After Mr. Fisher had disposed of a portion of the lots, he sold out his remaining interest in the town to George Frey. In some instances Frey afterwards transferred these properties to the church organizations for whom they were intended.

GERMAN REFORMED CHURCH.

This branch of the Presbyterian, or Calvinist, church was comparatively strong in this State at an early period. In 1743, the Reformed Synods of Holland proposed to the Presbyterian Synod of Philadelphia, a union of the Presbyterians, Dutch Reformed and German Reformed churches in America. This proposition the Presbyterians declined, and thus these churches, differing in but slight doctrinal points, remained separate.

There was a respectable number of members of the German Reformed church in and near Middletown at an early period, and ministers of this denomination sometimes preached from the pulpit of old St. Peter's Lutheran church. That an organization was proposed is evident from the fact that on May 22nd, 1770, George Frey and Catherine, his wife, sold lot No. 143, situated on the northwest corner of High and Pine streets, to John Backenstow (Bachentose), saddler, and Philip Baltimore (Parthemore), blacksmith, for five shillings, as a site for a German Calvinist or Presbyterian church and burying ground. The deed was acknowledged before Justice James Burd and witnessed by John Cline and James Walker. In this graveyard the dead of the denomination were buried for a number of years.

How They Celebrated the 4th of July in Middletown 106 Years Ago.

MIDDLETOWN, *July 5th, 1798.*

Yesterday being the twenty-second anniversary of American independence, in pursuance of notice previously given, the Light Infantry Company of this town, commanded by Captain Wolfley, paraded in the public square, for the purpose of celebrating the great festival in commemoration of American emancipation. From thence they marched, attended by a number of respectable citizens, to a commodious sylvan retreat on the bank of the Susquehanna, called the Locust Grove, on the plantation of George Fisher, Esq., to partake of an elegant repast, which was served up in a manner perfectly suited to the circumstances of time

St. Peter's Church, (erected 1767) Middletown, Pa.

St. Mary's Church, H. M. Herzog, pastor.

and place. During the repast (at which Major George Toot presided), the greatest harmony prevailed, and the most perfect festivity was conspicuous in every countenance. After dinner the following truly federal toasts were drank with the utmost cordiality, each accompanied by a discharge from Captain Wolfley's Light Infantry.

1. The Day Which Gave Birth to American Independence—may the anniversary thereof exhibit a perpetuation of the principles which gave rise to the same, throughout the remotest generations.

2. The President of the United States—may that distinguished wisdom and patriotic virtue, which contributed to promote him to the eminent dignity of first magistrate, continue to guide and influence him to discharge the great trust reposed in him, as may be most conducive of the happiness of the United States and the good of mankind.

3. The Constitution of the United States—may the blessings derived therefrom be so justly estimated by the American people, that we may be stimulated to preserve inviolate, and transmit the same unimpaired to our posterity, at the expense of our lives and fortunes—if necessary.

4. The Legislature of the United States—may wisdom direct their councils, unanimity crown their proceedings, and the welfare and prosperity of the United States be the result of their deliberations.

5. The American people—may they ever profess wisdom to discern, and fortitude to repel, the insidious machinations of foreign and domestic factions.

6. The Navy of the United States—may the spirit of '76 animate each warrior's breast with ardent zeal to guard our glorious constitution as the Israelites did the ark of old.

7. The Illustrious Washington, Prince of Patriots—may his long and arduous exertions in the service of his country meet their deserved reward, long life, health and prosperity in this world, and eternal happiness in the next.

8. Our Envoys to France—may the result of their mission prove an effectual antidote against the baneful influence of French policy, French enthusiasm and French fraternity.

9. Our Diplomatic Agents—may the disgrace of Monroe hold forth an instructive lesson to future ministers, that they may never deviate from the genuine principles of their instructions, nor listen to the insinuating but invidious flattery of foreign governments.

10. The Constituted Authorities—detection and universal detestation to those men who betray and calumniate the government they were chosen to administer and sworn to maintain.

11. Our National Character—may its purity never be contaminated by the polluted breath of faction, sedition or disaffection.

12. Agriculture—may she continue to improve and flourish under the auspicious sanction of wise rules and wholesome laws, until all nations shall acknowledge our affluence and esteem our friendship as profitable.

13. Commerce—may she diffuse her liberal benefits over the whole earth, protected and encouraged by all nations, and may her enemies

meet universal execration, and be excluded from the enjoyment of any of her gifts.

14. Arts and Sciences—may the cultivation thereof be assiduously pursued and amply encouraged by every description of men, till the United States become the seat of universal knowledge, religion and purity.

15. The Fair Daughters of America—may their charms never want virtue to detect artful blandishments of knaves and traitors.

V.

Although no actual settlements had been made in Lancaster county prior to 1709, a few Indian traders had (as has been previously mentioned) established their posts on the Susquehanna river.

In the year 1706, a number of Swiss Mennonites went to England and made an agreement with William Penn for lands to be taken up in this colony.

In 1709 the pioneers of this company emigrated to America and purchased a tract of ten thousand acres, for which they paid five hundred pounds sterling, and one shilling quit rent yearly, forever, for every hundred acres of the said ten thousand.* Their warrant was dated October 10th, 1710. On April 27th, 1711, the land was sub-divided among them, into so many parts as they had previously agreed upon.

The descendants of the Puritans boast that their ancestors fled from their persecutors, willing to encounter perils in the wilderness and perils by the heathen, rather than be deprived by ruthless intolerance of the free exercise of their religion. The descendants of the Swiss Mennonites, who amid hardships and trials, made the first settlements in the west end of Chester (afterwards Lancaster) county, can lay claim to more. Their ancestors did not seek for themselves and theirs only, the unmolested exercise of their faith and worship, but they in turn did not persecute others who differed from them in religious opinion. They pleaded for religious toleration, and their practice confirmed it.

One of these pioneers was Martin Kendig, ancestor of the Kendig family of Union street, Middletown. He was a man of considerable importance among the colonists, and owned a large amount of land, one

---

*Owing to Penn's pecuniary embarrassment he was obliged to mortgage his province. The mortgagees appointed commissioners to superintend their interests, viz: Edward Shippen, Samuel Carpenter, Richard Hill, and James Logan, who repaid the loan from the sale of lands and from his quit rents. Purchasers remonstrated against these quit rents as a burden unprecedented in any other American colony, but were told that by complying they supported the dignity of the government, and would be freed from other taxes.

These quit rents were not uniform, they rated from one shilling per hundred acres, to six shillings per annum. They were (with few exceptions) abolished in 1779.

tract of 1,060 acres, another of 530 acres, another of 265 acres. His dwelling was constructed of hewn walnut logs. It withstood the tooth of time for one hundred and ten years and had it not been removed in 1841, might have weathered the elements for a much longer period. Although the colonists had scarcely been fairly seated, they thought of their old homes, their country and friends. They remembered those that were in bonds and suffered adversity, and devised means to send some one to the Vaterland, to bring the residue of their families, their kindred and brothers in a land of trouble and oppression, to their new home, where peace reigned and the comforts of life could not fail. A meeting of the society was called, and Martin Kendig having offered, was sent to Europe, whence, after an absence of some months, he returned accompanied by a company of Swiss and some Germans. With this accession the settlement was considerably augmented, and now numbered about thirty families. They lived in the midst of the Mingo or Conestoga, Pequea and Shawnese Indians. This little colony improved their lands, planted orchards, erected dwellings, and a meeting house and school house, in which religious and secular instruction could be imparted. The Mennonites never invested money in rearing stately temples, or in building colleges in which to impart useful knowledge. They ever observed it religiously to have their children instructed in reading and writing, at least; to bring them up in habits of industry, and teach them such trades as were suitable to their wants, expedient, and adapted to their age and constitution. Their sons and daughters were kept under strict parental authority, and, as a consequence, were not led into temptations by which so many youths of both sexes are ruined.

Among those who located in the vicinity of the Swiss settlement, between the years 1718 and 1740, appear the names of Frantz, Schanck, Brenneman, Whitman, Funk, Landis, Eby, Burkholder, Bowman, Baumgardner, Earisman, Nisley, Carpenter (Zimmerman), Snavely, Ashleman, Kauffman, Schultz, Houser, Churtz, Bare, Weaver, Longanecker, Musselman, Miller, Staner, Light, Brand, Loughman, Klugh, Oberholtzer, Hershey, Brenner, Stouffer, Hummel, Baughman, Whistler, Schuck, Herr, Zeigler, Keagy, Kreemer, Ulweiler, Snyder, Espenshade, Groff, Keneagy, Beck and many others, which (spelling excepted) are now well known in Middletown.

The German emigration to Pennsylvania had commenced early in the century, the first comers settling in some parts of Lancaster county as early as 1720, but, being opposed to wars and fighting, during the numerous Indian raids of that time, they sought more congenial neighborhoods than that of Paxton.

A number of this nationality who were located in western New York, traveled through the forests to the Susquehanna, descended the river, and going up this stream, (the lands on each side of which they found occupied by the Scotch-Irish), settled about its head waters, in what are now Berks and Lebanon counties in 1723.

From 1740 to 1750 the Reformed Lutherans and Catholics commenced to gather in the unsettled portions of Lancaster county, and their names begin to appear among the inhabitants of Middletown about the opening of the Revolution.

"These men," says James Logan (writing in 1725 and 1727), "come in crowds—bold, indigent strangers from Germany, where many of them have been soldiers. All go to the best vacant tracts, and seize upon them as places of common spoil. They rarely approach me on their arrival to propose to purchase; when they are sought out and challenged for their right to occupancy, they allege it was published in Europe that we wanted and solicited for colonists and had a superabundance of land, and therefore they had come without the means to pay.— Many of them are Papists, the men well armed, and as a body, a warlike, morose race." These emigrations, he hopes "may be prevented in future by an act of Parliament, else the Colonies will in time be lost to the Crown." A prophecy which, half a century later, was fulfilled.

It is difficult for us in these days of toleration to understand the antagonisms existing between people of different nationalities, who had similarly come to this country as a haven of refuge, where they would be free to exercise the dogmas of their respective creeds without molestation. The English proprietors, supercilious and arrogant, refused to bear their proportion of the taxes—required the Germans to change their names before being naturalized—drove the Scotch-Irish on to the frontiers, and refused them land in the then eastern counties—and would not allow a Catholic to hold office. The Scotch-Irish—added to an insular contempt for all other nationalities—despised Quakers and Mennonists alike for their non-resistance doctrines. A feeling, which the traffic in redemptioners intensified to such an extent, that when those of their young people, who did not share their prejudices, wished to intermarry with the Germans, they strenuously objected. The Germans thus antagonized, opposed to the arrogance of the English, and bullying of the Scotch-Irish, a phlegmatic tenacity of purpose, which eventually overbore their assumptions, if not their egotism.

The Revolution cemented these uncongenial elements into a united resistance to arbitrary power; and at its close found them fused into the homogeneous mass which has made Pennsylvania the mother of statesmen, as well as the Keystone of the Federal arch.

VI.

The following is a literal transcript of one of the deeds (in possession of Hon. Robert J. Fisher, of York, Pa.), relating to the ground Middletown now stands on. Attached unto the deed is a large seal bearing upon it what I presume are the arms of the Penns, but which, not being versed in heraldry, I am unable to describe.—C. H. H.

Thomas Penn and Richard Penn, Efquires, true and absolute Proprietaries and Governors in Chief of the Province of Pennsylvania and

CHRONICLES OF MIDDLETOWN.   25

counties of Newcaftle, Kent, and Suffex on Delaware. To all unto whom these presents shall come, Greeting: Whereas by virtue of a warrant under the feal of our Land Office bearing date the twenty first day of March, 1742, there was furveyed and laid out unto one Jacob Job, a certain Tract of Land Situate in Pextang Townfhip in the county of Lancafter; And Whereas by virtue of one other warrant under the feal of our Land Office bearing date the Ninth day of January, 1743, a Survey was made unto one Thomas Cooper on a certain Tract of Land Situate in Pextang Townfhip, adjoining the above mentioned Tract within the faid county, Under Certain Conditions in the faid Warrant refpectively mentioned, which conditions not having been complied with by the faid Jacob Job and Thomas Cooper, nor either of them, the faid Warrants and furveys made in purfuance thereof, are becoming utterly void, as in and by the fame Warrants remaining in our Surveyor General's office, relation thereunto refpectively had, does manifeftly appear, And Whereaf afterwards in any by two feveral Warrants, bearing date the Nineteenth day of this inftant February. Upon application made to Us by John Fifher of the City of Philadelphia, Merchant, our Surveyor General was required to accept and receive into his Office the Surveys of the faid two Tracts of land fo made as aforfaid, and to make Returns thereof into our Secretary's Office for the ufe and behoof of the faid John Fisher, which Surveys being accordingly accepted by our Surveyor General and the faid two Tracts of Land (lying contiguous to each other) were by him duly returned into our Secretary's Office circumfcribed in one Tract, are included within the lines, Bounds and Limits, following (that is to say) Beginning at the mouth of Swataro creek and on the east side of the River Susquehanna and from thence extending up the said creek on the several courses thereof six hundred and eighty two perches to a post, thence by Samuel Kirkpatrick's Land south seventy degrees west one hundred and twenty two perches to a marked hickory and north twenty degrees west sixty four perches to a marked white oak, thence by the same and William Kirkpatrich's Land south seventy degrees west one hundred and seventy one perches to a marked white oak, thence by the said William Kirkpatrick's north seventy degrees west fifty perches to a marked hickory, thence by a line of marked trees west ninety six perches to a marked black oak, thence along a line of marked trees and by Samuel Mean's Land south twenty degrees west three hundred and forty nine perches to a white hickory marked by the side of the Susquehanna River, thence down the same river on the several courses thereof one hundred and eighty four perches to the place of beginning containing in the whole six hundred and ninety one acres and fifty three perches and the allowance of six acres per cent for roads and highways.

Now at the inftance and requeft of the faid John Fifher, that we would be pleafed to grant him a confirmation of the fame. Know ye that in Confideration of the Sum of One. Hundred and seven Pounds two shillings lawful money of Pennfylvania, to our ufe, paid by the faid

John Fifher, (the receipt whereof we hereby acknowledge and thereof do acquit and forever difcharge the said John Fifher, his Heirs and Affigns by thefe Presents) and of the yearly quit rent thereinafter mentioned We have given, granted, released and confirmed, And by these George the Second, over Great Britain, &c. And the Thirtieth year of Presents for Us, our Heirs and Succeffors, Do give, grant, releafe and confirm unto the faid John Fifher, His Heirs and Affignees forever, Six Hundred and ninety one acres and fifty three perches of land as the same we now set forth and describe as aforefaid With all Mines, Minerals, Quarries, Meadows, Marfhes, Savannahs, Swamps, Cripples, Woods, Under-woods, Timber and Trees, Ways, Waters, Watercourfes, Liberties, Profits, Commodities, Advantages, Hereditaments, and Appurtenances whatever thereunto belonging or in any wife appertaining and lying within the Bounds and Limits aforefaid [Three full and clear fifth Parts of all Royal Mines, free from all Deductions and Reprifals for digging and refining the fame; and alfo One-fifth Part of the Ore of all other Mines, delivered at the Pit's Mouth only accepted, and hereby reserved] and alfo free Leave, Right, and Liberty to and for the faid John Fifher his Heirs and Affigns, to hawk, hunt, fifh fowl, in and upon the hereby granted Land and Premifes, or upon any Part thereof: TO HAVE AND TO HOLD the faid Tract of Land and Premifes hereby granted (except as before excepted) with their Appurtenances unto the faid John Fifher, his Heirs and Affigns, to the only Ufe Behoof of the faid John Fifher his Heirs and Affigns forever TO BE HOLDEN of us, our Heirs and Succeffors, Proprietaries of *Pennfylvania,* as of our Manor of Conestoga in the County of Lancafter aforefaid, in free and common Soccage by Fealty only, in lieu of all other services, YIELDING AND PAYING therefore yearly unto us, our Heirs and Succeffors, at the Town of Lancafter in the faid County, at or upon the firft Day of March in every Year, from the firft Day of *March* next One Half-penny *Sterling* for every Acre of the fame, or Value thereof in Coin-Current, according as the Exchange fhall then be between our faid Province and the City of *London,* to fuch Perfon or Perfons as fhall, from Time to Time, be appointed to receive the fame. AND in Cafe of Non-Payment thereof, within ninety Days next after the fame fhall become due, that then it fhall and may be lawful for us, our Heirs and Succeffors, our and their Receiver or Receivers, into and upon the hereby granted Land and Premises to re-enter, and the fame to hold and poffefs, until the faid Quit-rent, and all the Arrears thereof, together with the Charges accruing by Means of fuch Non-Payment Re-entry be fully paid and difcharged. WITNESS the faid ANTHONY PALMER, Esquire. President of the Council of the faid Province.

Who as well in his own Right as by Virtue of certain powers and Authorities to him for this purpose, mutually granted by the faid Proprietaries Hath hereunto fet his Hand and caufed the Great Seal of the said Province to be hereunto affixed, at Philadelphia the twenty fourth

CHRONICLES OF MIDDLETOWN. 27

day of *February* in the year of our Lord One Thousand Seven Hundred and Forty-seven. The Twenty-Fifth Year of the Reign of King George the Second, over Great Britain, &. And the Thirtieth year of the faid Proprietaries Government.   Anthony Palmer.*
[On the back of this document is endorsed:] Patent to John Fisher of 691:53 in Lancaster County. Dated Feb. 24th, 1747: Consideration £107,2,0. Recorded at Philadelphia in Pat. Book A Vol 13, Page 364, April 5th, 1748.
Certificate of
C. Brock Dep. Rec. Dr.
and seal "Office of Pennsylvania Inrollment."

(There are several other endorsements as follows:)
Phila. Feb. 28th, 1757. Received of John Fisher twelve pounds nineteen shillings and two pence half penny sterling in full for nine years quit rent due on the within mentioned 691 A's 53 ps. of land to the 11th day of next month £12.19.2½ Stg.   E. PHYSICK.

Recd. October 1st, 1759, of Jno. Fisher two Pounds seventeen shillings and seven Pence Sterling in money of Pennsylvania in full for two years quit rent on the within mentioned Land the 1st of March last.
£2.17.7 Stg.   RICH FOCKLEY, R. C.

Rec. Philad., 14th May, 1760, of John Fisher, one pound eight shillings and 9½ Sterlg in money of Pennsylvania in full for one year quit rent due on the within mentioned Land to the 1st day of last March.
$£2,3.10 Curr cr.   E. PHYSICK

Recd. 4th March, 1761, of John Fisher, One pounds 8 9½ Sterlg. for one year's quit rent due on the within mentioned Land on the 1st instant.
£1.8.9½ Stg.   E. PHYSICK

Recd. 4th March, 1762, of John Fisher, 1. 8 9½ Sterlg. for one year's quit rent due on the within mentioned land to the 1st instant.
£1.8.9¼   E. PHYSICK.

Recd. 7th May, 1765, of John Fisher, £1.8.9½ pence Sterlg. in full for one year's quit rent on the within mentioned Land.
£1.8.9½ Stg.   E. PHYSICK

VII.

In connection with the deed, I give the following from the Family Record of the Fisher family (compiled by John Adams Fisher, Esq.):

John Fisher (abavus) came from England to Pennsylvania with William Penn on the first voyage of the ship Welcome in 1682. He had married Margaret —————— and had six children, Sarah, Alice, Anne, James, John and Thomas. The first four died without issue. Thomas married Margery Maud, in 1692, and had seven children.

His son John (proavus) married Catherine ──── and had four children, John, James, William and Anne. He died at Shippen street, Philadelphia, before the Revolution. James settled west of Harrisburg. Anne married Enoch Cummins.

His son John (avus) married 1st Elizabeth Light, and 2nd, Grace Lloyd. Had three children, John, William and George; his son John became a merchant in Jamaica, and had a son and daughter. William died without issue.

His youngest son George (pater) married Hannah Chamberlain, and settled at the mouth of the Swatara, in 1752, laid out the town of Middletown in 1755, and died in 1776. He left three children, George, John and Hannah. Hannah married J. Richardson. John left three children, John, George and Juliana.

George Fisher (2nd) married, first, Elizabeth Minshall, and second, Ann Shippen Jones. By his first wife he had four children, Hannah Wickersham, John Adams, George Washington and Elizabeth Minshall. By his second wife he had four children, Robert J., Edward H., Ann J., and Catherine. This is the George Fisher who founded Portsmouth, now an integral part of Middletown.

Of George Fisher, the founder of Middletown, we have scant data. He was a tall, handsome man, who chafed under the strict rule of the Friends or Quakers, and yearned after the pomps and vanities of the worldlings. Consequently he was at variance with his family, and to remove him from temptation, his father decided to send him to the tract of wild land, which he had purchased some five years previous, on what was then the sparsely settled frontier.

George, perforce, accepted the situation and with a train of three (Conestoga) wagons, drawn each by six horses, and loaded with the necessary supplies of provisions, farming and building implements, set out on his toilsome journey. There were no turnpikes in those days and but few settlers. It took him five days to reach his destination. The roads when it rained were deep in mud, and obstructed with numerous stumps some portions of the route, through marshy places, had been roughly corduroyed and as there were few bridges, most of the streams had to be forded; that part of the way west of Lancaster was particularly bad. It was difficult at one or two places to find passage between the huge boulders. Being Friends, the teamsters could not relieve their feelings by the customary objurgations.

At length, through much tribulation and weariness of flesh, they reached the Swatara, at Pineford, forded it and camped on the high ground on its western bank one evening in April, 1752.

Early the next morning, having selected a site, Fisher commenced preparations for the erection of his house. The whole tract was heavily timbered with fine oak, hickory, walnut, chestnut, locust, poplar and laurel trees, and in this locality was a dense growth of pine. In time the trees were cut down, fitted, and a log cabin rose, 18 by 18 feet square, and one and one-half stories high. Soon afterwards he built a log

Pineford Farm. Home of George Fisher, Founder of Middletown.

house, immediately in front, thirty by fifty feet, two stories high, and with a twelve foot wide porch on the south and east sides.*

A few Quaker families soon followed Fisher, and later, some Scotch and Irish traders came. The settlement began to grow, and so, with the approval of his father, he laid out a town, a short distance west of his residence. There were three streets, High, Main and Water running from east to west, and five, Union, Pine, Spruce, Race and Vine, from north to south.

It was difficult to secure a surveyor's chain and so a marked rope was used, which when dragged over the wet grass and then dried, made a variation in the size of the lots.

This was the site of an ancient Indian village of the Susquehanna nation. Some lodges of the Conoy or Ganawese were at the time located on the ground in the neighborhood of the square bounded by Pine, Spruce, Main and High streets.

These Indians quickly established friendly relations with the Quaker settlers, for they had heard of Penn and his honorable treatment of their forefathers. Fisher was also on good terms with the Mennonite settlers to the eastward.

In 1759 his parents conveyed the tract to him, as appears from (a synopsis of) the original parchment, which I copy verbatim, et literatim, et punctuatim.

On March 27th, 1759, "John Fisher and Grace, his wife, for and in Consideration of the Natural Love and Affection which they have and bear for the said George Fisher and for and in Consideration of the Sum of Four Shillings lawful money of Pennsylvania unto them the said John Fisher and Grace, his Wife, in hand well and truly paid by the said George Fisher at the sealing and delivery thereof the Receipt whereof is hereby Acknowledged and for divers other good Causes and Considerations them the said John Fisher and Grace his wife specially Moving HAVE given." (Here follows the wording of the original deed.) "together with all the Reversions and Remainders Rents Issues and Profits thereof and also all the Household Goods Utensils or Implements of Husbandry Horses Cows Sheep and Hogs of the said John Fisher or belonging to the said Plantation or Tract of Land or therewith used or occupied and also all the Estate Right Title Interest Use Possession Property Claim and Demand whatsoever."

Signed John Fisher
Grace Fisher

Sealed and Delivered
in the presence of
John Cooper,
Paul Isaac Voto.

On the 26th day of February one thousand seven hundred and sixty

---

*This latter dwelling was torn down in 1859, having stood 106 years. The wing or first cabin, was destroyed in 1875.

three before me William Coleman one of the Justices of ye Supreme Court of Pennsylvania Came the above named John Fisher and Grace his wife and Acknowledged the above written Indenture to be their Deed and desired the same may be Recorded as their Deed the said Grace thereunto Voluntarily Consenting. She being of full age secretly and apart examined and the contents of the said Indenture made known unto her Witness my Hand and Seal the day and year aforesaid.

"WILLIAM COLEMAN." (Seal)

"Entered in the Office for recording of Deeds for the County of Lancaster in Book L Page 226 etc. the 14th Day of July Anno Domini 1766 Witness my Hand and Seal of my said office.

"EDWARD SHIPPEN Recorder."

(Endorsed on back of deed:)
"Deed of Gift
John Fisher and Wife
to
George Fisher."

The town grew rapidly and its trade soon exceeded any other town on the river. The emigration westward was large and continuous, and all passed through the town, Main street being a part of the great highway between Philadelphia and Pittsburgh (the latter place being then a town of about 500 inhabitants).

Fisher occupied himself in clearing his new land and took part in the Indian wars which soon supervened. In 1776 some individuals of a party of travelers became suddenly violently ill, were taken into his house and cared for, but soon died. The record does not state the cause of their sickness but it was evidently contagious, for Fisher and his wife both contracted it, and died within a few hours of each other. They were buried on the farm, but no monument marks the place of their interment, and the location thereof will doubtless soon be forgotten.

(The following was given me by Mr. Boyd Hamilton:)

As early as 1750, certainly, and for some years previously, population grew apace in the immediate vicinity of the mouth of the Swatara creek. The locality was known to the provincial rulers as the "South End of Paxtang township, Lancaster county." A copy of what is said to be from the original assessment of taxables for the year 1749-50, has been placed in my hands. I have never seen the original, but presume this to be correct, and as such give it a place in this memoranda. It will be observed that all the names except Shultz, Sheets and Stern are Scotch-Irish.

Brown, Alexander,
Cannon, Kennedy,
Dickey, Moses,
Dickey, William,

Dugan, Thomas,
Herning, Peter,
Galbraith, Samuel,
Gorden, Charles,

Gray, John,
Hanna, Andrew,
Houston, Andrew,
Harris, William,
Jordon, Mathew,
Johnson, John,
Johnson, Francis,
Kirkpatrick, Will
Kinney, Patrick,
King, John,
Lusk, James,
Morrow, John,
Means, Thomas,
McKinney, Henry,
McClure, Richard,
Means, John,
McKnight, Timothy,
McElroy, H.,

Montgomery, John,
McKnight, James,
Shields, David,
Steel, William,
Stuart, Hugh,
Shultz, Martin,
Stern, Valentine,
Sellers, Henry,
Sheetz, George,
Sharp, William,
Shaw, Timothy,
Shields, John,
Tyler, Robert,
White, Alexander,
Wood, Samuel,
Wiley, Oliver,
Wilson, John,
Wilson, James,
Welsh, John.

The above roll contains 45 names. Estimated population 200 persons.

VIII.

After Braddock's defeat in July, 1775, the whole frontier was left comparatively defenceless, and the Indians scattered through the country committing depredations. It is impossible in these papers to go into detail; suffice it to say that much property was destroyed and hundreds of people killed and scalped in this county and those immediately surrounding it. The Proprietaries refused to allow their lands to be taxed to raise funds for the common protection, and the pacific principles of the Quakers, Dunkards, Mennonites, and Schwenckfelders, further complicated matters. The Quakers, in fact, having a majority of the Assembly, refused all aid. The people on the frontier, exasperated at their heartlessness, sent some of the mangled bodies of these victims of savage barbarity to Philadelphia, where they were carried through the streets placarded as some of the martyrs to the Quaker policy of non-resistance. A mob surrounded the house of Assembly, and placing the dead bodies in the door-way demanded immediate relief for the inhabitants of the border, without, however, moving the members. In 1756 and 1757 the Proprietaries and Assembly, forced by popular pressure, raised £135,000 for the defence of the province.

April 9th, 1756, the Governor was authorized to offer rewards for scalps. On the 14th of the same month he issued a proclamation offering the following bounties:

"For every male Indian aged over twelve delivered at a government fort or jail, $150.

"For every female prisoner or male prisoner under twelve, $130.

"For the scalp of every male Indian, $130.

"For every English Subject rescued from the Indians, and delivered at Philadelphia to the Governor, $150.

"For the scalp of every female Indian, $50.

"To every officer or soldier who shall rescue any English captives, or take Indian prisoners or scalps, one half of the said bounties."

To guard against Indian devastations a chain of forts and blockhouses were erected, at an expense of £85,000, along the Kitochtiny hills, from the river Delaware to the Maryland line. Of these the principal ones in Dauphin county were Forts Halifax, Hunter, McKee, Manady, Henry and Swatara.

In 1763 came the Pontiac war. It was in this war that the "Paxton Boys" became known, not only to the Province, but also to the country at large. The Indians, as any student of history knows, under the leadership of Pontiac, rose almost simultaneously. The whole frontier was ablaze; and Paxtang was truly the frontier, for west of the Susquehanna there was scarcely an inhabitant.

Authorized by the Governor, the Rev. John Elder, the pastor of Paxtang and Derry Presbyterian churches, organized his Rangers. As the Scotch-Irish, who then formed the population of Middletown attended these two churches alternately, many of them joined the Rangers.

The Quaker Assembly maintained its usual policy of do-nothingness, sympathizing with the Indians, and refusing aid to the settlers; one of their number characterizing these latter as "A parcel of Scotch-Irish who, if they were all killed, could well enough be spared."

(Extracts from old letters, &c., of 1763:)

"Imagination cannot conceive the perils with which the settlement at Paxton was surrounded from 1754 to 1765.—To portray each scene of horror would be impossible—the heart shrinks from the attempt. The settlers were goaded to desperation; murder followed murder."

"Rifles were loaded, horses were in readiness. They mounted; they called on their pastor to lead them. He was then in the 57th year of his age. Had you seen him you would have beheld a superior being—" "No man unless he were living in Paxton at the time could have an idea of the sufferings and anxieties of the people—" "Did we not brave the summer's heat and the winter's cold, and the savage tomahawk—were we tamely to look on and see our brethren murdered, and our fairest prospects blasted, while the inhabitants of Philadelphia, Philadelphia county, Bucks and Chester slept, and reaped their gain in safety?—The blood of a thousand of our fellow-creatures called for vengeance—What remains is to leave our cause with God and our guns."

(Extract from an address of the "Paxton Volunteers," in 1764, "to the candid and impartial world":)

"The Indians set fire to houses, barns, corn, hay, in short to every-

Old Fort.

thing that was combustible; so that ye whole country seemed to be in one general blaze, and involved in one common ruin. Great numbers of ye Back Settlers were murdered, scalped and butchered in the most shocking manner, and their dead bodies inhumanly mangled, some having their ribs divided from ye chine with the tomahawk, others left expiring in ye most exquisite tortures, with their legs and arms broken, their skulls fractured, and ye brains scattered on the ground. Many children were either spitted alive, and roasted, or covered under the ashes of a large fire before their helpless parents' eyes. Ye hearts of some were taken out and eaten reeking hot, while they were yet beating between their teeth, and others, where time and opportunity would admit of it, were skinned, boiled and eaten. Hundreds carried into ye most miserable captivity, and daily tortured to death in every method of cruelty which Indian barbarity can suggest.—The husband butchered in the presence of his helpless wife while ye children are clinging around his knees;—Ye widowed mother reserved to be a spectator of ye inhuman massacre of her tender family, before she receives ye friendly hatchet that closes her eyes on ye shocking scene.—Those that are with child ripped open and mangled in ye most indecent manner.—Hundreds of miserable refugees flying to ye nearest frontier town with a part of their families leaving the remainder of them in the hands of ye enemy, or wandering till they perish in ye woods.—Hundreds reduced from plentiful and independent circumstances, to a state of beggary and despair, taking shelter in the hovels and stables to secure their helpless families from ye inclemency of ye night or ye season; while others cannot even obtain this, but are obliged to make fires in ye woods and live worse than the savages themselves.—None but those who have been spectators or eye-witnesses of these shocking scenes can possibly have an adequate idea of our suffering."

Dauphin county was then Paxton township (or Paxtang, as some called it) of Lancaster county. Middletown and its vicinity was, about this time, 1763, the most thickly settled portion of what is now Dauphin county. It is fair to presume therefore that a large proportion of the "Paxton Boys" lived here.

These rangers scouted along the whole frontier, from fort to fort. They were so organized that while one-third was out, the other two-thirds could remain at home to protect the families from possible raids during their absence. They generally chose their officers immediately before proceeding on a scout, and during that scout rendered them implicit obedience. They adopted the Indian tactics in fighting, and these latter dreaded them, as they never did the regular troops, and avoided their vicinity.

They had several drawbacks to contend with; the Assembly, controlled by the Quakers, not only refused to pay them for their services, but were continually negotiating with, and sending presents to the Indians.

Below Middletown, on the Conestoga manor, were a number of so-called Christian Indians—the special pets of the Proprietaries—that the "Paxton Boys" suspected of harboring, concealing, and aiding the savages who were committing the murders and outrages in this section. Suspicion finally became a certainty, and they determined to capture the fiends who, red-handed, had the hardihood to remain in the vicinity of their crimes. They went for them—they resisted—in the melee the so-called tame Indians went under also.

Then the Assembly became exasperated and the men who could sit with folded arms, and see thousands of innocent whites butchered, wished to indict the rangers—who had thus rid the world of devils—for murder. But the sentiment, of the whole frontier, and that of the surrounding colonies was with them, and they remained at home unmolested. After this there were no more massacres.

At the opening of the Revolution most of the Paxton men sought the ranks of the army, from which but few of them returned to settle again in Paxton. As far as we have any record they lived useful and respected lives; some of them afterwards became prominent in this and other States; and through their posterity many of their names have since become noted in the history of the country.

But he who seeks for the descendants of the Scotch-Irish in Dauphin county finds but here and there a solitary isolated family, surrounded everywhere by an entirely different race; that of the German emigrants, who came about the close of the last century, and whose descendants inherit the language, the farms and the plodding industry and thrift of their forefathers. The ancient churches and graveyards of the Irish still remain as monuments of their former occupancy.

A PARALLEL.

In reading over Paper No. 9, I can't help thinking that to me these incidents of the past possess a vividness that it is hardly possible for an inhabitant of the present peaceful old "Keystone" to realize. So you will pardon me if, after quoting from a letter written by a resident of Lancaster county, Pa., in 1757, I make a few extracts from one written by an inhabitant of Uvalde county, Texas, in 1861; to show you how the same drama was performed, on a different stage, over a hundred years later, and a thousand miles further off. The actors on one side, being (judging from the names) descendants of the old pioneers of Pennsylvania; on the other, not alone the wild Commanches and Lipans, but also (and principally) the Government Indians from the reservation; the official in charge of whom (Maj. Neighbors) would believe no accusations brought against his pets by the "wild Texans," whom he looked upon much as the Quakers of a previous day did on the "Scotch-Irish." To make the parallel more complete, the nearest set-

tlement east of Uvalde was 60 miles distant, west 670 miles; south 65 miles, and north over 1,000.
(Letters to Edward Shippen and others, October 14th, 1757.)

"*Friends and Fellow Subjects:*

"I send you in a few lines the melancholy condition of the frontiers of this country. Last Thursday, the 12th inst., ten Indians came to Noah Frederick, while ploughing, killed and scalped, and carried away three of his children that were with him—the oldest but nine years old, and plundered his house—it being but two short miles to Capt. Smith's fort at Swatara Gap, and a little better than two miles to my house.

"Last Saturday evening an Indian came to the house of Philip Robinson, carrying a green bush before him, said Robinson's son being on the corner of his fort—the Indian perceiving that he was observed, fled; the watchman fired but missed him; this being about three-fourths of a mile from Manady fort; and yesterday morning two miles from Smith's Fort at Swatara, in Bethel township, as Jacob Farnwell was going to the house of Jacob Meylie to his own, was fired upon by two Indians and wounded, but escaped with his life; and a little after, in said township, as Frederick Hawley and Peter Sample were carrying away their goods in wagons, were met by a parcel of Indians and killed, lying dead in one place, and one man a little distance. But what more has been done has not come to my ears, only that the Indians were continuing their murders.

"The frontiers are employed at nothing but carrying off their effects so that some miles are now waste. We are willing but not able without help—you are able, if you be willing (that is, including the lower parts of the county,) to give such assistance as will enable us to recover our waste land. You may depend upon it, that, without assistance, we in a few days, will be on the wrongside of you, for I am now on the frontier, and I fear by to morrow night I will be left two miles.

"Gentlemen: Consider what you will do, and don't be long about it; And don't let the world say that we died as fools died. Our hands are not tied, but let us exert ourselves and do something for the honor of our country and the preservation of our fellow-subjects. I hope you will communicate our grievances to the lower part of the county for surely they will send us help, if they understood our grievances.

"I would have gone down myself, but dare not; my family is in such danger, I expect an answer by the bearer, if possible.

"I am, gentlemen, your very humble servant, "ADAM REED.

"P. S.—Before sending this away I have just received information that there are seven killed, and five children scalped alive, but have not the account of their names."

Extract from a letter in San Antonia, Texas, *Herald*, March 13th, 1861:

"Since my last, the Indians who went down the Sabinal have returned, going up the country. They stole all the horses on Rancheros' creek —a party of 40 men are in pursuit of them. The Indians who killed Robinson, Adams, Sanders, and Eastwood, and committed the other depredations and outrages I wrote you of continued on their course down the country, and crossed into Mexico. They treated old man Sanders as they did the others, cut out his heart, and scalped him; they also skinned one of his feet, and cut off his long flowing white beard. Settlers who have come in town to-day, state that this party overtook a man named Morrow on the Frio, below the Laredo road, shot him eight times—he probably killed one Indian; he is still living, and says that the party that attacked him were about 24 in number. They also killed a Mexican and wounded a Mexican boy somewhere below old Fort Merrill, and near the same place stole 65 head of horses. A party have but just returned from a scout in the lower country—another party is now fitting out, and will be ready to start in a day or so. We have never yet failed to overtake them when going up the country, nor do I think we will now. But this state of affairs cannot last—the State must furnish us the means, men, money and horses, or else the frontier will soon be a little nearer San Antonia than would perhaps be agreeable to the feelings of her citizens. Uvalde is willing to do what she can, but we cannot stand the whole brunt of this contest unassisted, while those whom our being on the frontier protects, look on in listless apathy.

The settlement on the Neuces is again broken up—not an individual remains. Below here for probably a distance of 100 miles, where there were a number of settlements, there is not a soul living.—There are no crops being made, and stock is neglected. What we are to do in the future, unless a change for the better takes place—and that very soon —God only knows. There may be some who will think this picture overdrawn; living remote from the scenes that are daily occurring here they will deem this exaggeration, and that we are unnecessarily alarmed. To such I would say, change places with us, bear what we have borne, year after year, without aid or assistance, and often not even sympathy for our misfortunes, or credit for our efforts from those whom our privation, toil and blood protected, and freed from the necessity of sharing in like dangers; and then see whether Uvalde has not just cause for complaint. We have done more actual and efficient service in proportion to our population, (we have 150 voters) than any other county on the border; we have raised and supported Ranging companies and never (save in one solitary instance,) have we received one cent from the State for our services. But we cannot do it forever. Long suffering and uncomplaining endurance sometimes cease to be virtues. We have waited and waited; and now we want aid, and that quickly. This state of things is but a foretaste of what we have to expect; these small parties are but the prelude to larger incursions, and therefore, as I before stated we will be unable to endure it much longer. You will soon have no frontier to protect, and then, when the evil is at your own

doors; when you suffer as we now suffer, you may wish for a few of those who once stood between you and danger, and whom you refused to aid.
C. H. HUTCHINSON."

IX.

Among the early citizens of Middletown was Col. James Burd. In spite of holding different political and religious views, the families of Burd and Fisher were very intimate, (an intimacy which was afterwards cemented by marriage connections and continued through successive generations). So when George Fisher (who had settled on his estate in 1752) laid out the town in 1755, Colonel Burd moved with his family and slaves on to his farm of "Tinian," about two miles from the center of the prospective town.

About 1760 he erected his residence on the bluff overlooking the Susquehanna just back of the town of Highspire which it antedates some fifty years. It is a stone structure thirty by forty feet and two and a half stories high, and is probably the oldest dwelling in the county of Dauphin.

It is one of the historic mansions of our State. The most notable men of the French and Indian and Revolutionary wars were entertained at "Tinian" right hospitably, for its owner was a man of mark in Provincial days.

The old iron knocker of Colonel Burd remains on the front door, while the interior presents little change.

One half a mile to the east of "Tinian" is "Walnut Hill," the home of the Cronchs and Jordans. It, too, was erected nearly a century and a half ago, and as the residence of Capt. James Cronch of the Revolution, Edward Cronch, a Representative in Congress, and Benjamin Jordan, a State Senator, all representative men, has an historic interest.

Colonel Burd was a Scotchman. He emigrated to this country when twenty-one years of age, married a daughter of Edward Shippen, Esq., and settled in Middletown some five years later.

He became a man of note in the province. Was successively captain, major, lieutenant colonel, and colonel of one of the only two regiments at that time in the service of the colony; took an active part at the commencement of the Revolution (was colonel of a battalion) and at the time of his death was one of the county judges.

He owned four slaves, viz: Lucy, aged 35 years; Cuff, aged 13 years; Dina, aged 7 years; Venus, aged two years. He was buried by the side of his wife in the old Presbyterian graveyard at the corner of Union and High streets, where they rested until June 4th, 1860, when they were removed by their descendants to the new Middletown cemetery, and reinterred. Near the entrance, on two large marble slabs lying side by side, are the following inscriptions:

Col. James Burd,
Born at Ormistown, Scotland,
March 10th, 1726,
Died at Tinian, Oct. 5th, 1798,
Aged 67 years, 6 months,
and 25 days.
Sarah Burd,
Born February 22nd, 1731,
Died at Tinian, Sept. 17, 1784,
Aged 53 years, 6 months,
And 25 days.

A few extracts from his correspondence, journal, &c., may prove interesting.
(To Edward Shippen.)
"Dear & Hon'rd Sir:
"We are in great Confusion here at present, we have received express last night that the Indians and French are in a large body in the cove, a little way from William Maxwell, esqur's, and that they immediately intend to fall down upon this country. We for these two days past have been working at our fort here, and believe shall work this day, this town is full of People, they being all moving in with their Famillys, 5 or 6 Famillys in a house. We are in great want of Arms and Ammunition, but with what we have are determined to give the Enemy as Warm a Reception as we Can, (there has) some of our people been taken Prisoners by this party, & have made their escape from them and come into us this morning.

"As our fort goes on here with great Vigour and expect to be finished in 16 days, in which we intend to throw all the Women and Children, it would be greatly Encouraging could we have Reason to expect assistance from Philadelphia by private Donation of Sweevells, a few great guns, small arms & ammunition, we would send our Wagons for them & we don't doubt upon proper application but something of this kind will be done for us from Philad'a.

"We have 100 men working at Fort Morris, with heart and hand every day. I am with Duty to Dady and Mammy, Love to Bro. and Sister, my dear wife and the little Babys, &c.,
"Dear Sir
"Your most affectionate son
"James Burd."
Directed to Edward Shippen, Sen'r, Esq., Lancaster.
(Gov. Morris to Capt. Burd.)

"P'da, 3rd Feb'ry, 1756.
"S'r:—I have just received ye melancholy Acc't of a fresh party of Indians falling again upon ye settlement on Juniata, & of their having murdered & carry'd off above 15 of ye people there, as I suppose you must have heard."

CHRONICLES OF MIDDLETOWN. 39

(To Gov. Morris.)
"Sir:—I am informed that they are entirely out of all manner of Provisions at Fort Granville, which is a very bad situation, as the enemy are Constantly Visiting them; they have wounded two men within sight of ye Fort & one of ye men's lives is despaired of, they would have Carried off one of them had not Lewt. Ward rushed out of the Fort and Rescued him. I could wish we had a Surgeon & Medicines we shall lose one-half of our men with perhaps slight wounds, purely for want of Assistance.

"I am respectfully,
Your Hon'rs
"Most Obed't humble Serv't,
"JAMES BURD.

"I hope ye Governor will excuse this scrall, as there is a Scarcity of Quills here."

In 1757 he writes a paper headed "A Proposition for the better securing of the Province of Pennsylvania from the inroads of the Indians, and finding them Employment at Home in their own Country, to prevent them from coming abroad to seek it. With some few reasons why our Present Situation can never be a Defenceable one against such an enemy."

Some of the suggestions in which were adopted by the Province.

Account of James Burd against Tedyuscung 1757.—Capt'n John Tedyouskunk (a Delaware chief) to James Burd, for Necessaries furnished him:

"To one Regimental coat,	£3	—	—
"One gold-lace hat and cockaid,	2	6	—
"1 p'r Shoes,	—	7	5
"1 Check Shirt,	—	12	—
"1 Ruffled Shirt,	1	15	—
"1 Plain do. for his wife,	—	15	—
"1 Cotton Handkr,	—	1	6
"pr britches,	—	16	—
"1 pr. linen do.,	—	6	—
"1 Riffle Gun,	5	—	—
"1 yd scarlet shallown for collars,	4	—	—
"1½ yds. half thicks for leggins,	—	6	6
"1 English Pipe Tomahawk,	—	12	—
"1 pr buckles,	—	1	6
	"15	2	0

Extracts from Colonel Burd's Journal:
"Thursday, 16th February, 1757.
"This morning sett out for Lancaster to visit the Troops from Susquehanna to Delaware.
"19th, Sunday.

"This day at 11 a. m. marched for Fort Swettarrow, got to Crawfords, 14 miles from Hunters', here I stayed all night, it rained hard.

"Had a number of applications from the country for protection otherwise they would immediately be obliged to fly from Settlements, appointed to meet them to hear their Complaints and proposals on Tuesday at 10 a. m. at Fort Swettarrow; the country is thick settled this march along the Blue mountains & very fine Plantations.

"20th, Monday.

"Marched this morning at 11 a. m., met a Serg't and ten men here, who marched with me back to Swettarrow, this day it rained much, got to Swettarrow Fort at 4 p. m., the roads extream bad, the soldiers march with great difficulty, found Capt. Lieut. Allen & 38 men here per report; this is 11 miles from Crawfords.

"21 Tuesday.

"Reviewed the garrison this morning at 10 a. m. and found 38 men, viz: 21 belonging to Capt. Lieut. Allen, & 17 detached from Capt. Weiser's Co.; of Capt. Allen's 13 men for 3 years no province arms fitt for use, no Kettles, nor blankets, 12 lbs poudder, and 25 lbs of lead, no poudder horns, pouches, nor cartouch boxes, no Tomahawks nor Province tools of any kind, 2 months provision.

"Some Soldiers Absent, and others hy'rd in their places, which has been a custom here, the soldiers under no discipline, Ordered a Serg't and 15 men to be always out upon the scout from hence to Crawfords, keeping along the blue mountain, altering their routs & a targeet to be erected 6 inches thick, in order to practice the soldiers in shouting.

"This day 12 m. d. the Country People came here. I promise them to station and officer & 25 men at Robertson's mill, this mill is situate in the centre between the Forts Swatarrow & Hunter, this gave the People Content."

From here he goes to Fort Henry, 17 miles and sends back a party to garrison Robertson's mill as promised. The journal continues with reports on condition of the different forts visited, &c.

"At Fort Williams I found a targett erected, ordered the Company to shoot at the mark, sett them the Example myself by wheeling around & fireing by the word of command. I shott a bullott into the centre of the mark the size of a Dollar, distance 100 yards."

He complains of the deep snows and excessive cold interfering with travel. Completes his inspection and reaches Philadelphia on Tuesday, March 7th.

His journal, as well as much of his correspondence, is full of interesting matter, but these papers are growing too voluminous, and one more extract will have to suffice.

"Ordered, in Aug., 1759, to march with 200 of my battalion to the mouth of the Redstone cr., where it empties itself into the river Monongahela, to cut a road somewhere from Gen. Braddock's road to that place as I shall judge best, and on my arrival there to erect a fort in order to open a communication by the river Monongahela to Pittsburg, for the more easy transportation of provisions, &c., from the provinces of Virginia and Maryland. Sent forward the detachment under the command of Lieut. Col. Shippen, leaving one officer and thirty men to bring our five wagons."

"When I have cut the road and finished the fort, I am to leave one officer and twenty-five men as a garrison, and march with the remainder of my battalion to Pittsburg."

He was ordered to pass by Fort Cumberland, and after inspecting the stores there, to continue on his route, which seems to have been along the road previously opened by Braddock, and which was afterwards nearly the route of the Cumberland turnpike.

X.

THE OLD LUTHERAN CHURCH.

St. Peter's Lutheran church is (except those at Derry, Paxton and Hanover, before alluded to) the oldest church edifice in the county.

Lot No. 135, (two hundred and fifty feet,) upon which the old church edifice stands, was deeded Sept. 18th, 1764, by George Fisher and Hannah his wife, to Peter Woltz, George Frey, and Deterick Schob, all of Lower Paxton, (now Swatara) township, Lancaster (now Dauphin) county, Province of Pennsylvania, for the sum of seven shillings and sixpence, with the additional rental of one grain of wheat per annum payable on each consecutive 1st of May. The deed was acknowledged before John Alison, Esq., and witnessed by Joseph Greenwood and Henry Renick. It is written on parchment and is in a good state of preservation.

In the same year a petition was sent to John Penn, Lieutenant Governor of the Province, praying for the privilege of erecting a church, and also of collecting funds for that purpose. The license reads as follows:

By the Honorable John Penn, Esquire, Lieutenant Governor and Commander in Chief of the Province of Pennsylvania, and counties of Newcastle, Kent and Sussex on the Delaware. Whereas, it has been presented to me, by the humble petition of Christian Roth and David Ettley, of Middletown, in the county of Lancaster; That, "The Lutherans of said town and adjacent, have deputized the said Petitioners to collect of the Good People of the said Province, such sums of money as they will please contribute towards building a Church in the said town. That there is no church for many miles round the said town. That the said Congregation had got a lot of ground. And that the said congregation was poor, and unable out of their own means to erect a Church, without assistance of others, as a great many of the members had been obliged to desert their respective places of abode; Praying that I would be pleased to grant the said petitioners, my License or Permission, to collect of the Good People of this Province, such sums of money as they would be pleased to contribute towards the said Pious Undertaking, &c."

And I, favoring the request, These are therefore to permit, and License the said Christian Roth and David Ettley, within the space of three years, from the Day of the Date hereof next ensuing, to make a collection of the Good People of this Province, who are willing to Contribute towards the Building of a Church, or a House of Worship, for the said Lutheran Congregation of Middletown, aforesaid, any sum or sums of money, not exceeding in the whole Twelve Hundred Pounds, Pennsylvania Currency.

Given under my hand and seal at Arms, at the City of Philadelphia, the twenty-eighth Day of September, in the year of our Lord, one thousand seven hundred and sixty-four; and in the fourth year of the Reign of our Sovereign Lord George, the third. By the Grace of God, of Great Britain, France and Ireland, King Defender of the Faith, &c.

JOHN PENN.

By His Honor's Command,
Joseph Shippen, Sec.

There is no record to show how much of this money was raised. The members were few, widely scattered, and as appears from the terms of the lease, very poor; in fact David Ettley, one of the committee, walked as far as Philadelphia on his collecting tour. Many of the settlers had but recently been driven from their clearings by the Indians, who roamed the surrounding forests, and who for years had been desolating this frontier with tomahawk, scalping knife and torch. The nearest churches were those of the Presbyterians at Paxton, Derry and Conewago, and the worshippers who visited them carried firearms, which they stacked inside during the sermon.

The church edifice was built in 1767. The corner-stone was laid by Justice (Col.) James Burd in the presence of the Revs. Theophilus Engeland, N. Harnell, and Conrad Bucher; and the church warden and elders, John Christ, Roth, John Metzgar, George Philip Shaage, Gottlieb David Ettley, and Jacob King, and also the building committee, Conrad Wolfley, Frederick Zeppernick, and George Frey. In the corner-stone was placed a German Bible; the shorter catechism of Martin Luther; three wafers; a half-pint bottle of wine; and some money in Pennsylvania currency.

The building was constructed of old red sandstone, was two stories in height, and had a gallery on the east, south and west sides, the pulpit occupying the north side. The main entrance was on Union street, but there was also a door on High street. A staircase led from each door to the gallery, meeting in the northeast corner thereof. The windows were small, as were also the panes of glass in them. The floor was composed of bricks nine inches square. The pews were narrow, with high, straight backs. The pulpit, a sort of marten box on an enlarged scale, was supported by a post eight or ten feet high, and reached by a

CHRONICLES OF MIDDLETOWN. 43

narrow winding stairs; over it, like a huge extinguisher, hung a sounding board. A pipe organ was introduced some years afterwards.

There was no provision made for heating, and when sixty years later, stoves were introduced, they were looked upon by the older members as a dangerous innovation. The first stoves were enormous affairs, capable of receiving into their interiors sticks of wood four feet in length.

The membership of "St. Peter's Kirche" (as the stone above the doorway has it), consisted, at this time (1767), of sixty-six old and sixty-three young persons.

In August, 1793, George Frey and Jacob King, acting for the congregation, purchased of George Gross and wife, the adjoining lot (No. 134), for £3 and a yearly rent of one grain of wheat. By mistake (?) the deed was made to Frey and King individually, but when they died their trustees and executors—John Landis, Charles Fisher, William Crabb and John Cassel for Frey's estate, and Jacob Snyder and Daniel Ehrisman for King's—conveyed it, by a deed bearing date October 7th, 1807, to the trustees of the church, viz: John Metzgar, Philip Ettele, John Blattenberger, Jacob Wolfley, Christian Eshenauer and Mark Snyder.

On March 10th, 1807, application was made by the congregation for a charter of incorporation. The paper was signed by John Blattenberger, Jr., John Croll, David Ettele, Ludwig ———, Martin Hemperly, John Heppich, George Lowman, Christian Lorentz, Jonas Metzgar, George Schneegantz, Jacob Snyder, George Shalkey, Nicholas Shuler, George Schuler, John Smuller, Christian Spayd, Ludwig Wolfley, Valentine Weirick and Matthias Walf. March 18th, the application was approved by Justices William Tilgman, J. Yates, Thomas Smith and H. H. Breckenridge, of the Supreme Court of Pennsylvania, and March 21st Governor Thomas McKean authorized Timothy Matlack, master of the rolls, to issue the charter prayed for.

In 1813 the steeple was built. For this purpose twelve hundred and eleven dollars and thirty-five cents were subscribed by one hundred and ninety-three persons, whose names (among which are those of the ancestors of many citizens of the town), are in the church records.

In 1826 Jane Hannegan sold lot No. 133 to the congregation. So that the old church and cemetery comprise three lots, viz: Nos. 133, 134, 135.

In 1830 the brick floor was replaced by a wooden one; the straight-backed pews gave way to more comfortable ones, a new pulpit was erected which had steps on either side, and a recess beneath where the pastor could retire and prepare himself for his duties, a semi-circular rail enclosing it.

In 1835 the lecture room was built. In 1850 the whole inside woodwork—pews, gallery and all—was removed.

The windows, which were formerly in two tiers, were made into one, and the doorway, facing High street, was converted into a window;

the pulpit was erected at the west end; a vestibule was made, from which enclosure stairways led to the gallery, and shut off the cold from the auditorium. The parsonage on High street was built in 1855. This old stone church is now only used occasionally, principally at the funerals of those older members who wish the services held within its walls.

On September 4th, 1867, the church celebrated its centennial anniversary, at which were present many distinguished clergymen of the Lutheran and other denominations, and persons prominent in the State. On this occasion one hundred grains of wheat, enclosed in a silken bag, were sent to the Hon. Robert T. Fisher, of York, Pa., the oldest of the legal heirs and representatives of George Fisher, who laid out the town, and of whom the church lot was purchased, as full satisfaction of one clause of the original deed, requiring a rental of one grain of wheat to be paid annually.

In 1872, the old building being inconveniently located, and not large enough to accommodate the increasing membership, town lots Nos. 149 and 150 were secured from the Frey estate at a yearly rental of about $16. At a congregational meeting March 7th, 1876, it was resolved to erect a new church edifice, and a building committee consisting of Jos. H. Nisley, William A. Croll, George A. Lauman, R. I. Young and J. E. Carmany was appointed. Plans were adopted June 11th, 1877; the cornerstone was laid September 6th of the same year, and the building completed and dedicated February 2nd, 1878.

It is on high ground at the southwest corner of Union and Spring streets; is of the Gothic style of architecture, and contains an auditorium, a chapel, or Sunday school room—with an annex, separated by a glass partition from the infant room—and a large and convenient library room. The pews are of chestnut, ash and poplar, fair-wood finish and arranged in a semi-circular form. The floor has a gradual slope from the vestibule to the front. The altar, railing and platform are of the same material and finish as the pews. The pulpit, constructed of ash and white walnut, is a beautiful piece of work. Three chandeliers, of the "Corona" pattern, swing from the ceiling. The handsome windows lighting the building are all of stained glass; three beautiful memorial ones, size twelve feet by twenty, are in the auditorium; the one on the east, facing the pulpit, is "In memory of John Croll by his daughters;" the south window is "In memory of Margaretta Cameron, wife of Simon Cameron;" the north window is "In memory of Sophia Young, by her son, James Young." The entire cost of the structure was $19,000. The architect was L. B. Valk, of New York; the builders, Christian Fisher and William Ruhl.

The pastors of the church have been: 1767-73, Rev. Theophilus Engeland; 1773-88, Rev. T. F. Illing; 1788-93, Rev. J. Kurtz; 1793-95, Rev. P. Pentz; 1795-1803, Rev. H. Miller; 1803-12, Rev.T. F. Sheaff; 1812-15, Rev. George Lochman, D. D.; 1815, Rev. A. H. Lochman, D. D.; 1830-34, Rev. J. Van Hoff; 1834-37, Rev. P. Saline; 1837-44, Rev.

S. D. Finckle; 1844-47, Rev. J. Voghbaugh; 1847-48, Rev. L. Gerhart; 1848-53, Rev. W. M. Baum, D. D.; 1853-56, Rev. Benjamin Saddler; 1856-65, Rev. C. J. Ehrehart; 1865-72, Rev. Peter Ruby; 1873-83, Rev. John W. Finkbiner; 1884-1890, Rev. H. C. Holloway; 1890-1904, Rev. F. W. Staley; 1905, Rev. S. T. Nicholas, the present pastor.

Early in the century this congregation seems to have awakened to the necessity of imparting religious instruction to the young, for a Sunday school was commenced in 1819. It was probably a crude affair, possessing little of the system and order which characterize such institutions to-day; the children were taught to read the Bible in English and German, and to sing in concert.

The first superintendent and teacher was Mr. Snell (or Snath). He was succeeded, in 1823, by John Croll. During the latter's incumbency, the lecture room was built, and the school removed thither; it was also organized as a Union Sunday school. In 1861 the building was enlarged to accommodate the increasing number of scholars. Mr. Croll was continuously in office until his death, October 12th, 1873. His successor, George A. Lauman, assumed the position in January, 1874. Died in August, 1888. Samuel Kiefer, assistant superintendent, took charge of the school until January 1st, 1889, when Isaac O. Nissley, the present incumbent was elected.

On the afternoon of the day the new church was dedicated (February 2nd, 1879), the Sunday school marched in procession from the old lecture room to their new quarters.

XI.

Port Royal, although in another township (Londonderry), and on the north side of the Swatara river, is connected with Portsmouth by two bridges, and is as much an integral part of Middletown as West Philadelphia is of Philadelphia, or Allegheny City of Pittsburg. The following I have transcribed from the original deed:

THOMAS PENN AND JOHN PENN, ESQUIRES, true and absolute Proprietors & Governors in chief of the Province of Pennsylvania & Counties of Newcastle, Kent & Sussex on Delaware. To all unto whom these presents shall come Greeting.

WHEREAS in pursuance of a warrant dated the third day of September, 1772, there was surveyed unto William Breden a certain Tract of Land called Port Royal Situate adjoining Swatara Creek & the River Susquehanna in Derry Township Lancaster County BEGINNING at a post at the side of Swatara Creek af'd thence by John Moyer's Land South seventy-seven Degrees East, one hundred & twelve perches to a marked Hickory thence by Daniel Clendenend's Land South forty-nine Degrees West One hundred & twenty perches to a Red Rock at low Water Mark at the side of said River & Creek along the several courses thereof two hundred and forty-two perches & an half to the place of Beginning Containing eighty-seven acres & a half & allowance NOW at the Instance and Request of the said William Breden that we would be pleased to grant him a Confirmation of the same. KNOW YE, that, in consideration of the Sum of fourteen Pounds fourteen Shillings lawful money of *Pennsylvania* to our use, paid by the said William Breden (the Receipt whereof we hereby acknowledge, and thereof do acquit and forever discharge the said William Breden his Heirs and Assigns, by these Presents) and of the yearly *quit rent* hereinafter mentioned and reserved, we HAVE given, granted, released and confirmed, and by these presents, for us, our Heirs and successors, Do give, grant release and confirm, unto the said William Breden, his Heirs and Assigns, the said Eighty-seven acres & an half of Land, as the same are now set forth, bounded and limited as aforesaid: With all Mines, Minerals, Quarries, Meadows, Marshes, Savannahs, Swamps, Cripples, Woods, Underwoods, Timber and Trees; Ways, Waters, Water Courses, Liberties, Profits, Commodities, Advantages, Hereditaments and Appurtenances whatsoever thereunto belonging, or in any wise appertaining and lying within the Bounds and Limits aforesaid (Three full and clear fifth Parts of all Royal mines, free from all Deductions and Reprisals for digging and refining the same; and also one-fifth Part of the Ore of all other Mines, delivered at the Pit's Mouth only excepted, and hereby reserved) and also free leave. Right and Liberty, to and for said William Breden, his Heirs and Assigns, to hawk, hunt, fish and fowl, in and upon the hereby granted Land and Premises, or upon any part thereof: TO HAVE AND TO HOLD the said Tract of Land and Premises hereby granted (except as before excepted) with their Appurtances unto the said William Breden his Heirs and Assigns. To the only Use and Behoof of the said William Breden his Heirs and Assigns forever TO BE HOLDEN of us our Heirs and Successors, Proprietaries of *Pennsylvania*, as of our Manor of Conestgoe, in the County of Lancaster aforesaid in free and common Socage by Fealty only, in lieu of all other Services, YIELDING and PAYING therefore unto us, our Heirs and Successors, at the town of Lancaster, in the said County, at or upon the first day of *March* in every year, from the first day of *March* next, One half penny *Sterling* for every acre of the same, or value thereof in Coin Current, according as the Exchange shall then be between our said Province and the City of LONDON, to such person or persons as shall, from time to time, be appointed to receive the same. AND, in case of non-payment thereof, within ninety days next after the same shall become due that then it shall and may be lawful for us, our Heirs and Successors, our and their Receiver or Receivers, into and upon the hereby granted land and premises to re-enter, and the same to hold and possess, until the said *quit-rent* and all the Arrears thereof, together with the Charges accruing by means of such Non-payment and Re-entry, be fully paid and discharged. WITNESS John Penn Esq; Governor of the said Province, who, as well in his own Right, as by virtue of certain Powers, and Authorities to him for this purpose, *inter alia*, granted by the said Thomas Penn, hath hereunto set his hand,

and caused the *Great Seal* of the said Province to be hereunto affixed, at Philadelphia, this the *twenty-ninth* Day of January, in the Year of our Lord *One thousand seven hundred and seventy-four*, and the 14th Year of the reign of King George the third, over Great Britain &c.

JOHN PENN

Recorded in the Rolls Office of and for the Province of Pennsylvania in Pat't Book A. A. Vol. 14, pa:118.

Witness my Hand & Seal of Office the 31st, January 1774.

WILL PARR, Record'r.

On the 10th of May, 1774, Breden sold his land to Henry Weaver, "miller," of Cærnarvon township, Lancaster county, Elijah Wickersham, merchant, and Joseph Leacock, of Philadelphia, as tenants in common. They laid out a town, naming it Port Royal, into four hundred and sixteen lots. On June 15th, 1774, Leacock sold his interest to Weaver and Wickersham, and upon the same day Weaver and Wickersham made an equitable division of the lots between them. Each took alternate lots: Weaver got two hundred and eleven lots, and Wickersham two hundred and five, with a large lot on Salmon street. Weaver took the even numbered lots and Wickersham the odd numbers.

December 17th, 1774, Elijah Wickersham sold to Samuel Pleasants all the annuities and rents of seven shillings for each lot of 205 lots. After Wickersham's death his executors sold to Charles Hurst, Charles Hurst sold to Susanna Radney; Susanna Radney sold to Doctor William Hurst, and he, on June 15th, 1809, sold to George Fisher for $900. After George Fisher's death, these lots came into possession of Hon. Robert J. Fisher, of York, Pa., who conveyed them to various parties, at different times, disposing of the last but a few months ago.

The other half of these lots (those belonging to Weaver), were sold separately by Martha T. Lorraine, of Clearfield county. She was one of the heirs of Lydia Lorraine, who purchased 200 lots from Elizabeth S. Swift, October 5, 1855, for $250. How Elizabeth Swift became possessed of them, the records of Dauphin county do not show.

A Philadelphia genealogist, in tracing some early Pennsylvania families contributes an interesting bit of history. The Murrays, of Swatara, were of Scotch descent, and appear first in 1732. They were Presbyterians, and active in the Revolutionary War, but Robert, a grandson of the emigrant, after going to North Carolina about 1750, came back, settled in New York, prospered as a merchant, became a Quaker, and, purchasing the tract of land known as "Murray Hill," gave his name to the fashionable centre on Fifth Avenue. It was his son, Lindley Murray, the Quaker, who wrote the grammar, prepared the spelling book, and compiled the "English Reader."

XII.

The experience gained by the men of Middletown during their long conflict on the frontier, was of value to them. Scarce ten years had elapsed, before the approaching throes of that travail of liberty which brought forth the Republic, began to be felt.

The population of Middletown and the surrounding country had not forgotten that their fathers fled from oppression. Their exodus was too recent, and some of those who had first sought an asylum here, were still living to tell their story, and rekindle and keep alive that love of freedom for which they had endured so much. Thus they were the first to protest against the machinations and encroachments of the British government.

On the 10th of June, 1774—*two years before the Declaration of Independence in Philadelphia*, at a meeting in Middletown, of which Col. James Burd was chairman, the following resolutions were passed:

"1. That the acts of the Parliament of Great Britain in divesting us of the right to give and grant our money, and assuming such power to themselves, are unconstitutional, unjust and oppressive.

"2. That it is an indispensable duty we owe to ourselves and posterity to oppose with decency and firmness every measure tending to deprive us of our just rights and privileges.

"3. That a closer union of the Colonies, and their faithful adhering to such measures as a general Congress shall judge proper, are the most likely means to procure redress of American grievances, and settle the rights of the Colonies on a permanent basis.

"4. That we will sincerely and heartily agree to, and abide by, the measures which shall be adopted by the members of the general Congress of the Colonies.

"5. That a committee be appointed to confer with similar committees, relative to the present exigency of affairs."

At the first meeting of the general committee of Lancaster county, December, 1774, which was composed of committees from all the townships, James Burd, Joseph Shearer and John Backenstoe represented Paxton township.

The Middletown resolutions were presented by Elijah Wickersham.

The influence of Philadelphia in the Revolutionary period over the rest of the State, has been greatly overrated. There was a knot of patriots there, but they were surrounded by a population which if not actively, was at least passively hostile to the patriot cause; in fact the counties of Philadelphia, Bucks and Chester, were hot beds of those who were not in sympathy with the party who favored absolute independence of the mother country. It was the intelligent people in the great border counties of Lancaster, Cumberland, &c., that took the initiative and inspired and sustained the able leaders in that city in the course which they pursued. In 1774 the population of the Province was 300,000 of which 120,000 was in Philadelphia, Chester and Bucks coun-

Liberty Engine House.

ties. The same year the excise tax of Lancaster county was twice as much as Bucks, and considerably more than Chester. Cumberland county, with but 20,000 population, pledged herself to put 3,000 men in the service, and borrowing £27,000, did so. Lancaster, Cumberland and York, before the Revolution ended, had sent to the field nearly twice as many men as the three original counties of Philadelphia, Chester and Bucks.

In view of these facts, it is fair to assume that the population, wealth and sentiment of the then new counties were the backbone of independence. The representation in the Provincial Assembly was most unequal; the three original counties had six members each—the eight outer counties had two members each. Thus three counties of the eleven into which the Province was divided, controlled its legislation. No wonder the exasperated Presbyterians and Lutherans complained of Quaker influence. It made them only the more ready to fight, so that this wrong with others, might be redressed.

It may be well to remember that Middletown was at this time the centre of business and population in this section of Lancaster county (Harrisburg had no existence until ten years later), and that most of the companies formed in the border counties, were either mustered here, or camped here, before their march eastward.

Within two days after the news of the battle of Lexington reached here, the Paxton men were organized for resistance.

In June, 1775, Congress authorized the raising of eight companies of riflemen in Pennsylvania. Each company was to consist of one captain, three lieutenants, four sergeants, four corporals, a drummer, a trumpeter and sixty-eight privates. Their pay was as follows: Captain, $20; lieutenant, $13½; sergeant, $8; corporal, $7⅓; private, $6 2-3 per month. They were to find their own arms and clothes.

Each enlisted man subscribed to the following: "*I have this day voluntarily enlisted myself as a soldier in the American Continental Army for one year, unless sooner discharged; and do bind myself to conform in all instances to such rules and regulations as are, or shall be established for the government of said army.*"

One of the first companies raised in the Colonies was that of Captain Matthew Smith, of Paxton. The first Pennsylvania battalion, of which they formed a part, reached Boston in August, 1775.

"They are," says Thatcher, a writer of that day, alluding to the Paxton Boys, "remarkably stout and hardy men, many of them exceeding six feet in height.

"They are dressed in white frocks or rifle shirts and round hats. These men are remarkable for the accuracy of their aim, striking a mark with great certainty at two hundred yards distance. At a review a company of them, while on a quick advance, fired their balls into objects of seven inches diameter, at the distance of two hundred and fifty yards. They are now stationed in our lines, and their shot have frequently proved fatal to British officers and soldiers who exposed themselves to view, even at more than double the distance of common musket shot."

John Joseph Henry, afterwards President Judge of Lancaster and Dauphin counties (the same who years later drew up George—Everhart—Frey's will), wrote an account of the campaign. He was a private in Captain Smith's company, as were also Emmanuel Bollinger, Valentine Weirick and other Middletown men. They led the advance and were in the attack on Quebec in 1775, were with Wayne in Georgia in 1772—at Savannah—at Charlestown, and started to return home when the last of the Pennsylvania Line embarked for Philadelphia, in July, 1783.

James Burd, of Tinian (now Ulrich's), was colonel of the "Fourth Battalion of Lancaster County Associators" (March 1776). As he had been for many years an officer of high rank in the Provincial service, this part of the newly formed State levies were placed under him, as undoubtedly of more experience than any officer within it. The battalion covered territory for eighty miles north and fifty miles east, made up of brave, intelligent and hardy material.

At the muster of the battalion on the 25th of March, the companies were commanded by the following captains: Joseph Shearer, James Cowden, Richard Manning, John Reed, James Murray, Albright Doebler, Jacob Fridley. The men were marched to and participated in the campaign "of the Jerseys" during the summer of 1776, as appears from a "return of the troops quartered in and near Philadelphia."

October 14th, 1776, Thomas Wharton, then President of Council, sent express to Colonel Burd, an order to collect his troops and hold "the battalion in perfect readiness to march at the shortest warning."

October 22nd, Colonel Burd transmits the order to Capt. James Murray. He (Colonel Burd) had been mortified and disappointed in an application for promotion, and had become unpopular with the militia of his command. He had influence enough to get his officers together, but very few of the rank and file made their appearance. Owing to this fact no further action was taken until December, when he sent the following orders to his captains:

TINIAN, 12 Decr, 1776
8 o'clock, A. M.

Gentlemen—upon my Return home Last Night I found an Express had been at my house with the Orders Transmitted you hear with, by wich you will observe that the whole associators in the Battalion with the Exceptions therein mentioned only are to March—In Consequence where of I hereby Request the whole of the Batt'n to be at Middletown Early on Monday Morning Next Prepaird from thence to March to Philadelphia. Agreeable to the Order of Council of Saifty. In the meantime I am Gentlemen. Your Obedient Humble Ser't.

James Burd, Col. 4th
Battallion of Lr. County.

N. B. I have also Orders to hire or Impress all the Wagons I can meet with thairfore I Request that all the Wagons fitt for Service be in Middletown on Monday Morning Early to goe with the Battalion.

"The season was stormy and inclement," but, without delay, a passionate, tumultuous gathering invaded the town. There were no arms to be had, and without weapons it was reasoned that no effective fighting could be done. Under such circumstances a large proportion of the men refused to march.

December 17, 1776, a great meeting was held in Lancaster, to "endeavor to fall on measures for marching the militia of the town and county to join General Washington."

December 27th, Colonel Burd writes to General Mifflin, that the rendezvous was at Middletown. "On December 16th, I intended to march with the battalion, from Monday, the 16th, to Sunday night, the 22nd, instant, and not one man turned out but eighteen, seven of whom were officers, myself included, except a small company of volunteers commanded by Captain Elder, of 33 men, whom I marched off. I put it to the vote of the eighteen if I should not march with them; it was carried against me that I should not." He then says that he was going to Lancaster to see Mifflin; all his officers protested against this step, so that "his influence" might be directed to get the battalion to march.

On the same date he informed William Atlee, Esq., at Lancaster, "you will observe that I have resigned the battalion, and the major did say at Middletown that he would also resign. How that may be I cannot say."

There is good reason to infer, from this evidence, that the people of this part of the State had reasons for dissatisfaction respecting the conduct of those managing the war.

The company commanded by Captain James Murray left Middletown on the day following the departure of Captain Elder, with his "33 men."

On the 24th a company of cavalry under Capt. John Hamilton who had marched that day fifty miles, arrived here and pushed on the next day.

After much confusion and loss of time, a portion of the quota was dispatched to the field. The detachments were placed under other officers, and no truer heroes were ever set in array against the enemy.

In the latter part of January, 1777, Col. Samuel Montgomery, with his Cumberland county regiment, 800 strong, camped here for two days.

On the 12th of August, Capt. John Rutherford with his company assembled here. This company, containing several Middletown men, had been in active service throughout the campaign of '76.

In 1778 Robert Elder (the Captain Elder alluded to by Colonel Burd), who had risen to be colonel of a battalion, camped here with his command, who were under the following officers: Captains, James Murray, Henry McKinney, Samuel Rutherford, ——— McClure, Robert Clark, Martin Weaver, James Stewart, John Gilchrist. Captain McClure commanded one, and Captain McKinney another of the companies raised in and about Middletown.

In the same year, the battalion commanded by Col. Alexander Lowry was ordered to Middletown, and encamped from March until June. The captains of it were Robert McKee, Andrew Boggs, Thomas Robinson, Joseph Work, David McQueen, Robert Craig, Abraham Scott, Hugh Peden, Abraham Forney, Martin Earhart. The whole force was nearly 800 men drawn from territory in the vicinity of Middletown (Conewago, Donegal and Elizabethtown). The camp was on Bomberger's (now Young's) farm, adjoining the town. The reason for this display of force was the protection of the army stores at the Middletown mills, where a vast amount of wheat and other supplies had been collected. Among the officers of the army who took an active part in affairs in and about Middletown, either immediately before, during or after the Revolution, were: Col. James Burd, Col. Jacob Cooke, Col. Cornelius Cox, Col. James Crouch, Col. Edward Crouch, Col. Joshua Elder, Col. Robert Elder, Capt. James Cowden, Capt. John Elder, Capt. John Rutherford, Capt. Joseph Shearer.

Although we cannot separate the Middletown volunteers from those coming from other parts of Paxton township, Lancaster county, yet we find on the muster rolls of the different battalions and companies, some few names which at that time or soon afterwards, were identified with her history, viz: Allison, Allen, Alliman, Burd, Brandon, Bollinger, Baker, Brown, Barnet, Bowman, Black, Bomberger, Cook, Crabb, Cooper, Crouch, Campbell, Davis, Duncan, Dickey, Elliot, Elder, Foster, Fulton, Fairman, Gross, Glover, Hays, Harrigan, Henry, Hamilton, Hogan, Hutchinson, Harris, Jamison, Jontz, Kerr, Kennedy, Lynch, Laird, Moore, Myers, Miller, Minsker, McCormick, McGuigan, McCann, McArthur, McClure, McClenachan, Means, McCord, Murray, McFarland, McNair, Martin, Poorman, Parks, Patterson, Postlethwait, Robinson, Ross, Rennick, Steel, Smith, Scott, Shearer, Sheets, Swinford, Thompson, Taylor, Wier, Walker, Weirich, Wilson, Wolf, Waggoner. The rest, although recorded, cannot be localized.

This was then the most important town in Paxton township of Lancaster county, and therefore it might naturally be supposed that there would be no difficulty in designating those who went from here into the Revolutionary army. There are many names which are familiar ones on our streets to-day and many others that were so a century ago, on the muster rolls of the various companies, but there being no particularization as to residence, I have (as yet) been unable to classify them. Could the dead of those forgotten battlefields, or in the deserted graveyards of Paxton, Derry and Conewago, speak, or had their tombstones longer resisted the gnawing tooth of time, we would know that of the more than two thousand patriotic men which Paxton township sent to the front, Middletown contributed her full quota.

Can you not in fancy see them—you, whose freedom they won—those brave, stalwart pioneers—as in fringed buckskin or faded blue and buff uniforms, with powder horns and patches, bullet pouches and muzzle-loading, flint-lock guns, they marched through the single, log cabin-lined street of old Middletown—the hardy frontiersmen of Pennsylvania—on their way to meet the veteran legions and mercenary allies of a power that had battled with, and (up to that time) beaten all nations that dared to oppose her.

> On Fame's eternal camping-ground
> Their silent tents are spread,
> And glory guards, with solemn round,
> The bivouac of the dead.
>
> Nor wreck, nor change, nor winter's blight
> Nor time's remorseless doom,
> Can dim one ray of holy light
> That gilds their glorious tomb.

XIII.
Wyoming Massacre.

May 25th, 1778, the Supreme Executive Council of Pennsylvania writes to the Board of War. After alluding to the fact that Colonel Grubb wishes a guard of one hundred men at Lebanon, and that the Hon. W. A. Atlee insists on keeping a guard at Lancaster until he has collected the Hessian prisoners, they add a postscript. "It is proposed to withdraw the guard at Middletown as soon as the Hessians are brought."

July 3d, 1778, occurred the "Wyoming Massacre." The Tories and Indians, commanded by Col. John Butler, defeated the settlers under Col. Zebulon Butler. (These latter were principally old men and boys, the able-bodied men being absent in the Continental army.) Then followed a massacre of the survivors, out of 400 but sixty escaped. (It is said that the war made 150 widows and 600 orphans in the Wyoming valley.) This remnant taking refuge in Forty-Fort, succeeded in effecting terms of capitulation, stipulating that their lives and property should be spared; but the Indians could never be bound by treaty, and after Col. John Butler and his army had left, burning and plundering commenced, and the remaining widows and orphans, a desolate band, with scarcely provisions for a day, took up their sad pilgrimage over the dreary wilderness of the mountains and the dismal "Shades of Death."*

Mr. Minor says:
"What a picture for the pencil! Every pathway through the wilderness thronged with women and children, old men and boys. The able men of middle life and activity were either away in the general service, or had fallen. There were few who were not in the engagement; so that in one drove of fugitives consisting of one hundred persons, there was

---
*On the head waters of the Lehigh, was an immense body of rather wet land, covered with a dense forest of pine. This place was called, by the forlorn fugitives from Wyoming, the "Shades of Death."

only one *man* with them. Let the painter stand on some eminence commanding a veiw at once of the valley and the mountain. Let him paint the throng climbing the heights; hurrying on, filled with terror, despair and sorrow. Take a single group, the affrighted mother, whose husband had fallen; an infant on her bosom; a child by the hand; an aged parent, slowly climbing the rugged way, behind her; hunger presses them sorely; in the rustling of every leaf they hear the approaching savage; the "Shades of Death" before them; the valley, all in flames behind them; their cottage, their barns, their harvests, all swept in this flood of ruin; their star of hope quenched in this blood shower of savage vengeance!"

These fugitives were the families of the Connecticut settlers in Wyoming, against whom a strong feeling existed at that time, the reasons for which do not concern these "Chronicles." William Maclay, the founder of the Democratic party, and (in 1779) the first Senator of Pennsylvania in the United States Senate, was among the number of those obliged to flee, and although so strongly prejudiced against the settlers that, in 1773, in writing to the Secretary of the Province, he says, that "if Hell is justly considered as the rendezvous of rascals, we cannot entertain a doubt of Wyoming being the place." In a letter sent from here (Paxton), to Timothy Matlack, Secretary to the Executive Council of Pennsylvania, July 12th, 1778, says:

"Dr Sir

"I write you this letter with reluctance, as I am certain it must give pain to any man of sensibility to be informed of the distressed situation of our Frontiers.—I will not trouble you with a recital of the inconvenience I suffered while I brought my family by water to this place. I never in my life saw such scenes of distress. The river, and the roads leading down to it, were covered with men, women and children, flying for their lives, many without any property at all, and none who had not lef the greatest part behind.—The panic and spirit of flight has reached even to this place. Many have moved even out of this township, and almost every one is thinking of some place of greater security.—Something, my dear sir, must be done to restore Confidence to the desponding and flying multitude, and to make them face the enemy. Depend on it, Sir, the County will be lost without some vigorous measures. For God's sake, for the sake of the Country, let Colonel Hunter be reinforced at Sunbury—send him but a single company, if you cannot do more. Mrs. Hunter came down with me. As he is now disencumbered of his family, I am convinced that he will do everything that can be expected from a brave and determined man. I must mention to you with freedom, an opinion that has prevailed, and done great hurt on the Frontiers, viz, that no men or relief would be sent to them. The miserable example of the Wyoming people, who have come down absolutely naked among us, has operated strongly, and the cry has been, let us move while we may, and let us carry some of our effects along with us.—Something in the way of charity ought to be done for the many miserable objects that crowd to the banks of this river, especially those who fled from Wyoming; they are a people, you know, I did not use to love, but I now most sincerely pity their distress.—I cannot but hope that the men will most cheerfully return, with the first troops that go up that way. We are told every hour of more and more murders committed by the straggling savages. We hope a great part of this vague intelligence may prove without foundation. The Express waits—am in great haste, Dear Sir, with sincere regard.

"Your most obedient and most
"humble servant,
"WM. MACLAY."

July 14th, 1778, Bartram Galbraith, writing from Lancaster to "George Bryan, Vice-President for the State of Pennsylvania," says: "Yesterday, at noon, I rec'd the alarming intelligence of eight or nine hundred British troops, Tories and Indians, coming down the East Branch of the Susquehanna, driving all before them; it is said they have taken three of our Forts at Wyoming, or near to it; out of which, four hundred of our men sallied out upon the enemy (not expecting them to be such a number), and that only sixty escaped, since which, the enemy have burnt the people's habitations thereabouts. On Sunday morning last, the banks of the Susquehanna from Middletown up to the blue Mountain, were entirely clad with the inhabitants of Northumberland County, who had moved off, as well as many in the river, in boats, canoes, rafts, &c. Indeed the inhabitants of Wiconisco valley, which is about twenty-five miles above Harris's ferry, in this county, were moving on Sunday last, and that the people lower down were thinking to follow. This I had from Captain Scott, a man of veracity who was up at Garver's mill for his sister, the wife of Colonel Hunter, and spake with a lieutenant of a company that was stationed at Wyoming, and was in the action; he also seen six of the wounded men that were brought down. In the mean time, I'm venturing the privilege of calling the class's of militia that were ordered to hold in readiness some time ago last March— It is really a melancholy affair for the inhabitants of Northumberland, as well as many of this county; for should they not get their crops cut, or some of them, the poor people will be entirely ruined; as many of them has been obliged to come off without the necessaries of life, or wherewithal to purchase, leaving their stocks behind, &c. In haste I wait the orders of Council,

"and am your ob't
"h'ble serv't
"BARTRAM GALBRAITH, LT.

Lancaster County."

At this time (1778) Middletown was the first place on the river, of any size, which the fugitives would reach and as the wounded, naked and famished refugees landed from their rude canoes, dugouts, and hastily improvised rafts, after days of exposure and suffering, and thronged on shore, what a cheering sight must the little burg with its single street, lined with one and two-story log houses, have seemed to them. There was a generous sympathy and hospitality among the old frontiermen, it was share and share alike; and although the newcomers, of some nationalities, from the wornout old world, were disposed to be close-fisted, their offspring, in the free air of that boundless domain, soon lost the grasping and mercenary proclivities of their progenitors. So they were welcomed with open hands, tables were bountifully spread with venison, bacon, hominy, corn-pone, milk and wild honey; with lashins of whiskey to wash it all down. And thus soothed and comforted, they rested; and forgot in sleep, for awhile at least, the horrors and woes of the recent past, and the loneliness and gloom (for many of them) of the future.

In 1779 General Sullivan was dispatched to carry the war into the Indian country, and (as was stated in a previous paper) the boats for this expedition were built in Middletown.

Philadelphia, May 13th, 1779, Ephraim Blaine writes to President Reed: "Sir, I have some time ago given orders to my assistant at Lancaster to send, and without delay, four hundred barrels of flour to Middletown," etc.

June 2nd, 1779, President Reed writes to Col. Samuel Hunter, requesting him, as Lieutenant of the county of Lancaster, to afford General Sullivan all the aid in his power; stating, incidentally, that it will be unnecessary to order out the militia of that county, as "there can be no danger from an enemy, from Middletown to Sunbury," etc.

On the next day, he (President Reed) writes to General Sullivan, "upon the subject of providing an escort for the stores from Middletown," etc.

July 28th, 1779, Colonel Hunter writes from Sunbury to Col. Matthew Smith, of Paxton, detailing fresh Indian outrages there, and concludes: "N. B. Rouse ye inhabitants there, or we are all ruined here.— S. H."

On the same date Francis Allison writes to Col. Joshua Elder, Sub. Lieutenant Lancaster county, to the same effect, ending: "If any relief can possibly be afforded it should be given instantly, otherwise the towns of Northumberland and Sunbury must be the barriers." Writing again. on the 29th, he says: "Hurry if possible, all the assistance possible, with utmost haste, or else the consequences on our side will be dreadful."

On the 30th, William Maclay writes from Paxton to Timothy Matlack, Secretary of the Council, ending: "I need not ask you what is to be done, Help, Help; or the towns of Sunbury and Northumberland must fall; our whole frontier laid open, and the communication with General Sullivan's army is cut off."

August 3rd, Col. Matthew Smith notifies President Reed of his arrival "at Sunbury with sixty Paxton Boys." He says: "The Distress of the people here is great—you may have some Conception, but can scarcely be told—the town now composes Northumberland County.

The Enemy have burnt Everywhere they have Been, houses, barns; rye and wheat in the fields, stacks of hay, &c., is all consumed—such devastation I have not yet seen" &c.

August 5th, William Maclay writes from Sunbury to Council, speaking of the arrival of this company; and says: "Every hour has brought us fresh accession of Numbers; We were near five hundred strong this morning, and the whole marched under the command of Colonel Smith, for Muncy, to seek them (the enemy) out."

In the summer of 1779, General Sullivan's expedition arrived at Wyoming; as they passed the fort, arms gleaming in the sun, their hundred and twenty boats arranged in regular order on the river, and their two thousand pack-horses in single file, they formed a military display surpassing any yet seen on the Susquehanna, and well calculated to make a deep impression on the minds of the savages.

They arrived at Tioga Point, August 11th, and hearing that the enemy were at Chemung, an Indian village twelve miles above, went up and discovered them lying in ambush below; the Indians were driven off, and, after destroying their grain, &c., the army returned to Tioga to wait for General Clinton's brigade, which came down the East Branch on the 22nd of August from New York, with 200 batteaux. The united forces now moved forward up the Tioga, into the Genesee country. They burnt the Indian towns of Katherine's-town, Candai, Kanandaiga, Kanaghias, Gaghsuguilahery; Jenise, their capital or chief town, and twenty-four others; laid waste their fields, and destroyed all their corn, a quantity not less than one hundred thousand bushels, and returned to "Fort Sullivan," at Tioga, September 30th, 1779. They were received by Colonel Shreeve (who had been left behind with two hundred men to guard the place), with a joyous salute, and "as grand an entertainment as the circumstances would admit."

The ravages committed by General Sullivan, made but a slight impression upon the savages; they hovered around the frontier until the close of the Revolution (1783).

August 6th, 1781, President Reed writes "to Captain Robinson of the Company of Rangers: I hope that by this time the ammunition and clothing sent to Captain Hambright, to be forwarded to Captain Scott at Middletown, and thence to Captain Hunter, has arrived safe," &c. He also writes to Capt. John Hambright: "Sir; your letter of the 25th ult., came safely to hand, and we were obliged to you for your care in forwarding the ammunition and clothing to Northumberland. We shall be glad you would inform yourself whether it has gone forward from Middletown."

To convey a better idea of the size of Middletown at this time, the tax lists for two years, viz: 1778 and 1782 are appended:†

---

†At this time most of the Scotch-Irish settlers were in the army, whence few of them returned to settle again in Middletown.

1778.

Backenstoe, John,
Caldhord, Matthew,
Cassel, Nicholas,
Craft, Philip,
Crabb, Thomas,
Creamer, Jacob,
Derr, Abraham,
Dowdel, Daniels,
Ettele, David,
Ettele, Philip,
Eater, Jacob,
Eakins, William,
Frain, Ulrich,
Frey, George,
Gross, Abraham,
Gross, Michael,
Hebright, Christian,
Harris, Henry,
Hemperly, Ludwig,
Hubley, Frederick,
King, Christian,
King, Jacob,
Kennedy, Dr. Robert,
Kalm, Margaret,
Lebernick, Frederick,
Lowman, George,
Lanning, Dr. John,
McKinley, Widow,
Moyer, Henry,
Metzgar, George,
Miller, Adam,
Miller, Peter,
Minshall, Thomas,
Mayer, John,
Parthemore, Philip,
Reigard, Peter,
Roth, Christian,
Singleton, Joseph,
Wolfley, Conrad,
Snodgrass, George,
Still, John,
Seabaugh, Christian,
Shertzer, Samuel,
Swinford, Albright,
Snyder, Mark,
Snyder, John,
Snyder, Jacob,
Snyder, Simon,
Shuster, Peter,
Shaffner, Henry,
Spayd, Christian,
Shockin, Philip,
Shertz, Christian,
Scott, Patrick,
Toot, Thomas,
Walton, Jacob,
Welker, Felty,
Weirich, Philip,
Wall, William.

1782.

Bombach, Conrad,
Bollinger, Emanuel,
Backenstrose, John,
Beitle, Michael,
Barnet, John,
Cassel, Nicholas,
Crabb, William,
Crabb, Thomas,
Conrad, Michael,
Cremer, Elizabeth,
Cryder, Christian,
Craft, Philip,
Conn, Daniel,
Davis, Henry,
Defrance, John,
Dowdel, Daniel,
Ettele, David,
Ettele, Philip,
Farr, Abraham,
Frey, George,
Gross, Abraham,
Gross, Michael,
Gross, George, Jr.,
Gross, George, Sr.,
Gregg, Joseph,
Harrigan, Patrick,
Hollenback, John,
Hubley, Frederich,
Heppich, Christian,
Hemperly, Ludwig,
Hemperly, Martin,
Harris, Henry,
Jamison, Alexander,
King, Christian,
Kennedy, Robert,
Kissinger, John,
Lytle, John,
Lowman, George,
Lipse, Anthony,
Lenning, Dr. John,
Moore, Thomas H.,
Minsker, John,
Minsker, Thomas,
McCann, Henry,
Miller, Jacob,
Miller, Peter,
Miller, Adam,
Myers, Henry,
McClure, David,
Parthemore, Philip,
Parks, Samuel,
Reichert, Peter,
Shaffner, Henry,
Scott, Patric,
Shertz, Christian,
Spayd, Christian,
Shuster, Peter,
Shertzler, Samuel,
Shockey, George,
Snyder, Jacob,
Snyder, John,
Snyder, Mark,
Seabaugh, Christian,
Sneaganc, George,
Tebemack, Frederick,
Wickersham, Abner,
Wolfley, Conrad,
Walker, Valentine,
Wells, William.

The roll of 1750—already given—contains 45 names. Estimated population, 200 persons. The roll of 1782 contains 70 names. Estimated population, 350.

In 1778 the following Middletown soldiers were among those detached from the army and, under Captain Crouch and others, sent to repel the Indians who were committing raids upon the frontiers of Pennsylvania. James McCord, Conrad Alleman, Martin Houser, Jacob Miller, Frederick Cassel, George Sheetz, Conrad Wolfley, Dr. Robert Kennedy, Adam Ritter, John Minsker, Albright Swineford, Christian King, John Ritter, Jacob Miller, John Swineford, George Sneagance, Robert Herron, George Williams, Simon Reardon, Richard Allison, Joseph Mark.

The roll of record in Dauphin county in 1785 contains 120 names; estimated population 600.

In 1799 Paxton township was divided and Swatara taken off.

These rolls, when compared with that of 1750 and other data, show the nationality of the earlier and subsequent settlers in and near Middletown.

XIV.

In 1777-1779, owing to the large number of tories in certain parts of the State, it was considered necessary by the Assembly to impose an oath of allegiance; a measure which is usually taken, particularly in civil war; in the late war it was only those suspected of disloyalty who were required to take such an oath, but in Revolutionary times, when the population was sparse, all were obliged to swear, as follows:

"We the subscribers, do swear (or affirm), that we renounce and refuse all allegiance to George the Third, King of Great Britain, his heirs and successors, and that we will be faithful and bear true allegiance to the Commonwealth of Pennsylvania, as a free and independent State, and that we will not at any time do or cause to be done, any matter or thing that will be prejudicial or injurious to the freedom and independence thereof as declared by Congress, and also, that we will discover, and make known to some justice of the peace of said State, all treason and traitorous conspiracies which we now know, or hereafter shall know, to be formed against this or any of the United States of America."

Each person taking the oath was given the subjoined certificate:

"I do hereby CERTIFY that ——————— hath voluntarily taken and subscribed the Oath or Affirmation of Allegiance and as directed by an Act of General Assembly of Pennsylvania, passed the 15th day of June, A. D. 1777. Witness my hand and seal the ——— day of ———————, 177—. ———————, [L. S.]

The following are a few of the names of the inhabitants of Middletown, and its immediate vicinity, who took the oath:

Allison, Robert,
Ashcraft, William,
Benner, Jacob,
Burd, James, Esq.,
Burd, Edward,
Brown, John,
Boland, John,
Crouch, Capt. James,
Chesney, John,
Crab, Thomas,
Cassel, Nicholas,
Carson, George,
Donley, John,
Deem, Adam,
Davis, Henry,
Dowdel, Daniel,
Derr, Conrad,
Ettele, Philip,
Ettelin, Gottleib David,
Flora, Peter,
Gross, Christian,
Hinds, John,
Hemperly, Ludwig,
Holmes, Abram,
Hemperly, Martin,
Johnston, Thomas,
Kirkpatrick, William,
Kennedy, Dr. Robt.,
King, Thomas,
Kirkpatrick, James,
Lewis, Michael,
Lindsay, William,
Lowman, George,
McClure, Jonathan,
McClure, Alexander,
McClure, Andrew,
McClure, William,
McClure, Roan,
McCord, Robert,
McClure, Richard,
McCord, James,
McClenaghan, William,
Moore, Howard,
Means, John,
Means, James,
Minsker, George,
Moore, John,
McGill, Robert,
Youngman, Jacob.
Means, Adam,
Moore, Thomas,
McNair, Thomas,
Plesson, Anthony,
Ryan, John, Jr.,
Raredon, Simon,
Shearer, Joseph,
Spade, Michael,
Shocken, George P.
Steel, John,
Steel, William,
Shuster, Peter,
Shoop, Barney,
Steever, Daniel,
Spade, Christian,
Thompson, Thomas,
Thompson, John,
Tate, Conrad,
Wickersham, Abner,
Wall, William,
Wertz, James,
Work, James,
Wolf, Michael,
Wierich, Valentine,

Those who would not take the oath were fined. Among the Quakers, Mennonites, Dunkards and others, who from conscientious scruples, doubt as to the final issue, or opposition to the cause of the colonies refused it, there were many who objected to paying the fine, and the Pennsylvania Archives show that the authorities had much difficulty in collecting it.

IMPROVEMENT OF THE SUSQUEHANNA.

September 5th, 1789, a meeting of the inhabitants was held in the Court House, to consider what steps should be taken to remove "the obstructions in the river Susquehanna," particularly at Conewago Falls. It was resolved that a subscription be raised for the purpose of "clearing" those falls, so that the river might be navigated as far down as Wright's Ferry (Columbia), and that certain responsible persons be appointed and meet at Mr. Archibald McAllister's in Paxton township, Dauphin county, on October 19th.

On this date "a number of the inhabitants of the counties of Lancaster, York, Cumberland, Northumberland, Dauphin, Huntingdon and Mifflin," met. Parties were selected to "raise subscriptions in their several counties," and a treasurer and five commissioners were appointed to carry the project into execution.

November 9th, the State Council instructed them as to the territory they were to examine, and the necessity of having their report of probable expense, &c., ready to be laid before the General Assembly during their "present session." This report was received, and March 31, 1790, the General Assembly instructed the President of the State, and Supreme and Executive Council, to appoint three suitable persons to re-examine, &c.

April 6th, 1790, Timothy Matlack, John Adlum, and Samuel Maclay were appointed commissioners to examine and survey the waters of the Quattapahilla, Swatara, part of the Susquehanna, &c. April 8th, instructions were given them.

April 23rd, Timothy Matlack and John Adlum, Esqrs., two of the commissioners apply to Council for the funds, provisions, tents, instruments, &c., necessary for their expedition.

Their estimate of time, provisions, &c., is as follows:

	Men.	Days.	Days.
From Sunbury down to Middletown 3 men, and stay there 13 days,	3	13	39
From Middletown to Sunbury and stay there,	5	6	30
From Sunbury to mouth of Consua	8	51	408
Three men returning with horses,	3	10	30
From Consua to Juniata,	5	78	390
Commissioners,	3	148	444
Day's provisions,			1,341

Provisions.	£	s	d		
25 bls of Flour,	25	00	00		
150 lbs of Chocolate boxes, &c.,	8	00	00		
160 lbs of Sugar,	7	10	00		
800 lbs of Pork and Bacon,	20	00	00		
Pease and Rice,	2	00	00		
Other small stores,	6	00	00		
				68	10 00
4 horses @ £12 10,	50	00	00		
4 pack saddles,	6	00	00		
Axes and adze,	2	05	00		
Rope, Nails, gimblets and small stores not in the Arsenal,	3	00	00		
(much too low.)					
Casks for packing, &c.,	4	00	00		
Boat,	15	00	00		
Men's pay, equal to 30 months, at 75s,	112	10	00		
Baggs, say 8, at 5d,	2	06	00		
				195	01 00
				£263	11 00

No rum is estimated, but there must be either in pay or something else as compensation.
Contingent expenses.
And carriages across from Connemach.
Carriages, &c., &c.
Powder and Lead.

Estimate of Time.

On the Quatapahill and Swatara, 7 days.
To the Juniata, including unavoidable delay at Middletown, 3 days.
To Sunbury, including the time for viewing Berry's Falls, McGee's Half Falls, Berger's Riffle and Shamokin Falls, 6 days.
(From Sunbury they estimate expenses to Sinamahonging exploring the Consua Toby's Creek, the Presquile, the Kiskeminetas Stoney Creek from the Juniata.)
Total number of days, 148.

And in this estimate very little, if any allowance is made for rainy weather, and everything is supposed to go straight forward, without delay of any kind.

The commissioners left Philadelphia May 6th, 1790. Met Maclay at Lebanon and commenced the survey, (which it is not necessary to give in detail). They found the people on the Quitapahilla opposed to them; and not disposed to aid them; had no time to go "in search of people of more good sense," and so came on down the Swatara, "which we found to be a very fine stream of water with much less fall than we had been led to expect," &c. "We found it necessary to stop at Middletown, to procure several articles of provisions, which detained us until Friday morning, when we set out for Sunbury."

In 1795, attention was again directed to the navigation of the Susquehanna. There was no definite action taken, however, until March, 1823, when an act was passed by the Legislature for the improvement of the river from Northumberland to tide-water, and Jabez Hyde, Jr., John McMeans, and Samuel L. Wilson were appointed commissioners to superintend the work. Jan. 14, 1826, they made their report, stating that contracts for the improvement of the river between Northumberland and Columbia will be incomplete until further appropriations are made; that contracts between Columbia and tide-water were nearly completed, and that when finished, "crafts will be able to descend from Columbia to the head of the Maryland Canal carrying from fifty to sixty tons at a stage of water at which, previous to the improvements, they could not arrive at the latter place, with more than one-half that quantity."

The total amount of expenditures made by these latter commissioners up to January 14th, 1828, was, from Northumberland to Columbia $1,201.50; and from Columbia to the mouth of the river $14,323.37; making a total of $15,524.87.

But altogether considerable sums were thus spent in improving the

CHRONICLES OF MIDDLETOWN. 63

navigation of the Susquehanna and its confluents, the anticipated benefits to be derived therefrom, owing doubtless to the subsequent construction of canals and railroads, running parallel therewith, were never realized.

SLAVES.

Slavery had existed in most, if not all, of the Colonies prior to the Revolution; but slave labor never was profitable in northern latitudes, and one by one the States north of Mason and Dixon's line abandoned it. March 1st, 1780, the Pennsylvania Assembly passed an act for its abolition. There were at the time quite a number of slaves owned in this State; in Paxton township of Lancaster county there were upwards of a hundred. In the immediate vicinity of Middletown, among other slave-holders, Colonel James Burd owned four, viz: Lucy, aged 35; Cuff, aged 13; Diana, aged 7; Venus, aged 2. Captain James Crouch owned eleven, viz: Bodly, aged 60 years; Sambo, aged 50; Phillis, aged 50; Jack, aged 30 years; Lucy, aged 30; Peter, aged 15; Nan, aged 12; Ket, aged 9; George, aged 7; Nell, aged 3; Isaac, aged 9 months. William Kirkpatrick owned one, viz: Richard, aged 27 years. Joshua Elder owned five, viz: Jack, aged 36 years; Pero, aged 29; Gin, aged 19; Susanna, aged 2; Silvia, aged 6 months.

XV.

(The following sketch was written by George Fisher, a son of the founder of Middletown. A more comprehensive biography of Mr. Frey may appear in the forthcoming volume.)

GEORGE EVERHARDT (FREY).

After Mr. Fisher, the founder of the town, settled on his estate, among the hands whom he hired to assist in ploughing his fields and clearing his new land, was George Everhardt, then a penniless German lad. George lived with Mr. Fisher some years until he had saved a little fund, when investing his money in a stock of trinkets, finery, and other articles suitable for Indian traffic, he mounted his pack and started up the Susquehanna. Passing the mountains, he encountered a party of soldiers from the garrison at Fort Hunter, a few miles above, who arrested him as a runaway redemptioner (a servant who had been sold for a time to pay his passage from Europe), a character common in those days, and far more consistent with George's appearance and language than that of a peddler, for what peddler, said they, would risk life and property thus alone and on foot, on this dangerous Indian frontier? "Ich bin frey, Ich bin frey" (I am free) repeated George earnestly in German, in reply to their charges.

He succeeded in convincing them of his independence, and went with them to the garrison, where he became quite a favorite; the soldiers knowing him by no other name than "Frey" which they had caught from his first reply to them.

He sold out his pack at a fine profit, and continued to repeat his adventures, still passing as George Frey, until he was able to start a little store in Middletown, and he afterwards erected a mill. Near the close of the Revolution, when the old Continental money was gradually depreciating, George, who always kept both eyes open, contrived to be on the right side of the account so that instead of losing, he gained immensely by the depreciation; and, in short, by dint of untiring industry, close economy, sharp bargains, and lucky financiering, he at length owned a great part of the real estate in and around the town. He had not, however, all the good things of this life; although he was married, Heaven had never blessed him with children—a circumstance which he bitterly deplored. The property, therefore, of the childless man, was destined to support and educate the fatherless children of a succeeding age. He died in 1806 and the brick building still standing on the ground adjoining St. Peter's Lutheran church, and now occupied by several families, was, after many years of expensive and vexatious litigation, built about the year 1840. It was used as an orphan asylum until 1874, when in a commanding and beautiful situation north of the town, the handsome and commodious "Emaus Institute," was erected. In a conspicuous position in the grounds surrounding it is a monument to the memory of George Frey (why his nickname was used instead of his patronymic is a conundrum).

Frey's Mill.

John Fisher, who was born November 3rd, 1760, and died February 27th, 1779, inherited jointly with his brother (George Fisher, Esq.) the patrimonial estate. He built a mill, constructed a dam (traces of which can be seen at low water, a short distance above the feeder dam of the Pennsylvania Canal Company) and dug a mill race. His original intention was to make a canal from the Swatara, so that boats could load and unload at his mill.

He associated with himself John Hollingsworth, a practical miller. In 1784 Fisher withdrew, and December 21st of that year, Hollingsworth went into partnership with George Frey. The new firm purchased of Dr. Fisher his improvements, together with four acres and twenty perches of land, for £500.

According to the articles of agreement entered into between Hollingsworth and Frey, they were to carry on a general milling business, manufacturing flour, middlings, &c., Hollingsworth was to do all the buying of grain, furnish all the barrels for flour, &c. Frey contracted not to retail any mill products at his store, but to send all such purchasers to the mill.

Matters progressed favorably for a while, but soon Hollingsworth detecting Frey violating the contract, forthwith demanded a dissolution

Residence of George Frey, Founder Emaus Orphan Home, Middletown, Pa.

of the partnership. On Frey's refusal, he brought suit for a partition of the property in the Dauphin Common Pleas Court. The judges of this court, Timothy Green, John Glonninger and Jonathan McClure, referred the case to the Supreme Court without deciding it. The suit was docketed in the Supreme Court, September term, 1787.

Hollingsworth had many creditors clamorous for pay; Frey brought forward counter suits against him, and assigned claims of Hollingsworth's creditors to eat up his part, so that finally he was obliged to make an assignment.

On November 19th, 1790, both parties entered into an agreement that judgment should be entered for Frey, unless Hollingsworth, or his assignee, Robert Ralston, should pay one-half of all the money which Frey had expended, or was entitled to on the mill, within six months from July 3rd, 1761; said amount to be determined by three arbitrators, viz: John Kean, Joshua Elder, and John Carson.

April 13th, 1791, the arbitrators brought in their report, granting George Frey £3646 6s 2¾d specie, that being the "one-half of his expenditures on lands, mills, and other appurtenances in question after giving John Hollingsworth credit for the money expended by him on the same lands."

Hollingsworth filed a bill of exception, which the Supreme Court overruled, July 2nd, 1791, and gave judgment on the report. He was now reduced to great straits; the mill property was worth considerably more than twice the amount he was to pay Frey, but he was unable to raise it, and thus was likely to lose all. It was not until five years later that he procured the requisite sum, which, September 26th, 1796, he sent his son to tender Frey; the latter refused to accept it. Then Hollingsworth brought an equity suit in the United States Circuit Court, October term, 1800, complaining that Frey had failed to produce his books and accounts in court, although notified to do so; that the conduct of the referees was improper in various particulars; that the books, accounts, &c., laid by Frey before the referees were untrue and fraudulent; that the latter had suppressed various material documents which he alone possessed; and that the value of the moiety of the property in dispute was at least £10,000. He asked for a perpetual injunction; for an account; for a partition of the premises, and for general relief.

The court decided that Hollingsworth had been guilty of gross negligence in allowing five years to elapse before proffering the amount awarded; "although he had previous notice, that he did not avail himself of an appeal to the discretion of the court, but suffered judgment to pass against him without making any objection," and dismissed the case. The decision was given by Judge Patterson, associate judge of court; Judge Peters, of the district court, dissenting.

Thus Frey became the sole owner. During the progress of the suit, to wit: June 24th, 1789, he purchased from John Fisher and wife "the privilege of cutting a canal or mill race" through their lands "for the purpose of conveying water to turn a mill or mills, or other water works;" granting to John Fisher, on the same day, the right to irrigate his meadow from said race. The deed was witnessed by John Joseph Henry and Frederick Oberlander. He rebuilt and enlarged the mill, increasing its capacity and making it the largest in Pennsylvania, if not in the United States, extending his race, making it a mile and a half in length, and constructed the present dam across the Swatara, above the Iron Mine Run. After the race and dam were completed, the former was found not to be large enough to carry the water required, consequently Frey had to go to the Legislature again for a permit to make it deeper. This was given on condition that he first secured the assent of the owner of the land.

The business transacted at this mill was enormous. Teams came here from far distant points. Flour was shipped (as appears from his books) to Pittsburgh, Philadelphia and Baltimore; to Maryland, Virginia and the Carolinas; in one instance at least, a ship load going to Europe. The river brought an immense trade—one item will give some idea of its magnitude—in 1790 (during the progress of the law suit) there were over three hundred and fifty thousand bushels of wheat brought down the Susquehanna and passed through Middletown for the Philadelphia market.

After George Frey's death the mill was run by the estate until 1843, when Thomas McAllen leased it; in 1845 William Ellinger; in 1847, George Allen; in 1848, John D. Heft, William Rewalt and Abraham Fisher leased it in partnership; in 1849, Philip Zimmerman was added to the firm; in 1850, John D. Heft leased it; in 1852, Henry Vogel and John K. Buser; in 1860, Edward Stover; in 1868, Michael Connelly and M. R. Alleman; then Fortney and Singer; then Edward Allen; then Gottleib Mayor; then the Swatara Mill Co., and finally the Middletown and Swatara Water Co., the present lessee.

THE STUBBS' FURNACES.

Among the first of the Friends (or Quakers) who followed George Fisher to his settlement on the Swatara river, were the Crabbs, Minshalls, Allisons and Stubbs. (Although members of the peaceful denomination which took the lead among the abolitionists and temperance reformers of a subsequent era, I find that none of them objected to a social glass, or a profitable investment in slave property.) Daniel and Thomas Stubbs, brothers, opened a store on the corner of what is now known as Union street and the Square. (The Rodfong property.) They seem to have done an extensive business. Both had families. In 1796 the brothers erected a furnace on what is still known, in the South ward, as the "Steel Furnace Lot." Thomas Stubbs was manager. They manufactured an excellent quality of steel, for which ready sale was found at remunerative prices. This is said to have been the first steel manufactured in America. June 6, 1803, Thomas married Mary Taylor. Oct. 11, 1804, she died. In 1805 a son of Daniel's, in partnership with John Elder, purchased the works, and erected a much larger establishment further up the Swatara, near Frey's mill. For a time they carried on the business successfully, but finally discontinued it. Their retorts or chambers were still standing some years ago.

XVI.

William Penn, in his proposals for a second settlement in the province of Pennsylvania, published in 1690, alludes to the practicability of effecting a communication by water between the Susquehanna and a branch of the Schuylkill. Canals and turnpikes were unknown at this period, even in Great Britain.

In the year 1762 David Rittenhouse surveyed and levelled a route for a canal to connect the waters of the Susquehanna and Schuylkill rivers by means of the Swatara and Tulpenhocken creeks. The Union Canal afterwards was constructed over a portion of this route—*the first which was surveyed for a canal in the colonies.*

The views of the projectors of this enterprise, were, if the difficulties to be encountered are considered, gigantic. They contemplated the junction of the waters of Lake Erie and the Ohio with the Delaware, on a route extending several hundred miles. A portage over the Allegheny mountains was recommended (an expedient which was subsequently adopted).

Duly to appreciate the enterprise of that age we must remember that the great valley of the Ohio was one boundless forest, uninhabited save by wild beasts, or wilder Indians; moneyed capital was almost unattainable; the term "engineering" was unknown to the vocabulary of those days; no canal was *yet* in existence (in England two had been commenced, but were unfinished) and public opinion looked upon them as visionary.

In 1769, a survey, authorized by the Provincial Legislature was made over a course reaching 582 miles to Pittsburg and Erie, and a report issued strongly advocating the execution of the project. But the Revolution, and the financial depression following the struggle, caused the plan to be postponed.

The great scheme of Pennsylvania was allowed to slumber until Sept. 29th, 1791 (about a century after William Penn's prophetic intimation) when the Legislature incorporated a company to connect the Susquehanna and Schuylkill by a canal, and slackwater navigation. Robert Morris, David Rittenhouse, William Smith, Tench Francis and others were named as commissioners. By a subsequent act of April 10th, 1792, a company was incorporated to effect a junction of the Delaware with the Schuylkill river by a canal extending from Norristown to Philadelphia, a distance of 17 miles. The Schuylkill river, from the former city to Reading, was to be *temporarily* improved; and thus form, with the works of the Susquehanna and Schulykill company, an uninterrupted water communication with the interior of the State; with the intention of extending the chain to Erie, and the Ohio.

68   CHRONICLES OF MIDDLETOWN.

Experience soon convinced the two companies that a greater length of canal was requisite, in consequence of the difficulty of improving the channels of the rivers; hence the company last mentioned determined to extend *their* canal from river to river, a distance of 70 miles. In conjunction with the former company, they nearly completed 15 miles of the most difficult parts of the two works; comprising much rock excavation, heavy embankments, extensive deep cuttings, and several locks (which were constructed with bricks). In consequence of commercial difficulties, both companies were compelled to suspend their operations, after the expenditure of $440,000.

Frequent abortive attempts were made, from the year 1795 on, to resume operations, but notwithstanding the subscription of $300,000, subsequently tendered by the State, they maintained only a languishing existence.

In the year 1811 the two bodies were united, and re-organized as the Union Canal Company. They were specially authorized to extend their canal from Philadelphia to Lake Erie, with the privilege of making such further extension, in any other part of the State, as they might deem expedient.

In 1819 and 1821, the State granted further aid by a guarantee of interest, and a monopoly of the lottery privilege. The additional subscriptions obtained in consequence of this legislative encouragement, enabled the managers to resume operations in 1821. The line was relocated, the dimensions of the canal changed, and the whole work finished in about six years from this period; after thirty-seven years had elapsed from the commencement of the work, and sixty-five from the date of the first survey.

The canal (including the Swatara feeder, &c.) was 89 miles in length from Middletown to a point on the Schuylkill a short distance below Reading. At Middletown it connected with the main line of the Pennsylvania canal; at Reading with the work of the Schulykill Navigation Company. The descent from the summit to the Schuylkill was 311 feet accomplished with 54 locks; to the Susquehanna 208 feet accomplished with 34 locks.

The summit (between the Swatara and Tulpehocken) was 6 miles 78 chains in length; to which must be added to the navigable feeder, which extended several miles to the coal mines at Pine Grove. On this section the canal passed through a tunnel 729 feet in length, hewn through the solid rock. *(This was the first tunnel constructed in the United States.)*

This summit was supplied by the water of the Swatara, conducted to it by the feeder already mentioned. As the summit was above the level of the feeder, two large water wheels and pumps were used for the purpose of raising water to the requisite height. Two steam engines, one of 120, the second of 100 horsepower, were provided for the purpose of supplying the feeder in case of accident to the water works.

In 1828 about $1,600,000 had been expended in the construction of the work in addition to the proceeds of the lottery, and excluding the sums expended on the old work.

A great error was committed in making the dimensions of this canal too small. It arose, partly from the great scarcity of water, and partly from erroneous views entertained by engineers and others having charge of the work. The locks of most of the State canals accommodated boats of 40 or 50 tons, while those of the Union being adapted only for boats of twenty-five tons, excluded the greater portion of those plying on the other canals. Between 1857 and 1860 it was enlarged. And there still being a scarcity of water three large reservoirs were constructed in 1866; two near Lebanon and one near Myerstown. However, the increasing competition by railroads gradually reduced its traffic to a minimum. It long since ceased to pay expenses, and was finally abandoned in 1885.

XVII.

THE TURNPIKE.

Soon after the settlements began to grow the necessity for roads was apparent, and a road was laid out from Lancaster to Shippensburg, passing through Middletown as early as 1736.

With the increase of travel came the necessity for turnpikes. The first turnpikes in this country were built in Lancaster county, Pennsylvania. The system of roadmaking known as macadamizing received its name from Mr. Loudon McAdam. He went from this country to England in 1783, and introduced his roads there.

The leading feature of his system was setting a limit in size and weight to the stones to be used in the roads, the weight limit being six ounces, each stone to pass through a three inch ring. Then covered with gravel and rolled with an iron roller.

THE CONESTOGA WAGON.

These spendid wagons were developed in Pennsylvania and took their name from the vicinity in which they were first in common use, viz: Conestoga, Lancaster county.

They had a canoe shaped bottom which fitted them specially for a hilly or mountainous country, for in them freight remained firmly in place at whatever angle the body might be. The wagon body was painted blue and had red side boards. The rear end could be lifted from its sockets; on it hung the feed-trough for the horses. On one side of the body was a small tool chest with a slanting lid. This held hammer, wrench, hatchet, saw, pincers, and other simple tools. The wheels had tires sometimes six inches broad. The wagon bodies were arched over with six or eight bows, of which the middle ones were the lowest; these were covered with a strong, pure white, hempen cover, corded down strongly at the sides and ends, and under the rear axle tree were suspended a tar bucket and water pail.

Sleek, powerful horses, of the Conestoga breed, were used by the prosperous teamsters. The horses were usually from four to seven in number, were often carefully matched, all dapple gray, or all bay. They were so intelligent, so well cared for, so perfectly broken, that they seemed to take pleasure in their work.

The heavy, broad harnesses were costly, of the best leather, trimmed with brass plates. Often each horse had a housing of deer skin or bear skin, edged with scarlet fringe, while the head stall was gay with ribbons and ivory rings, and colored worsted rosettes.

Bell-teams were common. An iron or brass arch was fastened upon the harness and collar, and bells were suspended from it. Each horse, save the saddle horse, had a full set of musical bells tied with gay ribbons.

The driver walking alongside, governed his team with an ease that was beautiful to see. These teamsters carried a whip, long and light, which, like everything used by them, was of the best material. It had a squirrel skin or silk cracker, was carried under the arm, and the Conestoga horses were guided more by the crack than the blow.

All chronicles agree that a fully equipped Conestoga wagon, in the days when they were in their prime, was a pleasing sight.

All the teamsters carried their own blankets, and many carried also a narrow mattress, about two feet wide, which they slept upon. This was strapped in a roll in the morning, and put into the wagon. Often the teamsters slept on the barroom floor, around the fireplace, feet to the fire. Some taverns had bunks with wooden covers, around the sides of the room. The teamster spread his lunch on the top or cover of his bunk; when he had finished he could lift the lid and he had a coffin-like box to sleep in, but this was an unusual luxury.

The number of these wagons was vast, at one time over three thousand ran constantly back and forward between Philadelphia and other Pennsylvania towns. Sometimes a number of them followed in close order, the leaders of one wagon with their noses in the trough of the wagon on ahead. To show the amount of this traffic, one man in Middletown spent his time in making the tar-buckets carried by these wagons. In one year Conrad Seebaugh, a cooper here, made for John Landis, who then (1807) kept store at the corner of the "Square," nine hundred fifty-pound firkins in which to pack the butter taken in at the store; and the rental of "Chamber's Ferry" about six miles above Middletown, where most of the travel crossed the Susquehanna, was over $750 per annum.

Main street was a portion of this great highway between Philadelphia and Pittsburgh. (One section of this road, that between the former city and Lancaster, was the first turnpike in the United States. It was commenced in 1792, and finished in 1794, at an expense of $465,000. It was macadamized, and substantial stone bridges spanned the streams crossing it.) Consequently a large proportion of the travel between the east and west passed through Middletown.

Long lines of "Conestoga" or "Pitt" wagons, gaily painted coaches, carriages, horsemen, pedestrians, and great droves of cattle and sheep, were always in sight. Hotels were to be found every few miles, whose jolly landlord knew all the teamsters, drovers, stage drivers, &c., that made the road their thoroughfare. Penn, Washington, Lafayette, Harrison, Webster, Stevens, and many other noted men have traveled over this route. For long distances, especially in the Alleghenies, the country was a dense forest, with only here and there an isolated clearing, but on the pike the travel was as dense and continuous as in the streets of a large town, and sometimes filled the road for miles, as the immense emigration and freightage to the west surged through.

There were several stage lines; the drivers were all armed, and carried horns, which they blew on arriving at or departing from a station. Each stage (and there were sometimes many each way a day) carried ten passengers and was drawn by four horses, which were changed every few miles.

When the railroad was completed between here and Philadelphia (about 1837) the stages ceased running; the traffic grew less and less with each succeeding year, until now its ancient glories exist only in the memories of a few ancient patriarchs, who tell marvelous stories of the "good and old times," and mourn o'er the degeneracy of the present. The turmoil of traffic, the beat of hoofs, the rumble of wheels, the tinkling of teamster's bells, the lowing of cattle, the bleating of sheep, the toot of stage horns, and the cries of the drovers have ceased. The deserted taverns and toll houses have disappeared; grass grows in the once dusty highway and (save an occasional peddler's cart or farmer's wagon) the road is silent and deserted.

XVIII.

The province of Pennsylvania as early as 1756 had put a tax on ardent spirits. Being violently opposed in the western counties, it was, after remaining for years a dead letter, finally repealed. On the 3rd of March, 1791, the Federal Government, at the suggestion of General Hamilton, Secretary of the Treasury, imposed a tax of four pence a gallon on all distilled liquors.

The Government was but recently established, and its powers were little understood. The cause of the Revolution had been an excise law, and the people of western Pennsylvania classed this in the same category as the tax on tea, etc. They were descendants of the Scotch and Scotch-Irish, and came naturally by their love of whiskey. There were no temperance societies in those days and there was nothing disreputable in drinking liquors; it was as common as to eat bread. Distilling was early commenced and extensively engaged in, and was considered as moral and respectable a business as any other. There was no market for rye, their principal crop; there were few roads, and the commerce was carried on by means of pack-horses; now, while a horse could carry but four bushels of grain across the mountains, he could carry the product of twenty-four bushels in the shape of alcohol. Whiskey, therefore, was the one article of traffic by means of which they were enabled to pay for their supplies of salt, sugar and iron. They had cultivated their fields at the risk of their lives, and protected themselves without assistance from the Federal Government; and now when they raised a little more grain than they actually needed, they were prevented doing what they pleased with the surplus.

That is the way in which they looked at the matter; and so when the excisemen, the tax collectors, came, liberty poles were erected; the people assembled in bands; chased off the intruders; singed their wigs; cut off the tails of their horses; put live coals in their boots; tarred and feathered them; burnt their offices, houses and barns; or compelled them to resign. The whole of that section of the State was aroused in armed opposition to the measure.

In Congress, May 8, 1792, material modifications were made in the law, lightening the duty, allowing monthly payments, etc. September 15th, of the same year, the President issued a proclamation, enjoining all persons to submit to the law, and desist from all unlawful proceedings. Government determined 1st, to prosecute delinquents; 2nd, to seize unexcised spirits on their way to market; and third, to make no purchase for the army except of such spirits as had paid duty. June 5th, 1794, Congress amended the law.

All was of no avail, the excitement still continued, and the people, led by prominent men of that day, and section, by united opposition practically nullified it, and demanded its repeal.

It became indispensable for the Government to treat the malcontents with more decision, and so finally the President ordered forward the army which had been collected in the east. It consisted of 15,000 men, regular troops and volunteers from Maryland, Virginia, New Jersey and Pennsylvania. Governor Lee, of Virginia, was in chief command. The other generals were Govenor Mifflin, of Pennsylvania; Governor Howell, of New Jersey; General Daniel Morgan and Adjutant General Hand, General Knox, Secretary of War, General Hamilton, Secretary of the Treasury, and Judge Peters, of the United States Court, also went out to Pittsburgh.

I have been thus diffuse, because history makes but slight mention of this rebellion, and little is known of it. President Washington passed through Middletown in October, 1794, and stopped at the tavern then owned by McCameron on the site now occupied by the Joseph Nisley property, then went on to Carlisle where he reviewed the troops. Among the troops who marched to suppress it was one company commanded by George Fisher, Esq., the founder of Portsmouth. As there were a number of volunteers from Middletown and its vicinity in this company I give an extract from the journal of one of its members, Captain Samuel Dewees. He says:

"Lawyer Fisher, Dentzel, Elder, a storekeeper of the name of Reitzel, and other citizens were engaged in raising a volunteer military company. Lawyer Fisher was elected captain, lawyer Dentzel, ensign, Reitzel, first lieutenant, and ———— ———— second lieutenant. The company was a large one, and each member uniformed and equipped himself in handsome style. Captain Fisher found out the residence of a drummer of the name of Warriour. Warriour had been a British drum-major, but had at an early stage of the Revolutionary struggle deserted from the British, and joined himself to the Continental army, and had beat the drum for it until the end of the war. Warriour was chosen drum-major in Captain Fisher's company and I was chosen fife-major. Warriour was decidedly the best drummer that I had ever seen or heard beat during the Revolution. His music was not of the loudest kind, but it was sharp, clear, well-timed, and rich in its spirit-stirring melodies. Captain Fisher's company was composed of patriotic, intelligent, respectable and wealthy young men, who prided themselves very much in exercising and perfecting themselves in the school of the soldiers.

"Captain Fisher received orders for his company to march on to Carlisle:—We crossed over the Susquehanna river in flats; these were a kind of boat twenty or thirty feet long, and ten or twelve feet wide, with sides a foot and a half or two feet high.

"Upon our arrival in Carlisle we pitched our tents upon the 'commons' beyond the 'spring' and very soon after the camp was formed, ten or twelve men were detached from our company to join General Washington's quarter-guard. President Washington had arrived that day, or the day previous, at Carlisle. He had been there, however, several times previous to our marching thither. Warriour and myself played the detached portion of our company up to the court house, where the General's body-guard was stationed, and then returned to camp.

"In a few days after our arrival at Carlisle, President Washington issued his orders for all to be in readiness to march. On the next or second day thereafter, in the morning, we were ordered to beat up the 'General.' This was a signal tune. As soon as we would commence to play it, all the men would set themselves about pulling up the tent pins, and arranging matters for a general strike. At a certain roll on this tune (called the 'General') all things being in readiness, the tents would be thrown down in one direction and all fall at once in the same movement, or as nearly so as could be done.

"This done, some of the soldiers would engage in rolling them up, whilst others would carry them to the wagon, and pack them, camp-kettles, &c., therein. When this task was accomplished the long-roll was beat and all formed into line. The army then formed by regiments into marching order, then marched and formed the line in the main street of Carlisle. The regiment to which Captain Fisher's company was attached, was formed in the main line of regiments, and upon the right of that line: Captain Fisher's company occupying the right of that regiment, constituted the extreme right of the entire line, and rested in the main street opposite the court house. The rear of the main column rested at a great distance from town on the old Philadelphia road, and beyond the 'Gallows-ground.' This line besides being formed preparatory to the march, was also established for the purpose of passing the review. All the officers were at their posts in front of the line in order to receive and salute the Commander-in-chief and suite. President Washington and the Governors of States then at Carlisle, formed the head of the line. The brigade and field officers that accompanied the President and Governors took their positions in the line preparatory to the review.

"All things being in readiness, the President and suite moved on to a review of the troops. The method of salute was, each regiment as the Commander-in-chief and suite drew near was ordered to 'present arms.' Field officers, captains, lieutenants, &c., in line in advance of the troops, saluted by bringing the hilts of their swords to their faces, and then throwing the points of their swords towards the ground at some little distance from their bodies on their right side, the musicians at the same time playing and beating a salute. The flag bearers at a certain roll of the drum would also salute by waving their colors to and fro. The musicians in this grand line of military varied very much in their salute. Some drummers no doubt knew what tune was a salute, and could have beaten it well, but their fifers could not play it; and some fifers knew how to play it, but their drummers could not beat it. An acquaintance of mine of the name of Shipe, who played the fife for a company from Philadelphia, could have played it, and well too (for many a time we had played it together during the Revolution), but his drummer knew nothing about it. Some musicians played and beat one thing, and some another. One fifer, I recollect (within hearing distance of us), played 'Yankee Doodle' and his drummer no doubt beat it well, too, but it was not a salute. When President Washington and his suite arrived at our regiment, I struck up and Warriour beat the old 'British Grenadiers march,' which was always the music played and beat, and offered to a superior officer as a salute during the Revolutionary War.

"President Washington eyed us keenly as he was passing up, and continued to do so, even when he had passed to some distance from us. After this duty was performed, upon the part of the soldiery, Washington, in conversation with the officers, asked Captain Fisher if his musicians (Warriour and myself) had not been in the Continental service during the Revolution? Captain Fisher informed him that we had been, upon which the President replied that he had thought so, from the playing and beating, and observed that we performed it the best of any in the army, and were the only musicians that played and beat the old (or usual) Revolutionary salute, which he said was as well played and beat as he had heard it during the Revolution. Captain Fisher was very proud of our having so far excelled as to attain the just praise of the President, and said to us upon his return: 'Boys, you have received the praise of President Washington to-day, for having excelled all the musicians in the line in playing and beating up Washington's favorite Revolutionary salute, for he says not a musician in the whole army has played it to-day but yourselves.' If Captain Fisher was proud of Washington's commendation of us, my readers may judge that we were not less proud of it than himself.

"In the course of an hour or two after the troops had been reviewed by President Washington, at Carlisle, the order of 'forward' was given. The whole army then took up its line of march westward, and in the evening of that day it reached Mount Rock and encamped. This place was about seven miles from Carlisle. The next day we passed through Shippensburg and reached Strasburg, at the foot of the mountain, where we encamped. I do not recollect whether we remained at this place longer than a night or not, but think that we were a day and two nights encamped there before we began to ascend the mountain.

"We broke our encampment at Strasburg, and set out upon the march up the mountains. It is nothing to travel over the mountains now to what it was then; the roads were both narrow and steep, as well as crooked. Owing to the zigzag nature of the road, soldiers in front could see many soldiers toward the rear, and the soldiers in the rear could see many of the soldiers that marched between it and the front. This march not being a forced one, ample time was given us to ascend to its summit.

"Soon after our arrival at that place (Bedford), portions of our army were reorganized. Here we lost our captain (Fisher), who was promoted to the rank of major. Lieutenant Reitzel became our captain, and Ensign Dentzel became lieutenant. After these changes were made we had to hold an election for ensign.

"Shortly after this there was intelligence received that the 'Whiskey Boys' in great numbers were lying in ambush awaiting our approach. The whole army received an ample supply of ammunition. The rifle companies were ordered to mould a great many bullets, and much preparation was made to repel any attack which the insurgents might feel disposed to make. The orders to march upon a certain day were general. Each man drew a double or triple quantity of provisions, and received orders to cook the same.

"All things being in readiness, we then took up the line of march, and pushed for the Allegheny mountains. I do not recollect anything worthy of notice until we were descending the western base of the Alleghenies in our approach to the 'Glades.' Here we had a hard time of it. It was now November, and the weather was not only quite cold, but it was windy and rain was falling. By an oversight we were pushed on a considerable distance in advance of our baggage wagons, and at length halted at an old waste barn that we supposed belonged to some one of the insurgents, for had it not been so our army would not have been permitted to burn the fences thereon. We collected rails and built fires, but owing to the rain and marshy nature of that section of country the ground around our fires with our continued tramping became quite miry.

"My readers may judge of the land's surface, and of the state of the roads through the 'Glades' when I inform them that when some of the wagons arrived in the forenoon, at where we had halted the night previous, they had each from twelve to twenty horses attached to them, and the axle-trees were sweeping or shoving the mud and water before them as they moved onwards. None but regular wagoners could have navigated these mud swamps, and none but regular teamsters, or men acquainted with bad roads, or roads in their worst state, can conceive the impassable state of the roads through the 'Glades' in the year 1794.

"We next made a halt at Greensburg, in Westmoreland county, and the next halt we made, was not far from the 'Bullock Plains,' known by many as Braddock's Fields. When we arrived there we formed camp and remained a few days. Whilst there, the soldiers, many of them, amused themselves by climbing up into the trees, for the purpose of cutting out bullets which had been lodged there in 1755, when General Braddock was defeated by the Indians. From Braddock's Fields we moved on to Fort Pitt (now Pittsburgh), and encamped within a mile of the town.

"Whilst we remained at Fort Pitt I obtained permission to visit the town every day or two. The old fort (Duquesne) which had been built for the protection of this post, I do not recollect whether it was occupied by any of our troops, but believe it was not. It was so built as to command the Allegheny and Monongahela Rivers above and at their junction, as also the Ohio river below. The hills around Pittsburgh, particularly those on the opposite sides of both rivers, were very high. The hills above Pittsburgh and between the two rivers were (some of them) quite high, and were called different names, as Grant's Hill, Scotch Hill, Forbes' Fields, &c.

"Instead of being met, as was threatened, by a formidable foe, we saw nothing in the form of enemies. The disaffected had disbanded and gone quietly to their homes. The insurrectionary spirit was every day growing weaker and weaker, and in proportion as this had manifested itself, the insurgent force had diminished. Mustering from seven to ten thousand men only, and they promiscuously and hastily drawn from their homes, young and old, without proper leaders, proper discipline, military stores, &c., they had thought it altogether futile to attempt to resist (or cope with) a well disciplined army of upwards of fifteen thousand strong. After a number of the more active leaders were captured, and handed over to the proper authorities, to be dealt with according to the laws of the land, the expedition was considered at an end. Governor Lee, believing that it was altogether necessary and loudly called for, left General Morgan with a strong detachment in the centre of this disaffected country. The main body of this army was then withdrawn from Pittsburgh, and the surrounding country, and were marched on their way homeward.

Many who sought discharges obtained them; some of them enlisted in the United States regular service and marched on to join General Wayne, who was then engaged in a war with the Indians on the Miami, in Ohio." In the spring the military were finally removed, order had been fully restored, the law was acquiesced in, and business resumed its wonted course.

XIX.

Let us go back about one hundred years and look at the old town in the days of stage coaches and canals; when telegraphs, electric lights, express companies and daily papers were unknown. To the good old era of the scythe and flail, the tallow candle and the tinder box; before lucifer matches, canned goods, reapers, petroleum, sewing machines, steel pens, ready-made clothing, and the thousand and one things that tend to demoralize this generation, and wean them from the simple habits of their ancestors, were dreamed of.

It was a jolly old burg then— no total abstinence societies or local option laws "froze the genial current of the soul." There was whiskey galore, and rows extempore; taverns every block, and streets, stores and inns were crowded with teamsters, raftsmen, boatmen and travelers. Yes, those were the flush times of Middletown, and we who live in these degenerate days can only mourn that we were not born sooner.

Commencing on the square—we find the old log house of George Rodfong's on the southeast corner, belonging to Joseph Struhman; he traded it to John Achey,[1] who lived here and carried on cabinet making in a shop on the same lot. He afterward moved to Ohio.

Where Joseph Nissley lived was a tavern. This was also the stage office for the Philadelphia and Pittsburgh stages and the postoffice, and was kept by John McCammon, who was postmaster for nearly twenty-seven years. On the same lot in the space now occupied by A. B. Croll's hardware store (northwest corner of the square and Main street) was a yard, with sheds for horses.

Dr. Laverty, Jr.'s (southwest corner Main and Square), was a log house built by Conrad Seabaugh's father, afterwards occupied by Jacob Schneider, a tobacconist. At the southwest corner Union street and Square he had a pottery. This Jacob Schneider bought a Redemptioner, a young woman named Schaab, whom his nephew afterwards married. She subsequently married a man named Koons. Her brother settled in Lebanon and died intestate, leaving considerable property, to which this sister's children or their descendants, if they could be found, are heirs.

Eugene Laverty's (northeast corner Union and Square) belonged to Mrs. Shackey. She left it to Mrs. Smuller, the late George Smuller's mother.

Jacob Dickert's (northwest corner Union and Square) was owned by

---
[1] He was married to Jacob Rife, Sr's. sister.

Dr. James McCammon. Before his time it had belonged to Dr. Meyrick. Here Simon Cameron once lived, and here his son, Donald, was born. The Rife property (southeast corner Main and Square) was a tavern, the "Washington House," kept by George Crabb.[2] Mrs. Wentz was landlady in 1807. Cummings in his "Sketches of a Tour to the Western Country," alludes to this hotel:

"January 30th, 1807.—After resting about an hour (at Elizabethtown), and not feeling at all fatigued, at half past four I proceeded for Middletown, eight miles farther, first loading one of the barrels of my gun with a running ball, as I had to pass near where one Eshelman[3] was robbed and murdered last fall. The road over the Conewago hills was bad, and by the time I arrived at the bridge over Conewago creek, three miles from Elizabethtown, my left foot began to pain me so that I was forced to slacken my pace, which made it dark before I arrived at Swatara creek; when the pain had much increased, which was occasioned by my stepping through the ice up to my knees in a run which crossed the road, which the darkness prevented my seeing.

"The boat was at the other side of the creek.

"In about half an hour, which appeared to me an age, the boat returned, and I gladly crossed the creek in a canoe hauled over by a rope exended from bank to bank, seventy yards, and in a few minutes after I found myself in Mrs. Wentz's excellent inn, the sign of General Washington, in Middletown. My foot being much blistered, I bathed it in cold water, and then injudiciously opened the blisters with a lancet and sponged them with spirits of turpentine. I then got a good supper and an excellent bed, but my foot pained me so much as to prevent my sleeping, so I rose early, unrefreshed and breakfasted with my landlady, an agreeable, well-bred woman.

"The view down the Susquehanna from Mrs. Wentz's back piazza is very fine. The town contains about a hundred houses, and is well and handsomely situated about half a mile above the conflux of Swatara creek with Susquehanna river, the former of which forms a good harbor for boats, which it is in contemplation to join to the Schuylkill by a canal, in order to give Philadelphia the benefit of the navigation of the Susquehanna through its long course above Middletown. If this is carried into effect, it will draw to Philadelphia a vast quantity of products which now goes to Baltimore.

"The Susquehanna is a noble river, here about a mile wide, with fine sloping wooded banks and abounds with rockfish, perch, mullet, eels, suckers, catfish and white salmon, which last is described as a fine fish from seven to fifteen pounds in weight, but a distinct species from the real salmon of northern rivers.

"Was it not that the Susquehanna abounds with falls, shallows and

---

[2] His wife was a sister to Walter Kendig's grandfather.

[3] An Eshelman still owns a farm on this road. He was married to Phillip Irwin's niece.

rapids which impede the navigation, it would be one of the most useful rivers in the world, as its different branches, from its different sources embrace a wonderful extent of country, settled or rapidly settling, and abounding in wheat and maize (Indian corn), which most probably will be always staples of the large and flourishing State of Pennsylvania.

"The road leads parallel to the Susquehanna in some places close to the river and never more distant from it than a quarter of a mile, along a very pleasant level bounded on the right by a ridge of low but steep wooded hills, approaching and receding at intervals, and affording a fine shelter from the northerly winds to the farms between them and the river, which perhaps is one reason that the orchards are so numerous and so fine in this tract.

"I have rarely seen in any country a road more pleasant than this, either from its own goodness or the richness and variety of the prospect. The Susquehanna on the left about three-quarters of a mile wide, sometimes appearing and sometimes concealed by orchards, groves or clumps of wood; the fine wooded islands on the river; the mountains rising abruptly from the margin of the river, in which they are charmingly reflected, altogether form scenery truly delightful.

"About six miles above Middletown the mountains terminate and the south bank of the river becomes more varied, though still hilly, and here on an elevated promontory, with a commanding view of the river, is a large and apparently fine stone house, owned by General Simpson, who resides in it on his farm and is proprietor of a ferry much frequented by the western wagoners, as the road that way is shorter by two miles than that by Harrisburg. He farms out the ferry on his side for about three hundred dollars per annum, while on this side the proprietor rents it at four hundred and seventy. The value of this ferry, called Chambers', may serve to convey some idea of the state of traveling in this country, particularly if one reflects that there are many other well frequented ferries where public roads cross the river within thirty miles both above and below this one, and which are all great avenues to the western country."[4]

Heckewelder, the Moravian missionary, who passed through Middletown in 1797, alludes to this ferry, and to the town, thus:

(April 3rd.) "Arrived at a seasonable hour in Middletown, where we remained over night. Middletown is an attractive village, having the Susquehanna on the west side, and on the east the Big Swatara creek, which flows into it about a mile below the village. The square and the cross streets are in good condition, and the streets running north and south are mostly built up. The houses are built of limestone or brick— the majority, however, are frame or log houses.

"On the morning of the 24th, we made an early start, and notwithstanding the rain, had good roads to Chambers' ferry, where we took breakfast and then crossing the Susquehanna. The country from Middletown to the ferry is very pleasing and exhibits some fine farms."

---

[4] John Benner, father of the late John and Jacob Benner, used to keep this ferry.

(Colonel Burd, Colonel Cronch, Captain Shearer, &c., officers in the Revolutionary army, all had estates in this vicinity.) The following persons "took out licenses to keep houses of public entertainment" in Middletown from 1793 to 1803, and some of them continued to do so many years after: Henry Moore, Ludwick Wolfley, Peter Kipe, John McCann, George McCormick, Frederick Rothfong, John Blattenberger, Christian Rodfong, Michael Hemperly, John McCammon, William Crabb, Benjamin McKinley, John Benner, John Smith, George Toot.

It was probably at the tavern of the first named (Henry Moore), that John Penn, son of Thomas Penn, and grandson of William Penn, stopped on his return from Carlisle in 1788. In his journal he says:

April 13th.—From hence the road lay thro' woods till the Susquehanna, at a distance, denoted that the (Chambers') ferry was at hand. I crossed the river about three and a half o'clock, surrounded by enchanting prospects. The ride to Middletown is along the eastern bank, and exhibits a striking example of the great in the opposite one, rising to a vast height and wooded close to the water's edge for many miles. From this vast forest, and the expansive bed of the river navigable to its source for craft carrying two tons burden, the ideas of grandeur and immensity rush forcibly upon the mind, mixed with the desert wilderness of an uninhabited scene. The first particular object on this road is Simpson's house, the owner of the ferry where I crossed. It is on a rock across the river. At Middletown I put up at one More's, who was a teacher formerly at Philadelphia of Latin and Greek. He talked very sensibly, chiefly on subjects which discovered him to be a warm Tory, and friend of passive obedience. Unlike many Tories, he is an enemy of the new Constitution. Here the Great Swatara joins the Susquehanna, and a very fine mill is kept at their confluence by Mr. Frey, a Dutchman, to whom I carried a letter from Mr. D. Clymer.

"April 14th.—Before my departure Mr. Frey showed me his excellent mill, and still more extraordinary mill stream, running from one part of the Swatara for above a mile till it rejoins it at the mouth. *It was cut by himself at great expense and trouble,* and is the only work of the kind in Pennsylvania. Middletown is in a situation as beautiful as it is adapted to trade, and already of a respectable size."

XX.

GEORGE FISHER.

[I will preface my sketch of Portsmouth by a short biography of its founder.]

George Fisher, Esq., was a great grandson of the John Fisher, who came from England to Pennsylvania with William Penn on the first voyage of the ship *Welcome*. He was born at "Pineford" (so called at a very early day, from the large grove of pine trees then standing on the

Fisher's Bridge, an old Middletown, (Pa.) Landmark.

west bank of the Swatara river, where the great road leading from Philadelphia to Fort Pitt passed the former stream by a fording), September 22d, 1766. His father, the founder of Middletown, and only surviving parent, died in 1777.

Having been thus deprived, at the early age of ten years, of both his parents, and having no relatives on the paternal side, he, with his brother John and sister Hannah, were by the will of their father, consigned to the care of a maternal uncle residing in Chester county, due provision having been made and directions left, for their care, maintenance and education until they became of age. With this uncle, George resided for some years, receiving such instruction as the disturbed condition of the country, and the limited advantages the schools of that day afforded.

Of this period of his life but little is known, although he sometimes alluded to the difficulties he and his brother had to encounter in securing even the rudiments of an education; and the hardships they endured in traveling twice a day through the unusually deep snows of the severe winter of 1777 and '78, to the rude, half-finished log school house, situated at the intersection of two public roads several miles from the residence of his uncle. Small, home-made linen wallets, thrown across their shoulders, contained in one end their few simple school books, and in the other, their homely fare, frequently consisting, to use his own words, of "small turn-over pies, hard enough to be used to play 'shinny' with."

On one occasion the master, as well as the scholars, was very much alarmed. Shortly after the assembling of the school on the morning after the battle of Brandywine, a regiment of British grenadiers passing along one of the roads, unexpectedly encountered a detachment of American militia, retreating from that battlefield, along the other. At the junction, immediately opposite the school house, an engagement ensued, and many bullets struck the logs, or passed through the solitary window of the building. The master, however, had presence of mind sufficient to counsel the children to throw themselves flat on the floor. They did so and fortunately all escaped injury.

Some few years after this occurrence, George was sent to Philadelphia and placed in the store of Israel Pemberton, then one of the wealthiest and most distinguished merchants of that city, with a view to his receiving a mercantile education. The employment was uncongenial to a boy of George's energetic temperament, and wholly unsuited to his inclinations, and he soon earnestly besought his relatives to take him from the city and place him in one of the chief institutions of learning of that day, and thus enable him to obtain such an education as would eventually aid him in selecting as the pursuit of his life, the legal profession, for which even at that early age, he manifested an ardent desire. He finally mentioned the subject to Mr. Pemberton, and enlisting his support, gained not only the consent of his connections, but also their promise to advance him what money was needed to carry out his desires.

He was first sent to an excellent preparatory school at Trenton, New Jersey, and finally to Dickinson College, at Carlisle, Pa. Upon the completion of his education, he entered the office of John Wilkes Kittera, Esq., an eminent lawyer, then residing in the town (now city) of Lancaster, as a student. He remained with Mr. Kittera until he was admitted to the bar at Lancaster, sometime in the summer or early in the fall of 1787. The precise date of his admission cannot now be ascertained, owing to the fact that the "minutes" of the several courts held in the county at that day have been lost. The record shows that shortly after, at the November term, 1787, of the Court of Common Pleas of Dauphin County, he was admitted to practice in the several courts of this county. After his admission, he designed settling in Savannah, Georgia, and pursuing his profession. With that object in view, he visited Middletown shortly afterwards, for the purpose of arranging his private affairs, and placing his patrimonial estate, near the town, in charge of some competent and trustworthy agent. Whilst thus engaged, an event occurred that changed his purpose and fixed his professional career in a totally different location.

He was one day called upon by a committee representing a large number of the Mennonist society, who had settled upon the rich lands of the Swatara valley, in Derry township, and the neighborhood of Middletown. The committee stated that, hearing of his arrival, they had been authorized to wait upon him, and ascertain whether he was as good a friend to the Mennonist settlers as his father had been, and if they found him to be similarly disposed, then to employ him as their counsel, to aid them in resisting the encroachments that the Irish settlers were making upon their lands, and the enjoyment of their religious rights.

He answered that he had every reason to entertain the same kind feelings toward their society that, as they had just declared, his father had always evinced towards them, and would willingly serve them and forward their interests to the best of his ability, but that his determination was fixed to remove to Savannah, as soon as he had completed the arrangement of his private affairs.

They replied that they thought he had better remain among the people in whose midst he was born, and who had strong feelings of friendship towards him on his father's account. As an earnest of that sentiment they proffered him ten gold Johannes ($80.00), as a retaining fee, if he would remain and act as their counsel in their approaching legal contests; at the same time assuring him of a continuance of their patronage and that of their brethren, then already becoming a numerous and comparatively wealthy class.

Thus urged, he changed his determination, accepted their retainer, and shortly afterwards settled at Harrisburg* (then called Louisburg), opened an office and commenced the practice of his profession.

The dockets of the several courts of Dauphin county for the year 1788 and 1789, show that he immediately obtained a very large and lu-

---

*His office was on the southwest corner of Market Square where the Presbyterian Church now stands.

crative practice in this county. In Northumberland county, also, his legal business was a heavy and paying one. He attended occasionally the courts of Cumberland, York and Lancaster counties; in fact, he said that for several years after his admission he attended the courts of all the counties north and west of Harrisburg, and assisted in trying nearly all the numerous and important ejectments, founded upon original titles to lands, in the counties mentioned.

He held a conspicuous place in settling the law of this State in reference to the titles to lands claimed or held by actual settlement, improvement, warrant, survey and patent, in which branch of the profession he held an equal rank with the most distinguished of that class of men who became at an early day in the legal history of Pennsylvania, eminent as "Land Lawyers."

For many years after he commenced the practice of the law, members of that profession made minutes of the decisions given by Judges of the Supreme Courts, when holding courts of *Nisi Prius*, on all important questions relating to land titles (no book of reports of these decisions being published until after 1790), which memoranda they carried in their saddle-bags, to be cited as authorities, as occasion should arise, in the cases in which they were severally engaged.

The judges and members of the bar then traveled in company, on horseback, from court to court, at all seasons of the year, and through all kinds of weather, over roads impassable by any other mode of conveyance, compelled frequently to ford the streams they encountered, and at times, when too full to be forded, crossing over them in canoes, swimming their horses alongside. As the country was but sparsely settled, and the accommodations of a very primitive character, each of them had a blanket, to be used as a covering on lying down at night—frequently upon some straw shake-down, on the floor of a rude log cabin, with their saddles as pillows, carrying also, in the holsters of the latter, a flask of brandy, a beef tongue, or a piece of dried venison and some crackers. On their return from Sunbury and other points on the Susquehanna, they occasionally jumped their horses on to rafts, and thus descended that stream, sometimes to its junction with the Juniata, sometimes to Harrisburg. Then they separated to return to their homes, there to remain until the approach of court again summoned them to renew their labors, in the comparatively distant frontier counties of the State.

In these journeys many hairbreadth escapes and ludicrous incidents occurred, which at after times, were recounted with great zest, particularly when some apt delineator pictured a ludicrous reminiscence, the actors in which were present.

They were, as a class, vigorous in body, as is abundantly proved by the long lives of uninterrupted good health that most of them enjoyed. Highly polished, highly cultivated and richly endowed, their unsurpassed mental powers enabled them to achieve the enviable reputation they so justly enjoyed, not only during their lives, but after they had passed from this sphere of action. They were emphatically "gentlemen of the old school," and though of convivial temperaments, lovers of wine and good living, seldom, or never, indulged to excess; whilst in their social intercourse with each other, the *esprit de corps* which so eminently distinguished the profession of that day, always shone forth conspicuously. The intimate and confidential friends they had been in their advancing years, they continued until they severally sank to honored graves.

After the division of Northumberland county, Mr. Fisher continued to practice in Union county as well, until the year 1826, when he ceased to visit these counties. In the spring of 1830, after a highly successful career at the bar for upward of forty years, and after establishing two of his sons in the same pursuit, to wit: John Adams (who became eminent in his profession and practiced in Dauphin and Lebanon counties for over forty years), at Harrisburg, and Robert J. Fisher (afterwards President Judge of the district composed of the counties of York and Adams), at York, Pa., he removed from Harrisburg to the patrimonial estate and place of his birth, "Pineford," with the intention of devoting the remainder of his years to agricultural pursuits, for which he had, throughout life evinced great partiality. He was, however, sought out in his retirement, and occasionally induced to aid in the trial of important cases, as well at Lebanon as in Dauphin county, until about the year 1838, when he ceased practice in the courts of Lebanon, and finally, in 1840, at Harrisburg also.

He, however, again appeared, and for the last time in any court, in the Supreme Court of Pennsylvania, at Harrisburg, at May Term, 1845, to participate in the argument of the Commonwealth *vs.* Church, reported in 1 Barr, 105; a case in which he had large interests at stake, the dam therein complained of forcing the water of the the Swatara upon the opposite banks, and causing serious injury to the lots of the town of Port Royal, of which he owned the one-half.

Having then reached his eightieth year, the force and brightness of his intellect, added to the power and volume of his voice, as then exhibited, called forth expressions of surprise from all who heard the lucid and very able legal argument made by him.

He continued to reside at "Pineford," in the enjoyment of a ripe and vigorous old age, until the effects of an accidental fall which he had at Harrisburg in the autumn of 1852, caused his death. He died February 5, 1853, in the eighty-seventh year of his age, in the house where he had first seen the light of day, and where his father and mother had lived and died before the American Revolution.

He had always expressed a desire to be buried by the side of his parents in the family burying ground on the estate, but in view of the fact that the property was then expected to be sold, and thus pass out of the hands of the family, it was thought best to inter him at Harrisburg. He was therefore taken to the house of his son, John Adams, and from there, February 9th, to Mount Kalmia cemetery. His funeral was (up to that time) probably the largest ever seen in Harrisburg, and was attended by all the judges, members of the bar, officers of the several courts, the surviving members of his family and a large number of sympathizing friends. The lot is enclosed by an iron railing and an appropriate monument marks his grave.

Devoted to his profession, the subject of this sketch never sought or held any civil office. Revering the character of Washington (for whom his first vote after attaining manhood had been given, as first President of the United States,) and his principal intimacies and associations being with the surviving soldiers and statesmen of the Revolution, he imbibed in early life the political principles entertained by those patriots, as well as by many of the eminent men of that day, and remained the earnest and firm supporter of the administration of Washington and of his successor, the elder Adams. Nay, he may be said to have adhered through a long life to those principles, never attaching himself to or being recognized as being a member of any of the political parties which sprang into existence upon the defeat and dissolution of the old Federal party.

The only public station he ever filled was that of major in a battalion of volunteers from the counties of Dauphin and York, during the "Western Expedition" (elsewhere alluded to), upon the disbandment of the army he returned to Harrisburg and resumed the practice of his profession. In November, 1795, he was married to Elizabeth, a daughter of Thomas Minshall, Esq., of York county, who had been a representative in the Provincial Assembly of Pennsylvania, in the years 1768, 1769 and 1770, who had also been commissioned one of the justices of York county, in October, 1774, and by virtue of such commission, one of the judges of the county court of that county. This lady was also a descendent of one of the oldest Quaker families of the State, her ancestors having emigrated from England between the years 1675 and 1681, and settled at Chester, Pa. She died in December, 1803, leaving three children.

After her decease, to wit: In January, 1805, he was again married, at Philadelphia, by the Rt. Rev. Bishop White, to Ann Shippen Jones, a daughter of Robert Strettle Jones, A. M. (and granddaughter of Isaac Jones, Charter Mayor of Philadelphia in 1767 and 1768), and Ann his wife, who was a daughter of Joseph Shippen (and a lineal descendent of Edward Shippen, first Charter Mayor of that city). By this lady, who was one of the most beautiful women of her day, he had five children, four of whom, with their mother, survived him.

Mr. Fisher was possessed of a graceful and commanding figure and handsome manly features, being endowed by nature with a powerful and melodious voice and mental powers of the first order, he was not only distinguished at the bar for the acuteness and soundness of his legal arguments, but also for the great distinctness, energy and—when occasion required it—eloquence, with which his forensic efforts were delivered. Being naturally of a very convivial disposition, fond of the society of men of worth, refinement and intelligence, he was, particularly during his residence at Harrisburg, noted for his hospitality and constant habit of entertaining handsomely at his house many of the men of worth and distinction of this State, with most of whom he was on terms of the closest intimacy and friendship.

"I have seen at his table," says an eminent lawyer, "among other distinguished veterans of the Revolution, the venerable General Arthur St. Clair, Colonel Henry Miller, Alexander Graydon, &c. At a later day, Chief Justice Tilghman, Justices Yeates and Breckenridge, David Watts, and Thomas Duncan, of Carlisle; William Montgomery and Charles Smith, of Lancaster; Marks John Biddle, of Reading; Charles Hall, of Sunbury; Benjamin R. Morgan, George Vaux, John R. Coates, Nicholas Biddle, and John Hallowell, of Philadelphia. And at a still later period Chief Justice Gibson, Justice Rogers, James Buchanan, John M. Scott, George Cowden, William M. Meredith, and other gentleman of Philadelphia, as well as from different sections of the State."

After his death, many gratifying memorials of the esteem in which he had been held during life, were received by members of his family, from distinguished gentlemen residing in different parts of the country. Most, if not all, of these letters, were couched in terms expressive of the highest respect and esteem for his memory; and of sincere condolence with the surviving members of his family for the great loss they had sustained. From among these testimonials, all breathing the same spirit, two are here selected. One of them, written by William M. Meredith, of Philadelphia, says:

"The death of your father, at a ripe age, was to be expected in the order of nature, and scarcely to be regretted on his own account, as, at eighty-six, life is scarcely desirable. It is always a shock to lose those whom we love, and I therefore offer you my condolence on the occasion. I had learned early to esteem your father and his estimable lady, from my own parents; and their uniform kindness to me when I passed my winters at Harrisburg many years ago, increased my attachment and respect for them; and I have thought it would be agreeable to you to know that among all who know your father—and there are many here among our elder respectable citizens—there has been a general expression of kindness and respect, in which I entirely and sincerely participate."

The other was written by Jacob B. Weidman, Esq., of Lebanon, to Jacob Haldeman, of Harrisburg, who, in transmitting the letter of the former gentleman to one of the family of the deceased, says: "Agreeing fully with Mr. Weidman in all he has said in regard to your father, I take the liberty of sending his letter to you." The letter thus referred to states:

"Since the date of your last letter, an old, mutual and highly esteemed friend, George Fisher, has gone to his fathers; and has terminated a long and very useful life. It is true that he grew to be a very old man, and was by the present generation nearly forgotten, if he was ever known to them. But time was when he enjoyed a reputation at the bar, in then Western Pennsylvania, second to no man for legal attainments.

When he, Thomas Duncan, David Watts, Charles Hall, Charles Huston, Steel, Dunlop and others were the pride of the State and the lions of the profession. I remember the day when Fisher and Hall were the selected specimens of manly perfection and comeliness. Both were highly polished gentlemen of the old school, and the powerful and eloquent men of the bar. Fisher was a soldier, too, in the 'Western Expedition,' as well as the lawyer who girded on his armor, and labored —bravely and arduously labored—to establish the principles of the new form of Government upon the newly laid foundations declared in the Constitutions of the United States, and of the Commonwealth of Pennsylvania, then recently formed. He, whilst the frontiersman was felling the trees of the forest, and turning the haunts of wild beasts and merciless savages into smiling fields and homes for civilized men, with his brother lawyers was engaged in cementing the foundations of this Republican Temple. And yet those "Old Fogies" are forgotten! This should not be—every man of them is entitled to a monument in commemoration of his talents, integrity of purpose, moral worth and undoubted patriotism."

XXI.

In 1779 the town is noticed in the Colonial records as being a supply depot for the army during the Revolution.

In 1789 the question of fixing permanently the seat of the Federal Government was strongly agitated in Congress then in session in New York. In the House of Representatives Mr. Goodhue offered the following resolution:

"*Resolved*—In the opinion of this committee, that the permanent seat of Government of the United States ought to be at some convenient place on the east bank of the Susquehanna river, in the State of Pennsylvania, &c."

Mr. Heister moved to insert after the words "Susquehanna river" the words "*Between Harrisburg and Middletown inclusive.*"

A lengthy and spirited debate followed, participated in by nearly all the principal members of the House; those from the Northern and Eastern States generally favoring the amendment, and those from the South opposing it. The amendment was finally lost.

Several other amendments were proposed and lost and the original resolution was carried.

The resolution went to the Senate, which body struck out all relating to the Susquehanna, and inserted a clause fixing the permanent seat of Government at Germantown, Pa.

The House at first agreed to the clause, but refused to concur with some subsequent action of the Senate thereon and pending further consideration of the subject, Congress adjourned *sine die* for that year.

In 1790 the question was again brought up before Congress, and created intense excitement throughout the country. The Northern and

Eastern members were opposed to the seat of government being located south of the Susquehanna while the Southern and Western members were opposed to its being either north or east of that river. The sectional feeling became so strong that the safety of the Union was endangered, and Washington, Jefferson, Hamilton and other patriots sought to effect a compromise, but were unsuccessful.

At last, through the instrumentality of Mr. Jefferson, the votes of one or two Northern members were changed and a bill passed fixing the site on the banks of the Potomac, at such place as should be selected by commissioners under the direction of the President.

In 1793 an epidemic prevailed at Harrisburg, which being supposed to be caused by a mill dam belonging to two men named Landis, it was determined at a meeting of the citizens, January 16th, 1795, to remove the cause; and two thousand six hundred pounds were ordered to be assessed on the property of the citizens; said sum to be offered to the Landises for their mill and appurtenances, and if refused the dam was to be prostrated by force.

In the list of about three hundred and fifty citizens, I find George Fisher assessed £40, by far the largest amount set against any name (except Joshua Elder's) the others not averaging over £5 each. I merely mention this fact to show that Mr. Fisher—the founder of Portsmouth—was at that time a heavy property holder in Harrisburg.

(Extracts from the *Oracle of Dauphin*, a newspaper published between the years 1792 and 1832. The advertisements, &c., unless otherwise specified, being by inhabitants of Middletown:)

April 4, 1798.—John Wier, of Harrisburg, advertises that he has moved his store next door, but one, to George Fisher, Esq., opposite the lower market house.

May 30.—A meeting of the inhabitants of Middletown (Dauphin county) and its vicinity was held on the 19th inst., and three persons appointed to prepare an address to the President of the United States, which was signed by 147 respectable citizens. The following is a copy of the address:

"*To the President of the United States:*

"The address of the inhabitants of Middletown and vicinity in the county of Dauphin and State of Pennsylvania:

"SIR: At a period so interesting as the present, when the political situation of the United States is become so precarious with respect to the belligerent powers, and especially the French Republic—at a time when a haughty nation, evidently aspiring to a dominion of the universe and the subjugating of all nations, and repeatedly committing the most aggravated and unprovoked depredations on our commerce—refusing to attend to the just remonstrances of our government, treating with the most pointed neglect and contempt its representatives, who are furnished with the most ample powers and instructions for adjusting and terminating all our differences amicably, and with unparalleled effrontry declaring to the world that we are a divided people, dissatisfied with our government, and under the arbitrary influence of a foreign nation. At such a time it becomes a duty incumbent on every true and unprejudiced American to come forward and by an open and candid avowal of his sentiments, endeavor to rescue his country from the odium attempted to be cast upon it by such calumnious aspersions.

"We, therefore, the subscribers, impressed with a proper regard for the welfare and happiness of our country, do beg you, sir, to accept this public testimony of our entire approbation of the measures adopted by the executive, and that relying with the fullest confidence on your wisdom, integrity, and patriotic exertions, in concert with other branches of the Legislature, we shall deem it our indispensable duty to be ready on all occasions with cheerfulness to contribute as much as within our power lies, to the support of government and the vindication and maintenance of our national honor and independence. With these sentiments, sir, we offer our sincere and unfeigned wishes for your personal happiness and prosperity, and that your services in a political capacity may ever meet the deserved approbation of your country."

June 6.—Answer of the President of the United States to the address from Middletown:

"*To the inhabitants of Middletown and vicinity, in the county of Dauphin and State of Pennsylvania:*

"GENTLEMEN: This concise but comprehensive address contains every assurance which the government can desire, from the best citizens at a critical moment. To me it is particularly obliging, and deserves my thanks. To the public it must be satisfactory and will receive its applause.

JOHN ADAMS.

"*Philadelphia, May 30th, 1798.*"

May 19.—Thomas Minshall offers eight dollars reward for a runaway apprentice.

June 6.—Nathan Skeer informs the public that he has opened a ferry two miles above Middletown on the Susquehanna.

August 14.—George Fisher, of Harrisburg, requests those who have borrowed muskets, bayonets and cartouch-boxes from him, to return them.

December 19.—Died—Colonel Robert McKee, at his residence near Middletown.

January 28, 1799.—George Toot notifies John Hull, waggoner, to come and get his horse and pay charges or he will be sold.

January 14.—Henry Shepler, of Harrisburg, informs the public that his stage, via Middletown, to Lancaster, will run but once a week instead of twice, during February and March.

February 25.—At an election held in Hummelstown by the Second regiment of Dauphin county, Major George Toot, of Middletown, was elected lieutenant colonel.

March 27.—Frederick Rodfong & Co. give notice of a dissolution of partnership.

April 8.—Cornelius Cox, assessor, gives notice that he will be at the house of William Crabb, on the 26th, to hear appeals from property valuation.

October 25.—The property of Jonathan McClure advertised to be sold November 15th at the public house of John McCommon (by Henry Orth, sheriff).

November 9.—George Fisher cautions the public not to purchase the above property as it belongs to him, and McClure's lease will expire in the ensuing April.

In the edition of December 23rd is this anecdote: "Two or three of the inhabitants of this town (Middletown) were spending the evening at a neighbor's house, the man of the house was reading in your paper an account of the Norwegian who died in the one hundred and sixtieth year of his age; a person sitting present, who lived some thirty or forty miles distant (who was noted for shooting on the wing) said he knew a man in his neighborhood who was one hundred and twenty years of age, and his grandmother was yet alive. One of the company observed that she must be the widow of Methuselah." The same paper announces the death of General Washington on the 14th inst. [News traveled fast in those days.]

January 6, 1800.—Prices current [the only one given in the county].

Middletown, Jan. 4th, 1800.

Wheat,	$1 43	per	bushel
Rye,	66	"	"
Corn,	50	"	"
Plaster of Paris,	1 33	"	"
Salt,	5 33	"	barrel
Shad, 8 to	10 00	"	"
Whiskey,	47	"	gallon
Bacon,	9	"	pound
Bar Iron,	100 00	"	ton

January 9th, 1800, the citizens of Middletown and surrounding country testified their sorrow at the death of General Washington by meeting at the house of George Fisher, Esq., and moving therefrom in the following order to the meeting house:

Trumpeter.
Cavalry on foot, swords drawn.
Infantry, arms reversed, by platoons inverted.
Rifle company, arms reversed.
Militia officers in uniform.
Music.
Standard.
Surgeons.
Clergy.
Pallbearers.
Young ladies in white.
Ancient citizens first.
Citizens in general by two.
Boys in pairs.

Having arrived at meetinghouse, the troops formed lines right and left, when the clergy, pallbearers and citizens entered, followed by the troops, while the Dead March from Saul was performed by the organist. The exercises were opened by a short prayer, and singing part of the 90th Psalm. Rev. Mr. Snowden and Rev. Mr. Moeller then delivered impressive and well adapted addresses.

December 21, 1799.—Daniel Sweigart (Harrisburg) notified his creditors to meet him January 3rd, 1800.

January 1, 1800.—Crabb & Minshall gave notice of dissolution of partnership. Thomas Minshall will carry on the business. (Coppersmith.)

February 28.—Prices current:

Middletown, Feb. 28th, 1800.

Wheat,	$1 50	per	bushel
Rye,	67	"	"
Corn,	50	"	"
Oats,	33	"	"
Plaster of Paris,	1 33	"	"
Salt,	1 67	"	"
Whiskey,	47	"	gallon
Bacon,	9	"	pound
Bar Iron,	106 67	"	ton

WAGES.

In connection with this "Market report" it may not be amiss to give a short account of the wages paid in those halcyon days.

In 1793 the Schuylkill and Susquehanna Canal Company advertised for workmen, offering $5 a month for the winter months and $6 for summer, with board and lodging. The next year there was a debate in the House of Representatives, which brought out the fact that soldiers got but $3 a month. A Vermont member, discussing the proposal to raise it to $4, said that in his State men were hired for £18 a year, or $4 a month with board and clothing. Mr. Wadsworth, of Pennsylvania, said: "In the State north of Pennsylvania, the wages of the common laborer are not, upon the whole, superior to those of the common soldier." In 1797 a Rhode Island farmer hired a good farm hand at $3 and $5 a month was paid to those who got employment for the eight busy months of the farmer's year.

A strong boy could be had at that time, in Connecticut, at $1 a month through those months, and he earned it by working from daylight until eight or nine o'clock at night. He could buy a coarse cotton shirt with the earnings of three such months. Women picked the wool off the bushes and briers where the sheep had left it, and spun and knit it into mittens to earn $1 a year by this toilsome business. They hired out as help for 25 cents a month, and their board.

By a day's hard work at the spinning wheel a woman and girl together would earn twelve cents. Matthew Carey, in his letter on the

Charities of Philadelphia (1829) gives a painful picture of the working classes at the time. Every avenue of employment was choked with applicants. Men left the cities to find work on the canals at from sixty to seventy-five cents a day, and to encounter the malaria, which laid them low in numbers. The highest wages paid to women was 25 cents a day; and even women who made clothes for the arsenal were paid by the government at no higher rates. When the ladies of the city begged for an improvement of this rate, the Secretary hesitated, lest it should disarrange the relations of capital and labor throughout the country.

To return to the *Oracle,* the edition of February 24th, 1800, contains a transcript of General Washington's will; the value of the scheduled property was $530,000.

March 31.—Wm. Crubb is married to Miss Kendrick, of Lancaster.

April 7.—Robert Candor's property (near Middletown), 130 acres, for sale.

June 20.—Wm. Crabb, "Surveyor of the Revenue," gives notice of his appointment, and notifies citizens to make returns of their dwelling houses, lands, slaves, &c.

August 11.—Sale of George Cross property in Middletown, adjoining the property of Ludwick Wolfley and John Snyder, deceased. To take place at the public house of John McCammon on August 23rd.

September 17.—Sale of Thomas Moore, deceased, property in Middletown, adjoining properties of Charles McMurtrie, James Russel and George McCormick to take place October 8th.

October 20.—Middletown's vote for sheriff 313; for member of Congress, 206.

April 6, 1801.—George Fisher advertised a three-story brick dwelling house for sale, next door to Captain Lee's tavern.

June 6.—Lieutenant Wm. Carson, U. S. Reg. Inf., advertises a deserter from the redezvous in Middletown.

September 2.—Barbara Knatcher's new stage line between Harrisburg and Lancaster. Leave Harrisburg, Mondays and Fridays at 5 o'clock. Breakfast at Mr. Crabb's, in Middletown; arrive at Lancaster in the evening. Returning, leave Lancaster Tuesdays and Saturdays at 5 a. m.; dine at Mr. Crabb's, Middletown; arrive same evening at Harrisburg. Through fare $2. 14 pounds baggage allowed. (150 pounds baggage at passenger rates.) Baggage at the owner's risk.

September 8.—Robert and John Spear will sell October 24th, 213 acres of land, farm buildings, &c., four miles from Middletown, adjoining land of Colonel Robert McGee, deceased, James Scott, now James Templeton, &c.

November 2, 1801.—Henry Shepler (Old Stage Line), advertises stages to start three times a week. Fare to and from Lancaster, $1.00.

December 25.—Stephen Hays, Thomas Smith, James Russel and George McCormick, heirs and administrators of Henry Moore, deceased, offer the following properties in Middletown for sale:

One two-story log house, now occupied as a tavern by John Benner.
One two-story log house, adjoining, occupied by Charles Brandon, Esq.
One two-story log house, adjoining, occupied by George McCormick.
One lot of five acres adjoining George McCormick.
One lot of four acres on main cross street.
One lot of eight lots on main cross street and Water street.
Sale at 10 a. m., January 15th, 1802.

XXII.
HARBORTON.

"The subscriber having laid out a new town at the confluence of the Swatara with the Susquehanna, in the county of Dauphin, proposes to dispose of the lots at sixty dollars each, when deeds in fee simple are delivered for them. As the object of the proprietor is to promote immediate improvement, and not present emolument, and as many of the lots will now sell for from one hundred to three hundred dollars, and none of less value than forty dollars, the preference will be determined by drawing the several numbers from a wheel.

"The navigation of the Susquehanna thus far down is perfectly safe; but from this to Columbia (a distance of twenty-one miles) it is obstructed by the Swatara and Conewago falls, and many other rapids, so as to render it precarious and hazardous, and sometimes impracticable.

"The well known harbor formed by the mouth of the Swatara is not only the most capacious, but the only safe one on the river, and produce to more than a million dollars value annually floats down the Susquehanna; a great proportion of which, it is presumed, will be transported from here to the Philadelphia market, on the turnpike road now making, and nearly completed to Lancaster (a distance of twenty-four miles) and by the contemplated canal from the Susquehanna to the Schuylkill, which will enter the harbor through this town. The extensive command of water here for the turning of mill-machinery and other water works, and its vicinity to the great iron works, owned by Messrs. Coleman and Grubb, added to the facility with which an abundant supply of Susquehanna and Juniata coal may be had; when all combined, will fully justify the assertion that no town on the Susquehanna offers more advantages, and none more certain prospects of gain, to the enterprising merchant and mechanic than this.

"The site is an inclined plain, gradually rising from the margin of a bank, from ten to fifteen feet above low water, to a summit of fifty feet, commanding many beautiful prospects, as well land as water, and is as healthy as any on the river.

"Tickets may be had of the subscriber, and other places, where plans of the town may be seen. GEORGE FISHER.
"Feb. 16th, 1809."

Previous to this time, as far back as 1755, all the territory lying near the mouth of the Swatara was known as Middletown. From the head of the river to this point navigation was comparatively safe, but in consequence of the numerous and dangerous falls, it was supposed the Susquehanna could not be safely descended below the Swatara. This being the southern limit of navigation, all the marketable produce of the Susquehanna and its tributaries was brought here for sale, and distributed, and a brisk trade sprang up, which extended not only to the surrounding country, but even to Maryland and Virginia. Those who have read the preceding papers will remember that, as early as 1690, William Penn alludes to the traffic then carried on by the Indians of the interior with the Atlantic coast, via the Swatara and Tulpehocken. With the advent of the whites this trade increased until in 1760 it exceeded that of any other point on the river.

For a long period it was the great lumber mart of the Susquehanna. Every spring and fall the mouth of the Swatara was crowded with rafts and arks, loaded with boards, shingles, grain, whiskey, plaster, and other marketable products of the up river country; and not only was the mouth filled, but the shores of the river some distance below, and for two miles above the "point" were lined with every kind of river craft.

During the rafting season all was bustle and activity, and the handling, counting and measuring of the lumber, grain, etc., gave employment to large numbers of men, some of whom came from great distances to work, returning to their homes when the busy season was over. The spring and fall freshets were harvest times for the merchants and tavernkeepers. Laborers were in demand, and received good wages; and most of them were liberal patrons of the stores and inns. The "Yankees," as all the up-river men were styled, were generally a boisterous class; and, when released from the restraint of their homes, usually took a spree, spending their hard earnings freely; but, before returning to their families, laid in a supply of necessaries for home consumption, sufficient to last until they could take another trip.

A row of store houses lined the road facing the Swatara (some of which have been altered into dwelling houses, and are still standing, but so changed in appearance as not to be recognized) and these were frequently filled, from floor to roof, with grain, whiskey, &c. These articles, with lumber of all kinds, were transported from this point in every direction, teams coming from Delaware, Maryland and Virginia.

After the war, trade again revived, and flourished extensively until 1796, after which it gradually declined. Until then, the mouth of the Swatara was considered the termination of navigation of the Susquehanna and its tributary streams. Below this it was believed to be impracticable on account of the numerous and dangerous falls and cataracts impeding its bed. In 1796 an enterprising German miller named Kreider, from the neighborhood of Huntingdon, appeared in the Swatara with the first ark ever built in those waters, fully freighted with flour, with which he safely descended to Baltimore. His success becoming known throughout the interior, many arks were constructed, and the next year numbers of them, fully freighted arrived at tide-water.

Thomas Burbridge, a merchant of Wyoming, in the following year (1797) freighted and ran, in one season, ninety-one arks loaded with coal, a few of which failed to reach their destination for want of skillful pilots.

Much of the trade with this place was carried on in keel-boats (or Durham boats, as they were sometimes called, after their first projector) and they were the only ones that ascended as well as descended the river.

The Susquehanna is almost a mile wide, has a very rocky bed, and in low or moderate stages of the water is very shallow. Consequently a boat drawing one or two feet of water would soon strike upon the rocks and be wrecked unless kept in the channel. This channel is a peculiar one shifting from side to side of the river, with a swifter current running through it, and even when the river is low, has usually about five feet depth of water in it.

These boats were fifty or sixty feet in length, and required a crew of eight expert polemen and a steersman to each boat. To force them up against the swift current, about ten miles a day, the boatmen, generally four on each side, used setting poles about twelve feet long. Standing near the bow of the boat, they thrust the larger end against the bed of the river at an inclination, and placing the upper end against their shoulders, pushed the boat forward by walking from the bow to the stern, making her move just her own length. The impetus kept the boat from falling back until having drawn their poles up, they walked forward again to the bow, and repeated the operation and so on to the end of the day.

Considerable trading was done by these boats during their trips. Their approach to the villages along their route was signalled by the blowing of a horn, and those who were desirous of making purchases, or of disposing of any surplus products were offered an opportunity.

Supplies were then transported from Philadelphia across to the mouth of the Swatara, via Lancaster, in Conestoga wagons, occupying about four days in transit; there they were loaded on the boats, and thence pushed by toilsome steps against the current of the Susquehanna for days. (The material then requiring the labor of hundreds of men and animals, and taking several weeks to transport; two men with a single locomotive and train of cars now carry a similar distance in a few hours.)

In order to avoid the rapids known as the "Conewago Falls," a short canal was made, reaching from the head of the falls to York Haven, on the York county side of the river. This enabled these small boats to pass up and down in safety; but on the completion of the Pennsylvania canal, that channel was abandoned.

On the 17th of March, 1814, George Fisher and wife conveyed to

John Swar, of Lancaster county, that portion of "a certain tract of two hundred and twenty acres, on which the town of Portsmouth is laid off." John Swar and Anna, his wife, deeded the lots to other parties, at different times. (Part of them back to George Fisher, as appears from deeds now in my possession.)

On March 3rd, 1857, Portsmouth then having a population of seven hundred and fifty, was consolidated with Middletown.

XXIII.

In the "Square" was held the annual fair (alluded to in No. 4). These fairs were great commercial marts; the country was sparsely settled, there were no railroads or canals, and but few turnpikes, consequently the news from the outside world came in driblets, and the social intercourse of the inhabitants, particularly that of the female portion thereof, was limited to their own immediate neighborhood. (Although a neighborhood included a much wider radius then than what we consider such now, and the uncorseted maids and matrons of that day thought little of riding fifteen or twenty miles on horseback to make a call; while the male portion of the community—spite of indulgences which would cause a modern cold water apostle unspeakable anguish —footed greater distances.)

So the coming of the annual fair was hailed with delight by old and young, and the "yearly market" for this whole section being held in Middletown, to it, in carryall and wagon, on horseback and on foot, the crowds came trooping from the surrounding country, and from towns as far distant as Carlisle, Reading, Lancaster and York.

The "Square" was the center of attraction, but the adjacent lots in the vicinity, and the neighboring streets, were also filled. Here came the drovers with horses, cattle, sheep, hogs, &c.; the dealers in all kinds of wares; the showmen with inchoate and peripatetic menageries, circuses, theatres, &c. There were eating booths and drinking booths, dancing booths and gambling booths. There were English, Dutch, French, Scotch-Irish, and Yankees; Indians from the forests, and African slaves from the adjoining plantations; there were farmers in smocks and sundowns, wagoners in blouses and caps; and traders in brass-buttoned swallow-tails and bell-crowned beavers; there were children in pinafores and round-a-bouts; women in shortwaisted homespun frocks and simple wimples, and other women in shortwaisted silk gowns, and Leghorn coal-scuttles. Some of the crowd were engaged in trading, some in swindling, and most of them in murdering the English language. They were scenes of fun and frolic, noise and bustle, turmoil and carousal. The advent of canals and railroads, with the resulting facilities of intercommunication, caused these fairs to be gradually discontinued.

A Scene at the Middletown Fair Grounds.

CHRONICLES OF MIDDLETOWN. 97

The brick building at the northeast corner of the Square and Main street—belonging to Mrs. Oberland, she willed it to her sister Mrs. Gilliard, mother of the late John and Jacob Benner. In 1807 John Landis kept store on this spot.

East of the Square, north side of Main street (in the building recently remodeled by Dr. Mish) Hood and Thompson kept store. They were succeeded by Ross, he by McNair & Hicks, and they by McNair & Metzgar.

Old Middletown Bank.—This stone building was built by Ephraim Heller for his residence. He was inspector of liquors, and justice of the peace.

In the log house which once stood next door east of the bank, Ephraim Heller kept store. The brick building now occupying its site, was built by Simon Cameron, and here his son Simon and his daughters Margaret (now Mrs. Haldeman) and Virginia (now Mrs. McVey) were born.

C. F. Beard.—(Main street, north side, opposite.) This building was once occupied by the Swatara Bank. The following is an account of its organization:

SWATARA BANK.

"At a large and respectable meeting of the inhabitants of Middletown and the adjoining neighborhood, in the county of Dauphin, the 19th day of November, 1813, convened to take into consideration the propriety of establishing a bank in said town. James Hamilton was appointed chairman and Elisha Green secretary.

"The meeting fully sensible of the result of a disposable capital, combined with the many advantages afforded by the junction of the Swatara with the Susquehanna, at the now contemplated town of Portsmouth, where a large proportion of the immense produce of the country up the Susquehanna is offered for sale, confidently believe that the establishment of a bank here, will not only greatly promote the commercial prosperity of Pennsylvania and industrious and enterprising farmers, mechanics, and manufacturers, but will contribute much to the improvement of the navigation of the river, and to the advancement of the canal and lock navigation of the State.

"*Therefore Resolved*, that a bank be established at Middletown aforesaid, with a capital of $250,000, divided into shares of $50 each, to be conducted by the president and twelve directors, and to be styled the Bank of Swatara.

"*Resolved*, that the books be opened at Middletown, on Tuesday, the 14th day of December next, by Jacob Snyder and Elisha Greene, at the house of John McCammon, for the subscription of fifteen hundred shares; at Hummelstown, on the same day by Christian Spayd and Thomas Fox, at John Fox's for five hundred shares; at Lebanon, in the county of Lebanon, on the same day, by William Allison and Abraham Doebler, at the house of Abraham Doebler, for five hundred shares; at Lancaster, the same day, by James Hamilton and James

Humes, at the house of John Duchman, for one thousand shares; at Elizabethtown, the same day, by John McCammon and Jacob Gish, for five hundred shares; at Manheim, the same day, by Ephraim Heller and Wendle Shelley, at the house of ——— ———, for five hundred shares; at Millerstown, in the county of Lebanon, the same day, by William Lowman and Joseph Wallace, at the house of Christian Capel, for five hundred shares.

"*Resolved,* that five dollars be paid to the commissioners for each and every share of stock at the time of subscription.

"*Resolved,* that James Hamilton, William Allison, E. Heller, and E. Greene, be a committee to draft a constitution for the said bank, which shall be printed and submitted to the stock holders at the time of subscribing.

"*Resolved,* that these resolutions be signed by the chairman and secretary, and be published in the English and German newspapers in the counties of Dauphin, Lebanon, and Lancaster."

The bank was chartered by the Legislature early in 1814, with a capital of $400,000, divided into 8,000 shares at $50 each. $100,000 was paid up, and Thomas R. Buchanan, George Bower, Isaac W. Van Leer, Henry Berry, George Fisher (Harrisburg), John Shelley (Londonderry), James Wilson (Derry), Jacob Hershey (Derry), James Hamilton, Christian Spayd, Elisha Greene, Ephraim Heller and William Lowman, appointed to receive subscriptions to the stock. The amount was subscribed and the bank organized with James Hamilton as president and John Neilson cashier.

Shortly after commencing business the institution was robbed of forty thousand dollars in unsigned notes. The thief, a man named Rennock, was caught at Myerstown, Lebanon county, and the money recovered. Rennock was convicted and sentenced to a lengthy imprisonment in the penitentiary.

After several years' successful business the bank discontinued operations, and its affairs were wound up by Mr. Neilson, who afterward became cashier of the State Treasury.

XXIV.

The brick dwelling (north side of Main, east of Beard's) was erected by George Beidler (afterwards the first United States postmaster at Guthrie, on the opening of Oklahoma Territory), on the site of a log house, occupied about one hundred years ago by John Metzger, a saddler and harnessmaker. His son Jonas resided next door, in a log building since torn down.

William A. Croll's (next east of Beidler's).—In this building resided Christian Spayd. He was principal of the Frey estate, a justice of the peace and for four years postmaster.

The Post Office.

This institution was not carried on with the exactitude and system which now prevails. There were no postage stamps, postal cards, or stamped envelopes.—There were no envelopes—the letter was folded the address written on the outside of the same sheet, and it was fastened with a wafer, or sealing wax. The postage was regulated by the distance a letter had to go, and could be prepaid or not, at the option of the sender. Six, twelve, eighteen and twenty-five cents on single letters were common rates. There was no money-order system. The letters were not classified, but thrown promiscuously into the mail bag, and each postmaster had to hunt for those belonging to his particular office. The Middletown post office was established in October, 1800. The first postmaster was William Crabb. He was succeeded in 1801 by Peter Thurston. In the spring of 1803, John McCammon was appointed. He held the office about twenty-seven years, and was succeeded in December, 1829, by William Lauman, and his widow, Elizabeth Lauman succeeded him in December, 1832. In June, 1834, Elizabeth Crabb took the office. In April, 1836, Christian Spayd was appointed. He was succeeded by Edward S. Kendig in March, 1840. In June, 1841, John Hicks was appointed. In January, 1845, Edward S. Kendig; in February, 1849, Catharine A. Stouch; in May, 1857, Maria L. Lauman; in April, 1861, Walter H. Kendig; on April 19th, 1863, John J. Walborn; April, 1866, Jackson H. Kirlin; March, 1867, Clara Monaghan (did not qualify); April, 1867, Rachel McKibbon; in April, 1883, Mrs. McKibbon (who had held office from the time it became a Presidential one) resigned and Miss Eveline Wiestling was appointed; October 22nd, 1895, Israel K. Deckard succeeded her; September 8th, 1900, Edward K. Demmy, the present incumbent, was appointed.

In 1850 Portsmouth, then a separate town, petitioned for a post office, the petition was granted, and Dr. John Ringland was appointed; in October, 1851, he resigned and F. H. Neiman was appointed. He was succeeded by his sister, S. E. Neiman. She held the office until April, 1857, when Portsmouth being included in the borough of Middletown, the office was abolished.

To return to W. A. Croll's residence. This stone house was built by George Everhart (Frey); here he kept a store and tavern. His clerk, Christoph Frederick Oberlander, who afterwards became his partner, died October, 1795, and is buried in the old (first) Lutheran graveyard. In this building, March 3d, 1768, a man named Henry Cowan had a quarrel with a negro, a slave of Colonel Burd's; he pursued him to the Colonel's residence, and in the affray which followed was killed. On the 6th of March an inquest was held in Frey's house by the coroner of Lancaster county, Mathias Slough. The members of the jury were Richard McClure, Henry Renick, Thomas McCord, William Dickey, John Steel, John Bachentose, Conrad Wolfley, John Steel, Sr., William Kerr, John Duncan, Thomas McArthur, Joseph Cook, John Myers and

John Laird. The negro was convicted of murder, imprisoned, and afterward sold out of the Province. Several of the members of this jury became officers of the Pennsylvania Line during the Revolution.

In the residence of the late Dr. A. N. Brenneman lived Dr. Mercer Brown.

DOCTORS.

Among the earliest physicians here were Dr. Romer, who located before 1770. Dr. John Fisher (son of George Fisher, the founder of Middletown), born November 3d, 1766, died February 27th, 1797. Dr. Charles Fisher, who was born September 8, 1766, and died May 8th, 1808. Dr. James McCammon began practicing at the beginning of the century, having been born in 1788, and died November 7, 1813. Contemporaneous with him was Dr. Abraham Price. He was born April 27, 1787, and died April 3d, 1821. A little later was Dr. Abraham McClelland, who died October 20th, 1828, aged thirty-seven years. Dr. Mercer Brown, long in practice, was born February 22, 1795, and died February 9th, 1871. Dr. Benjamin Weistling, over forty years in continuous practice, was born September 16th, 1805, and died July 31st, 1883. Dr. Meyrick practiced from about 1795 to 1815, and Dr. Simonton read medicine with him. Dr. John Ringland, born January 29th, 1825, practiced twenty-four years, when owing to a bodily infirmity he was obliged to retire. He died April 17th, 1899. Contemporary with him were Dr. Theodore C. Laverty and Dr. William H. Beane. The former was born May 12th, 1831, practiced forty-six years, and died August 14th, 1900. The latter was born June 25th, 1837, practiced thirty years, and died November 7th, 1899. Dr. Charles E. Pease was born May 9th, 1857, and died September 13th, 1904. Dr. John H. Myers was born May 14th, 1872, died April 20th, 1901.

The next house east of Dr. Brenneman's is the residence of the late Adolphus Fisher; his father, Dr. Charles Fisher, bought this property of John Eshleman in 1802, and lived in it until his death.

The late William M. Lauman's (southwest corner Main and Pine streets) belonged to Mr. Rife, father of Abraham Rife, and was sold by him to George Remley. Here the late Dr. Benjamin Weistling once lived.

The Nisley property (northwest corner of Main and Pine streets) was then a log house but longer than the present brick building. It was owned by Mrs. Crabb, who lived in the lower part; in the upper end the two Misses Job resided, and taught school from 1815 to 1828. They were elderly ladies at this time, and daughters of Adam Job. His father, Jacob Job, was one of the oldest settlers in this neighborhood, his land warrant being dated in 1742.

One of their scholars says of them: "The alphabet, spelling, and reading short sentences were all they professed to teach; a majority of the children were sent to keep them out of mischief. It was their invariable rule to wash the faces and comb the heads of those who came in what they did not consider proper trim, and it was with no gentle hand that these operations were performed. They were strict Presbyterians, and when the Rev. Mr. Sharon, who ministered to the neighboring churches of Derry and Paxton, paid them a pastoral visit during school hours he would always address the scholars and afterwards pray. He was provided with a pillow to kneel on, while we had the bare floor; as his petitions were generally rather long, we were glad when he finished, particularly so because school would then be dismissed, in order that some refreshment might be provided for him." The old ladies lie side by side in the abandoned graveyard on High street near Union.

Of the other pedagogues of this time, the same gentleman I quoted says: "The Rev. John F. Hay was a first-class teacher, and to him the larger children were sent. He was very strict in enforcing his rules, and in requiring perfect lessons. Mr. Jacob Wilson was a man of good common sense, but not much education; he had, however, a wonderful knack in bringing on the pupils as far as he undertook to teach. Many of his scholars were young men and women, but he was no respector of persons, and I have seen him flog young men taller than himself. He earned the title of 'Bully Wilson' among his scholars, yet was a kind man withal, and if we were well-behaved and had perfect lessons, we never had any trouble. About the same time a Mr. Samuel Dennis, a New England man, a graduate of Yale college, kept school in the basement of the old Bethel church. He was an excellent teacher and instructed the pupils in the higher branches of mathematics, Latin, Greek, &c. The trustees afterwards allowed him the use of the school house on Pine street, displacing a Mr. Mendenhall, but the supporters of the latter one day entered the building, and after forcibly removing Mr. Dennis, reinstalled Mendenhall. Upon this Mr. Dennis left town in disgust."

A Mrs. Ward was the first school teacher here that we have any record of. Jacob Peeler, a nailmaker, taught school in 1808 and '09, during the winter months.

"There were no free schools, and teaching was different from what it is now. The teacher sometimes provided his own schoolroom, bought his own fuel, made his own fires and kept the room in order. A quarter's schooling consisted of thirteen weeks, and no week was complete unless we made five days and a half. If we missed the half day on Saturday, we had a full day the next Saturday. There were no steel pens at that time and no printed copy books; the teacher made all the pens from goose quills and 'set copies' after school hours. For all this he received from $1.50 to $2.00 a quarter for each scholar. Those who were too poor to pay for the education of their children, the county made provision for, and the teacher was obliged to go to the county seat to get his pay from the commissioners."

When the school law was passed in 1834, Middletown was one of the first places to adopt it. The first directors were Dr. Mercer Brown, president; John Croll, secretary; Christian Spayd, treasurer; John Romberger, E. J. Ramsey and Peter Kob. John Ross was appointed a delegate to represent the district in the joint meeting of the commissioners at the court house in Harrisburg, on the first Tuesday of November of that year. He was instructed to vote for the laying of a tax for the support of the common schools. There was very little opposition to this school law. Among the most active in its favor were Gen. Simon Cameron, Henry Smith, George Smuller, John Bomberger and Martin Kendig; the latter representing the county in the Legislature during the Buckshot War. In 1835 Michael Lazarus was elected to represent the district in convention at the county commissioners' office, with instructions to vote for levying a tax, and such other measures as might be necessary for carrying into effect a general system of education.

The property on the southeast corner of Main and Pine streets belonged to Joseph Brestle.[1]

The Farmers' Hotel (northeast corner Main and Pine streets), now kept by Martin Snyder, was the Black Horse Tavern, owned by David Kiseker.[2] It was a favorite stopping place for teamsters.

Next door, east of Snyder's, was Thomas Dunham's tin shop.

About where S. L. Yetter's insurance office stands was then Remley's blacksmith shop.

Where Miss Meesy's brick house is (north side of Main street), there stood a two-story log tavern, the "Pennsylvania House," of which Martin Kendig was landlord. From its porch in 1836 General Harrison in response to an address of welcome delivered by George Fisher, Esq., made a short speech to those assembled to greet him. It afterwards belonged to John McCammon[3] and was kept successively by ———— Carlisle, Henry Chesny and Christian Caslow. In this building *The Middletown Argus*, the first newspaper printed here, was established by Mr. Wilson in 1834. He did the editorial work and his wife helped set type. It was discontinued in 1835. Here also George Rodfong carried on cabinet making, and Henry Schreiner had a saddler's shop.

In the property of the late John Heistand, John Shuler had a tailor shop.

In Frank Fisher's property George L. McClure[4] lived.

---

[1] Uncle Joseph Brestle.
[2] Mrs. Maria McCord's father.
[3] Mrs. R. McKibben's father. It was at Mr. McCammon's hotel, (N. W. cor. of the square) that the Marquis de Lafayette took dinner in 1825.
[4] Father of William McClure, Esq.

Where Eby's brick residence is (south side Main street, nearly opposite Miss Meesey's), Michael Heikel liven and had a butcher shop back. S. L. Yetter's was owned by Parthemore. Here James Ringland[5] kept a store.

At Ashenfelter's, Wolf had a wagon-making shop.

On the late Samuel Singer's lot, in a one-story log house, was Robert Henry's (afterwards Matthew McClure's) coppersmith and tin shop.

In the Singer residence John Snyder lived.

G. W. Baker's—Daniel Ehrisman—'Squire Heller had lived here before him.

S. S. Selser's property (southwest corner Spruce and Main), John Myers[6] kept a butcher shop.[7]

Where Daniel Sweigart's residence now stands was then a garden. Here on certain nights of the year the shade of a woman in white, who was said to have died of a broken heart, walked. There was also a man without a head, who had a habit of walking after dark along the run where Spruce street now is.

Kleindopf's (next east), Valentine Weirick lived. He had been a soldier of the Revolution and was then watchman at the Swatara Bank. This then was a one-story house; afterwards Mrs. Bombaugh lived here, her adopted daughter Eliza Bell[8] married DeWitt, who raised it to two stories, and put up the back building.

The late Joseph Brestle's property, (southeast corner Main and Spruce), was then an open lot, the next house (east) was owned by Peter (brother of Jacob) Schneider, and a man named Smith kept tavern here. It subsequently became the residence of the Rev. Mr. Seibert (German Reformed), and then of Mrs. Eshenower.[9]

John Keener's house, lately torn down, was owned by Adam Hemperly, who lived there. The Schneider property adjoined Keener's lot.

The Deckard property (east of Kleindopf's) George Selser[10] resided and carried on nailmaking. He had a small sawmill near the "sluice" on the race, and was the first to manufacture sawed plastering lath here.

XXV.

In the Hendrickson property Mr. Remley lived; after him Michael Hemperly.

At Brandt's (north side Main, east of Deckard's), Mrs. Flanigan resided. Afterwards Dr. Redfield's widow (Ezra J. Ramsey's sister) lived here and taught school.

---

[5] Dr. John Ringland's and Mrs. S. L. Yetter's father.
[6] Mrs. Farrington's father.
[7] The same shop had been owned by his father.
[8] Sister of Mrs. Geo. Lauman.
[9] Aunt to Christian King and Mrs. Jacob Benner.
[10] Father of Samuel Selser, Sr.

Where Mrs. Barnitz's brick residence it, was a one-story log house. Here Mrs. Shuster (a sister of Christian Spayd's) and her sister, Mrs. McMurtrie[1] lived. The next house above was Mrs. Shuster's son's (afterwards Christian Alleman's) blacksmith shop. Back of this was David McMurtrie's butcher shop.

At William Starry's lived John Remley, a chairmaker. He married Mrs. McClure.[2]

At Christian Hoffer's (south side Main street) lived Adam Toot. After him Henry Leham occupied the house and at the back end of the lot (on Water street) had a cooper shop.

Hoffman's (east of Starry's, north side of Main street), lived Kauffman's. In the upper end Joshua Heppich[3] had a shoemaker's shop and chandlery.

Roop's (south side Main street, north of Hoffer's), Jacob Strouse lived and carried on cabinet making.

John S. Roop's property (southwest corner Race and Main streets) was occupied by Hemperly, a nurseryman, who had a nursery near the race ground.

In the Hemperly building (northwest corner Race and Main streets) Rachael Marker lived at the lower end; at the upper Simon Zurger, a stonecutter, had his shop. After him it was occupied by Joseph Martin.

Hatz's (southeast corner Race and Main streets), Martin Kendig built and kept tavern. It was owned afterwards by David McKibben.

At the late Lewis Hemperly's residence (northeast corner Race and Main streets), Peter Kob kept the "Jackson House" and had a butcher shop back.

Where the late Mrs. Longenecker lived (next Hemperly's) was a yard, in the next house lived Burnheiter's; afterward Philip Blattenberger.

In the late S. Selser, Sr.'s, residence John Conrad lived. It belonged to George Lauman.[4]

In the Croll property nearly opposite was Isaac Gibson, an auctioneer. Here afterwards Alex. Black kept the "Cross-Keys" tavern.

Aungst's (southeast corner Vine and Main streets), Conrad Seabaugh[5] lived and had a cooper shop back.[6] This property was afterwards owned by the late Samuel Keller.[7] (He and his brother Sebastian were first cousins to Simon Cameron.)

West Main Street: Mr. Bauder's stone house (north side Main, west

---

[1] Miss Ellen McMurtrie's grandmother.

[2] Her daughter Martha married Benjamin Eby, brother of Jacob Eby, (Harrisburg) and Ephraim Eby (Phila.).

[3] John Heppich's father.

[4] Prof. George Fisher's grandfather.

[5] Brother of Mrs. Gilliard.

[6] Mrs. Benner, mother of John & Jacob, was a sister of Seabaugh's.

[7] Their mothers were sisters. Martin Kendig married Sarah Seabaugh, one of his daughters.

CHRONICLES OF MIDDLETOWN. 105

of Joseph Nisley's), John Stubbs lived, afterwards George Lowman. In the old Bethel parsonage (south side, opposite J. Nisley's), Thomas Elliot[8] lived.

The old brick building now occupied as a public school house (south side Main, west of parsonage), was built by Elisha Greene. He resided here and kept store; was a justice of the peace. It was afterwards Joseph Ross' drygoods store. Joseph Ross was the father of Christian K. Ross, who was born here. In this connection it may not be amiss to give a slight synopsis of a pathetic story.

CHARLEY ROSS.

Christian K. Ross resided in Germantown, a suburb and part of Philadelphia. On July 1st, 1874, his son, Charles Brewster Ross, was abducted by two men who soon after commenced correspondence with Mr. Ross, demanding $20,000 for his return. Every means, save that of compounding with the kidnappers, was tried to recover him. Citizens of Philadelphia offered $20,000 reward for the child stealers; $5,000 was offered for Charley; immense numbers of photographs and descriptions of the missing child were scattered broadcast over the land; the press in the United States and abroad advertised him; many in remote quarters of the world became interested in the case; police, detectives and citizens everywhere were on the alert; money was lavished in the search, but all without avail.

December 14th, 1874, William Mosher and Joseph Dauglass were shot while committing a burglary on Long Island and one of them lived long enough to reveal the fact that they were the abductors, but gave no clue to his whereabouts. No trace of the missing child has ever been found.

(His father's description of him is here given.) "Charley was born May 4th, 1870, and was about four years and two months old when he was stolen. His body and limbs were straight and well formed; his face round and full; his chin small, with a noticeable dimple; his hands very regular and prettily dimpled; small well formed neck; broad, full forehead; bright, dark brown eyes, with considerable fullness over them; clear, white skin; healthy complexion; light flaxen hair of a silky texture, easily curled in ringlets when extending to the neck; hair darker at the roots, a slight cowlick on the left side when it was parted; very light eyebrows. He talked plainly, but was shy and retiring, and had a habit of putting his arm up to his eyes when approached by strangers. He had no marks upon his person except those of vaccination. He had a good constitution, and when taken away was full of flesh and in good health—never having been sick after he was six months old."

Harry Ettele's (south side Main, west of Ross building), was a one-story log house. Mrs. Heppich[9] lived here.

---

[8] Dr. Brenneman's wife's father.
[9] John Heppich's grandmother.

Gingerich's (north side Main, west of Stehman's), John Snyder lived.[10]

In the Leiby property (where John Few resides, northeast corner Spring and Main), William Lowman, a hatter, lived. He kept the stage office and postoffice, succeeding Mr. McCammon. His son, William (who was a merchant in Philadelphia), donated the bell to the new Lutheran church, corner Spring and Union streets, and willed $1,000 for the purchase of an organ. He also left property valued at $10,000, the returns from which were to be used in keeping the old Lutheran church (northwest corner Union and High streets) in repair. Owing to some legal technicality, these bequests have never been realized by the church. On this site afterwards was Ettele's[11] hat shop.

Where the Wiestling residence is (north side Main, west of Gingerich's), old Mr. McCammon lived.

East of Mrs. Flora Saul's property (southeast corner Main and Spring streets), on the same lot, was a building owned by a German, Joseph Sneegontz. On this corner was afterwards a blacksmith shop,[12] carried on by Joseph Laubach and Jos. Campbell.[13]

Beck's (southwest corner Spring and Main streets), George Croll lived and had a cabinet maker's shop.

The next house (west on Main street) was occupied by John Snavely's father, a tailor.

The late Michael Lauman's residence (northwest corner Main and Spring streets) and adjoining lot were left to his father by his grandmother, Mrs. Michael Conrad.[14] Here stood two log houses which were burned in 1855; in the one occupied by Henry Stehman,[15] at that time burgess, the records of the borough were destroyed.

Misses Croll's (west of M. Lauman's): Here Abner Croll lived. In the first house across the run, north side Main and west of Spring, John Croll lived. He built the house where the Misses Croll now reside. He and Abner Croll[16] were partners in the tannery, which was situated between the two houses spoken of.

Where George Ettele's residence is (south side Main, near the run), James Crawford,[17] a stonemason and bricklayer lived, after him Christian Siple,[18] a gunsmith.

In the late George Barnitz's residence (south side Main street), Christian Lawrence lived.

---

[10] Joseph Campbell's grandfather.
[11] Father of George and Harry Ettele.
[12] Here Michael Lauman learned his trade.
[13] Joseph Campbell's father.
[14] Prof. George Fisher's great-grandmother.
[15] Father of D. W. & H. C. Stehman.
[16] John Croll, Henry Croll and Abner Croll were brothers, Abner Croll was William A. Croll, Esq's. father.
[17] Dr. John Ringland's uncle.
[18] Henry Siple, Sr's. father and William and Henry Siple's grandfather.

The next house, west of Barnitz's, near the run, was a stone one, and was first used as a stillhouse, afterwards John Dennis, a weaver, had a shop and lived there.

On the north side of Main street, west of John Croll's, Emanuel Bolling, an old soldier of the Revolution, lived. When he first came here there were but four persons buried in the old (first) Lutheran cemetery (southeast corner High and Pine streets). He is supposed to have built the old tannery (faint traces of which still exist near Rife's tanyard), before Croll commenced.

Near the Christ residence was old Mr. McCammon's orchard. Here John Jemison, a poor Irishman, lived in a shanty which Mr. McCammon erected for him. He afterwards went to Indiana, and Neddy Lum, a colored man, who had been a servant to Col. Tom Jordan,[19] succeeded him.

Opposite the American Tube and Iron Company's works (north side Main street) was the old Wolfley farm. Here there was another tannery owned by Jacob Wolfley.[20]

Joseph Heister, afterwards Governor of Pennsylvania, had several hundred acres in this vicinity. He owned the Bomberger farm and the "Oak Lane" farm. One of his heirs (J. Murray Rush, of Philadelphia) sold them to subsequent owners.

XXVI.

On Water street there were but few houses. On the northwest corner of Spruce and Water stands the United Brethren Church.

Where Prof. H. B. Garver's residence is (north side Water, west of Spruce), Jacob Albert lived and had a weaver shop.

At the late James Keener's (south side of Water), stood an old log house occupied by Samuel Freeman.

Where Scott Hemperley's house stands (northwest corner Water and Pine streets), John Bomberger[1] (Jacob E. Bomberger, the late Harrisburg banker's father), lived. On the southeast corner of the same streets he had his wagonmaker's shop.

At John Parthemore's (south side of Water between Spruce and Pine streets), John Starr's grandfather lived.

Where the late Jacob Landis lived (Pine street north of Water), William Wandlass, a Scotchman, once lived. He was the first cooper in town, opening a shop here in 1769. (With him Conrad Seabaugh learned his trade.) At the northeast corner of Water and Pine streets, where the brick house stands, was an old cellar where he soaked his poles.

Next (east side of Pine street, north of Landis') lived a family named Snyder. Here afterwards resided Aunt Sallie Freeman.

[19] A brother of Edward Jordan.
[20] Mrs. Rachael McKibben's uncle.
[1] He was Mrs. Magdalene Ringland's father and John Heppich's uncle.

108   CHRONICLES OF MIDDLETOWN.

On the west side of Pine street, where the North ward brick school house stands was a little low log building then used for school purposes; on one side was a small gallery, approached by a narrow stairs; here refractory scholars were compelled to sit.

North side of the school house, in the building now the property of Mrs. A. Ackerman, lived Rev. John F. Hay the school teacher. He was afterwards the founder of Cottage Hill Seminary, at York, Pa.

In Miss Ida Evans' property (the frame building north of F. Myers' brick residence), Mrs. Esther Lauman,[2] George and William Lauman's mother, lived.

On Water street west of Hemperley's stood a small house wherein dwelt Mrs. Patty Allen. Afterwards Anna Marshall lived here and kept a candy shop, well patronized by the school children.

Where John Peters resides (north side of Water, west of Hemperley's) there lived an old colored man named Major Fetterman.

Kline's (northeast corner Water and Union), George Etter[3] built and lived in.

Mrs. Connelly's residence (northwest corner Water and Union), John Pricer, a shoemaker, built and lived in. Philip Irwin, George and William Lauman, Henry Techtmoyer and others learned their trade with him.

Mr. Pricer (who although an excellent man and a good workman, had an irascible temper) owned a black muley cow. One day Abe Simcox, one of his apprentices, procuring a couple of horns at a neighboring tannery, affixed them neatly to muley's head in the place where the horns ought to grow; then with the aid of a bucket of whitewash, he painted several spots on her. Pricer coming into the stable at dusk and seeing a strange cow there, attempted to put her out. She resisted and he grasped her by the horns, which being unprepared to resist such a strain, tore loose. Horrified he dashed them down and rushed into the shop. "Abe, whose cow is that in the stable?" "Why ours, ain't it?" replied Abe, looking up in innocent surprise. "No it ain't ours by a good deal!" shouted Pricer, "it's a strange cow, and what's more, I've gone and pulled the horns off her!" The burst of laughter which greeted this remark showed Pricer that he had been imposed on, and it is reported that Abe used a cushion on his workbench for several days afterwards.

Dr. J. Ruhl's (southwest corner Water and Union streets), was also built by John Pricer. Here David McKibben[4] lived. Mr. McKibben had a large warehouse where Condriet's sawmill afterwards stood. After the railroads had, to a great extent, destroyed the grain commission business, he converted it into a planing mill and was the first person in town to use the steam engine for manufacturing purposes. This mill was afterwards turned into a sawmill and was destroyed by fire in 1846.

---

[2] Abner Lauman's grandmother.
[3] Washington Etter's father.
[4] Mrs. Rachel McKibben's husband.

CHRONICLES OF MIDDLETOWN. 109

In the low building once standing on the north side of Water street near the Bethel church, Elisha Green had a cooper shop. Afterwards it was Isaac Simcox's tailor shop.

Where the Bethel church now stands (northeast corner Spring and Water streets), Burgoyne lived. He was one of the oldest settlers and owned the tannery, afterward owned by Daniel Dowdel; purchased in 1830 by Jacob Rife, Sr., and now owned by the Rife Brothers.

High Street: On the west side of Pine street, above High, John Blattenberger had a rope walk.

Old Lutheran parsonage (north side High, between Pine and Union). This was then a log structure; there was a Lutheran school in one end and Philips, the organist lived in the other. (The first organist in the Lutheran church was Michael Conrad.[5]) After Philips, Jacob Wilson lived in the upper end and taught in the lower.

In Kleindopf's (north side High, west of the parsonage), Monaghan,[6] a tailor, lived.

In the house next, east of the Coleman property, (south side High street) lived John Schlich.

In the Keever residence (northeast corner Spring and High streets), James McBride lived; afterwards the widow, Mary Jontz, resided here; she married William Peck and moved to Wayne county, Ohio.

The late Mrs. Bretz's residence (north side High, east of Keever's), Jacob Bomberger[7] built for Jacob Erb; he afterwards lived here himself.

Where the Wood property is (southwest corner Spring and High streets), Elberti carried on tailoring; it was afterwards owned by Martin Peck. Northwest of Demmy's stood a hay shed owned by Philip Ettele.

Spring Street: At the north end of this street (above High) stood a hay shed owned by John McCammon, used to store away hay to supply the stage horses.

Where the residence of William Carr now stands was a log house belonging to Philip Ettele. In a log house opposite George Critson, a shoemaker, lived.

The late Frank Swartz's property (east side Spring, south of Main) was owned by Mrs. Blattenberger.

Walter Fortney's property (west side Spring, south of Main). Where this residence is there then stood George Gross' large barn. South of this Youngblood's lived.

The property occupied by the late Dr. Robert Long[8] (west side Spring south of Main), Joshua Heppich sold to Richard McGlennan, who afterwards had a shoe shop here.

---

[5] Michael Lauman's grandfather.
[6] John Monaghan's grandfather.
[7] Mrs. Jacob Rife, Sr's. father.
[8] Here John Heppich was born.

In the Barr residence (east side Spring, south of Main) Henry Siple,[9] Sr., lived.

Mrs. M. Myers' residence was Leonard Alleman's cooper shop; afterwards Wolfe's wagonmaker shop.

Next door north of John Rife's residence (northwest corner Spring and Water) was David Rohrer's[10] locksmith shop.

Next north of Rohrer's was Goodyear,[11] a cabinet maker.

The house (southwest corner Spring and Water streets), Mrs. Sedgwick built; here she lived and taught school.

Mrs. Fralich's residence was owned by F. Murray; there was a tavern here.

Where H. S. Roth lives (west side Spring, opposite Postoffice avenue) Jacob Rife, Sr., resided.[12]

In the Hipple property (east side, south of Water) dwelt John Jemmison.

Jacob Ehrisman owned several lots here and lived on this street.

On the southwest corner Spring and Union, where the new Lutheran church now stands, were the grounds of the (2nd) Emaus Orphan House. (This latter is now occupied as a residence.)

Union Street: James Billet's[13] residence at the north end of this street was originally the Ebenezer Methodist church edifice.

The Mish property (southeast corner Union and High streets), originally a Moravian church lot, was then in the possession of a Mr. Ressler.

Ebersole's (northeast corner Union and High streets) was the residence of Mr. Ettele.

At Balsbaugh's, Mr. Ressler lived; afterwards John Blattenberger. On this property was afterwards George Smuller's residence and tailor shop.

The late John Benner's residence (southwest corner Union and High streets) was a vacant lot on which James Campbell had a gun shop. During the many years that elapsed between the death of George Fisher, the founder of Middletown, and the return of his son, the residence at "Pineford" was rented, part of the time to Mr. Benner, the father of John and Jacob, and they were born in the old two-story log house (the first building in Middletown), which was afterwards torn down by Edward Fisher.

Where John Heppich's residence is (west side Union, south of Benner's) was Remley & Peck's blacksmith shop and Thomas Jontz's wagon shop. Here afterwards was a weaver shop. It was subsequently occu-

---

[9] Father of Wm. H. Siple, of Wilkinsburg, Pa.
[10] Father of Capt. Jeremiah Rohrer, of Lancaster.
[11] George Rodfong learned his trade with him.
[12] Here Mrs. Susan Brady was born.
[13] George A. Lauman's mother.

pied by the new Lutherans, after the split in 1835, as a meeting house or church until 1838, when they erected Christ Church.

Alpheus Long's (west side Union, south of Heppich's); here John Benner had a cooper shop. Before his time it was occupied by Michael Lazarus.

The late William Lauman's residence (west side Union, south of Long's) was owned first by Mrs. Shackey; afterwards occupied as a tailor shop by Jacob Shurtz;[14] Dr. Watson lived here at the same time and had an office on the opposite side of the street near Balsbaugh's.

M. H. Gingerich's, a one-story stone house, stood on this site, occupied by Jontz, a turner. His principal business was turning out tarbuckets for Conestoga wagons. Before him Jacob Hamaker lived here; he built the first canal boat constructed in this town; it was conveyed to the canal by being placed on rollers.

Abner Croll's butcher shop was then occupied by Peter Myers and Henry Croll as a butcher shop.

North of the late Henry Croll, Sr.'s, residence (northwest corner Union and the square) there lived Thomas Allison, a school teacher.

In G. W. Elberti's residence (west side Union, south of square) his father, Lawrence Elberti, lived.

At Mrs. Harry Hinney's (east side Union, north of Water) James Russel lived.

Mrs. John Cole's residence was James Ringland's residence;[15] afterwards John Jos. Walborn,[16] a justice of the peace, lived here.

The Garret property (west side of Union, south of square), Stubbs built. It was afterwards owned by Mrs. Ramsey, who taught school here. This was Simon Cameron's first place of residence in Middletown.

Where the Wendling and Wolfe properties stand John McFarland had a turner shop; it was afterwards Fortney's hat shop.

Baker's residence (west side Union, north of Ringland's Hall) was built by Polly Kain. She was a great knitter; it is said that being summoned to Harrisburg as a witness, she walked there and back, and knit six pairs of the long woolen stockings it was then the fashion to wear, while attending the court.

At T. M. Yost's, William King had a tannery, which he afterwards rented to John Wolfley.

Manning's, James McCord, a chairmaker, lived.

Miss Annie Kendig's residence, James Hamilton built. He erected a stillhouse back of it. He owned several warehouses and built a grist mill lately occupied by Israel Deckard. Here, afterwards, Barney Duffy kept the "Lamb Tavern;" he had a bowling alley and a shuffleboard, and it was a great place of resort for watermen in the spring, and for laborers on the canal while it was building.

---

[14] Jacob Shurtz's grandfather.
[15] Here Dr. John Ringland was born.
[16] Cornelius Walborn's father.

J. W. Rewalt's property (northwest corner Spring and Union) was a distillery, owned either by Wagner or Stubbs.

Where the late Seymour Raymond's residence stands (east side Union opposite Spring) was a large log house belonging to John Elder,[17] and sold by him to John Wolfley.

The site of Arthur King's and Dr. D. W. C. Laverty's residences (south of the new Lutheran church) was a large pond; there was once a brickyard here.

Below Raymond's, where the late Dr. Ringland's residence is, was a small log house. There were no houses between this and the canal, and on the west side of the street none below Rewalt's.

In Portsmouth William Rewalt[18] kept a store where Wesley McCreary's restaurant now is.

Wagner's ferry was near where the Pennsylvania Canal lock used to be; during high water this was a rope ferry. The double house, the late Washington Etter's[19] property, was the ferry house. There was also a low water ferry at Seagrave's; on the Port Royal side of this ferry was a tavern kept by Mrs. Grote.

At the outlet lock Mr. Gutterman lived and kept a grocery.

There was an old brewery at the run near the lock, kept by Mr. Baer.

Across the canal there was a landing at Dunning's, on the Swatara front.

At the period we are writing of the "Red Tavern," owned by Frank Murray, stood at the point; there was another at Mrs. Snyder's; near here was the "Cross Keys Tavern," kept by Mrs. McFaun.

On the river above the ferry stood the "Lochman House."

There were several warehouses standing along the bank of the Swatara, above the Pennsylvania Canal, and between it and the outlet lock.

Where Moyer's cabinet maker's shop formerly was, the first store in Portsmouth was kept by James Ringland. In after years Kunkle and others kept branch stores here in summer time for accommodation of the watermen. Later Captain Hawk converted one of the warehouses into a permanent dwelling and store and put his son-in-law, McBarron, in as partner, and still later Fisher & Boyd opened a store in the "Red" warehouse on the canal basin, where Young's Opera House now stands.

[17] Mrs. R. C. McKibben's sister.
[18] John Rewalt's father.
[19] A. L. Etter's father.

NOTE:—In concluding the series of papers entitled "About a Century ago," we wish to return our thanks to those who have furnished the information contained therein. We are particularly indebted to William Remly; leaving here at the age of twenty-two, and returning after an absence of fifty years, his recollections of the home of his boyhood were remarkably vivid. We are also under obligations to Mrs. Irvin, Mrs. McKibben, Mrs. Adolphus Fishel, Messrs. Michael Lauman, Dr. John Ringland, S. Selser, Sr., and others. In order to secure accuracy the papers were submitted as a whole to some thirteen of the older residents of Middletown, all now dead.

One of Middletown's Handsome Homes.

XXVII.

George Everhardt (Frey) was born March 3, 1732, in Klatte, in the county of Darmstadt, Kingdom of Wirtemberg. According to his contemporaries he came to this country as a redemptioner in 1749, served his time and then (see chapter 17)—

The Emaus Orphan House.

This institution was the first of its kind in this country. It owes its existence to George Frey, who by will provided for its erection and maintenance. The will in substance is as follows:

He bequeaths all his property, to wit: A grist mill with six acres of land on the Swatara, and the right to a mill race through the Fisher estate; 498¼ acres purchased from Blair McClenachan; 284½ acres purchased from Andrew McClure, Roan McClure and Jonathan McClure; 120 acres "contiguous to the town of Middletown;" four houses in Middletown, to wit: One occupied by himself, one by Charles McDowell, one by Memucan J. Howell, and one by Michael Hemperly; 120 lots in Middletown, 207 acres in Northumberland county; about 300 acres on Penn's creek, and all his personal property; in trust to John Landis, merchant; Dr. Charles Fisher, of Middletown; Jacob Rife, farmer, of Derry township; John Cassel, of Swatara township, yeoman; in trust, to erect and support an Orphan House, which shall be called "Emaus," and provide for the education of as many poor orphan children as the rents and profits of the said estate would allow; excepting a house and lot, and such furniture, money, etc., as his wife may need.

He orders that the trustees, a principal and a tutor, shall be members of the institution. That they shall within two years after his death, "at furthest" carry his will into effect.

He directs that if at any time, from any cause, a vacancy should occur among these officials, they shall elect a freeholder and resident of Dauphin county to fill such vacancy, a record of which transaction, and the cause therefore, shall be kept and laid before the judges of the Court of Common Pleas at its next session thereafter, and if said judges disapprove of the board's action, a new election shall take place within one month after such decision.

The Duties of the Trustees.

They are to examine and verify the accounts of the principal. For sufficient cause they may remove him and elect another in his stead. Once in two months at least, they shall meet at the Orphan House, liquidate the accounts, examine thoroughly into all matters pertaining to the agriculture, &c., and suggest any changes of advantage to the trust; for which service they are to receive a specified sum per day.

They have power, together with the principal, to build or finish the

Orphan House. They must be economical and yet at the same time provide for the comfort of the inmates. If they find the funds inadequate, they have power to erect mills, machinery or water works on the race, or any other buildings on the lots or farms, that they deem necessary or beneficial to the institution, but no part of the estate can be sold; it must remain "undivided forever."

When the Orphan House is ready, they must receive into it for maintenance and education (free of all expense to the children or their relatives), all such poor, but healthy orphan children, as are of the age of five and under twelve years; and, if they have sufficient funds, poor children whose parents are unable to maintain or educate them.

The children must be educated in the Lutheran religion, and in the German language; no other language shall be taught.

The children may remain there—the boys until they are fifteen, and the girls fourteen years of age, when they shall each receive a freedom suit.

THE DUTIES OF THE PRINCIPAL.

He shall have immediate superintendence and management of the whole estate; shall oversee and direct the agricultural concerns thereof, subject to the advice of the trustees; shall keep regular bank accounts of all receipts and expenditures, and submit such accounts at least every two months, to the inspection of the trustees.

He shall reside in one of the four houses mentioned, and shall have a free table for himself and family furnished out of the proceeds of the estate, and a stipulated salary yearly.

He shall exercise a supervision over the mills and other water works erected on the race, and keep an exact account of all receipts and expenditures relative thereto.

If his own children labor for the institution, they shall have reasonable wages therefor.

If he has been faithful in office and becomes superannuated in the service of the estate, he shall be supported out of the funds of the institution, and if he has a son who is equally capable and trustworthy, he shall be appointed instead of his father.

DUTIES OF THE TUTOR.

At 6 o'clock in the morning he shall assemble the children in a suitable room, sing and pray with them, concluding with the Lord's prayer; then exercises in the Christian belief and Lutheran catechism; then breakfast; two hours of school, teaching reading, writing, arithmetic and catechism; at 9 A. M., they shall work in the garden. The officers of the institution are instructed to lay off ten acres contiguous to the Orphan House, for that purpose, "which shall be cultivated principally as a kitchengarden."

A portion of the garden shall be devoted to fruits; hemp and flax shall also be raised; all for the use of the institution, any surplus to be disposed of for the benefit of the same; at 11 A. M., thanksgiving, "knee prayers, and belief, as in the morning, shall be repeated." The children shall then dine. School for two hours; then work again in the garden; at 6 P. M., singing, "and ceremonial of the morning shall be repeated." "In winter, after supper, the girls about six years old, shall be taught to spin. When the children have been taught to read, one of the boys shall repeat a chapter out of the Bible."

An orphan shall not be permitted to leave the institution without leave from the tutor, and if stubborn, disobedient or incorrigible, the trustees shall bind him (or her) out to a trade.

The tutor if sending the children on errands, must send two together. They must be corrected for lying, bad language, &c.

When the principal needs help on the farm the tutor shall send as many children as he may require to assist him—between school hours.

When the funds of the institution justify it, weaving shall be introduced, and the "children shall be clothed in home manufactures—the boys in brown—the under garments of the girls shall be linsey wolsey, their upper garments of blue striped cotton stuffs;" the clothing to be given annually at Easter.

A female teacher shall instruct the girls in needlework, knitting and spinning. The children must assist in keeping the house in order.

No books shall be used except those which inculcate good morals and sound religious principles. When a child is fourteen years old, it shall be confirmed and admitted to the sacrament.

The tutor must be a married man and reside in the institution, and shall have a free table furnished himself and family out of the funds of the estate, and a specified salary annually. If he should become superannuated during his service, he shall be supported during life and an allowance made him annually.

Duties of the Trustees, Principal and Tutor Conjointly.

They have the power of modifying the mode of instruction, if necessary, so that they conform to the orthodox belief of the church and the method practiced in its schools.

If any charges are brought against any of said officials they shall be examined into, and if the accused is found guilty, he shall be removed and another elected in his stead.

They shall annually submit at the first Court of Quarter Sessions in the county, which meets after the first of the year, an itemized statement of all the accounts of the estate and institution for the preceding year, accompanied by sufficient vouchers. And (if required by the court) a statement of the children admitted, maintained and educated; their sex, ages, &c. The court is requested to appoint three respectable "members of the grand jury," to examine and settle said accounts. If the balance is in favor of the accountants, to be placed to their credit; if against them, then go to their debit for the ensuing year. If the trustees, principal and tutor refuse or neglect to exhibit such accounts, the court is to compel them to do so.

The court is requested to appoint "a respectable freeholder," as a visitor to the Orphan House, who shall have the right to inspect all the properties belonging to the estate, twice a year, at such times as he shall select. He shall give the officials of the estate and institution forty-eight hours' notice of his visit, and one of them shall accompany him in his tour of inspection, and answer all questions he may propound to him. The visitor shall report to the next court, a detailed statement of the result of his observations; and the court may either approve his report, or if necessary on account of neglect, or gross violation of duty, summarily remove any of the officials from office, at its discretion; such vacancies to be filled as before provided. When Middletown shall be incorporated as a borough, the power of the court to appoint a visitor shall cease, and all said visitor's powers be transferred to the burgess of said town, forever.

If the institution should "fail" on account of the death, emigration or removal of officials, or any other cause, the Governor of the State is authorized to appoint other officers, who shall have all the rights, privileges, emoluments specified in the will.

The tract of land in Northumberland county, is directed to be sold, and the money arising from such sale to be used for the benefit of the institution.

Should any future legacy or fund be given to the Emaus Orphan House, the name of the donor (if permitted), the amount of donation and the time when given, shall be entered in a book kept for that purpose, and on the anniversary of such donation, the clergyman holding service in the institution, shall publicly "mention the circumstances of such bounty."

The trustees shall be respectable freeholders of Dauphin county, and regular members of some Protestant church. The principal and tutor must be of good moral character, and "regular members of the Evangelical Lutheran religion."

John Cassel, yeoman, is appointed principal; and the trustees, principal and tutor, are ordered to petition the Governor and Legislature for an act of incorporation, under the title of the Emaus Orphan House.

A codicil provides that all the real estate owned by him, not otherwise mentioned; and all now in litigation (when recovered), shall be sold, and the proceeds, together with all the moneys due him (when collected), placed in the hands of the trustees for the use of the institution. John Crabb, Sr., is appointed agent to collect all money due him, for which service he is to receive ten pounds out of every hundred he collects. The said John Crabb is to reside with his (Frey's) family, and to have £100 per annum in addition to the percentage above specified, during the time he is collecting. He is also allowed to keep a horse, and to be allowed his reasonable expenses.

The German school in Middletown under the control of Frederick

Miller is to be continued until the Orphan House is completed.
The will was executed May 12th, 1806, in the presence of John Blattenberger, Abraham Rife and Charles Brandon, who were all his neighbors. George Frey died the following day, May 13th, 1806. This will was drawn up and written by John Joseph Henry, President Judge of Dauphin county, who presided over these courts from 1793 until about 1810. It was, as may be judged from the summary, an elaborate document, containing minute and special directions.

Immediately after his death a suit was brought, on a feigned issue, to test the validity of the will. After a sharp contest a verdict was given, April 16, 1807, in favor of the will, admitting it to probate, but invalidating the codicil, and so far in favor of the contestants.

The delay occasioned by this suit would have been a trifling matter but for the debt incurred in prosecuting it. The attorneys for the trustees charged $4,800 for their services. The sum added to other charges, made the liabilities of the estate at the end of the first year some $8,000. This amount, large as it was, might easily have been paid had a proper application of the personal estate been made. The money estate was estimated at $27,000; to be added to this was $2,666.67 realized by the sale of the tract of land in Union county. Of the rest of his personal estate there is not any precise statement. The power of his wife over that was unlimited, at least her privilege was made to do duty for all her real expenditures, and for many other transactions of which she knew less than nothing. Much of this was shown in the fierce legal contest which followed, and which was continued for quite a quarter of a century. It is obvious, however, that the money arising therefrom, was entirely diverted from the institution it was intended for, and instead of going into its treasury, was used by the trustees or their agents for private purposes.

So much of the land was sold by distress, to pay debts, prior to the accounting of 1829, that its acreage was considerably decreased. Considering that Frey was not in debt at his death, the charge of "mismanagement and dishonesty in management," is not astonishing.

Instead of applying the revenues of the estate to the liquidation of the debt, and the establishment of the Orphan House, they were squandered. Thus the debt not only remained but was increasing. Upon legal processes for the payment of debts, mostly created by the trustees, houses, lots and lands were sold prior to 1835, to the amount of $17,683.87.

The trustees also failed to comply with the requisitions of the will, to file an annual account of all receipts and expenditures of the institution for presentation to the court of Dauphin county. The first eighteen months only, did they file a full account. The receipts for that period were $4,882.19 and the expenditures $4,724.47.

Notwithstanding the fact that the will of Mr. Frey had been tried and established on a feigned issue, the children of a deceased brother, encouraged to believe that the will could not be carried into effect and that eventually they must recover, ventured a suit to get the estate into their possession. Some of these children sold out their claims, and the purchasers united with those who did not sell, in an ejectment to the August term of the court, 1826, more than twenty years after the testator's death. Christian Spayd, the principal of the estate, and the defendant in the ejectment, was a nephew of George Frey, and claimed one-fourth of the estate as his share; the plaintiffs—and among them were some of the trustees—claimed three-fourths. It was thus the interest of both parties that the plaintiffs should recover, as then each party would receive the shares respectively claimed. Owing to this state of things, no proper defense was made, and a verdict was rendered for the plaintiffs, for three-fourths of the estate. The charge of the court had been in favor of the defendant, and against the recovery of the heirs, consequently, on motion, without argument, a new trial was granted; the judge asserting that he would not permit such gross injustice to be done whilst he was on the bench.

For some years the Lutheran church had been endeavoring to secure such an administration of the affairs of the estate as would meet the ends contemplated by the testator. On account of the resistance made, and the difficulties thrown in their way by the trustees, with the usual delay of legal proceedings, nearly fifteen years elapsed before the trustees' accounts were finally agreed upon.

On the 25th of May, 1829, the Supreme Court appointed Francis R. Shunk, William Clark and Valentine Hummel, auditors to examine the accounts of John Cassel and Christian Spayd, the former having been principal from 1806 to 1814, and the latter from 1814 to the time of the auditors' appointment.

On the 22nd of November, 1830, these auditors reported. They found a balance in Cassel's favor of $711.84 and in Spayd's favor of $9,029.67. The report of the auditors was set aside by the decision of the Supreme Court, in November, 1834, Chief Justice Gibson in delivering the opinion of the court said:

"Had the respondents (Cassel and Spayd) performed their respective duties and accomplished the purpose of the trust, these balances, though sufficiently startling, might have been deemed to have accrued consistently with good management and fair dealing. But when we find that not a single step has been taken for three and twenty years towards a dispensation of the founder's bounty, that not a single orphan has had the benefit of it, and that the Orphan House built by the founder has been suffered to rot, till it is not worth the cost of repairing; that a considerable part of the estate has been dilapidated and sold by the Sheriff, a part of it to one of the respondents, and other parts of it to some of the trustees; and that the respondents having taken the profits without having fully accounted for them, yet claim to be let in as creditors on the fund to an amount that would bankrupt it, we are astounded by the magnitude and boldness of the pretension." He pronounced the value of the realty in 1826, "worth one hundred thousand dollars;" observing that there had been expended "in taking care of it, to the time of adjudication (1833), nearly or quite $100,000."

Instead of confirming the auditors' report the court declared John Cassel a debtor to the estate of more than $15,000, and Christian Spayd a debtor of more than $12,000; with five years' proceeds of the estate to account for. Amounts which neither of them was able to pay, or ever did pay.

Whilst the suit of the relatives against the estate was pending, the plaintiffs in the ejectment, who call themselves heirs, desired to effect a compromise with the Lutheran Synod of Pennsylvania and West Pennsylvania. At their request a meeting of representatives from the heirs and two Synods was held at York, Pa., on the 25th of March, 1835. The representatives of the heirs presented the committees of the Synods at this meeting the following proposals, viz:

"That if they were permitted to get possession of the estate, they would appoint and authorize Abraham Bombaugh and Daniel Hummel to sell the entire estate, and would appropriate the money arising from the sale in the following manner: The one-twentieth part thereof to be paid over to the Directors of the Poor in and for Dauphin county, and the residue to be divided into two equal shares, one of said shares to be paid over to the heirs of George Frey, and the other to be paid over for the benefit of the Lutheran Church in Pennsylvania; to be invested, and the annual interest of it applied to the maintenance and education of orphans, and other poor and pious young men for the gospel ministry."

The representatives of the Synods, consisting of J. George Schmucker, D. D., President of the Synod of West Pennsylvania; John C. Baker, D. D., President of the Synod of Pennsylvania; and S. S. Schmucker, D. D., Frederick Smith and John Barnitz, committee of the Synod of West Pennsylvania, promised to lay the proposal of the heirs before their respective Synods for their decision.

A special meeting of the Synod of West Pennsylvania was called on the 14th of June, 1835, to consider the proposal. The Synod of Pennsylvania held its annual convention the same month, at Germantown, and in reference to this proposition adopted the following:

"WHEREAS, the reputed heirs of Geo. Frey have proposed to this body a compromise, &c., &c. Therefore the members of this body have, and it is hereby resolved, that they will accede to the proposed compromise, for the following reasons.

"1st. Because the last will and testament of said George Frey expressly declares that the institution contemplated by him, should be connected with the Lutheran church in Pennsylvania; that its principal and teacher must be members of the Lutheran church, and its instruction be accommodated, from time to time, to the orthodox belief of the church, and the method practiced in its schools.

"2nd. Because, although the compromise sets aside some of the localities and minor circumstances of the will, it accomplishes the grand moral and religious design of the testator.

"3rd. Because after an experiment of twenty-nine years, the church has failed in her attempts to coerce the parties to execute the design of the testator under the will, and there is but little prospect of having the residue of the estate applied with better success to the said design." The action of the Synod of West Pennsylvania was substantially the same.

Pending these negotiations, however, the old board of trustees, which was favorable to the compromise, resigned, and in July of the same year the Supreme Court appointed a new board, of which Dr. Mercer Brown was principal. The new board was averse to the compromise of the heirs with the church, consequently it failed. Subsequently the trustees themselves compromised with the heirs, and agreed to pay them $4,500.00 to have the ejectment discontinued, and all claims released and surrendered, forever. This compromise was afterwards authorized by legal enactments.

Thus it was not until after many years of expensive litigation, that the building on Spring street near Union, was erected. George Frey had commenced to build his "Orphan House" about a quarter of a mile east of the edifice on Spring street, and a log building, thirty by forty feet, and two stories in height, was already under roof when he died. He had also established the German school, alluded to in the latter part of his will, in which all poor children of that parentage or nationality were taught, free of charge. The erection of the Orphan House being delayed, this school was maintained by the trustees for a number of years, the teacher receiving his stipulated salary, and having, much of the time, but a mere shadow of a school.

On the completion of the (second) Orphan House, in 1837 "on high ground between the towns of Middletown and Portsmouth," Rev. S. D. Finkel took charge of it. He continued his connection therewith for three or four years, during which period he had under his care from *two* to *five* orphan children, who were supported by the estate. This was the first benefit conferred by the bequest on orphans, since it was left for them thirty years previous.

In 1839 the governing body was incorporated. Owing to some error the tutor's name was omitted as a corporate member. (This has never since been rectified.)

In the will the trustees held office for life, and were a self-perpetuating body—by the act of incorporation their term of office was limited to eight years, and the appointing power given to the court of Dauphin county; thus a trustee is appointed every two years. The act also provided for the teaching of the English language in the institution, and a leasing of a portion of the real estate for any term not exceeding one hundred years; the grist and sawmills and the farms for not exceeding six years; and any portion of ground along the canal or railroad, of not more than ten acres with or without the additional privilege of water power, for any term not exceeding twenty years.

In 1840, in consequence of debts amounting to about $8,000, the Orphan House was again discontinued. Shortly afterwards, June 2nd, 1840, permission was obtained from the Legislature to connect a private school with it. The building was enlarged and virtually converted into an academy. For fifteen years the tutor was nothing more than the teacher of a select school, receiving a part of his support from the estate; in consideration of which he taught a few poor children gratuitously.

The following names are those of the scholars who attended this private school during the sessions of 1841 and 1847.

1841.

M. R. Alleman,
—— Balsbaugh,
John Brown,
David Brown,
J. Best,
Brua Cameron,
Don Cameron,
B. F. Etter,
G. Ettele,
M. Flora,
L. Heiner,

John S. Croll,
H. Harrison,
J. Heck,
James Jordon,
R. M. McKibben,
J. Wolfe,
George C. Kunkle,
Christian Kunkle,
Walter Kendig,
Christian King,
George Minshall,

—— Mumma,
John Ross,
S. Snyder,
J. Snyder,
J. C. Stouch,
Henry Smith,
John Shelley,
L. Shelley,
J. Smuller,
John Wolfley,
A. B. Wood.

1847.

Charles Allen,
Henry Alleman,
M. Benner,
Sarah Brown,
Rebecca Brown,
J. Baker,
W. Boyer,
Maria Croll,
Lizzie Croll,
Susan Croll,
William Croll,
G. Kain,
W. Kain,
Margaret Cameron,
Virginia Cameron,
S. Detweiler,
J. Embig,
G. Ettla,

F. Fortney,
F. Fenstermacher,
John Gross,
Joseph Hoyer,
Louisa Kendig,
Clara Kendig,
Annie Kendig,
Joseph Nisley,
Abner Croll,
Edward Martin,
M. Kunkle,
J. Mengus,
David McMurtrie,
Frank Murray,
Jacob Nisley,
Annie Wolfley,
Andrew Patterson,
S. Patterson, Sr.,

S. Patterson, Jr.,
Frank Peebles,
Magdalene Ringland,
John Ross,
Harriet Ross,
Sophia Rife,
S. Rutherford,
Mary Rewalt,
Mary Smuller,
D. Swar,
Mary Watson,
Mary Weistling,
Evaline Weistling,
Robert Weistling,
Benjamin Weistling,
Catherine Zimmerman,
J. Detweiler.

In 1846, in view of the fact that although no children were maintained by the estate, yet its indebtedness had increased, the Legislature was memorialized and an act passed for the appointment of the trustees on the nomination of the two Lutheran Synods lying east and west of the Susquehanna. The trustees opposed this act and carried it up to the Supreme Court, where it was declared unconstitutional.

Subsequent to this, Thomas Moore, a citizen of Dauphin county, offered before the Supreme Court, to contract to pay off the entire indebtedness of the estate, from its proceeds, in seven years, and to give ample security for the fulfillment of said obligation. The then principal, Dr. Mercer Brown, believing he could do equally as well, undertook it, and succeeded; in 1855 the estate was clear of debt, and a balance of $1,500 remained in the treasury. The orphan department was again resumed, and two children were admitted.

In spite of this, and of all previous legislation, the institution continued to languish, and when Rev. C. J. Ehrehart took charge of the Lutheran congregation here, in 1856, he found but two orphans supported by the estate. It was mainly due to his exertions that the Orphan House at last commenced to fulfil the purpose of its founder. During his tutorship, the number of children was gradually increased until, in the spring of 1861, twenty children were maintained. Too much praise cannot be awarded him.

After the union of Portsmouth and Middletown the ground between them was laid off in lots, and was rapidly built upon and settled, until it became the populous center of the town. This rendered the location of the Orphan House unsatisfactory, and there being no land in the immediate vicinity available for agricultural purposes, the inmates thereof could not be instructed in one of the branches that the founder had insisted on. It was decided to remove the institution to a more favorable site. In 1872, thirty acres of ground were purchased of James Young, for $4,500 and the erection of a new edifice commenced. It cost $15,000, was completed early in the winter of 1873, and occupied December 17th, of the same year.

It is a massive structure erected on an elevation half a mile north of Middletown known as the Red Hill. It is constructed of brick, is three stories in height, and built in the form of an L. The main building is 60 feet front by 36½ feet deep; the wing is of a similar height, and 40 by 36 feet. A large and high porch adorns the front and the whole is surmounted by a mansard roof.

Inside there are twenty-eight rooms. The halls are wide, as are also the stairways which spring from their centers. The ceilings are high, and all apartments commodious and well lighted. The heating and ventilating arrangements are perfect. There is a reception room, a parlor, a sewing-room, library, dining-room, school-room, play-room, wash-room, kitchen, and a number of dormitories. A dry, arched basement extends under the whole building.

The family and children's apartments are neatly and tastefully fitted up. The library is comparatively small, but contains a good selection of books. The school-room is supplied with all the modern educational

CHRONICLES OF MIDDLETOWN. 123

appliances, globes, charts, blackboards, &c.; it is a cheerful looking, pleasant apartment, its windows are filled with flowers. The school course embraces history, geography, grammar, physiology, spelling, reading, writing and drawing. A literary and scientific department has been added by order of the Legislature. There are two school sessions, of three hours each, every day except Saturday. In the dining-room religious exercises precede and follow each meal; substantial, well-prepared and well cooked viands, that compare favorably with the average hotel meals, are served. The play-room (although the founder made no provision for recreation) is a feature of the establishment that more pretentious institutions would do well to copy. The dormitory beds, covered with white counterpanes and snowy linen; the pantries, the kitchen, the cellars, but more than all, the comfortably dressed contented looking children, their almost perfect health, and the air of exquisite neatness, order and cleanliness which pervade every department, show executive ability in the present management.

The view from the windows of the institution is a fine one.

> Look here, at the Round Top's bald old crown,
>   Lit up by the sun rays' quiver;
> And there, where Swatara's flashing down,
>   Until lost in the broad blue river.
> Mark the puffing rings of smoke up-curl
>   As a far faint whistle sounding,
> Notes where, fire fed, with flash and whirl,
>   Man's iron steed goes bounding.
> In near, see many a sun-browned roof,
>   Dwarfed chimney, and low steeple;
> Down where time's shuttle, 'mid warp and woof,
>   Life's web weaves the town's people.
> East, west, north, south, o'er the wide expanse,
>   The eye grasps a picture worth telling,
> Of dotted white homesteads, groves (orchards perchance,)
>   With close fence-locked fields, where the grain waves glance;
> 'Neath the soft breezes sinking and swelling.

The grounds immediately surrounding the institution are well kept, and protected by a neat pale fence. In the enclosure on the southern side, is a flourishing young peach orchard; in front is a lawn, and east are the gardens. There is also a fine spring house, and all necessary out buildings. The instructions of the founder, as modified by subsequent legislation, are consistently and faithfully carried out, and everything is provided that is considered necessary for the comfort and convenience of the inmates. The three farms, cultivated by tenant farmers, under the immediate supervision of the principal, are well tilled and productive. The barns, stables, etc., are comparatively recent erections, and provided with all modern improvements. In fact the whole estate is well conducted, and reflects credit on those controlling it.

Thus although the past history of the Orphan House is not pleasant reading, the present showing of what an honest and competent administration of its affairs can accomplish, is gratifying, and encourages the hope that this institution—which offers shelter, food and instruction to those deprived of their most natural guardians, and fits them for the active duties of life—has a bright future before it.

The following persons have been trustees and officers of the institution:

TRUSTEES.

The original trustees were: John Landis, Charles Fisher, Jacob Rife and John Cassel. Their successors previous to 1835 were: William Crabb, Sr., Joseph Burd, John Elliot, Jacob Hershey, Ephraim Heller, John Smith and George Lauman.

Trustees subsequent to 1835: Simon Salade, Martin Kendig, Joseph Ross, George Etter, John Snyder, Benjamin Jordan, Simon Cameron, John Eshenauer, Daniel Kendig, John Pricer, Adolphus Fisher, John Jos. Walborn, John Croll, Jacob L. Nisley, J. E. Carmany, Thomas Moore, Henry Alleman, Samuel Kiefer, Joseph H. Nisley, Simon C. Peters, Christian W. Esehenauer, Adam Ulrich.

Present trustees: Simon C. Peters, Henry Alleman, F. W. Lusman, Arthur King.

PRINCIPALS.

John Cassel, from 1806 to 1814.
Christian Spayd, from 1814 to 1835.
Dr. Mercer Brown, from 1835 to 1866.
William A. Croll, from 1866 to the present time.

TUTORS.

1837-40, Rev. S. D. Finckel, D. D., Rev. Samuel Spreecher, D. D., Mr. Jonathan Cory, Rev. Samuel Schaeffer, Mr. Whittlesey; 1847-55, Rev. William Heilig; 1855-59, Rev. M. Valentine; 1859-62, Rev. C. J. Ehrehart; 1862-64, John T. Ross; 1865-66, Lewis F. Steinmetz; 1866-70, Michael R. Alleman; 1870-71, S. L. Yetter; 1871, G. A. Lauman; 1889, Grant W. Nitrauer; 1894, E. J. Miller; 1900, John Croll, the present tutor.

XXVIII.

The Union canal, which was abandoned in 1885, had one of its termini here. An outlet from the basin of the canal to the Swatara river was made, to allow the boats, rafts, and arks access to and from the Susquehanna. The lock was situate between the railroad—near where it crosses the Swatara—and the old collector's office. (For a full description of this canal see Chapter No. 19.)

THE PENNSYLVANIA CANAL

Also passed through this portion of the borough, and here crossed the Swatara by means of an aqueduct, the piers supporting which also sustained an iron wagon bridge.

In 1822 an act was passed authorizing the construction of this canal at the expense of the State. July 4th, 1826, ground was broken for it with great ceremony. In 1827, the canal commissioners were instructed to take measures to build a railroad, to connect the different sections of the canal. In 1828, water was let into this division and a railroad was commenced, to run from Philadelphia, through Lancaster to Columbia. It was an important link in the chain of public improvements inaugurated by the State. Millions of dollars were spent on both the canal and railroad, the expenditure being made necessary by the completion of the Erie canal, which was taking the commerce of Philadelphia to New York. In 1832, portions of the Columbia railroad were completed, and horse cars were run on it; it took them nine hours to travel from Philadelphia to Columbia, and it was not until 1836 that locomotives were regularly put to work on it, to the exclusion of horse power. In 1834, the entire line between Philadelphia and Pittsburgh was opened to trade and travel.

It consisted of eighty-two miles of railroad between Philadelphia and Columbia; one hundred and seventy-two miles of canal from Columbia to Hollidaysburg; thirty-six miles of railroad over the Alleghenies, from Hollidaysburg to Johnstown; and one hundred and four miles of canal from Johnstown to Pittsburgh, making a total length of three hundred and ninety-four miles.

That portion of the road over the mountains is worthy of a brief description. It was known as the Portage railroad; in a distance of thirty-nine miles and a fraction it overcame, in ascent and descent, an aggregate of 2,570 feet, 1,398 of which was on the eastern, and 1,172 on the western side of the mountain. The top of the mountain, which was some 200 feet higher than the culminating point of the railroad, is 2,700 feet above the Delaware river at Philadelphia. The ascent and descent were overcome by ten inclined planes. The shortest plane was 1,585 feet and 130 feet high; the longest 3,100 feet and 307 feet high. There was on the line a tunnel 870 feet long and 20 feet high; one viaduct, that over the Horseshoe Bend, was a semi-circular arch of 80 feet span. All the viaducts and culverts were built of the most substantial masonry. The cars were elevated by stationary steam engines at the head of each plane, and on the intervening levels locomotives and horses were used. The total cost of this (Portage) road exceeded $1,500,000.

Goods were then shipped in Philadelphia, in sections of boats, which were transported to Columbia on railroad trucks prepared for the purpose; at Columbia they were placed in the canal, and connected together, forming a complete boat; then towed to Hollidaysburg, where they were again put upon trucks, and thence carried by the Portage road to Johnstown, where they were re-placed in the canal, and towed to Pittsburgh.

A large basin for the reception of boats, arks and other water craft was located in Portsmouth, and an outlet lock of great capacity constructed to the Swatara. Upon the completion of this lock, that of the Union canal was abandoned and suffered to go to decay, and there is nothing left to show that there ever was one here.

The construction of this line of public works cost the State nearly fourteen and a half millions of dollars. It was afterwards sold to the Pennsylvania Railroad Company, who finally abandoned the whole line in 1903.

THE BREAKWATER.

During the palmy days of the lumber trade, several efforts were made to have a dam, or breakwater, constructed across the Susquehanna, a short distance below the Swatara, as a harbor for lumber where it would be safe at all seasons. The project, however, never took definite shape.

THE HARRISBURG, PORTSMOUTH, MOUNT JOY AND LANCASTER RAILROAD.

This road, surveyed about 1832, was strenuously opposed by the farmers along its line, they objecting to having their farms cut up or divided. It was however partially finished, at different points, in 1836, and in August of that year the section between Middletown and Harrisburg was completed. A horsecar was at first run over it, the horses being attached by a rope to the car, and driven alongside the track. In September a locomotive called the "John Bull" was brought here by canal, on a flatboat landed at the wharf where B. S. Peters & Son's brick building now stands, and drawn from thence to the railroad by employes and citizens. It was a small, black affair with two driving wheels, the piston connected inside of the wheel; was built in England, and was scarcely more than a toy compared with the powerful "modocs" of the present day. Instead of the heavy T rail and sleepers now employed, flat bars of iron, two and a half inches wide, and three quarters of an inch thick, spiked onto string pieces running lengthwise with the line of the road, were used. The first car was about the size of a one-horse street car, with the entrance at the side, and would accommodate from twelve to eighteen passengers; a high seat outside was provided for the conductor and brakeman; three or four cars constituted a train. Just below the old Railroad house was a turn-table, and when preparing for a start the conductor blew a horn.

When the locomotive made its first trip there was great rejoicing; Governor Ritner, the heads of the State departments, and other prominent citizens were brought here and handsomely entertained at Peter Young's tavern (now occupied by J. A. Kramer). The distance was covered in twenty minutes. Afterwards, on Saturdays and Sundays, excursions were run to Harrisburg and back every two hours; the single car attached was always crowded.

The next two locomotives put on the road were built by Matthew Baldwin, of Philadelphia; they were named after the principal towns on the road, and were used for both freight and passengers. Then two freight engines, named Henry Clay and David R. Porter, were purchased from Norris & Son's, Philadelphia. They were heavier and lower than the first, and although with but two driving wheels, had the piston connected on the outside, as they are now constructed. Owing to the heavy work at Elizabethtown, the tunnel there was not fully completed until August, 1838. (During its construction passengers were conveyed around it in stage coaches.) After August 8th, the trip between Philadelphia and the State Capital could be made in seven hours. General Simon Cameron, Dr. Mercer Brown, Henry Smith, Martin Kendig, and many other citizens of Middletown, took a great interest in the enterprise.

THE PENNSYLVANIA RAILROAD.

In Port Royal is the junction of the Mount Joy and Columbia divisions of this road. After crossing the Swatara on a substantial stone bridge of four arches, the road passes through Middletown.

This road was incorporated in 1846. The charter was granted February 25th, 1847; and on the 10th of December, 1852, cars were run through from Philadelphia to Pittsburgh, connections being formed between the eastern and western divisions by the use of the Portage (State) road over the mountains.

The Pennsylvania Company's road over the Alleghenies was opened early in 1854. In 1857 the company became the purchaser of the main line of the State works.

In the years immediately following the completion of the road, it was greatly improved; the tracks doubled, other lines leased or bought, depots and extensions built, and later the line was straightened, re-graded, and entirely relaid with steel rails.

Soon after the breaking out of the "Great Rebellion," the president of the Road, Colonel Thomas A. Scott, was summoned to Washington by President Lincoln, and for some time the whole railroad transportation of troops, army supplies and war material was under his supervision and direction.

Years ago the Pennsylvania Railroad had but a single iron track and a few wooden stations between Philadelphia and Pittsburgh; now handsome brick and stone depots line its route, and four tracks of steel bind its eastern termini in Philadelphia, New York, Baltimore, Washington and Richmond, with its western in Pittsburgh, Erie, Cleveland, Toledo, Chicago, Cincinnati, Indianapolis, Louisville, St. Louis, &c.

XXIX.

THE MUD PIKE.

This turnpike followed the course of the Susquehanna from Columbia to Portsmouth, and thence until it crossed the main Philadelphia and Pittsburgh pike a short distance west of the town. It was kept in good repair until the railroad was laid out, when, as the latter occupied much of the pike, it was abandoned, and what was left of it was turned over to the townships through which it passed.

Very few persons have any idea of the difficulties of transportation prior to the era of canals and railroads. One hundred years ago, it was not uncommon to see hundreds of pack horses pass through here westward loaded with merchandise, salt, iron, &c. The iron was carried on horseback, being bent over and around their bodies. Two men could manage ten or fifteen horses, carrying each about two hundred pounds, by tying one to the other in single file; one of the men taking charge of the lead horse to pioneer, and the other the hinder one, to keep an eye on the adjustment of the loads, and to stir up any that appeared to lag. The horses were fitted with pack saddles, and a bell collar ornamented each animal's neck; at night after their loads had been removed they were hobbled and then turned loose. Each horse could carry two bushels of coarse alum salt, weighing 84 pounds to the bushel. The common price of a bushel of salt in the west at an early period was a cow and a calf, and before weights were used, the salt was measured into the half bushel by hand as lightly as possible, no one being permitted to walk heavily over the floor while the operation was going on.

When wagons were first introduced the carriers considered them as great an invasion of their rights, and were as indignant as the teamsters were some forty years later when canal boats, and afterwards railroads, took their trade.

In those early years turnpikes were not the miserable apologies for roads that are called such now, but were well graded, rounded from the center to the gutters on each side, with all the necessary crossings for water, and thoroughly macadamized. Such were the roads and such the conveyances by which all the internal commerce of the country was then carried on.

The Middletown Furnace,

On the west bank of the Pennsylvania canal, between Wood and Lawrence streets, was built by Jonathan Warner, January 12, 1855. He sold it to James Wood and Robert B. Sterling, who transacted business under the firm name of Wood & Co. February 2, 1864, Wood & Co. disposed of it to John and Richard Meily. January 8, 1874, Meily & Co. transferred it to Lyman Nutting. July 9th, 1880, Lyman Nutting sold out to Michael Schall; and he in December of the same year transferred it to the Conewago Iron Company. This furnace stood idle for some time, and was finally torn down in 1903.

It had a forty-five foot stack, an eleven foot bosh, and a capacity of six hundred and fifty tons pig-iron per month.

The residence of the secretary which was once called the "Mansion House," was built by Martin Kendig; after his death, his administra-

The P. R. R. Company's New Depot, Middletown, Pa.

tor, Martin Kendig, Jr., sold it May 30, 1851, to George M. Lauman. He disposed of it, April 25, 1856, to Wood & Co.

This brick edifice bears an air of faded gentility sadly out of place with its present environment; surrounded, as it once was by orchards, groves, and fields, and overlooking a wide expanse of country, it must have been a desirable residence.

The Slab Mill.

On the mill race opposite the foot of Race street once stood a saw mill, known as the "Slab Mill." Although a rough looking affair, for a long time it did a flourishing business. Christian Spayd, when principal of the Frey estate (from 1814 to 1835), built it, obtaining the material for its construction from the (1st) Emaus Orphan House, which stood on what is now known as the "Race Ground," west of Keener's brickyard. The logs of this latter building were used in the frame work, and the stone from its cellar walls in the abutments of the mill.

It was for several years run by the estate. In 1844 it was leased by George and G. W. Etter (father and son); in 1846, by Joseph Brestle; in 1848, by the firm of Jacob Landis, Samuel Landis, and John P. Farrington; in 1850, by Samuel Landis; in 1852, by Philip Zimmerman; in 1856, by Benjamin Kendig; in 1860, by Edward Stover; in 1868, by Connelly and Alleman. This latter firm tore down the old slab structure, and erected the mill which finally passed under the control of Kendig & Lauman and was destroyed by fire (1885) while occupied by them.

The Lath Mill.

About 1835, George Selser (father of Samuel Selser, Sr.) had a small sawmill on the sluice-way, near this mill, and was the first to manufacture sawed plastering lath in this section of the country.

The Furnace Saw Mill

Once stood near "Gamber's Grist Mill," better known to-day as "Deckard's Mill." It was erected by John Gamber. For a long time most of the timbers used in Middletown for building purposes, were cut either here, or at the slab mill. It was run successively by Daniel Kendig & Co.; Samuel Landis, and Kendig & Hendrickson; was torn down in 1860.

The Feeder Dam.

The dam across the Swatara which supplied a feeder to the Pennsylvania canal and the Cameron Company's furnace and grist mill was planned by John F. Houston (cousin of H. H. Houston, a native of Columbia, Pa.), a graduate of Amherst, and a civil engineer. He entered as a rodman on the Pennsylvania canal at Middletown in 1832; and succeeded Mr. McCutcheon in charge of that enterprise in 1833. When the canal was finished, he was ordered to the Gap, and remained there until the road was completed in 1835. He then worked on the Tidewater (Susquehanna) canal; then on the W. & G. R. R. In 1838, he returned to the State service, and was engaged on the Delaware canal under Mr. Hutchinson. His last work was settling the accounts of the abandoned road known as the "Gettysburg Tape Worm." He married Catherine, youngest daughter of George Fisher, Esq., of Middletown, and died in 1876.

XXX.

January 20, 1802, Peter Shuster, postmaster, commenced advertising letters remaining in Middletown postoffice, viz: "Holden Collins, Elizabeth Cowan, Wm. & Jas. Hamilton, John Montgomery, Wm. Stout, Mr. Thompson, and Jacob White."

June 21, 1802, Daniel Shelley died on Shelley's Island, sixty-six years of age. Outlived four wives, had eighteen children.

July 5th, Samuel B. Davis (Harrisburg), advertises "Seneca French Creek Oil" to cure consumption, dropsy, rheumatism, &c. Seen in the light of our present knowledge, the following may prove interesting:

OIL FIELDS OF PENNSYLVANIA.

The commandant of Fort Duquesne writing (probably about 1755) to General Montcalm says: "While descending the Allegheny, fifteen leagues below the mouth of the Conewago, and three above Fort Venango, we were invited by the chief of the Senecas to attend a religious ceremony of his tribe. We landed and drew up our canoes on a point where a small stream entered the river. The tribe appeared unusually solemn.—The scene was really sublime.—The surface of the stream burst into a complete conflagration.—At the sight the Indians gave forth a triumphant shout that made the hills and valleys re-echo again! Here then is revived the ancient fire worship of the East;— here then are the Children of the Sun."

The *Democratic Archives* (1842): "The Seneca oil from the oil springs on Oil creek was used by the Seneca Indians as an unguent. It is almost as celebrated as the far-famed Naptha of the Caspian Sea. With it the Senecas mixed their war paints which gave them a hideous glistening appearance, and added great permanency to the paint, as it rendered it impervious to water."

The *Lancaster Journal*, August 12th, 1795, says: "The American troops in marching that way halted at the spring, collected the oil and bathed their joints with it. This gave them great relief and freed them immediately from the rheumatic complaints, with which many of them were affected. The troops drank freely of the waters, and they operated as a gentle purge."

The *New York Journal of Commerce* (in 1830) thus alludes to Oil

CHRONICLES OF MIDDLETOWN.

creek: "Springs exist on its margin, from which there is a constant flow of oil, floating on the surface of the water and running into the creek, which may be seen for a great distance down the stream. The oil is burned in lamps, and used in various ways, but is particularly valued for its medicinal qualities.—Considerable quantities are annually brought to this city and sold to the apothecaries."

August 31st, John Cassel, stone cutter, is now manufacturing burr mill stones for sale.

December 13th, Wm. Hamilton is appointed printer of the State Senate.

January 8th, 1803, Wm. Crabb advertises house and shop of Thomas Minshall on Market Square and Main cross street (Union) for sale. To let house and lot of Christian Rodfong, lately occupied by Mr. Thomas Stubbs, "on the main road from Middletown to the landing (Portsmouth) at the junction of the two main streets, suitable for a tavern." Also the house adjoining this property.

March 28, John Cowden, B. F. Young, Joseph Priestley, Wm. Spring and Thos. Cooper (Northumberland) solicit subscriptions for the purpose of stocking the Connecticut with salmon.

February 21st. "For sale a healthy negro wench; she is an excellent washer, baker and cook, and well acquainted with all kinds of house work. For terms apply to the printer hereof."

April 19th, William Crabb, tax collector, notifies the inhabitants of Harrisburg, Lower Paxton, Swatara, Derry, West Hanover, Middle and Upper Paxton townships, who have not paid their house and land taxes, to come to his office, in Middletown, and settle before May 1st.

June 13th, George Shuler, coppersmith and tinplate worker, has for sale stills, washing kettles, coloring, planking, fuller's, fish and tea kettles.

July 18th, Christian Swartz (near Middletown) advertises six stray steers.

December 31st. "Died on Thursday morning last, after a lingering illness, Mrs. Eliza Fisher, consort of George Fisher, Esq., of this borough, in the thirty-sixth year of her age. By this unexpected decree of Providence her husband is deprived of an amiable wife, several young children of an affectionate mother, and her relations and acquaintances of a kind and sincere friend."

September 22nd, John Bomberger, Jacob Bomberger and Michael Bomberger, executors, offer a plantation of 132 acres, one mile from Middletown, and adjoining lands of George Fisher, Esq., and others.

House (two story log), barn, orchard, timber and ploughed land. To be sold by direction of the last will of John Bomberger, deceased.

December 31st, blacksmiths, nailers, &c., are notified by James Biddle to leave their orders for stone coal with James Hamilton, Middletown, before February 1st, 1805.

April 17th, John Fox (Hummelstown) acknowledges receipt of money from John Smuller (Middletown).

April 6th, Alexander Boggs wants several journeyman nailers.

June 29th, 1805, "Married in Phila. on Wednesday evening the 19th inst., by the Rt. Rev. Bishop White, Geo. Fisher, Esq., attorney at law, of this place (Harrisburg), to the amiable, beautiful and accomplished Miss Nancy Jones, of Philadelphia."

Fourth of July Celebration in 1805.

"On the 4th inst., the citizens of Middletown, wishing to keep in perpetual remembrance the happy epoch which ranked America among the nations of the earth, made previous arrangements by appointing managers, &c. The dawn was hailed by a general volley of musketry, and at 2 o'clock p. m., they repaired to Locust Grove, where, by the judicious arrangement of the managers, a sumptuous repast was prepared for them; after appointing Edward Crouch, Esq., President, and James Russel, Vice-President, the following toasts were drank, under discharges of musketry, and the numerous plaudits of the citizens:

"1. The Day We Celebrate—May the torrid rays of Cancer be annually hailed by freeman, which led to the discovery of principles, and laid open the imposition of governments.

"2. The President of the United States—May wisdom and virtue guide and direct him to the discharge of his important offices with honor to himself and advantage to his country.

"3. The Memory of General Washington—While virtue, talents and worth will be revered among mankind, the great birthday of the world's emancipation will naturally bring a tear to his urn.

"4. Prosperity to Pennsylvania, viz:—Agriculture, commerce, manufactures, social life, improvement of inland navigation, turn-pike roads, a new governor.

"5. Thomas McKean, Governor of this Commonwealth—Should he be re-elected may he no longer continue his political warfare under false colors.

"6. Simon Snyder, Candidate for Governor—Should a majority of the electors think him worthy, may he convince the people he is a statesman, as well as a mechanic.

"7. The Judiciary of Pennsylvania—May she be stripped of all her monkish and technical trappings, and know of no other precedent but 'do unto others as ye would that others do unto you.'

"8. Our Brethren in Captivity at Tripoli—May their freedom be speedily purchased with American powder and ball.

"9. May the intercourse of public virtue soon put a period to party faction.

"10. May our rulers be actuated by the love of country more than by the 'loaves and fishes.'

"11. The Memory of Benjamin Franklin—'Where liberty dwells there is my country.'

"12. May those who would sacrifice our liberties to the privileged few be detested as traitors, and despised as fools.

"13. The infernal traffic of human beings, as it is incompatible with the name, may it meet the execration of every freeman.

"14. The United States of America—As they have heretofore, may they continue to be the wonder of the world.

"15. The Sons of Columbia—May they always live together in the strictest ties of unity, and still be able and willing to resent serious injuries when offered them.

"16. The Fair Daughters of Columbia—May no enemy to his country be ever rewarded with their smiles.

"17. The Enemies of Our Independence—May they be obliged to breakfast on green crab-apples, dine on green persimmons, and sup on red-pepper, until they change their principles.

"VOLUNTEERS.

"*By the President.*—The Tree of Liberty—May it shoot forth its branches until the shade thereof covers the human race.

"*Vice-President.*—May the Federals remember the language near six years since, of old tories, apostate whigs, refugees, &c.

"*James Hamilton.*—May the freeman of Pennsylvania on the second Tuesday in October next, spell the name of Simon Snyder without missing a letter.

"*Daniel Stubbs.*—American Steel—May the disorganizer be put in the furnace of renovation, raised to a blood-heat, wrapped in flagiston till fully converted, and drawn out well blistered.

"*William Allison.*—The Second Tuesday in October next—There is a time when the hoary head of inverterate abuse will neither draw reverence, nor obtain protection.

"After spending the day in the greatest hilarity and social harmony, they formed a grand procession and marched to the center of the town; from thence they repaired to their respective homes, each impressed with the lively sense that the importance of the day still pervades the breasts of our citizens, and thankful that twenty-nine revolving seasons have found us free."

XXXI.

August 31st, 1805, Middletown. The Constitutional Republicans are notified to hold township meetings on Saturday, the 7th of September next, and at that time to appoint deputies to a general meeting of delegates, to be held at Hummelstown on Saturday the 14th of September, 1805, in order to fix on a general ticket—"Let us show ourselves worthy of enjoying the blessings of a free government; let us transmit the present constitution unimpaired to our children;—and let no friend to McKean and the constitution be absent from the poll on the 8th day of October next."

JOHN GINGERICH, *President,*
DAVID DETWEILER, *V. President.*
JOHN ELLIOTT, *Sec'y.*

November, 1808.—The stockholders of the Lancaster, Elizabethtown, and Middletown turnpike Company are notified to pay up their arrearages to finish the road, otherwise "their names will appear in the papers."

February, 1809.—George Fisher, Esq., having laid out a new town named Harborton, at the confluence of the Swatara with the Susquehanna, in Dauphin county, proposes to dispose of the lots at $60 each. (The name Harborton was subsequently changed to Portsmouth.)

April.—Mr. John Gingerich, of Londonderry township, offers to sell the time of a stout healthy negro boy, aged about fourteen years.

Andrew Miller, of Paxton, offers to sell a mulatto wench who has five years to serve, and has a child five or six months old, which will be sold along.

(In an old account book of Mr. Geo. Fisher's for 1806, I find under the date of July 18th this entry: "Wm. Crabb, Middletown, Dr., to a negro wench sold at £56 5s.)

May.—Edward Crouch, of Middletown, appointed one of the directors of the branch bank established in Harrisburg by the Philadelphia bank. (This was the first banking institution in that town.)

July.—Died on Tuesday evening, last, in Middletown, Mr. George Lauman, mason. His death was occasioned by the severe kick of a horse.

October.—The Middletown races are advertised to commence on Wednesday, the 22nd, on which day a subscription purse of $60 will be run for in three mile heats.

May, 1811.—The "Yearly Market" at Middletown is advertised to commence on the 11th of June, at which time and place a great number of valuable horses, cows, sheep, lambs, calves and hogs, with many articles suitable to the taste of the season, such as pickled oysters, roast beef, punch and wine, will be offered for sale. The market is to be enlivened with all kinds of music.

Sunday, January 30th, 1825, notice was received that General Lafayette and suite were on their way to the State Capital, whereupon Messrs. Hawkins and Askey of the joint committee of the Legislature, and M. C. Rodgers, Esq., Secretary of the Commonwealth, proceeded in carriages to Middletown for the purpose of meeting the General and his party. Dinner was prepared for them in Middletown, and an outrider sent forward to ascertain whether he was upon the road. At about half past ten Lafayette and secretary, General Spangler, Colonel Spangler, and Dr. King, a committee deputed to escort him from York, were received at Middletown and took dinner. In the evening he arrived at

Harrisburg, where he was taken to the Governor's residence. Here he remained several days receiving those hospitalities which the people of this country were proud to tender to one of their most disinterested defenders. On the 31st he was waited upon by the members of the Harrisburg bar in a body, when George Fisher, Esq., on their behalf, made an appropriate address, to which the General replied. It would take up too much space to enumerate in detail what transpired during his stay there. On Wednesday, February 2nd, he left with his party for York.

Between March, 1823, and January 14th, 1828, the State expended $1,201.50 in improving the navigation of the Susquehanna between Columbia and Northumberland, and from Columbia to tidewater, $14,323.37.

In 1825 some citizens of Baltimore formed a company for the purpose of running a line of steamboats on the Susquehanna between the towns of Northumberland and Middletown and three light-draught steamboats, the "Codorus," "Susquehanna," and "Pioneer," were built and put in the river at York Haven. Of one of these boats, the "Codorus," Henry K. Strong, Esq., in a letter to the Secretary of War (Hon. Lewis Cass), dated July 14th, 1834, says: "Eight years ago, a sheet-iron steamboat built at York, in this State, was put upon the river, about twelve miles below Harrisburg, and forty from tide-water, and was propelled by steam to the line separating the States of Pennsylvania and New York, nearly two-thirds of the whole distance from the Chesapeake it was *the first that ever sailed upon American waters.*"

The boats continued to make trips at short intervals, during the medium stage of the water, until April, 1826, when one of them—the "Susquehanna"—exploded her boiler near Berwick, Columbia county, killing and wounding several of her passengers, among whom was Christian Brobst, Esq., member of the Legislature from Columbia county. This seems to have cast a damper on the enterprise, and shortly afterwards the boats were removed from the river.

In 1827 a small side wheel steamboat plied on the river in this vicinity during the summer, but not proving a success financially, was taken off and returned to Philadelphia, where it had been purchased.

XXXII.

Old Advertisements.

Lancaster, Elizabethtown and Middletown Turnpike.

Notice is Hereby Given

That in pursuance of an act of the General Assembly of the commonwealth of Pennsylvania, entitled "An act to enable the Governor of this commonwealth to incorporate a company, for making an artificial turnpike or road, by the best and nearest route from the borough of Lancaster, through Elizabethtown to Middletown," books will be opened in the borough of Lancaster, at the house of Adam Weber; at Elizabethtown, at the house of George Redsecker; at Middletown, at the house of William Crabb, on Monday the 14th of May next, at ten o'clock in the forenoon, and be kept open until 5 o'clock in the afternoon of the same day, and every succeeding day, for three days, for the purpose of receiving subscriptions for making the same road; each share of stock being one hundred dollars, 10 dollars of which to be paid on each share, at the time of subscribing.

William Crabb,
Jas. Hamilton,
Elisha Green,
D. Montgomery, Jr.,
George Redsecker,
John Carolus,
Adam Weaver,
Abram Witmer,
John Gundacker,
George Frey,

John Pedan,
Ad. Reigart, Jr.,
Samuel Humes,
Wm. Kirkpatrick,
Christ Mayer,
John Swarr,
Peter Gonter,
Jacob Dickert,
Wm. Montgomery,
W. G. Lattimer.

March 30th, 1804.

May 4th, 1805, "Lancaster, Elizabethtown and Middletown Turnpike Road." A meeting of the stockholders is requested on Monday, the 3rd of June next, at the house lately kept by Michael Nicholas, commonly called the Cross-road Tavern, and now kept by Nathan Lightner. The object of the meeting is to elect officers, and to organize the company; it is therefore hoped that the stockholders will generally attend. (Signed by the Commissioners.) April 23rd, 1805.

NOTICE.

At a meeting of a number of the stockholders of the Lancaster, Elizabethtown and Middletown Turnpike road, held at the house of Nathaniel Lightner, on Monday the 3rd day of June (inst.), agreeably to previous notice given; the following persons were duly elected to the offices annexed to their respective names, to serve for one year from the date hereof, viz:

President, WILLIAM MONTGOMERY,
Treasurer, CHRISTOPHER MAYER.

MANAGERS.

William Crabb,
Thomas Stubbs,
Christian Ober,
John Wolfley,
John Pedan,

Gerhart Bubach,
John Swar,
Henry Lecher,
Abraham Witmer,
Martin Greider.

Take Notice.

The president and managers are requested to meet at the house of N. Lightner, on Saturday, the 15th instant, for the purpose of taking into consideration proper measures for commencing operations on said road.

JOHN SWAR, *Chairman.*
WM. BOYD, *Secretary.*
Middletown, June 3rd, 1805.

Lancaster and Middletown Turnpike Road.

Agreeably to a resolution of the managers, at their last meeting, they will meet at the house of Adam Weaver, in the borough of Lancaster, on the 22nd day of July next, at 9 o'clock in the morning, and proceed from thence to lay out the tract of said road.
June 21st, 1805.

Lancaster and Middletown Turnpike Road.

August 9th.—The managers are requested to meet at the house of Nathaniel Lightner, on Monday, the 26th of Aug. instant, at 10 o'clock in the forenoon. WM. MONTGOMERY, *President.*

The Cameron Furnace.

April 26th, 1803, George Roup sold to Abraham Landis a tract of land containing 20 acres and 116 perches (part of the Port Royal purchase). August 24th of that year Landis sold it to James Hamilton for $900. August 30th, 1830, Frederick Watts, administrator of Hamilton's estate, sold it to John Gamber, "miller," for $4,000. March 20th, 1840, John Gamber, "iron master," sold it to Israel and Michael Kinsman and Daniel Cohich (1-3 to Israel Kinsman, 1-3 to E. W. Robinson and 1-6 each to Michael Kinsman and Daniel Cohich). He also sold to the same parties and in the same proportions, a number of lots which he had purchased from "George Fisher and Ann Shippen his wife" (through which he, by Act of Assembly of June 16th, 1836, built a canal slip to his furnace) for $2,200. The total purchase money received by Gamber was $40,000. February 5th, 1841, D. Cohich transferred his interest to I. Kinsman; March 30th, 1841, I. Kinsman sold to M. Kinsman, and September 8th, 1841, M. Kinsman sold to John Jewett. (Jewitt's deed is not recorded, and we have no trace whatever of his disposition of the property.) October 11th, 1853, George W. Robinson, by power of attorney, sold his interest to George and Christian Landis and John Care; these parties sold to J. D. Cameron.

The Cameron Furnace, situated in Port Royal, on the hill overlooking Middletown, was built on a portion of this tract. It stood on the site of the two long known as the Christiana Furnaces, which were built by John Gamber soon after he came into possession of the land (1830-31). He named them after his daughter. They were originally charcoal furnaces; the Gingerich farm and much other woodland was cleared to furnish the charcoal.*

After Jewitt came into possession of these furnaces, Gamber rented and ran them for a short time; then Grubb & Cabine; then Care & Landis. Burr, who built the Harrisburg bridge, constructed the latter works, which were afterwards owned by Joseph H. Landis, James Young and J. Donald Cameron, doing business under the name of the "Cameron Furnace Co."

This furnace had a forty-seven and a half foot stack, a thirteen and a half foot bosh, and a capacity of seven hundred tons of pig per month. It was torn down in 1904 and its site is now occupied by the brick plant.

THE CAMERON GRIST MILL.

This mill (familiarly known to-day as "Deckard's Mill," from the fact that Israel Deckard leased and ran it from 1862 to 1886), on the east bank of the Swatara opposite Frey's mill, was on a portion of the same tract of land occupied by the Cameron furnace, and always had a similar ownership. It was built by James Hamilton in 1803. It was originally supplied by water conveyed through a race on the east bank of the Swatara, fed by a tumbling dam about three feet high, which crossed the river about a quarter of a mile above the present feeder-dam, where the ravine comes through the hills on the east side. This dam, as well as later the feeder-dam, were provided with booms, and many hundred feet of logs were floated to and from it. It was torn down in 1903.

James Hamilton, the builder of the mill, was born on the Swatara, in 1754. During the Revolution he was first, second lieutenant in Capt. John Murray's company, Pennsylvania Rifle Battalion; was afterwards captain in the First Pennsylvania; was taken prisoner by the British at the battle of Brandywine; was subsequently exchanged; was promoted major in the Second Pennsylvania, December 10th, 1778. At the surrender of Yorktown, October 19th, 1781, "Major Hamilton with a detachment marched into the town, took possession of the batteries and Bay to the lakes. If this was not the first steamboat ever constructed, hoisted the American flag." He afterwards went with the Pennsylvania troops under Gen. Anthony Wayne to Georgia and South Carolina, where he served until the close of the war, in April, 1783.

In 1803 he returned to his native State and settled at Middletown. He was quite a prominent man in the early history of the town; dealt extensively in lumber and grain, was president of the Swatara Bank in 1804, and built the brick dwelling on North Union street, which stood on the site of the handsome residence now occupied by Dr. John W. Rewalt.

---

*The Round Top was despoiled of its timber to supply charcoal for the Mount Vernon furnace, (situated about four miles east of Middletown,) when it was run by the Grubbs.

He afterwards removed to Middlesex township, Columbia county, where he died in 1830, at the age of 76.

An Old Ferry House.

In Port Royal on the point of land at the mouth of the Swatara stood, until recent years, a large old building built of yellow pine logs and weatherboarded, which withstood the elements for over a century. It was two stories and a half in height, with high pitched roof, and contained a number of rooms. Its early history could not be ascertained and in the flush times of the lumber trade, when the Swatara was filled and the Susquehanna at this point, lined for miles with rafts, keel-boats and arks—this was a tavern, and a great place of resort for boatmen, raftsmen and travelers on the river road. John and Christian Zimmerman, William Embick, Stephen Atherton, Isaac Lightheiser and Frederick Karper were among its later landlords. There was another ferry here, and on the western shore of the Swatara, immediately opposite, stood Frank Murray's tavern.

From Scott's Geographical Description of Pennsylvania, published in 1805, I cull the following: "Middletown, a considerable post town, situated near the northwest branch of the Swatara, about two miles above its confluence with the Susquehanna. The inhabitants carry on a brisk trade in wheat and flour, by means of the Susquehanna and its east and northwest branches. Contiguous to the town is one of the largest merchant mills in the United States. Middletown is 15 miles southeast of Harrisburg, 92 W. by N. of Philadelphia, and 142 miles from Washington city."

(An accurate geographer, if his information was as correct in all other respects, it must have been invaluable.—C. H. H.)

XXXIII.

Although Wesley and Whitfield commenced their field preaching in 1739, yet it was not until 1759 that Robert Strawbridge, Philip Embury and Thomas Webb established Methodist societies in this country. They came to America, not as missionaries, but two of them to earn a living, and the third (Capt. Thomas Webb) in the service of his King. They were soon followed by others.

The difficulties encountered by these early pioneers were both physical and moral. Much of the country through which they were compelled to travel was overhung with malaria; good roads were rare, many of them being made by burning the brush, and blazing the trees: Rivers were plenty, and fords were few; of bridges there were hardly any. In spring the circuit-rider was often knee deep in mud; and in winter, if without a compass, hopelessly adrift in the snow. The cabins where they could lodge were few; some of them with the latch string pulled in, some of them the resorts of horse thieves and desperadoes. In some sections the Indian prowled with wolf-like ferocity. The rude hospitality of the settler was given with a warm heart, but often with dirty hands. The rough blanket which was laid over the itinerant sleeper, was often biting with vermin, or the worst forms of cutaneous disease. Often he was hungry, sometimes asking a blessing upon a crust of bread, sometimes for days without as much as that. Asbury's meagre pittance of sixty-four dollars a year, was a fair sample of a preacher's pay.

But the moral difficulties which confronted them were greater than the physical. Their position from 1770 to 1784 was one of peculiar peril. Wesley pronounced disloyalty a sin, and the Methodist preachers here were held responsible for his opinions; they were all supposed to be Tories, and were known to be opposed to slavery. Now while the loyalists were far more numerous than the readers of Bancroft would ever dream, the patriots were suspicious, aggressive and violent. In some localities the Methodist places of meeting were stoned, the windows broken, guns and squibs fired, or boards placed over the chimneys. Some of the preachers were imprisoned, others beaten and injured for life, others nearly killed. Even Asbury was forced to seek shelter in Delaware, and in 1784, when Coke and Whatcoat arrived, he alone remained of those who had come from England.

Even at that time outspoken utterances against slavery required no little courage, but the same spirit filled them as that which animated George Dougherty when, in 1798, he carried through the annual conference at Sparta, Georgia, the resolution that "If any preacher should desert his station through fear, in time of sickness or danger, the conference should never employ that man again." They were a brave, ardent and faithful class, those early Methodist itinerants; men whom no mobs could frighten, no difficulties daunt; and sometimes the bullies and desperadoes got the worst of it, particularly when they encountered a preacher of the Cartright stamp, who believed in what is now termed "muscular Christianity," and who smote them with the "sword of the Lord and of Gideon."

The Methodist itinerants visited Middletown more than a century ago, and *the first Methodist preaching in the county*, antedating that at Halifax by twenty-one years, occurred here. As early as 1780, this was a preaching place of "York Circuit," then embracing a large area of country, and parts of what are now several counties, the preachers crossing the river a few miles below Middletown. Services were held at the dwelling house of Dr. Romer, on High street, then occupied by Eli Rigg, one of the first Methodists in the town.

Sometimes two or three months would elapse ere the itinerant made his appearance. In good weather, however, and with no sickness on the part of the circuit riders, services were held every four weeks. Little is known of the progress of the church here for several years, but early in the last century Middletown became part of Dauphin circuit.

March 12th, 1814, Arnold S. Johns, Eli Rigg, Andrew Alexander,

John Funk and William Foulk, trustees of the Methodist Episcopal congregation of Middletown, purchased of Philip Ettla, a lot of ground at the northern extremity of Union street, containing seven hundred and thirty square yards, for sixty dollars. (This lot had been sold to Ettla, June 22nd, 1793, by Frederick Zeppernick for £3, and was part of a tract of sixty acres deeded to Zeppernick, March 5th, 1767, by George Fisher and wife.) A small frame church was erected on this lot shortly afterwards, and was dedicated in the year 1816, by Rev. John Goforth, preacher in charge of Dauphin circuit. Here the Methodists worshipped for about forty years. This was the second church edifice erected in Middletown. In 1839 the building was remodeled and improved. Rev. Curry preached the sermon at the reopening.

At that time this location was not far from the centre of the town, but after the canal and railroad were constructed, that part of Middletown, which was then called Portsmouth, began to grow, and the larger part of the members residing in that vicinity, in 1851, the cornerstone of a new church edifice was laid on Ann street above Catherine.

In 1856 Middletown was taken from the Dauphin circuit, and with Hummelstown and one or two other points, constituted a new charge, with Rev. George G. Rakestraw, as pastor. He found an unfinished church, heavily encumbered and with about twenty members; but by dint of earnest effort, in which he was supported by a small congregation, a satisfactory arrangement was made with the contractor, Mr. George Rodfong. The building was finished and dedicated May 10th, 1854, Rev. D. W. Bartine officiating.

In 1857 Middletown was taken from the circuit and made a station with Rev. George G. Rakestraw as its first pastor. During this year an act of incorporation was procured from the Dauphin County Court, and the following trustees are named therein: D. J. Boynton, Thomas Fairman, Seymour Raymond, N. T. Wood, Yetman Eaves, John Seibert and Henry Lynch. The corporate name is "The Middletown Methodist Episcopal Church."

This church not being of sufficient capacity for the increasing congregation, early in the year 1883 it was determined to build a larger and better house of worship. June 11th, the trustees, Thomas Fairman, Seymour Raymond, Benjamin S. Peters, George W. Ettele, John Fratts, John Atkinson and A. S. Matheson, purchased lot No. 298, at the southeast corner of Ann and Catherine streets, of Adam Baumbach for $2,500. The following committee were selected to superintend the erection of a building thereon, viz: Rev. L. B. Brown, Seymour Raymond, B. S. Peters, John Atkinson and A. S. Matheson.

August 3rd, 1883, the cornerstone was laid in the presence of a very large concourse of people, with Masonic ceremonies. In it were placed a Bible, a Methodist Episcopal hymn book, a Methodist Episcopal year book, a Methodist Episcopal discipine, a copy of the *Christian Advocate*, *Our Church Monthly*, Middletown *Press*, Middletown *Journal*, names of the members of the church and Sunday schools, history of the three church buildings, and a program of the exercises.

The work was immediately commenced and so vigorously pushed that the edifice was completed and ready for occupancy by the time for the meeting of the succeeding annual conference. The church was dedicated by Bishop Thomas Bowman, D. D., LL. D., Sunday, April 27, 1884.

The building is a handsome one, is eighty-five feet long and fifty-five feet wide, with an annex four feet in depth in the rear. It is built of brick, trimmed with Gettysburg gray granite, is two stories high and roofed with slate. Four doors give easy ingress and egress. Two wide stairways, protected with heavy balustrades of walnut lead to the auditorium. This room is filled with the softened mellow light entering through nine Gothic windows of cathedral glass. The ceiling is high and peaked, following the slope of the roof. The pews are constructed of walnut and ash; the pulpit, chancel and pulpit furniture are of solid carved walnut. The choir is back of the pulpit, slightly higher and facing the congregation. In a recess behind the choir is a large and handsome pipe organ. The arrangements for heating and ventilation cannot be surpassed; a battery located in the basement automatically opens or closes the ventilators, thus maintaining an even temperature. The Sunday school room on the first floor, is very complete; it is divided by glass partitions into three departments, and at the opening and closing of the school these are all thrown into one. The infant school is in the rear of the main school; both are well furnished. The other two rooms are used as class rooms. The library is also in the rear of the Sunday school room, and is well stocked with books.

The architect was William Miller, of Harrisburg; the builder, William Starry.

The pastors of the church have been: 1856-58, George E. Rakestraw; 1858-60, S. W. Kurtz; 1860, William B. Gregg; 1861-63, J. S. Lame; 1863-65, J. M. Wheeler; 1865-67, S. T. Kemble; 1867-69, Allen Johns; 1869, L. B. Hughes; 1870-72, J. Montgomery; 1872-74, T. B. Miller; 1874-77, S. G. Grove; 1877-79, J. T. Swindells; 1879-82, W. H. Fries; 1882-85, L. B. Brown; 1885-86, M. L. Graves; 1886, David McKee; 1890, William Rink; 1891, S. H. Evans; 1895; William Ridgway; 1898, J. T. Gray; 1900, W. H. Pickop; 1902, R. H. Crawford; 1905, W. E. Yeager, the present pastor.

SUNDAY SCHOOLS.

The history of the Methodist church is so identified with that of the Sunday school, that I am tempted to give a slight sketch of the latter institution.

Hannah Ball, a young Methodist, at High Wycombe, England, organized a Sunday school in 1767, fourteen years before Robert Raikes began his at Gloucester; and it was Sophia Cook, a member of the Wesleyan

Society at Gloucester, who afterwards became the wife of Samuel Branburn, one of Mr. Wesley's most efficient ministers, who first suggested to Robert Raikes the idea of a Sunday school, who was also his first teacher, and first led his ragamuffin school through the streets of Gloucester to the parish church.

When Raikes organized his Sunday school in 1781, from John Wesley it received its principal support. "It seems," says he, "these schools will be *our great means of reviving religion* throughout the nation." The Sunday school was first noted in print by Raikes in 1783. In January, 1785, Wesley, in his *Armenian Magazine*, commended it to his societies as a promising field of usefulness. Before 1787 he had Sunday schools among his people numbering seven or eight hundred pupils. The Methodist Church also originated the system of gratuitous teaching, recommended by John Wesley in England, and Francis Asbury in America, and by the South Carolina conference in 1790, which was the first great advance in the spirit and method of Sunday school work. John Fletcher conceived the idea of a Sunday school literature; Dr. Vincent originated the uniform and international system of lessons; the Sunday School Institute was first suggested by Dr. Kidder.

Bishop Asbury established the first Robert Raikes Sunday school on this continent, at the house of Thomas Crenshaw, in Hanover county, Virginia, but Ludwig Hacker started a Sunday school in Pennsylvania (thirty years before Robert Raikes established his), which flourished for over twenty-five years. Joseph Alleine opened a similar school in England fifty-nine years before that; the Pilgrim Fathers established the first Sunday school in Massachusetts fourteen years before that; Borromeo, Archbishop of Milan, established them throughout his large diocese before that; John Knox inaugurated the Sunday schools of Scotland, "with readers," twenty-three years before that; Martin Luther's celebrated Sunday school at Wirtemburg existed thirty-three years before that; the catumenical schools of Origen and Tertullian were in operation thirteen hundred years before that. If necessary we can trace it back for forty centuries. But these schools degenerating into mere training places for endless formalities and soulless catechisms, were finally abandoned altogether, and it was two hundred and fifty years after the Reformation, before the Sunday school of to-day took a definite form in the brain of Robert Raikes.

After the removal of the Union Sunday school from the Ebenezer Methodist church (see paper No. 21), it ceased to have any Methodist connection. Some time afterwards a union school was opened in the school house, southeast corner of Ann and Wood streets, but the church was poor and weak, and it was not until Middletown was made a station that a sustained effort was made.

June 7th, 1856, a Sunday school was organized in the new (second) church, the basement not being completed.

The first officers were: Superintendent, Thomas Fairman; assistant superintendent, Solomon Heiney; secretary, Yetman Eaves; librarian,

D. J. Boynton; assistant librarian, Reuben Miller; treasurer, G. G. Rakestraw; teachers, Harry Fisher, David Boyle, J. Horner, B. Black, J. S. Steese, Wm. Embich, J. A. Platt, V. Foreman, A. E. Fairman, F. A. Murray, Mercy Woughter, Sara Eaves, Annie Wolfley, Matrona Fisher, Harriet Fairman, Mrs. Reed, Lydia Hughes, Mary J. Bennett, Angeline Lochman, Margaret Henderson, Mary Fairman and about eighty scholars. July 20, Seymour Raymond was made assistant superintendent. In September following the school numbered 32 teachers and 150 scholars.

In May, 1862, a mission school was started in Port Royal, with Seymour Raymond as superintendent; in a short while it numbered 140 scholars. In 1864 so many of the male members of the Sunday school had gone into the army that the superintendent had to relinquish its control, to take charge of the parent school.

The superintendents have been: 1856, Thomas Fairman; 1857-62-63-64, N. T. Wood; 1858-70, D. J. Boynton; 1860-61, 1865-69, 1871-83, Seymour Raymond; 1883-1903, Joseph F. Raymond; 1904, H. V. B. Garver, the present incumbent.

XXXIV.

About 1825 Rev. John Winebrenner, a minister of the German Reformed Church, but who had withdrawn therefrom and entertained and preached views on experimental religion which differed somewhat from those held by the church, resided at Harrisburg. At the request of the friends of Mrs. Black, who had been at one time a member of his congregation, and who had died on the farm of George Fisher, Esq., Mr. Winebrenner came to Middletown to preach the funeral sermon. The feeling against him was so strong that some of the older citizens refused to have anything to do with him, on the ground that he was not a minister in good standing in any church. John McCammon, however, on being asked whether he would walk with Mr. Winebrenner on the occasion, cheerfully consented, and they were afterwards warm friends. The funeral services were held in the Lutheran church and some of the young men of the town were so favorably impressed with Mr. Winebrenner, they invited him to preach. The doors of the Lutheran church were, however, closed against him, but Mrs. Flanagan, who had charge of the Ebenezer Methodist meeting house, opened that building to him, and under his ministrations a great revival commenced. He continued preaching alternately with the Methodist circuit preachers for several years. About 1832 his friends deemed it advisable to have an edifice of their own. In the meantime, however, some friends of Mr. Winebrenner residing in Middletown, Harrisburg and vicinity met at Linglestown and organized a new church or sect, adopting the doctrines taught by Mr. Winebrenner and styled themselves the "Church of God," but for many years they were generally known as "Winebrennarians." Mr. Wine-

Church of God, Middletown, Pa.

brenner always disapproved of this term, and all his followers are now known as members of the "Church of God." The first members of this congregation (in 1827), were Susanna Smuller, ———— Bare, Elizabeth King, Jacob Rife, Joshua Heppich, Jacob Benner, John Benner, Henry Siple, Joseph Ross, George Smuller, George Etter, Conrad Seabaugh, George Baker, John McFarland, Eliza Longhead and Eva Crist.

The first church edifice of this new denomination ever built, was erected in Middletown in 1832, on lot No. 23, on the east side of Union street, about midway between Water street and Centre Square. It was a frame structure, lathed and plastered on the outside. There were two entrances at the front, reached by high stairs or steps. The pulpit was placed between the doors at the end of the building towards the street, and those entering faced the audience. The building had a basement in which the Sunday school was held, and at one time a week-day school was taught therein by Samuel Dennis.

In 1848, by a change of grade in the street, so much filling was done in front of the church that the high steps were no longer necessary, and the entrance to the building was made much easier. In 1852 the edifice was enlarged by extending the front to the line of the street, casing the whole outside with brick, and making a vestibule and gallery. The latter was constructed so as to be shut off entirely from the auditorium, if desired, and was of sufficient capacity for Sabbath school and prayer meetings. The internal arrangements were so changed that the pulpit was at the end opposite the entrance. On account of the gradual giving away of the wall, the church council, in June, 1873, appointed a committee to ascertain the cost of repairing the building; and at the meeting of council, in July following, it reported that it was inexpedient to spend any money on repairs. Shortly afterwards it was decided to erect a new church edifice, at a cost not exceeding ten thousand dollars; and to begin its erection when eight thousand dollars were subscribed.

The lot section was on the northeast corner of Spring and Water streets, which was purchased for twelve hundred dollars. In November, 1873, eight thousand and thirty-eight dollars had been subscribed. Ground was broken June 9th, 1874, and the cornerstone laid June 8th. During the following winter the regular services, prayer meetings and Sunday schools were held in the basement; and in the winter of 1875 and 1876, the auditorium was thrown open for the use of the great concourse of people attending the union meetings. It is a brick structure, and the steeple is one hundred and sixty-eight feet high, surmounted by a ball and vane. The roof is of slate, both on main building and steeple. The walls are frescoed and the windows of ground and stained glass. The seats of the basement are of iron and walnut and chestnut wood, with movable backs. Those of the audience room are of the same material, but fixed. The pulpit and reading desk are made of walnut and chestnut.

Among the pastors have been Elders John Winebrenner, Smitmer, Kyle, Edward West, McCartney, Croll, Mackey, William Miller, Joseph

Adams, Jacob Flake, William Mooney, A. Swartz, Edward H. Thomas, William Mullineux, A. Snyder, D. A. L. Laverty and B. F. Beck. Since 1867 the pastors have been: 1867, J. Stamm; 1867-70, J. Keller; 1870-72, J. Haifleigh; 1872-75, George Sigler; 1875-77; W. L. Jones; 1877-79, J. Miller; 1879-80, W. P. Winbigler; 1880-83, D. S. Shoop; 1883-85, J. B. Lockwood; 1885, O. H. Betts; 1888, G. W. Getz; 1891, J. M. Carvell; 1893, C. I. Behney; 1894, J. H. Esterline; 1896, George Sigler; 1903, W. J. Schaner; 1905, Harry Hoover, the present pastor.

Bethel Sunday School.

In the early part of the year 1832 (eight years after the formation of the "American Sunday School Union"), a Union Sunday school, one of the first in the country, was commenced in the old Ebenezer Methodist church. It opened with seventy scholars, six male and four female teachers. November 25 of the same year it was moved to the Bethel church edifice, and, the schoolroom in the basement not being completed, met in the auditorium.

Its male superintendents up to the present time have been: Joshua Heppich, George Smuller, Martin Peck, Augustus H. Shote, Lawrence Elberti, Jacob Rife, Sr., John Heppich, D. W. Stehman, J. W. Baxstresser and H. G. Schreiner. Its female superintendents were Desidary Metzgar and Margaret A. Shott. Its earliest secretaries were W. J. McCammon, Daniel Kendig and Henry Schreiner. Augustus H. Shott was the first librarian and continued in that position for many years. The scholars in 1832 from November 25th to the close of the year were.

Scholars.	Parents.
Brestle, Michael,	Peter Brestle,
Brestle, Mary,	Joseph Brestle,
Brestle, Ann,	Joseph Brestle (uncle),
Bomberger, Jacob,	John Bomberger,
Brown, David,	Mercer Brown,
Boyer, Washington,	Mrs. Wiman (G. M.),
Boner, Amanda,	William Glover,
Crawford, Jane,	James Crawford,
Crawford, Sarah,	James Crawford,
Cameron, W. Brua,	Simon Cameron,
Cameron, Rachael,	Simon Cameron,
Crawford, Thomas,	James Crawford,
Carr, Margaret,	Margaret Carr,
Davis, Daniel,	Henry Hawk (stepfather),
Ettley, David,	Philip Ettley,
Ettley, Mary D.,	Philip Ettley,
Etter, Franklin,	George Etter,
Etter, John,	George Etter,
Etter, Harriet,	George Etter,

CHRONICLES OF MIDDLETOWN 147

SCHOLARS.	PARENTS.
Etter, Anna Eliza,	George Etter,
Elder, John,	John Elder,
Elliot, William,	Thomas Elliot,
Earisman, Elizabeth,	Jacob Earisman,
Earisman, Charlotte,	Jacob Earisman,
Earisman, Christian,	Jacob Earisman,
Gross, Elizabeth,	George Gross,
Glover, Washington,	William Glover,
Glover, Susan,	William Glover,
Glover, John A.,	William Glover,
Heppich, Catharine,	Joseph Heppich,
Heppich, John,	Joseph Heppich,
Hemperly, Harriet,	Michael Hemperly,
Hemperly, Lena,	Michael Hemperly,
Hemperly, John,	Michael Hemperly,
Hogan, Richard,	Richard Hogan,
Heppich, Christian,	Jacob Heppich,
King, Christian,	Elizabeth King,
Kendig, Daniel,	Martin Kendig,
Kendig, Ann,	Daniel Kendig,
Kendig, Benjamin,	Daniel Kendig,
Kisseker, Sarah A.,	Eliza Kisseker,
Kisseker, Margaret,	Eliza Kisseker,
Kunkle, Christian,	Benjamin Kunkle,
Kobb, Sarah,	Peter Kobb,
Lowman, Frederick,	William Lowman,
Lowman, Edward,	William Lowman,
Lemon, James,	Samuel Lemon,
Metzgar, Laura,	Jonas Metzgar,
Murray, Rachel,	Francis Murray,
Murray, Sarah,	Francis Murray,
Miller, Sarah,	Conrad Miller (grandfather),
McCammon, Elisha,	John McCammon,
McCammon, David,	John McCammon,
McClure, David,	Mary McClure,
McClure, William,	Mary McClure,
McGlennan, John,	Richard McGlennan,
Murphy, John,	Benjamin Murphy,
Morton, James,	
Minshall, Geo. A.,	Geo. Smuller (guardian),
McMurtrie, Wm.,	Simon Cameron,
Mundal, David,	David McMurtrie,
Russel, James,	John Mundal (brother),
Russel, William,	James Russel,
Ross, Joseph,	James Russel,
Ross, William,	Joseph Ross,
	Joseph Ross,

Scholars.	Parents.
Ross, Christian,	Joseph Ross,
Redfield, Philander,	Anna Redfield,
Seabaugh, John,	Conrad Seabaugh,
Seabaugh, Samuel,	Conrad Seabaugh,
Shott, John,	Margaret Shott,
Snyderly, Christian,	Widow Sndyerly,
Snyder, Jacob,	Widow Snyder,
Snyder, John,	Widow Snyder,
Snyder, Jeremiah,	Francis Murray (uncle),
Snyder, Maria,	John Snyder,
Snyder, Sarah,	John Snyder,
Sellers, George,	George Sellers,
Sellers, Hiram,	George Sellers,
Sellers, Sarah,	George Sellers,
Sellers, Mary,	George Sellers,
Simcox, Abraham,	Henry Schreiner (uncle),
Stoner, Henrietta,	Joseph Ross (uncle),
Smith, Sarah,	Henry Smith,
Smith, Elizabeth,	Henry Smith,
Smith, Ann,	Henry Smith,
Smith, Catherine,	Henry Smith,
Schuster, Susan,	Christian Schuster,
Schuler, John,	John Schuler,
Spayd, George,	Christian Spayd,
Thompson, Sarah,	John McCammon,
Thomas, William,	Mr. Thomas,
Woodruff, John,	Caleb Woodruff,
Woodruff, Caleb,	Caleb Woodruff,
Williams, Samuel,	Major Williams (uncle),
Yorger, George,	Simon Yorger,
Yorger, Emanuel.	Simon Yorger.

XXXV.

War of 1812.

This war arose, as is well known, from the assumption by England of the right to search American vessels, and to take therefrom all seamen whom her officers claimed as British subjects. Congress declared war June 18, 1812; authorized a call for 100,000 troops and voted $5,000,000 for war purposes.

On March 12th (one month before this action by Congress), Governor Snyder of Pennsylvania issued his proclamation calling for 14,000 men. More than three times the number of volunteers responded. In 1812-13 they were not needed, but upon the destruction of Washington and threatened attack upon Baltimore in 1814, the troop from this county marched to York and Baltimore. News of the signing of the treaty of peace (December 24, 1814) reached here February 11, 1815, and in March, after an absence of about six months, the boys returned home.

Among others from Middletown who marched on that occasion were: Christian Spayd, brigade inspector; Captain Peter Snyder, John Snyder, John Lehigh, George Hathorn, Joshua Heppich, Michael Cassel, Jacob Brown, John McElrato, David Weirich, John Wolf, David Moser, John Grunden, David Ettele, Michael Hemperly, John Conrad, Daniel Bollinger, Jacob Bollinger, John Smith, Lawrence Elberti, Geo. Johntz, Michael Gross, John Cassel, W. Curry, George Remley, George Critzen, Charles Hughes, Christian Karp, Philip Youngblood, Thomas McNair.

INCORPORATION OF THE BOROUGH.

The borough was incorporated February 19, 1826, with the following boundaries: "Beginning at a stone at the east end of the town on the south side of Main street, thence south six degrees east forty-one perches to a stone; thence south eighty-six degrees west sixty perches to an apple tree; thence south sixty-six degrees west eighty-two perches to a stone; thence south twenty-two degrees east two perches and five-tenths to a stone; thence south sixty-seven and a half degrees west thirty-two perches to a stone; thence north twenty-four degrees west across Main street sixty-one perches to a stone; thence north thirty-four degrees east six perches to a stone; thence north thirty-two degrees west twenty-one perches to a stone; thence north seventy degrees east thirty-two perches to a stone; thence north thirty-two degrees west two perches to a stone; thence north sixty-five degrees east one hundred and eight perches and five tenths to a stone; thence north eighty-six degrees east sixty-one perches and five-tenths to a stone; thence south eight degrees west forty-six perches to a stone; and thence along the south side of the said Main street south eighty-nine degrees east seven perches and five-tenths to the place of beginning."

The first borough election was held the second Tuesday of April following, at the tavern of David Kissecker. By legislative act of March 9th, 1857, the limits and boundaries were so extended as to include the town of Portsmouth and lands contiguous and adjacent to the said borough and town. Thus the borough boundaries were then made to comprise the following limits: "Beginning at a point on the river Susquehanna, and at low watermark thereof, opposite to the termination of a certain lane between the lands of George Crist and company, and land now or lately the property of A. Welsh; thence by lands of same and J. Rife, John J. Walborn, and Stephen Wilson, north eighteen and one-quarter degrees east, two hundred and seven perches to the center of the Middletown and Harrisburg Turnpike road; thence by said turnpike road south seventy-eight degrees east, forty-six perches to a stone; thence north sixty-four degrees east twelve perches; thence north sixty-one and one quarter degrees east sixty perches to George Crist's lane; thence by lands of Christ Brown, Croll and others, north twenty-seven and one-quarter degrees west one hundred and seventy-two and one-half perches to lane at side of Red Hill; thence by said lane north sixty-nine degrees east one hundred and one perches to the great road leading from Middletown to Hummelstown; thence south one-half degree east three hundred and twenty-one perches to center of Swatara creek; thence down the said creek or river, the several courses thereof, to the junction of the said creek and the Susquehanna river at low water mark thereof seven hundred and thirty-eight perches; thence up the said Susquehanna river the several courses thereof to the place of beginning."

The same act divided the borough into three wards, viz: All that part of the said borough lying north of a line commencing at a point on the Middletown and Harrisburg Turnpike, and running directly through Water street to a point on the Swatara creek, to be called the North ward, and all that part lying south of said line, and north of a line commencing in the lane forming the western boundary of the borough opposite the extension of Ann street, directly through said extension and through Ann street to a point on Swatara creek to be called the Middle ward, and all that part lying south of the said Ann street line to be called the South ward.

The first election under the newly extended wards and borough occurred on the third Friday in March, 1857, when three councilmen were elected from each ward, and were by lot divided into three classes, to serve one, two and three years respectively. Thereafter one was annually elected from each ward for a term of three years. The first elections were held as follows: In the North ward, at the brick schoolhouse on Pine street; in the Middle ward, at Union Hall on Elizabeth street; and in the South ward, at the town schoolhouse, corner of Spring and Ann streets.

The fourteenth section of this act, extending the limits of the borough, and giving council power to survey, lay out, enact and ordain streets, roads, lanes, alleys, courts and sewers, was specially exempted from applying to the tract of land included within the borough limits (as created by this act) late the estate of George Fisher, deceased, called and known by the name of "Pine Ford."

The Mexican War.

Then annexation of Texas—a measure which, although opposed by a powerful minority in that republic, was earnestly desired by the slave oligarchy in the United States, who hoped by its subsequent division into four or five States, to increase their representation, strengthen their rapidly declining power, and maintain their supremacy in the national councils—was successfully accomplished December 24, 1845.

Texas had originally been a province of Mexico; and that country had never recognized its independence, consequently war ensued. In 1846 Congress appropriated $10,000,000 to carry on the war, and authorized President Polk to accept 50,000 volunteers. Of this number Pennsylvania was awarded two regiments. The people of Middletown were staunch Whigs, and were not enthusiastic supporters of the war. Few of them responded and I have been given the names of but nine who went from this place, viz: Henry Stentz, Christian R. Spayd, Abraham Simcox, John Kincey, Daniel O'Donnell, James Murphy, George M. Lauman, Jacob Furman and William Black. They participated in several engagements. Henry Stentz was wounded, lay for some weeks in the hospital at Vera Cruz, and was discharged from there April 13th, 1847; Christian R. Spayd died in the city of Mexico, and Abraham Simcox returned home at the close of the war in 1848. Of the others I have no record, except that George M. Lauman was appointed paymaster.

XXXVI.

It was soon after his arrival in 1682 that William Penn divided his province of Pennsylvania into three counties, viz: Bucks, Chester, and Philadelphia. By the act of May 10th, 1729, Lancaster county was separated from Chester. In 1784 a proposition being made to the Assembly to form the present county of Dauphin out of a portion of Lancaster, the inhabitants of Middletown sent in the following memorial:

"*To the Honorable the Representatives of the Freemen of the Commonwealth of Pennsylvania in General Assembly:* The petition of the inhabitants of Lancaster county humbly showeth, that

"WHEREAS, The said county being very extensive, and the increase of the inhabitants becoming very great, renders the attendance upon courts and other business burdensome and expensive to your petitioners, occasioned by their situation being so far distant from the county town.

AND WHEREAS, It seems to be the intention of a respectable number of the inhabitants of the county to make application to the Honorable House for redress of this burdensome grievance, to have the county divided into two separate counties for the ease and welfare of the said inhabitants; and when any grievances or inconveniences arise to the inhabitants of the State, petition to the Honorable House is the mode to make them known to your Honors; and as by experience we are made sensible of your strong inclination to remove any inconvenience that at any time and from time to time, may arise to your constituents; you first being made sensible that the inconvenience complained of is real and well founded, we make no doubt but that you would permit us humbly to intimate to you our ideas of the mode of relief, which we would beg leave to do, leaving the ultimate determination to your better judgment.

"If you should think proper to divide the county, we would presume to recommend the town of Middletown, in the lower end of Paxton township, as by far the most proper place for the county town, for many clear and obvious reasons, which we think would naturally occur to the Honorable House, but lest they should not, we beg to mention ours.

"First, Middletown will be as central as any other place that can be thought of. Then its situation upon the river Susquehanna, accommodated with the finest, indeed, we may venture to say, the only fine safe harbor upon said river, and public utility of the said river Susquehanna to the State of Pennsylvania and to the city of Philadelphia in particular, is unquestionable; that river being a fine navigable river for boats from ten to twelve tons burden coming down said river, the river Juniata and other streams leading into the Susquehanna some hundreds of miles from a fine fertile country on all sides of the river; and we must further presume that time is not far distant when a communication will be effected from this river to the western waters of the great Lake Erie, attended with very trifling land carriage between the heads of the two waters.

"Another great advantage to the State and particularly to the city of Philadelphia, will naturally accrue, and that is, instead of great quantity of produce of different kind being carried from the counties of York and Cumberland to the town of Baltimore, they will be carried through the channel of the town of Middletown to the city of Philadelphia.

"It may not be improper to observe that Middletown is situated at the very lowest end of navigable water of said river Susquehanna, so that the trade of that extensive river will at all events centre in that town and be carried from thence to the city of Philadelphia, and consequently will draw off from the city a very considerable quantity of merchandise of all kinds to the new country upon and beyond the Susquehanna river.

"And, further, that it is not improbable that in time the trade will be carried from Middletown to the city of Philadelphia, by water carriage, via the river Swatara and other waters to the river Schuylkill, as we stand informed that this water communication was viewed some years ago by a number of gentlemen of eminence appointed by the House of Assembly for that purpose, and reported very practicable.

"And also that Middletown has the great advantage of being seated upon such high ground that they need never be apprehensive of an inundation, even in the lowest part of the town, by the overflowing of the Susquehanna and Swatara rivers.

"That the Honorable House may appoint Middletown for the county town is the earnest desire of your petitioners, and by granting the same we, as in duty bound, shall ever pray, etc.

"Lancaster county, March ye 2nd., 1784.

"Ezra Patterson, "Ludwig Sulwink,
"Jacob Schneider, "Daniel Croll,
"Charles Brandon, "Frederick Seybold,
"Nicholas Cassel, "Anthony Baume,

"Jacob Schrader,
"John Burnharter,
"George Miller,
"Edward Moyer,
"Conrad Bombach,
"Jacob Shautz,
"Lenox Stawl,
"Jacob Kraft,
"Jacob Hershey,
"John Nobel,
"Emanuel Conrad,
"John Bachenstose,
"John Bowman,

"John McCann,
"Martin Cox,
"Daniel Walter,
"James Moon,
"Thomas Edminston,
"Jacob Smith,
"Henry McCann, Jr.,
"Daniel Dowdel,
"Frederick Schuyler,
"Sebastian Hendrie,
"James Van Hoerst,
"James Foster,
"Daniel Weylster."

There are but few signatures to this petition, and there is a notable absence of the names of then prominent citizens. It is possible that other memorials were sent in, but—owing to causes which I may hereafter allude to—not probable.

By an act passed March 4th, 1785, the Assembly created the county of Dauphin and fixed the county seat at Harrisburg.

This was the turning point in the destinies of Middletown and the latter place. The former was at the time a town containing eighty or ninety houses (and four or five hundred inhabitants), at Harris' ferry there was but one building. Then the heaviest trade on the Susquehanna centered in Middletown, and the immense emigration surging westward, passed through it; the larger portion of which, deflecting at Chambers' ferry, avoided Harris' alltogether. The effect of the act of 1787 was marked, as a couple of extracts will indicate.

In 1787 (*two years after the county seat was located*), the Rev. Manasseh Cutter, who passed through on his way to the Ohio, thus writes in his journal:

"It (Harrisburg) contains about one hundred houses, all built in less than three years, many of them brick, built in the Philadelphia style; all appear very neat. A great number of taverns, with handsome signs; houses all two-story. About one-half of the people are English. People were going to meeting; they meet in private houses; have no churches yet."

John Penn, son of Thomas Penn, and grandson of William Penn, stopped at Harrisburg over night during a journey he made from Philadelphia to Carlisle, in 1788. In his journal he says:

"Mr. Harris, the owner and founder of this town, informed me that *three years ago there was but one house built,* and seemed to possess that pride and pleasure in his success which Æneas envied. One good point of view is the tavern almost close to the river. This was the house which stood alone so many years. It is called the Compass, and is one of the first public houses in Pennsylvania. The room I had is twenty-two feet square and high in proportion."

In 1795, 1796 and 1797 the Duke de la Rochefoucald-Liancourt, of France, was traveling in America. He discourses thus of Harrisburg: "Mr. Harris, lord of the manor in which Harrisburg stands, availed himself of Mr. Frey's error to procure his town advantages that the other neglected. No sooner was it in contemplation to form the tract of country, separated from Lancaster, into a distinct county, than he offered to the government of Pennsylvania to sacrifice not only a ferry on the Susquehanna, of which he was possessed, and the profits of which he lawfully enjoyed, but also—land in and about the town. This offer induced the government of Pennsylvania to make this the chief town of the county, though it has neither an anchoring place for the ships that sail up and down the river, nor can afford them the smallest shelter.

"The new county obtained the name of Dauphin. The first houses were built here in 1782, and their number at present amounts to three hundred."

XXXVII.

The Catholic Church.

The first organized Catholic colony in this country, and one of the first to establish religious toleration, was that of Lord Baltimore, founded in 1632.

From Maryland the church crossed into Pennsylvania, and we find a considerable Catholic settlement at Conewago about 1740, from which points priests visited Central Pennsylvania and soon began the erection of churches, among the first of which were St. Mary's at Lancaster, and St. Peter's at Elizabethtown. The Catholics of Lancaster were organized in 1740 and St. Peter's congregation at Elizabethtown seven years later. It was at this church that the Catholics of Middletown and its vicinity worshipped for over a century, and therefore a short account of it is here given.

St. Peter's church was organized as early as 1752, when the scattered Catholics of the district assembled at a little log cabin, erected by Henry Eckenroth on his farm about three miles from Elizabethtown, and called the "Church of the Assumption." It was at first a mission attached to St. Mary's church, Lancaster, and visited by the priests of that parish, which then included Middletown, Columbia, Harrisburg, Lebanon, &c., in fact the whole of Central Pennsylvania.

At that time the wayfarer between these and more distant points would occasionally meet a solitary priest, on horseback, journeying to visit his few parishioners, to give them religious instructions and hold services in their widely separated cabins and hamlets. The records show that some of them were never again heard of; alone they sank to rest, the soughing of the wind through the forest aisles their only requiem, the falling leaves or drifting snow their only shroud.

In 1757, in answer to a request of the Governor for a statement of the number of Catholics in the Province of Pennsylvania, Father Farmer counted those in Lancaster county as:

	Men.	Women.
Germans,	108	94
Irish,	22	27

The congregation of St. Mary's was composed principally of Germans, and the priest spoke and preached in both the German and English languages, or it sometimes happens that there were two priests, each of whom attended to one nationality.

In 1795 Rev. Ludwig Barth was appointed by Bishop Carroll to St. Mary's, Lancaster. He immediately began to take steps for the erection of a new church at the then growing mission of Elizabethtown. In this he was much encouraged by Bishop Carroll. There were then from 150 to 200 communicants. In 1796 a site was selected in the village, and May 30, 1799, the cornerstone was laid by Rev. Father Barth. The church committee were Henry Eckenroth, John Kauffman and Andrew Gross. Among the more prominent members who acted on the committee of the building were: Dominick Eagle, Stephen Felix, John Witman, Charles Wade, John Lynch, George Carolus, Adam Gross, Simon Eckenroth and John Wagner.

To show the devotion of those early Catholics, it is related (either of this church or St. Mary's, Lancaster) that the women came daily to mix the mortar, while the men gathered the stones from the adjoining farms and carried them to the site of the building.

Father Barth administered the affairs of the mission until 1807. One of his associates, Rev. Michael Egan, became first bishop of Philadelphia in 1808. Upon his death Father Barth was urged to accept the mitre, but declined. He died in September, 1844, aged 80 years, in the 54th year of his priesthood. He was succeeded by Revs. Beschter, Bryan, Hogan, Schenfelder, Burgess and Holland. Then Rev. Bernard Keenan took charge of St. Mary's and its mission, and was pastor over 53 years, dying, universally regretted in 1877. In 1832 Father Keenan gave Rev. M. Curran charge of St. Peter's. He, finding the church too small, began the erection of an addition. In this improvement the poor Irishmen, then engaged on the railroad, assisted. It was finished in 1834. In 1847 Rev. Pierce Maher attended this mission. In 1840 Father F. X. Marshall succeeded. During his pastorate a parsonage and a new altar and pulpit for the church were erected. Rev. Michael Filan was his successor. In October, 1855, Rev. John McCosker took charge of Elizabethtown and missions. The number of Catholics at Middletown had considerably increased and "Father John" took a special delight in building up that mission.

St. Mary's Church (Middletown).

There is a tradition that in 1779, when General Sullivan was here preparing for his expedition, a priest celebrated mass for some of the workmen, but nothing definite could be learned.

The earliest Catholics in the vicinity of Middletown that we have any record of were: Henrietta Brandon, John Luck, John McCristal, Bernard Mooney, Patrick Boyle, John McGuigan and their families. They were occasionally visited, after 1795, by priests from Elizabethtown and Conewago.

Those settlers were probably drawn into the current of emigration westward, for in 1846-47 there were but three Catholic families in town, viz: Those of Patrick O'Donnel, Richard McGranigan and Luke Norton, although in the neighborhood were the Doughertys, Sweenys, Witmans, Youtzs, Cannons, McGarveys, Bradleys, Hollands, Gross, Flynns, McCanns, McMillans, Allwines, Schaeffers, &c., some of whom had been settled here for many years. In the absence of any priest these families would ride, drive, or the male members, cane in hand, would walk to Elizabethtown or Harrisburg to church. Services were first held at private houses (notably at Luke Norton's) then at the brick school house on Furnace Hill, and afterwards at the old school house on the southwest corner of Ann and Wood streets.

In 1857 a lot was secured, and Father John McCosker, to whose untiring efforts the congregation is in a great measure indebted for their church, began to collect means to build it.

The cornerstone of "St. Mary of the Seven Dolors" was laid Sunday, September 20, 1857, by Rt. Rev. John Newman, bishop of the diocese of Philadelphia, assisted by Doctor O'Hara, Rev. John McCosker, and several other priests. Doctor O'Hara (afterwards Bishop of Scranton, Pa.) preached the sermon on this occasion, and also at the consecration of the church.

It is located on high ground, at the western end of Ann street, above Lawrence; is a brick structure, of Gothic style with an organ gallery. It has a seating capacity on the first floor of over two hundred, and is a handsome, well-ventilated edifice. Edward Hodnett built it for nine thousand dollars. It was opened for divine service in the spring of 1859, Rev. John McCosker officiating. In 1861 Father McCosker was appointed chaplain of the fifty-fifth regiment, Pennsylvania volunteers, which was assigned to duty in South Carolina. Before starting on his journey he was presented with a handsome sword and belt by James Young. He served faithfully until, overcome by hardship and disease, he returned to Philadelphia and soon afterward died.

In November, 1861, Rev. Hugh McGorian, who had been on the missions in Australia and Van Dieman's Land, came to America, and was appointed pastor of Middletown and Elizabethtown. February 19, 1864, he died. His successors (each surviving a short time) were: Revs. R. V. O'Connor, Eugene Sullivan, Thos. Walsh and Patrick McSwiggan. Rev. J. J. McIlvaine then took charge. Owing to his exer-

CHRONICLES OF MIDDLETOWN. 157

tions the debt was paid off. After him, December, 1869, Rev. P. J. Nunan was appointed. He was followed, February, 1870, by Rev. Charles McMonigle, who remained here until September, 1873, when he left to take charge of St. Patrick's, at York, Pa. The first mission was held in the church, November 10, 1864, by Rev. Father Wendelin, a Benedictine monk, under the auspices of Rt. Rev. Bishop Shanahan, of Harrisburg, when a considerable number were confirmed. In commemoration thereof a large cross has been erected in the church, bearing the date of the mission, and the text, "Abide in my love."—John v:10. After Rev. McMonigle's departure, Rev. J. J. McIlvaine again took charge and remained until the close of 1877, when sickness compelled him to quit.

From 1877 to 1879 the church was supplied by different priests. In 1879 Rev. J. C. Foin was appointed. Father Foin served from 1879 to 1889. During his incumbency a piece of ground containing nearly three acres was purchased at the eastern end of Main street, and laid out as a Catholic cemetery. It was consecrated by him, June 26, 1885, he being delegated to do so by Rt. Rev. Bishop J. F. Shanahan. (Previous to this acquisition the members of St. Mary's had to take their dead to Elizabethtown for interment.) It is enclosed by a neat fence and is well cared for.

Since Father Foin's incumbency the priests have been:
1889 to 1891, Rev. James A. Huber.
1891 to 1892, Rev. C. Kenny.
1892 to 1895, Rev. B. J. Campbell.
1895 to 1897, Rev. James M. Barr.
1897 to 1900, Rev. P. J. Costigan.
1900, Rev. S. Clement Burger.
1900 to 1901, Rev. L. Stein.
In 1901, Rev. H. M. Herzog, the present pastor, was appointed.
In 1902 a handsome rectory was built.

XXXVIII.

[The Harrisburg *Telegraph*, some time ago, contained the following, which we transfer to Chronicles as a portion of the town's history. The Pineford spoken of gave its name to the farm of George Fisher, and was just above the old rope ferry crossing the Swatara, which Fisher's bridge now spans.]

("The road referred to especially was probably that which commenced at now Paxtang street, from Race street to Paxtang creek and continued on the low ground through Highspire—the run there being known as Renick's run—to the Swatara. Most of this road was absorbed by the original incorporators of the Harrisburg and Middletown turnpike. The "back road is yet in existence. The paper is in the handwriting of Robert Baker, the first signer.")

The Humble Petition of the Inhabitants of Paxton to the Honorable Court of Quarter Sessions, Sitting in Lancaster ye first Tuesday in Feb'y in the Ye r of our Lord one thousand seven hundred & fourtey five:

WHEREAS, we understand that there is application made to your Worships for a Road to John Harrises from the pine fourd upon the Swatara to Coume Down on the River Side within the Bottoms, which we Luck upon to be an unsuportable Burden that we are unable to Bair, for maney Reasons; first, because of the maney Grate Swamps & mudey Runs that is to be Bridged ; secondly when they are Bridged there is no Expectation of them standing one Season, by Reason of the floods, thirdly because the most of the Way is so soft that a Leetil time Wagons would Cut it so that we never will be able to make it good or maintain it, & besides all this, sum years ago John Harris sued for & obtained a Road from his house to the pine ford & notwithstanding of all our Labour & pains in Cutting & Bridging of the s'd Road, we acknowledge that it is not Good, nor scarcely passable by the Direct Survey; Whereas a small vareyation might have mist those places that is not passable. We are Bold to assert that not six Rod might a mist sum of them.

We beg Lave of Your Worships to hear us patiently to Represent our Case fairley as it is; & first, we have briefly shown sum of the Evils that will attend that Road on the River side, within the Bottom ; & secondly that the Road already surveyed & Cut from John Harrises to the pine fourd is not Good; & now wou'd humbly shew whie this Latter Road is not Good & scarcely can be made Good ; & first, because there was contending parties about the farries, to Witt John Harris & Thomas Renicks; & the s'd Harris haveing obtained an order of court for his Back Road & all the men appointed for the laying out of it was strangers to these Woods..............owne: & he being Renickses special frind & near kinsman, the worst way he piloted them the Less it answered Harrises intent & the more Renixes ; and besides all this, the very same day that this Back Road was Laid out the Sherieph held a vandew of Peter Allon's Goods; & there was few or none of the near neighbours at home to shew them a Better way which we presume sum of your pettisnors can do, and notwithstanding of all the objections that may be made, that we did not varey a small matter when we Cutt the Road in anwer to that; so we would had we not been Divided; theye that was for Renickes was punctual for the survey, sum threatened to stop it if we Left the survey & others affraid if they Left the survey they wou'd have to coume & Cutt it again; Therefore your peitisinors Humbley Begs that there may be a final stop put to the Riverside Road, & we acknowledge that it is the Glorey of a Countrey to have Good Roads ; & we promise to be as assistive as possable we can, & Dos purpose a Better Way & as near as aney yet purpos'd, & we can shew your Worships a Reason for it, the Distance between Susquehanna & Swatara is but a Littel way, & the Waters or Runs falling botth wais we can

CHRONICLES OF MIDDLETOWN.   159

find Champion Drye ground between the two, not that we are ———
own Royd for another, but that, that will be for a publick good.
Your Worships Compliance to our petitisions will oblige your Humble
Petitisioners Ever for to pray:

Robert Baker,	David Shields,	Samuel McCorkel,
John Shields,	John Barnett,	Thomas Forster,
Richard McClure,	Michael Graham,	Jeremiah Sturgeon,
Oliver Willey,	Andrew Colwell,	John Lowry,
Andrew Hannah,	Alexander Meharg,	James L. ———,
Thomas Smith,	John Killcreest,	Wm. Chambers,
William Sharp,	James Kern,	James Gilchrist,
Matthew Shields,	William S———,	Jacob S———,
James Morgan,	Thomas Farrell,	Wm. McMillan,
John Gray,	Andrew Scott,	John Willey,
James Polk,	Thomas Elder,	Alexander Cully,
Robert Smith,	Thomas Dugal,	William Barnett,
James Eaken,	James Coler,	John Cavet,
Samuel ———,	Robert Gray,	Samuel Sturgeon,
William Chambers,	Timothy Shaw,	Alexander Osborn,
John Johnson,	John Forster,	Thomas Simpson,
Thomas Morrison,	Anthony Sharp,	William Scott,
George Alexander,	Henry McIlroy,	Thomas W. ———,
Pat. Montgomery,	Robert Armstrong,	Andrew Foster,
Joseph Scott,	John Porience,	Nehemiah Steen.

MIDDLETOWN MILITIA.

(Half a century ago.*)

The "Swatara Guards"—an infantry company, flourished for a number of years. They were a fine body of men, well drilled, under the command of a capable officer who took great interest in the company. The uniform was a blue swallow-tailed coat, faced with yellow, and trimmed with yellow cord and innumerable "bullet buttons." Large yellow epaulettes covered the shoulders. The pants were blue also, with a yellow stripe down the sides. The cap was high and stiff, with a large brass plate in front, and a heavy plume of scarlet feathers, a foot or more in height. A small pompon was afterwards substituted for the plume. When on parade a good deal of powder was burnt in firing by platoons and by company in the market square, where they were generally dismissed. This company was also furnished with a brass field-piece, which was served by a detail of members.

A rifle company was also in existence. Their uniform was a long

---

*This extract is from the Salamagundi papers, written by Dr. John Ringland, and copied from an old scrap book kindly loaned me by Mrs. McCord.

green frock coat, and dark pants, the bottoms faced on the outside with leather or oil-cloth, so as to resemble boot-legs; the cap was sealskin with the hair on and of a gig-top style, with black ostrich feathers for plume. They were also well-drilled, and marched and shot well. The target used by the companies was made of boards, and was about the size of an ordinary door; on it was painted the life size figure of a man. The prize for the best shot among the rifles was the privilege of wearing a set of white ostrich feathers along with the black. Our friend, Mr. George Rodfong, was a good shot and on more than one occasion "showed the white feather."

"Battalion" and "General Review" days of militia were the days of the year. The "bone and sinew" then reported themselves for the annual inspection, review, drill and parade. As for uniform, each dressed according to his inclination, some wore coats and some did not; the coats were of all colors, shapes and material—from white to black, and from linen to broadcloth. Hats and caps of every style covered the heads. Some of the yeomen wore boots, some shoes, and others went barefoot. As for weapons, they were various, muskets, rifles, double and single barrel shotguns, canes, hoop-poles, corn-stalks, and umbrellas—the latter frequently hoisted to protect their bearers from the rays of the sun, or occasional showers. The officers generally provided themselves with a sword, scabbard and belt. The drill and inspection were on a par with the arms and accoutrements. The generals, colonels and other mounted officers charged furiously on their fiery, untamed steeds, conscious that the fate of the nation depended upon them. The different regiments having formed their lines, marched through town to the parade ground or "commons" followed by all the children old enough to accompany them. The "common" was the ground lying between Ann street and the canal, in what was then Portsmouth, and in which but few houses had been erected. Their military evolutions were executed with wonderful precision, no two obeying the word of command at the same time, unless by accident, and such a thing as keeping step was unknown. The firing, considering that there was scarcely a charge of powder in the whole line, was equally well done. After inspection, an hour's rest was given, when arms were grounded and ranks broken. From the numerous hucksters who always thronged the field on those occasions, plentiful supplies of lemonade, small-beer, Monongahela whiskey, brandy, rum or gin, were obtained by the tired soldiers, whose subsequent evolutions were somewhat tangled.

XXXIX.

In 1825 a schism occurred in St. Peter's Lutheran church under its pastor, Rev. Peter Sahm. A great religious revival was in progress in the town, and meetings were nightly held in the lecture room, which was always well filled. Many members of the church made professions of

St. Peter's Lutheran Church, Middletown, Pa.

a change of heart. This was an innovation, and some of the more conservative members looked upon the movement as heretical. Finally the opposition to the meetings became so great, that many of the members left the church, and started a new congregation, called "Christ Church."

In 1838, Philip Ettele, Adam Hemperly, Henry Brenneman and John Wolf, trustees of Christ church, bought from John Bomberger, Jacob Bomberger, Jonas Metzgar, John Snyder, Christian Lehman and Benjamin Kunkle, a lot of ground on the northwest corner of Spruce and Water streets, for $150.00, built thereon a brick church, and continued to worship here for many years. The membership gradually declined owing to deaths and removals until it was no longer able to support a pastor; and finally those remaining connected themselves with other churches.

On December 13th, 1861, the trustees of Christ church sold the building to Rev. C. J. Ehrehart, who conducted a flourishing private school here, known as the Middletown Academy, for several years.

January 17th, 1866, Ehrehart sold to James Young, M. B. Rambler, Jacob L. Nisley, W. R. Alleman, John C. Carmany and G. W. Etter, for $906, and April 5th, 1867, these gentlemen sold to Valentine Baumbach, David Peters and John Snyder, trustees of the United Brethren in Christ church for $1,200.

This congregation had, in 1852, erected a frame church on Duck street south of Water a lot belonging to John Shoop. It gradually increased in membership, until it was able to effect the purchase aforesaid, which after it came into their possession was entirely renovated and remodeled. For many years only a circuit, this is now a prosperous station.

On August 23rd, 1872, the surviving trustees of Christ church, viz: Benjamin Kunkel and Adam Hemperly, conveyed to Solomon L. Swartz, Joseph Weirich and David Detweiler, trustees of the United Brethren church, the cemetery north of the church.

In 1892 the congregation having grown too large for the building, the church built the present edifice. It is a large and handsome structure with a belfry tower and all modern appliances, steam heat, electric lights, stained glass windows, etc.

The first Quarterly Conference of this station met May 2nd, 1874. The following names were placed upon the roll as members. Rev. J. Baltzell, Rev. H. C. Phillips, Rev. Jacob Focht, Rev. Solomon Swartz, Augustus Parthemore, A. H. Reider, John Mathias, John H. Baker, Howard P. Focht, Benjamin Bletz, John Maginnis, David A. Detweiler and Harry S. Roop. A. H. Reider was elected secretary.

The first stationed pastor was, 1874-76, Rev. H. C. Phillips; 1876, Rev. J. R. Reitzel; 1876-77, Rev. Israel Groff; 1877-78, Rev. H. W. Zimmerman; 1878-80, Rev. James M. Lesher (who is now a missionary in Africa); 1880-83, Rev. James G. Fritz; 1883-85, Rev. A. H. Kauffman; 1885-86, Rev. Theodore Wagner; 1886, Rev. Z. C. Mower; 1888-

89, Rev. Thomas Garland; 1890-95, Rev. J. G. Smoker; 1896-1904, Rev. E. Ludwick; 1904, Rev. D. S. Eshleman, the present pastor. A flourishing Sunday school is connected with the church. Its superintendents since 1871 have been: 1871-73, E. B. Bierbower; 1873-76, Andrew Poorman; 1876-77, J. R. Reitzel; 1877-78, John H. Baker; 1878-79, D. A. Detweiler; 1879-80, Aaron Robb; 1880-93, D. A. Detweiler; 1894-96, Charles Orth; 1897-1900, J. C. Detweiler; 1901-2, J. R. Snyder; 1903-5, D. B. Kieffer, who still holds that position. Immediately north of the church is a new and neat parsonage.

THE MENNONITES.

A congregation of New Mennonites afterwards purchased the abandoned frame church on Duck street south of Water. The membership was small and meetings were held once a month. After a short interval the services were discontinued and the building removed.

Speaking of the Mennonites, as the members of this denomination were, next to the Scotch-Irish Presbyterians, the earliest settlers in this county, and as they are still numerically strong in the neighborhood of Middletown, a short sketch of them may not prove uninteresting.

The Mennonites are a set of German Baptists, who derive their name from Menno Simonis. He was born in Friesland in 1505. In 1537, having been previously a Catholic priest, he united with the Baptists. A few years previous to his union with them, this sect had been led away by their zeal into the most fanatical excesses at Munster. Menno collected the more sober-minded into regular societies, who formed an independent church under the name of Mennonites, or Mennonists.

Menno traveled through Germany and Holland, disseminating his doctrines and gathering many followers. He died at Oldeslohe in Holstein, in 1561. Before his death his followers had divided themselves into two parties, differing in regard to the rigor of discipline. Other sub-divisions occurred after his death. These sects were only tolerated in Europe on the payment of exorbitant tribute, and still suffered many grievances and impositions. William Penn, both in person and in writing, first proclaimed to them that there was liberty of conscience in Pennsylvania. Some of them, about the year 1698, and others in 1703 to 1711, partly for conscience's sake, and partly for their temporal interest, removed here. Finding their expectations fully answered in this plentiful country, they informed their friends in Germany, who came over in great numbers, and settled chiefly in Lancaster and the neighboring counties.

In 1770 Morgan Edwards estimated that they had in Pennsylvania 42 churches and numbered about 4,050 persons. They are remarkable for their sobriety, industry, economy and good morals, and are very useful members of the community.

The Aymish.

The Aymish, or Omish, are a sect of the Mennonists who profess to follow more rigidly the primitive customs of the apostolic church. They derive their name from Aymen, their founder, and were originally known as Aymenites; they wear long beards, and reject all superfluities, both in dress, diet and property. They have always been remarkable for industry, frugality, temperance, honesty and simplicity. When they first came over and settled near Pequea creek, land was easily acquired, and it was in the power of each individual to be a large proprietor, but this neither agreed with their profession nor practice.

In the year of 1720, a thousand acres were offered to an influential member of the Aymish faith by the proprietary agent, but he refused the grant, saying: "It is beyond my desire, as also my ability to clear; if clear, beyond my power to cultivate; if cultivated, it would yield more than my family can consume; and as the rules of our society forbid the disposal of the surplus, I cannot accept your liberal offer; but you may divide it among my married children, who at present reside with me."

When the sect came to the country they had neither churches nor burial grounds. "A church," said they, "we do not require, for in the depth of the thicket, in the forest, on the water, in the field, in the dwelling, God is always present."

Many of their descendants, however, have deviated from the ancient practice, and have both churches and burial grounds.

During the Revolution, owing to their refusal to take up arms, pay the fines imposed on them, or swear allegiance to the Continental government, they were continually embroiled with the authorities; as a reference to the early State records will show. According to the census of 1880, they had 300 churches, 350 preachers and 50,000 members.

The Dunkards.

As a few of the earlier inhabitants of Middletown belonged to this sect, and as there are yet some remaining in its neighborhood, I append a short account of them.

The word Dunker of Tunker is a corruption of *Taeufer*, Baptist.

In the year 1708, Alexander Mack, of Schreisheim, and seven others, in Schwardzenam, Germany, met together regularly to examine the New Testament, and to ascertain the obligations it imposes on professing Christians, determining to lay aside all preconceived opinions and traditional observances. Their inquiries resulted in the formation of the society now called Dunkards or First-day German Baptists.

Persecuted as they grew into importance, some were driven into Holland, some to Creyels, in the duchy of Cleves, and the mother church voluntarily removed to Scrustervin, Friesland; and thence emigrated to America in 1719, and dispersed to different parts—to Germantown, Skippack, Oley, Conestoga and elsewhere. Soon after a church was established at Muelback (Mill creek), Lancaster county. One division of this sect, that at Ephrata, Lancaster county (about thirty miles from here), deserves special mention, from the fact that they succored and comforted the distressed families of Paxton during the French and Indian wars. Although opposed to bearing arms, they opened their houses cheerfully to the fugitives. The government tendered them its thanks, and Governor Penn offered them a whole manor of land, but they would not receive it.

This society owned a farm, a grist mill, paper mill, oil mill and fulling mill; they established a printing office—the second German press in the State—where they printed many books, tracts and hymns.

During the Revolution they were decided Whigs, and after the battle of Brandywine, the whole establishment was thrown open to receive the wounded Americans; their Sabbath school house was converted into a hospital, and great numbers of the sick were transported there in wagons. The army sent to the mill for paper for cartridges, but finding none seized the printed sheets, and they were fired off against the British, at the battle of Germantown.

XL.

THE PROTESTANT EPISCOPAL CHURCH.

In July 1899, Dr. Hope, then rector of Steelton, held the first service of this church in Odd Fellows' hall. In a few weeks Ward Reese was sent to Middletown by Bishop Talbot and continued to hold services regularly at the same place. Early in September there was a meeting of the congregation, at which Archdeacon Baker was present. The name St. Michael and All Angels was then given the church. The Middletown mission, in October, was made part of the Steelton mission, and placed under the care of Rev. W. H. Holloway. (Mr. Reese, after getting the Middletown mission in working order, left here to continued his studies at school.) After Mr. Holloway took charge of the work, a room in Smith's Hall was rented and services held there regularly until the spring of 1903, when the hall, having been sold, the mission was removed to the frame building at the southwest corner of Union and Brown streets, where they still continue to worship. Rev. Holloway remained until January, 1902. He was followed by the Rev. F. Lyne. He was succeeded in January, 1903, by Rev. J. H. Earp, who remained until April, 1904, his successor being the present rector, Rev. R. F. Gibson.

OLD SAW MILLS.

Just north of the Pennsylvania Railroad Company's stone bridge over the Swatara river, lately stood a large sawmill. Originally this was the site of a warehouse built by Mr. McKibben. It was turned into a sawmill. It was first run by Church, Landis and Kunkle, then by Christian Landis and Washington Etter, then by Etter, Carmany and Siple, then by Cramer, Mann and Company, then by L. M. Condriet. It was abandoned and torn down about 1886.

In 1856-7, E. and J. McCreary built a sawmill on the Susquehanna river, near the old ferry house. In 1866 they tore down this mill and removed to Royalton. It was burned down in 1873; was rebuilt and enlarged and sash and door factory and planing mill attached. Had circular, gang and upright saws. Sawed sixty-five rafts in one year. Burnt down in 1885.

William Murray and Martin and Daniel Kendig built a sawmill at "the point," where the Susquehanna and Swatara rivers join, in 1846. They were succeeded by Kendig, Lescure and Zimmerman. This was a large mill. Sawed in one year one hundred and four rafts. Was burnt down twice.

A dilapidated looking building, still standing on the south bank of the Swatara, near Frey's grist mill, was a planing mill, built and run by Boynton and Co., then run by Christ and Brown. Burnt down. Then Kendig bought out Brown and rebuilt. Afterwards run by Kendig, Bricker and Lauman. Abandoned in 1892. Where this mill stands was once a foundry built by McBarron and Jenkins, afterwards D. Peterson ran it. (He was a burgess of the old borough before consolidation.)

West of this mill stood a sash and door factory, owned first by Shott and Rohrer, then by Shott and Ulrich. Afterwards sold to the planing mill firm of Kendig, Bricker and Lauman.

Wm. Rewalt (Dr. J. W. Rewalt's father), built a lot of cars on the ground now occupied by the Middletown Car Works.

E. and J. McCreary had a boatyard at the weigh lock in 1850.

John Watson had a boatyard where the Reading Railroad freight depot now stands. (Here Elijah McCreary learned his trade, March 10th, 1844.)

Henry Frick had a boatyard where C. H. Hoffer's barn now stands.

On Hill Island, opposite the town, was built, in 1844, the largest mill on the river, by the firm of Jacob M. Haldeman (of Harrisburg), Harry Etter (of York), Martin Croll and George Crist. Croll and Haldeman bought out Etter, then Crist and Haldeman bought out Croll. Then Daniel Lamb bought out Haldeman. Then Croll bought out Lamb. This mill cut principally ship timbers, which were shipped by arks to Port Deposit, thence by schooners to Philadelphia, Baltimore and New York. Its capacity was over one hundred rafts per annum. It had four run of saws, also lath and pale saws, and one set of gang saws. In one year it cut one hundred and five rafts. The mill was subsequently run by Crist and Brandt. During their ownership, the building, which was then full of tobacco, went down the river in the flood of 1865, and lodged above Marietta, and was a total loss. It was the only mill run by water power. Crist at this time had two other sawmills at New Cumberland. In addition to his Middletown properties, he owned a farm on the island.

A sawmill was built on Brown street and the Union canal by Watson,

166   CHRONICLES OF MIDDLETOWN.

Johnson and Yingst in 1857. It ran in connection with the boatyard until 1868, when it was bought by W. D. Hendrickson and V. C. Coolbaugh, and run under the name of Daniel Kendig and Company, in connection with planing mill and lumber yard until 1873, when the two last mentioned properties were sold to Kendig, Bricker and Lauman. The sawmill was run under the name of Daniel Kendig and Company until 1876. Then under the name of Coolbaugh and Hendrickson, until 1888, when the Pennsylvania Railroad closed the Union Canal and obliged them to quit business.

A planing mill and lumber yard were located on the ground where Sweigard's coal yard is now, in 1869, by Rider and Ramsey. In 1870 John L. Nisley joined the firm. This mill was burned down in 1871.

Fisher and Ramsey had a planing mill and sash factory on Wilson street about where the Weaver blacksmith shop now stands. Watson also built a boatyard and screw-dock about where the iron county bridge crosses the Swatara. He built many large canal boats here, which being too large to pass the locks of the Pennsylvania Canal, were floated down the river during high water to Havre de Grace.

Farrington and Mumma had a mill at Royalton, where Tom Holland's property, known as "Brenneman's store" is. There was a ropewalk owned by T. Jackson and Son near the mill at Royalton.

XLI.
BURGESS AND COUNCILMEN.

The first Record Book of the borough was destroyed by fire in 1855, when the residence of Henry Stehman, then burgess, was burned; consequently the records are incomplete, and we can only give a list of officials and the dates of their election subsequent to that time.

March 16th, 1855.
Burgess.
Henry Stehman.
Council.
Isaac Bear, Christian Fisher, Adam Hemperly, Jr., John Cobaugh, Abraham Landis, Eli May, David Lehman, George W. Elberti, Joseph Brestle.

March 21st, 1856.
Burgess.
Henry Stehman.
Council.
Henry Croll, G. W. Elberti, William Croll, George Barnet, Dr. John Ringland, Adam Hemperly, Jr., Levi Hummel, John Yingst.

March 20th, 1857.
Burgess.
John K. Shott.
Council.
North Ward—Wm. M. Lowman, George Rodfong, Samuel Detweiler.
Middle Ward—John Monaghan, John E. Carmany, James Young.
South Ward—Stephen Wilson, Elijah McCreary, Charles McClain.

1858 (Lost).
Burgess.
John K. Shott.
March 18th, 1859.
Burgess.
Jeremiah Rohrer.

Council.
North Ward—Jacob Rife (1 year), Abraham Brandt (3 years).
Middle Ward—Henry Smith (3 years).
South Ward—George Whitman (2 years), James Hipple (3 years).
March 17th, 1860.
Burgess.
Thomas Wilson.
Council.
North Ward—Christian Fisher.
Middle Ward—John Monaghan.
South Ward—Elijah McCreary.
March 16th, 1861.
Burgess.
E. J. Ramsey.
Council.
North Ward—J. H. Nisley.
Middle Ward—James Young.
South Ward—M. B. Rambler.
March 21st, 1862.
Burgess.
E. J. Ramsey.
Council.
North Ward—Jacob Ebersole.
Middle Ward—M. Buckingham.
South Ward—Daniel Hake.
1863 (Lost).
Burgess.
Edward S. Kendig.
March 18th, 1864.
Burgess.
Yetman Eves.
Council.
North Ward—John Hendrickson.
Middle Ward—Henry Detweiler.
South Ward—Henry Baumbach.
March 16th, 1865.
Burgess.
E. J. Ramsey.
Council.
North Ward—Jacob Ebersole.
Middle Ward—William Hendrickson.
South Ward—Joseph Stewart.

March 16th, 1866.
Burgess.
Charles Churchman.
Council.
North Ward—Joseph Brestle, Frederick Koerper.
Middle Ward—John Monaghan, John Ringland.
South Ward—James Witherow.
March 15th, 1867.
Burgess.
George Smuller.
Council.
North Ward—Dr. M. Brown, Levi Hummel.
Middle Ward—John Raymond.
South Ward—M. B. Rambler, C. W. Churchman.
March 20th, 1868.
Burgess.
John McCreary.
Council.
North Ward—Caleb Roe.
Middle Ward—Samuel Landis.
South Ward—Joseph Stewart.
October 12th, 1869.
Burgess.
D. J. Boynton.
Council.
North Ward—(John F. Rife, Eli May)—(?)
Middle Ward—Kirk Few, Sr., John Carmany.
South Ward—Henry Hipple, D. J. Hake.
October 11th, 1870.
Burgess.
Henry Raymond.
Council.
North Ward—Jacob H. Baxtresser.
Middle Ward—Joseph Campbell.
South Ward— ——— Ziegler.
October 10th, 1871.
Burgess.
Henry Raymond.

Council.
North Ward— A. N. Breneman,
J. W. Rife.
Middle Ward—Kirk Few, Sr.
South Ward—George D. Yentzer.

1872.

Time changed to third Friday in March, 1872; all borough officers hold over till then.

March 21st, 1873.
Burgess.
Henry Raymond.
Council.
North Ward—Henry Hinney.
Middle Ward—W. D. Hendrickson, John Klineline.
South Ward—George Yentzer, Samuel Brandt, Al. Fortney.

February 17th, 1874.
Burgess.
H. C. Raymond.
Council.
North Ward—Dr. A. N. Breneman.
Middle Ward—Samuel Landis.
South Ward—F. P. Norton.

February 16th, 1875.
Burgess.
William H. Embich.
Council.
North Ward—George Rodfong, Sr., Joseph Brestle.
Middle Ward—John K. Shott.
South Ward—A. Myers.

February 15th, 1876.
Burgess.
H. C. Raymond.
Council.
North Ward—J. A. Swartz.
Middle Ward—John Klineline.
South Ward—A. B. Fortney.

February 20th, 1877.
Burgess.
John W. Rife.

Council.
North Ward—Lauman, Kauffman.
Middle Ward — Landis, Hendrickson.
South Ward—Norton.

February 19th, 1878.
Burgess.
John W. Rife.
Council.
North Ward—C. H. Hoffer.
Middle Ward—C. W. King.
South Ward—A. Poorman.

February 19th, 1879.
Burgess.
Christian Shireman.
Council.
North Ward—William Lauman.
Middle Ward—D. A. Detweiler.
South Ward—H. L. Rehrer.

February 17th, 1880.
Burgess.
Charles Churchman.
Council.
North Ward—Jacob Rife.
Middle Ward—W. H. Siple.
South Ward—Joseph Stewart.

February 15th, 1881.
Burgess.
S. L. Yetter.
Council.
North Ward—C. H. Hoffer.
Middle Ward—Elias Earisman.
South Ward—A. Roush.

February 21st, 1882.
Burgess.
S. L. Yetter.
Council.
North Ward—John Few.
Middle Ward—W. H. Kendig, D. A. Detweiler.
South Ward—E. Nagle.

February 20th, 1883.
Burgess.
Henry Hipple.

Council.
North Ward—John Baker.
Middle Ward—H. B. Campbell.
South Ward—H. L. Rehrer, Joseph Stewart.

February 19th, 1884.
Burgess.
Joseph Hewitt.
Council.
North Ward—Frederick Wagner.
Middle Ward—Elias Earisman.
South Ward—H. L. Rehrer.

February 17th, 1885.
Burgess.
J. H. Cobaugh.
Council.
North Ward—D. W. Stehman, J. V. Heistand.
Middle Ward—Martin Kendig.
South Ward—John Kohr.

February 16th, 1886.
Burgess.
J. H. Cobaugh.
Council.
North Ward—John G. Fisher.
Middle Ward—H. B. Campbell.
South Ward—J. J. Norton, H. H. Parsons.

February 15th, 1887.
Burgess.
J. H. Cobaugh.
Council.
North Ward—Dr. W. H. Beane, Dr. D. W. C. Laverty.
Middle Ward—L. C. Keim.
South Ward—George Gotshall.

February 21st, 1888.
Burgess.
C. H. Hutchinson.
Council.
North Ward—E. K. Demmy.
Middle Ward—H. Hipple.
South Ward—E. McCreary.

February 19th, 1889.
Burgess.
C. H. Hutchinson.
Council.
North Ward—J. McDonald.
Middle Ward—A. McNair.
South Ward—E. K. Demmy.

February 18th, 1890.
Burgess.
C. H. Hutchinson.
Council.
North Ward—H. Croll.
Middle Ward—A. J. Lerch.
South Ward—R. Benson.

February 17th, 1891.
Burgess.
S. L. Yetter.
Council.
North Ward—H. Croll.
Middle Ward—F. K. Mohler.
South Ward—John Beachler.

February 16th, 1892.
Burgess.
S. L. Yetter.
Council.
North Ward—J. McDonald.
Middle Ward—J. Atkinson.
South Ward—E. K. Demmy.

February 21st, 1893.
Burgess.
James H. Nicely.
Council.
First Ward—R. Benson.
Second Ward—A. J. Lerch.
Third Ward—M. B. Schaeffer.

February 20th, 1894.
Burgess.
J. H. Nicely.
Council.
First Ward—F. B. Hampton.
Second Ward—J. L. Nisley.
Third Ward—L. Fenical.

During Nicely's incumbency the official term of the Burgess was extended to three years. Nicely dying, W. W. Kurtz was elected to fill out his unexpired term.

February 17th, 1895.
Council.
First Ward—M. H. Hartman.
Second Ward—I. K. Longenecker.
Third Ward—E. O. Hendrickson.

February 18th, 1896.
First Ward—G. W. Botts.
Second Ward—W. H. Bausman.
Third Ward—M. Schaeffer.

February 16th, 1897.
Burgess.
Jacob Welsh.
Council.
First Ward—J. Hubley.
Second Ward—J. Ackerman.
Third Ward—J. L. Nisley.

February 15th, 1898.
Council.
First Ward—W. C. Bowers.
Second Ward—W. M. Hipple.
Third Ward—C. Ashenfelter.

February 21st, 1899.
Council.
First Ward—G. W. Botts.

Second Ward—H. W. Bausman.
Third Ward—M. Snyder.

February 20th, 1900.
Burgess.
Oliver M. Swartz.
Council.
First Ward—M. Schaeffer.
Second Ward—C. Long.
Third Ward—J. L. Nisley.

February 19th, 1901.
Council.
First Ward—W. H. Martin.
Second Ward—J. Atkinson.
Third Ward—D. Seiders.

February 18th, 1902.
Council.
First Ward—W. Hipple.
Second Ward—W. C. Fleming.
Third Ward—E. J. Swartz.

February 17th, 1903.
Burgess.
John L. Whisler.
Council.
First Ward—J. Clouser.
Second Ward—W. Weaver.
Third Ward—J. L. Nisley.

XLII.

WATER RIGHT OUT OF FREY'S MILL RACE.

This indenture made the twenty-fourth day of June, in the year of our Lord, one thousand seven hundred and eighty-nine, between George Frey, of Paxton township, in the county of Dauphin and State of Pennsylvania, merchant of the one part, and John Fisher, of the township, county and State aforesaid, yeoman of the other part. Whereas the said John Fisher and Margery, his wife, by their indenture bearing equal date herewith, for the considerations therein mentioned, did grant and convey unto the said George Frey, his heirs and assigns, the privilege of cutting a canal or mill race through a certain piece or plot of ground for the purpose of conveying water to turn a mill or mills or other water works, which piece or plot of ground is commencing on the western bank of Swatara creek bounded and described as followeth, viz: Beginning at a post on the western bank of Swatara creek, near the division line of the said John Fisher and Blair McClenachan's land, extending along and near the division line aforesaid, south sixty-six degrees, west thirty-eight and a half perches to a post, thence by various courses and distances thhrough the other lands of the said John Fisher (party hereto), to the lot of ground on which the mill of the said George Frey now stands, and did also grant to him the said George Frey, his heirs and assigns, the sole and exclusive right of all the water that can be conveyed out of Swatara creek by the above mentioned canal or mill race through the lands of him, the said John Fisher, his heirs and assigns, as in and by the above mentioned indenture indented to be recorded, reference thereto being had, may more fully appear.

Now this indenture witnesseth that the said George Frey, for and in consideration of the sum of five shillings to him in hand well and truly paid by the said John Fisher, at and before the ensealing and delivery of these presents, the receipt and payment whereof is hereby acknowledged. As for other good causes him thereunto moving hath granted, bargained, sold and confirmed, and by these presents doth grant, bargain, sell and confirm, unto the said John Fisher and his heirs, the liberty and privilege of laying one pipe or tube the bore of which is to be six inches in diameter at any one place between the place of beginning aforesaid and the post which makes the first corner in the above mentioned line, the distance whereof is thirty-eight perches, for the purpose of conveying from and out of the said canal or mill race so much water as will pass through the said pipe or tube for the watering the meadow of the said John Fisher contiguous to the race aforesaid, but for no other use, interest or purpose whatsoever; and also to permit and suffer the said John Fisher and his heirs to erect and build a bridge or bridges at, upon and across the canal or mill race aforesaid, for the convenience of him, the said John Fisher, but in such a manner as not to injure the said canal or mill race or to impede or obstruct the passing and repassing of boats or other craft thereon.

To have and to hold the said liberty and privilege hereby granted, or intended so to be, to him, the said John Fisher, his heirs and assigns, forever, and the said George Frey, for himself and his heirs, executors and administrators, doth hereby covenant, promise, grant and agree to and with the said John Fisher, his heirs and assigns, that he, the said George Frey and his heirs, the said above liberty and privilege and premises unto the said John Fisher, his heirs and assigns, against him the said George Frey, his heirs, and against all and every other person lawfully claiming the said premises, shall and will warrant and forever defend by these presents.

In witness whereof the parties to these presents have hereto interchangeably set their hands and seals the day and year first written.

GEORGE FREY.

Sealed and delivered in the presence of Jno. Jos. Henry, C. Fred Oberlander.

Received on the day of the foregoing indenture of and from the above

named John Fisher the sum of five shillings in full for the consideration in the foregoing deed specified. GEORGE FREY.
Attest:—JNO. JOS. HENRY,
C. FRED. OBERLANDER.
On the reverse of this deed is the following:
Dauphin County:
Be it remembered that on the twenty-fourth day of June, one thousand seven hundred and eighty-nine before me, Jacob Cook, Esquire, one of the Justices of the Court of Common for said county, personally came George Frey and acknowledged the within indenture to be his act and deed and desired the same might be recorded as such. In witness whereof I have hereunto set my name and seal the day and year aforesaid. JACOB COOK.
Dauphin County, ss:
Recorded August 28th, 1848, in the office for recording of deeds be in and for said county in Deed Book S, Vol. 2, Page 266.
In testimony whereof, I have hereunto set my hand and affixed the seal of said office at Harrisburg the day and year aforesaid.
ROBERT F. BLACK, *Recorder.*

NOTE:—This document is on ordinary writing paper and is in a very dilapidated condition. In phraseology and punctuation it is a verbatim copy of the original.

XLIII.

The Great Rebellion cannot be attributed to the efforts of the abolitionists, for, as far back as 1776, John Adams wrote to his friend Gates, "All our misfortunes arise from a single source—the resistance of the southern colonies to a republican government."

Unlike New England, the Middle States, or their children of the west, which were settled by the freedom loving refugees from tyranny in Europe, most of the early Southern States filled up with adventurers, Royalists, Cavaliers, from England; Huguenot noblemen and their retainers from France, and the worn out, impoverished nobility of Spain. The institution of slavery increased and perpetuated a governing class, that was rapidly turning this whole section of our country into the estates of a landed and slave-holding oligarchy, which controlled not only the legislation of the South, but also that of the nation. Slavery kept out immigration, hindered development, and tended gradually to enervate and emasculate the population of the territories where it existed. The free States, oppressed by no such incubus, rapidly grew in wealth, power and intelligence; the northern democracy, the "mud-sills," from being subservient had become aggressive. The serf-begotten aristocracy saw that the power which they had so long wielded was slipping from their grasp. They endeavored to retain it by annexation of fresh territory—by legislation—finding all of no avail they resolved on separation.

On November 6th, 1860, the vote of Middletown was: Lincoln (Republican), 227; Breckenridge (Democratic), 184; Bell (Union), 34. January 21st, 1861, there was a large mass meeting of citizens at Union Hall. Colonel John Raymond called the assembly to order and nominated Mercer Brown for president. Thirty-three vice-presidents were chosen. The secretaries were Benjamin Whitman, Thomas Wilson, William Ross and Henry Raymond. Addresses were made by Messrs. Christ, Buckingham, Eves, Seymour, Raymond, John Raymond, Henry Raymond, and Frederick Lauman. The meeting passed strong Union resolutions.

April 12th, 1861, news was received here of the attack that morning on Fort Sumter by the rebels. April 15th, President Lincoln issued his proclamation calling for 75,000 volunteers.

There was great excitement in town. Volunteers, singly and in groups, left to join different companies. The bands played. Ladies marching to the depot sang patriotic songs as the trains filled with soldiers passed, and sent a delegate to offer their services to the government to care for the sick and wounded, if necessary. On Sunday, national songs were sung and patriotic sermons preached in the different churches. Subscriptions were started to provide for the families of those who enlisted, several persons offering $500 each. A full company, under Major Rehrer, was formed.

April 22nd, this company, the J. D. Cameron Infantry, was organized, tendered themselves to the Governor, and were accepted.

Sunday, May 5th, the company left Middletown for Camp Curtin, to which place they were conveyed by canal boats, accompanied by a brass band, and at least two hundred citizens. Before leaving the wharf here the company was addressed by Rev. J. S. Lame (M. E. minister), in the presence of over a thousand spectators. "Then amidst the beating of drums, blare of trumpets, waving of handkerchiefs, farewells, tears, and shouts of sympathizing friends, the boats moved off bearing away their freight of American patriots. Fathers and husbands, brothers and sons, have left their homes to fight their country's battles."—*Dauphin Journal.*

May 24th, the company received their uniforms, viz: A light gray coat, fine cassimere pantaloons, and caps to match, the outfit being presented by J. D. Cameron, Esq. Their subsequent history is that of the regiment of which they formed a part.

EXTRACTS FROM THE *Dauphin Journal.*

The *Dauphin Journal* of May 9th, 1861, says: "In addition to the above company a number of young men from this town joined the Cameron Guards and the State Capital Guards; and another company, to be called the Middletown Rifle Company, is now being formed." In Company E, of the First Pennsylvania Regiment, organized April 20, 1861, was Elijah S. Embich; in the Second Pennsylvania Regiment, in Company I, were James Harvey, Henry Brestle and Lot B. Allen. There were others whose names I have been unable to obtain. Neither of these regiments were in any general engagement, and at the expiration of three months, their term of enlistment, the men were returned home and mustered out of the service.

On the same day (May 9th) the *Journal* says: "J. Rohrer, Esq., is now drilling a company at Union Hall. Mr. R. has had considerable military experience and will make an excellent officer. Captain D. J. Boynton is getting up a rifle company to hold themselves in readiness for any emergency.

"May 23d—The Invincibles meet regularly for drill at Union Hall, and the company is making rapid progress under Capt. Rohrer.

"June 6th.—Gen. Philip Irwin, of this place, appointed sutler in U. S. Army. Among the deputies selected by the General is W. H. Kendig, postmaster. William C. Ross, of this place appointed to a clerkship in U. S. Arsenal, Philadelphia. On last Monday (3rd) a number of the patriotic ladies of Middletown made havelocks for the J. D. Cameron Guards.

"August 22nd.—Mr. Joseph Rife has been promoted to a second lieutenancy in the regular army.

"August 29th.—Mr. L. B. Allen has been authorized to recruit a company of cavalry, to be attached to Col. E. C. William's regiment. A meeting will be held at Union Hall this evening, when all who desire to enlist are invited to attend. Headquarters at Raymond & Kendig's Hotel.

"October 3rd.—We are pleased to learn that Rev. John McCosker, pastor of the Catholic churches at this place and Elizabethtown, has been appointed by Gov. Curtin a chaplain to one of the Pennsylvania regiments. Honor could not have fallen upon a worthier recipient; he commands the respect and esteem of all who are acquainted with him, and the army will contain no better Union man, nor one who will be more devoted to the welfare of those under his spiritual charge.

On Saturday evening (September 28th) a meeting was held in Union Hall, to get volunteers for Colonel McCarter's regiment, of Lebanon. The meeting was addressed by Captain D. J. Boynton and Rev. Lame. Several young men enrolled their names. Colonel McCarter is a minister of the gospel. Those wishing to join will report immediately to A. Black of this place, or Henry Pear. Colonel McCarter is expected to deliver an address in this borough this week.

"October 24th.—A number of our most respectable young men have joined this company (Col. McCarter's) and a few more, of good, moral character, are wanted to fill it.

"October 31st.—Lieut. J. R. Rife, now at Fort Columbus, N. Y., is promoted to a first lieutenancy in the regular army. Col. McCarter's regiment, in camp at Lebanon, has received orders to move on Friday (Nov. 1st). Capt. D. J. Boynton's company, of this place, is attached to this regiment.

"November 7th.—Rev. John McCosker is appointed chaplain to the ninety-fifth (Col. Goslin's) regiment. Shortly after his appointment he was the recipient of a handsome sword and belt, presented to him by Mr. James Young, of this place, as a slight token of the donor's regard for the many estimable qualities possessed by the reverend gentleman. A number of young men from this place are at Camp Cameron, attached to a cavalry regiment.

"November 28th.—Middletown has now two hundred and twenty-five volunteers in the U. S. service. Mr. Alvan McNair, Co. D, 6th cavalry regiment, in writing to his father from Bladensburg, Md., says: 'I like the service very well, and although a minor, am determined to fight for my country. You need not go to the trouble to get me out of the army, for I have made up my mind to stick to Uncle Sam until this outrageous rebellion is crushed.' There had been an effort made to get the writer out of the army on the plea of his being a minor. We admire the pluck of that young man.

"December 12th.—A box of knit wool socks, sent as Christmas gifts to the soldiers by

Mrs. James Young,	Mrs. D. Beaverson,	Mrs. Ehrehart,
Mrs. D. Fortney,	Mrs. Daniel Kendig,	Mrs. Aple,
Miss Clem. Fortney,	Mrs. S. Henderson,	Mrs. J. K. Buser,
Miss Lizzie Arnold,	Mrs. M. Rambler,	Mrs. John Ulrich,
Mrs. J. Beitleman,	Miss S. M. Eves.	Mrs. Edward Kendig,
Mrs. Gray Kultz,	Mrs. Catherine Wolfle,	Miss M. Kissecker,
Mrs. Jno. Snavely,	Mrs. M. G. Shott,	Mrs. Stouch,
Miss Violet Ramsey,	Mrs. Wash. Snyder,	Mrs. McCammon,
Miss Mary E. Murr,	Mrs. Rogers,	Mrs. F. Fisher,
Mrs. J. Eves,	Mrs. Atkinson,	Mrs. Elizabeth Snyder
Mrs. A. Poorman,	Miss May Fairman,	Mrs. R. C. McKibben,
Mrs. Dr. Shaeffer,	Mrs. Lorish,	Miss S. S. Thompson,
Mrs. C. Neff,	Mrs. Thomas Fairman,	Mrs. B. Graham,
Mrs. Kleiss,	Mrs. Wm. Embick,	Miss Eliza Wagner,
	Mrs. W. Etter,	Miss B. J. Brown.

"December 19th.—Lieut Shipley, of this place, complimented by Col. H. Brown, commander at Fort Pickens, for coolness and bravery displayed during two days' engagement.

"December 26th.—Capt. D. J. Boynton returns thanks to Morris Johnson, E. S. Kendig, George Crist, D. Kendig, James Young, S. Landis, George Lenhart and others, of Middletown, for sword presented to him."

March 20, 1862, the following advertisement is quoted in the *Dauphin Journal:*

"ESTATE SALE—EIGHTY NEGROES.

"On Monday, 14th February, 1862, at 10 o'clock a. m., will be sold at the residence of the late William Seabrook, Sr., Esq., on Edisto Island (S. C.), a prime gang of eighty negroes, accustomed to the cultivation of Sea Island cotton, belonging to the estate of the late Robert C. Seabrook, Esq. Terms: For the negroes, one-third cash; balance in one and two years, with interest from day of sale, secured by bond mortgage and personal security. Purchasers to pay for paper.

"The sale did not take place as advertised, owing to the arrival of U. S. troops, and the following is written at the bottom of the bill:

"'As the above property has not been disposed of I bequeath it to Father McCosker, chaplain 55th regiment, P. V.

'MRS. SARAH SEABROOK.'

"May 22nd.—George F. Ross, of this place, appointed aide-de-camp to Col. Crocker, acting Brig. Gen. 6th Div., Iowa Vols.

"June 12th.—Rev. John McCosker, chaplain of 56th Pa. Vols., died in Philadelphia, in his 32nd year. Dr. Jas. A. Lowe, of our town, appointed surgeon at the military hospital of St. Joseph's, Phila. Soldiers' aid association formed. Dr. B. J. Wiestling called to the chair; T. J. Ross, Sec.; Rev. C. J. Ehrehart, Treas. Resolved, That we organize a society to be called the Soldiers' Aid Society of Middletown, and that the present officers be permanent officers of the society. Dr. John Ringland and J. J. Walborn, Esq., appointed a committee to wait on the surgeons at Camp Curtin and ascertained from them the wants of the sick and wounded soldiers. An executive committee consisting of four persons from each ward was appointed—two ladies and two gentlemen—viz: N. Ward—Mrs. Brua Cameron, Mrs. J. W. Stofer, Dr. J. Ringland, J. J. Walborn, Esq. M. Ward—Mrs. J. E. Carmany, Miss M. Kissecker, Henry Smith, Seymour Raymond. S. Ward—Miss S. Eves, Mrs. George Whitman, Jno. Snavely, E. McCreary. Dr. Wiestling's residence was selected as the depot for all contributions.

"July 3rd.—Amount realized from festival of Soldiers' Aid Society was $217.42. "J. T. Ross, Sec. S. A. Soc.

"At a meeting of the Soldiers' Aid Society, in the council chamber, Dr. Wiestling was authorized to make bandages of the muslin in his possession and Drs. J. Ringland and J. Schaeffer appointed a committee to purchase 'Sharpee.' A committee consisting of Rev. C. J. Ehrehart, Dr. Ringland and Dr. Schaeffer to inquire into the expediency of establishing a hospital in our borough. Also resolved, That the ladies be requested to meet in council chamber Tuesday morning 7.30 a. m., and divide themselves into committees for the purchase of materials and manufacture of needed garments. The president was also instructed to extend aid to any sick or wounded soldiers brought here in need.

"July 17th.—July 12th a citizens' meeting held at Union Hall for the purpose of encouraging enlistments in response to the call of the President for 300,000 additional men. Rev. J. S. Lame was chosen president, and J. J. Walborn, Esq., secretary. Rev. O. C. McLane moved that committees be appointed to arrange for another meeting. Rev. C. J. Ehrehart gave patriotic address. On motion of Mr. P. Irwin audience joined in singing the 'Star Spangled Banner,' led by William Smith. On Tuesday evening a large and enthusiastic meeting was held at Union Hall. Daniel Kendig was called to the chair; Messrs. Jacob Rife and Henry Smith, vice-president; Dr. J. Ringland and J. J. Walborn, Esq.,

Rescue Hose House.

secretaries. After organization, singing the 'Star Spangled Banner,' and prayer by Rev. D. A. L. Laverty, Rev. George T. Cain delivered a very eloquent and stirring address. Patriotic resolutions were offered by J. J. Walborn, Esq., and adopted. The audience was then addressed by Rev. D. A. L. Laverty, and after singing the 'Red, White and Blue,' adjourned."

"December 24, 1863.—A meeting was held December 18th at Union Hall. Committees were appointed to solicit subscriptions, and receive and ship goods to the soldiers from this place now in the Army of the Potomac. Committees to raise funds for this purpose: North Ward—Mrs. J. W. Stofer, Mrs. Maj. Brua Cameron, Miss Eva Wiestling. Middle Ward—Mrs. W. H. Kendig, Mrs. Kate Church, Miss Maggie Kissecker. South Ward—Mrs. Eves, Mrs. Rambler, Mrs. Fisher. Committee to receive, pack and ship goods—Capt. J. K. Shott, Messrs. J. L. Nisley and John H. Snavely. The ladies met with great success and on December 29th five barrels and six mammoth boxes of turkeys, geese, ducks, chicken, butter, bread, cakes, pies, tobacco, preserved fruits, &c., were shipped.

"January 21, 1864.—Major Brua Cameron, son of Hon. Simon Cameron, died at Lochiel (his father's residence) on Wednesday, the 13th inst. The deceased was thirty-eight years of age, and was a resident of this place, where he leaves a wife and several children. He held a commission as paymaster in the army, with the rank of major. He had a great many warm, personal friends here, and was well and favorably known throughout the state. His remains were interred in the Middletown cemetery on Friday afternoon, followed by the largest funeral procession ever witnessed in this place. Peace to his ashes.

"January 28th.—A meeting was held in the North ward, in the Presbyterian church. John Heppich was chairman. Patriotic speeches were made by Dr. Wiestling, Messrs. J. L. Nisley, J. J. Walborn, T. C. Search and others.

"February 17th.—George Rodfong enlisted in the signal service corps for three years. Lieut. J. H. Waltz (93rd Penna.) opens a recruiting office at C. Neff's tavern, in this borough.

"March 10th.—Dr. George F. Mish, surgeon 15th Penna. (Anderson) Cavalry, home on furlough.

"May 19th.—Middletown Guards, organized in the Fall of 1862, paid off.

"June 6th.—The Pennsylvania Reserve Corps returned home, after three years' service.

"June 23rd.—A picnic given to Company G, Sixth Reserves, at Fisher's woods. At 9 o'clock the soldiers, forty in number, formed in line at the market house and with martial music marched to the beautiful grove. They were met and escorted by Baumbach's brass band. Exercises: Singing 'The Star Spangled Banner,' by the Lutheran choir;

(The file of the *Journal* from July 17, 1862, to Aug. 13, 1863, is missing.—C. H. H.)

Rev. McKinney, late chaplain of the Ninth Penna. Cavalry, addressed them; song by the choir; Rev. Rakestraw, of the Methodist church, then addressed them, alluding and pointing to the worn and tattered flag, which was in the rear of the speakers, as evidence of what they had passed through; song; banquet. The number in attendance was 1,500. The committee of arrangements were: N. Ward—Dr. John Ringland, J. L. Nisley, T. C. Lerch, Mrs. B. F. Kendig, Mrs. A. Hemperly, Mrs. J. H. Nisley. M. Ward—Samuel Landis, Dr. J. H. Nonamacher, John Monaghan, Mrs. Yetman Eves, Mrs. Morris Johnson, Mrs. Henry Siple. S. Ward—Dr. J. H. Schaeffer, John H. Snavely, B. S. Peters, Mrs. F. Fisher, Miss Murr, Miss C. Fortney. D. R. Ettla presented each soldier with a fine silk badge."

The news of Lee's surrender, April 9, 1865, was received here with ringing of bells. The schools were dismissed, and "all gave themselves up to the general joy." The citizens were preparing for a grand demonstration over the return of peace, when the news of the assassination of President Lincoln (April 14th) reached here. Says the *Journal* of the 20th: "The news of the assassination of our noble chief—our second Washington—reached us on Saturday morning at the breakfast table. We can never forget the sad, horror-stricken expression on the faces of the people as they wended their way to the depot to ascertain if the horrible intelligence was true; men looked into each other's faces as though each was moving to the grave with the body of a near and dear relation. It could not be true; the change from speechless amazement to wild indignation was not a wide one; a cry for vengeance went up, the day of retribution has come, we take back every word uttered touching a humane policy towards the active promoters and sustainers of the rebellion."

The funeral train passed through here at 11.30 a. m. Saturday, April 22. A handsome arch of spruce was sprung across the track at this place, bearing the inscription in large black letters, "For Freedom Fallen!" Several hundred citizens assembled to see the train pass through town. It consisted of nine elegant cars, elaborately draped in mourning. Watchmen were stationed every half mile.

July 4, 1865, there was a parade of returned soldiers, cavalry, infantry and artillery. Several salutes were fired. The soldiers met at Smith's Hall, formed in line and marched through the principal street to Center Square where the "Declaration of Independence" was read, followed by an address by the Rev. G. Rakestraw.

"July 29th.—A meeting was held to raise funds to erect a monument to Middletown soldiers who fell in war."

XLIV.

Soon after the incorporation of the borough, February 19th, 1828, an engine was procured, and a fire company organized under the name of the "Union." The engine was small but very effective for its class, and was built in Philadelphia by Philip Mason in 1875.

An ordinance was passed by the borough council, requiring the owner of each house to provide "fire buckets," one for each story; they were made of heavy leather; were long and narrow, and held two or three gallons each, they were painted in different colors, each having the name of the owner and "Union Fire Company" inscribed upon it. (Some of these buckets are still in existence.) They were kept hanging in some convenient place, frequently in the hall or entry, and it was the householder's duty, in case of an alarm, to carry or send them to the fire. Double lines of the townsfolk were then formed to the nearest pumps, and the buckets were passed from hand to hand, to and from the engine. The women were the most effective workers, they standing at their posts and handling buckets, while the men were running around giving orders. The machine remained in use until 1868, and on several occasions did good service. It passed afterwards into the possession of Raymond & Campbell. Its subsequent fate I do not know.

United States Engine House.

In 1861 a meeting of citizens of Portsmouth was held, at which steps were taken to provide better facilities for extinguishing fires. Those present subscribed liberally, and a committee appointed to solicit subscriptions were so successful that David R. Ettla, then a resident of Philadelphia, was selected to visit the manufacturers, and secure an engine. He made a contract there with Mr. Agnew to build a suction engine after the pattern of the old "United States," of that city (of which company he was a member). It was built and delivered and then turned over to a company for service.

The company purchased a hose-carriage and hose, but becoming financially embarrassed soon afterwards disbanded. The engine was sold and taken to Harrisburg; it was there used by the "Friendship Fire Company" several times, but was soon afterwards destroyed by fire, together with the building in which it was placed.

The Good Will Engine.

On November 16th, 1866, on the petition of one hundred and eighty-three freeholders of the borough, an appropriation of two thousand dollars was made to purchase a fire engine and erect an engine house. For four hundred and fifty dollars an engine with hose-carriage, etc., was purchased from George Smuller; and Christian Fisher, for nine hundred and eighty dollars, contracted for and erected an engine house at the northwest corner of Union and Emaus streets. (The building was afterwards moved to Catherine street, above Emaus.) The engine was never very effective, and was afterwards stored in a stable on Susquehanna street, then to the furniture factory, and was finally broken up and the metal part sold.

The Liberty Fire Engine Company.

As may be judged the borough was but poorly provided with means to check or subdue any conflagration, therefore in the year 1874 a number of the residents resolved to raise a sufficient sum of money to purchase a steam fire engine. The firms of Raymond & Campbell, Fisher & Smith, Shott & Ulrich, Daniel Kendig & Co., Etter, Carmany & Siple, Kendig, Bricker & Lauman, Coolbaugh & Hendrickson, with James Young, Benjamin Peters, M. B. Rambler, Geo. Hendrickson, and some eighteen other citizens, subscribed about $60 each. The necessary amount was raised, and a committee went to Philadelphia and purchased at Harkness' bazar, for $1,500.00 the Liberty engine.

The Liberty Steam Fire Company was organized November 7th, 1874, and incorporated by a decree of the court in January, 1875. Its presidents have been: 1874-75, D. R. Ettla; 1876, H. G. Raymond; 1877-78, W. G. Kennard; 1879, Rufus Franks; 1880-82, W. G. Kennard; 1883, Emanuel Kling; 1884-86, A. J. Lerch; 1887, John Hipple; 1888, George Patton; 1889, Samuel Nusky; 1890-94, A. J. Lerch; 1895, John P. Seitz; 1896-1901, J. S. Kennard; 1902, W. H. Koons; 1903-05, A. L. Etter.

In 1886 A. J. Lerch, D. H. Bucher, Samuel Nuskey, H. H. Rakestraw, William Schuetz, Frank J. Stipe and F. B. Bailey made applications for a charter which was granted January, 1887.

In 1889, a building committee was appointed: A. J. Lerch, H. S. Michaels, J. S. Hipple, S. H. Nusky, James P. Hipple. A substantial brick building was erected and dedicated July 4th, 1891.

In 1901 the steam fire engine was sold and a chemical engine was purchased in Baltimore from the makers. The committee for the purchase of the chemical was H. A. Lenhart, J. S. Kennard, W. E. Raymond, J. P. Seitz and O. M. Swartz.

In 1902 a bell tower and hosedrier was erected. The assembly-room is handsomely furnished and the building provided with all the modern appliances.

The North Ward Hose Company.

That portion of Middletown lying above Water street and formerly known as the North ward, is at some distance from the center of the borough, and in case of fire, comparatively unprotected. Appreciating this condition of affairs, a number of the property holders met together in the North ward schoolhouse, March 18th, 1886, and organized the North Ward Hose Company, with the following officers: President, William A. Croll; vice-president, Samuel Singer; secretary, Edward L. Croll; treasurer, D. W. Stehman; foreman, E. S. Baker; first assistant foreman, S. S. Selser; second assistant foreman, J. H. Horst. A committee was appointed to solicit money by subscription to purchase a carriage and hose. The citizens responded liberally; a hose-carriage was made by H. Saul, the necessary quantity of hose was purchased, and the company was ready for active service by June 3, 1886. A bell was donated by Raymond & Campbell. The total cost of the building was over $1,000. The carriage was kept in Nissley's barn, but shortly afterwards a piece of land was leased from Frey estate and a neat two-story frame building was erected on Pine street north of Union. This building was afterwards moved to a lot purchased by the company on the north side of Water street.

The company was reorganized June 3rd, 1889, and assumed the name of the old Union Hose Company (whose constitution is now in their possession) and was incorporated August 30th, 1897.

February 2nd, 1903, at a regular meeting of the company, it was resolved to erect a new edifice, and a building committee was appointed consisting of E. O. Hendrickson, W. J. Roop and Frank Winnaugle. The old structure was sold in May, 1904, contract for new building awarded July 15th, 1904, ground broken in the same month and the present handsome brick structure was completed March 6th, 1905.

The Rescue Hose Company.

At the request of W. G. Kennard, a meeting of citizens of the South (now the First) ward was held July 16th, 1888, at the colored school-house, chairman, Dr. J. C. Lingle; secretary, H. H. Rakestraw. An organization was effected and the following officers elected: President, Wm. G. Kennard; vice-president, Dr. J. C. Lingle; secretary, H. H. Rakestraw; assistant secretary, H. W. Myers; treasurer, B. F. Brandt; foreman, John Core; assistant foreman, David Brandt; second assistant foreman, James P. Hipple; third assistant foreman, W. Hickernell, Jr.; trustees, F. B. Hampton, Chas. Gottschall, Elijah McCreary, Sr., J. H. Welsh, and J. J. Norton. The name of the company adopted was the Rescue No. 3. On Monday following adopted constitution. A committee consisting of W. G. Kennard, Elijah McCreary, Sr., John Fishburn, Dr. J. C. Lingle, H. H. Rakestraw, B. F. Brandt, A. Baumbach, Charles Ulrich, Jr., H. Welsh, and H. W. Myers appointed to raise means to purchase carriage and build a hose house.

The first lot selected was on property of McCreary Brothers on Mud Pike. Afterwards a lot on State street was bought from Colonel James Young. After the foundation trenches were dug the canal company claimed a portion of the ground, making the lot too short. The company then purchased the present site on South Union street from George Fisher.

On motion of J. J. Norton the resolution appointing a building committee was rescinded and the president and trustees were empowered to act.

The first fair to raise money was held in September, 1888, and cleared $544.75.

The company was incorporated October 3rd, 1888.

In December a second fair was held, and the company purchased five hundred feet of hose from Eureka Co.

On March 4th, 1889, building committee reported building complete and all bills paid.

W. G. Kennard was president until his death in October, 1898, when J. H. Welsh, the vice-president, was elected and has filled that office till the present time.

In 1898 the company joined the Fire Association.

In September, 1899, erected a hose tower, and moved bell-tower into it at a cost of $350.00.

In May, 1900, committee appointed to confer with the other two companies, and form a fireman's relief association—was organized and incorporated November 12th, 1900.

In December, 1900, organized a drum corps, John Core, leader, under direction of the trustees.

In April, 1903, added a bath room complete.

In 1904, put in steam heat and added a kitchen.

May, 1905, joined fire department.

XLV.
WAR RECORD.
THIRTY-FIFTH REGIMENT.

Sixth Reserve. (Three years' service.)

It is a remarkable coincidence, that although recruited in different sections of the State, six of the ten companies of this regiment were organized on the same day—April 22nd, 1861—as follows: The "Iron Guard," Company A, in Columbia county; "Northern Invincibles," Company F, in Bradford county; the "J. D. Cameron Infantry," Company G (Middletown), Dauphin county; the "Tioga Invincibles," Company H, Tioga county; the "Towanda Rifles," Company I, Bradford county; and the "Susquehanna Volunteers," Company K, in Susquehanna county. The remaining companies, B, C, D, and E, were from Snyder, Wayne, Franklin and Montour counties respectively. The men, with but few exceptions, had no previous military experience.

On the 22nd of June the regimental organization was effected. On the 11th of July the regiment received orders to march to Greencastle, Pa.; it arrived there on the following day and was placed in Camp Biddle, where it remained drilling until the 22nd, when it moved by Cumberland Valley and Northern Central Railroads, via Baltimore, to Washington.

In its passage through Baltimore one of its members was wounded by the accidental discharge of a musket, the men supposing they were attacked, as their predecessors had been on the 19th, were with difficulty kept from firing on the mob in the streets. The command was halted, the cause of the accident ascertained, and the march quietly resumed.

The regiment reached Washington on the 24th, encamped east of the

Capitol, and was mustered into the United States service on the 27th. It then moved to Tenallytown, where General McCall had his headquarters, and was organizing his division of the Pennsylvania Reserves. Here it was engaged in performing guard and picket duty and assisting in the construction of forts. General McCall, in his report at this time, to General McClellan, says of the Sixth: "The regiment is very well drilled. The malaria arising from the low grounds about Washington soon transformed the hardy healthy men of the regiment into an invalid organization with a sick roll numbering hundreds."

The sick were assigned to the Third Brigade of General McCall's Division. On the 9th of October it marched, with the division, across Chain Bridge and encamped near Langley. A commendable degree of proficiency in discipline was attained, which was severely tested on many well-fought fields. On the 19th, a reconnaissance was made for the double purpose of driving in the enemy's pickets and securing forage. This accomplished, it returned to camp on the 21st, but soon to go forth and confront the foe, who was reported in force near Dranesville. The order was given on the 19th of December to march at 6 a. m. of the following day, and leaving camp in buoyant spirits, the regiment proceeded to the Leesburg pike, where the column was formed and speedily moved towards the field of battle. The Ninth Reserves was posted on the right, the Sixth in the center, the Kane Rifles on the left, and the Tenth and Twelfth in reserve.

While possession was being taken by the Reserves, the enemy opened fire from a battery posted on the Centreville road, which was promptly responded to by a section of Easton's Battery of the First Pennsylvania Artillery, the first discharge eliciting cheers from the entire line. Immediately after, the Sixth then on the pike, with its right resting a short distance from the intersection of the Alexandria road, was ordered forward, and after crossing a field and ascending a gentle slope, entered a wood, into which it advanced a short distance, when the Ninth was met slowly retiring. Volley after volley was exchanged with the enemy, without an attempt by either party to advance. At length a charge was ordered upon his battery. At the word "forward" the regiment bounded over the fence in front, crossed the open field, and in a moment had driven him from his position in confusion, capturing one caisson and some prisoners. Thus the initial victory of the Reserves was won.*

During the next two months but little occurred to vary the monotony of camp life, constant drill and guard, picket and fatigue duty, were regularly performed. Remaining in Camp Pierpont until the 10th of March, when the Army of the Potomac advanced upon the rebel fortifications at Centerville and Manassas, it marched sixteen miles to Hunter's Mills, remaining there until the 14th, when ordered to Alexandria, where it arrived on the 16th, after one of the most fatiguing marches,

---

*Jacob A. Embich, now high constable, beat the first long roll for the regiment after this first victory of the Army of the Potomac.

through rain and mud, shelterless and hungry, experienced during its whole term of service. The regiment changed its camp on the 27th, to a beautiful grove near Bailey's Cross Roads, and had secured comfortable quarters by appropriating the tents of an unoccupied camp in the vicinity, when orders came on the 10th of April to march to Manassas. Moving through Fairfax Court House and Centreville and crossing Bull Run at Blackburn's Ford, the command reached Manassas Junction on the 12th. These points were full of interest to the men, in consequence of being the winter quarters of the rebel army.

On the 18th, the command marched, following the line of the Orange and Alexandria Railroad, to Catlett's Station. Remaining there until the 2nd of May, it advanced with the division through Hartwood to Falmouth, where it arrived on the 3rd, and encamped a mile north of the town. Comfortable and pleasant quarters were constructed of lumber obtained from an adjoining mill. Extensive preparations were being made for an advance upon Richmond from Fredericksburg, the troops being clothed and equipped for the campaign in the best possible manner. But these plans were all frustrated by the advance of Stonewall Jackson down the Shenandoah Valley, and his defeat of Banks. It was then determined to send the Reserves, by water, to the support of McClellan's army operating on the Peninsula.

On the 13th of June the regiment embarked for White House, where it arrived on the following day. Here had been accumulated vast stores for the supply of McClellan's army. The First and Second Brigades had already arrived and had moved forward. Upon the arrival of the Third Brigade the post was in a state of considerable alarm, Stuart having, on the night previous, made his famous cavalry raid in McClellan's rear, temporarily cutting his line of supply. The Sixth Regiment was detailed to remain behind, when the brigade marched to join McClellan's column, and was stationed at Tunstall's Station, four miles from White House, on the Richmond and York River Railroad. On the 19th, five companies were ordered to fall back to White House, and the companies remaining at Tunstall's were set to work throwing up earthworks for their protection. The advance of the rebels on the right flank of the Union army rendered the White House no longer tenable as a base of supplies, and preparations were hastily made for its evacuation. On the evening of the 28th, everything wore a gloomy aspect. Railroad and telegraph communication with the front was severed, and Dispatch Station was in possession of the enemy. Innumerable transports, laden to their fullest capacity with government stores, were moving away, and huge piles, remaining for want of transportation, were prepared for destruction by surrounding them with hay and saturating them with whiskey. The dense clouds of black smoke grandly rolling up towards the sky, at length indicated the nature of operations at White House.

At four p. m., Colonel Sinclair, in command of the companies at Tunstall's Station, received orders to march to White House without delay. On the way he was twice urged forward by orders from General Stoneman, and finally directed to throw away everything except arms and cartridge boxes, and move at double-quick. The enemy followed closely, but made no demonstration. Upon its arrival at the landing, the command immediately embarked, the other five companies having already departed. The view of the shore was inexpressibly grand, and in strong contrast with the appearance it presented a few days previous. Where everything had been one busy scene of action—the whole plain a vast storehouse, was now swept by the destructive flames.

Proceeding via Fortress Monroe and James river, the regiment, passing on the way the wrecks of the *Congress* and *Cumberland,* vividly recalling the struggle of these two noble crafts with the powerful ironclad *Merrimac,* arrived at Harrison's Landing on the 1st of July. During the night the wagon trains from McClellan's discomfited columns began to arrive, and towards morning brigade after brigade came pouring in. A sad spectacle was presented as the worn and thinned regiments, just from the fields of the seven days' battles, many not larger than a full company, came toiling in through the mud. The wounded, barely able to walk, yet eager to escape capture, dragged themselves along and reached the landing in a state well nigh to death. The meeting of the Sixth with its comrades of the division was touching indeed, their greatly reduced numbers enabling the regiment to fully realize how dreadfful had been the late contest before Richmond.

On the 4th the Sixth was transferred to the First Brigade. The regiment at this time exchanged its arms for the Springfield rifles, and did skirmish duty alternately with the Kane Rifles. The band which had hitherto been connected with it, was on the 10th, mustered out of service. From the Peninsula it moved by water on the night of the 14th of August, reached Acquia creek on the morning of the 16th, and the same day was sent by rail to Falmouth. At dark on the evening of the 21st, with the division, it marched towards Kelly's Ford, on the Rappahannock, but by attempting to take a short route, the command became detached and scattered, so that nearly the whole night was spent in fruitless wanderings. The next day a long and unusually severe march was made, reaching Kelly's Ford at dark. The march was resumed on the following day in the direction of Rappahannock Station, which place was reached just in time to see a column of rebels beat a hasty retreat under a galling fire from Captain Matthew's Battery, First Pennsylvania Artillery. On the 24th, it reached Warrenton and encamped on the Sulphur Springs road, remaining several days.

The regiment was sent out on the 26th to guard a signal station on a neighboring mountain, but finding no trace of the signal party, returned to camp. The contending forces were preparing for a desperate encounter upon the field of Bull Run. On the 27th, the division marched on the Alexandria and Lynchburg pike, crossed the line of the enemy's march, and encamped at New Baltimore. On the morning of the 28th, as the command approached Gainsville, it was suddenly brought to a halt by a rebel battery, which opened fire from a wood some distance to the left of the Centreville pike. A line of battle was immediately formed and Captain Cooper's Rifled Battery replied with telling effect, soon silencing the enemy's guns. A portion of the Sixth was deployed as skirmishers, and moved forward across the open fields. No further demonstrations were made, and the command reached the Alexandria pike, where it bivouacked for the night.

On the morning of the 29th, the command was early under arms, and moving towards the enemy's positions near Groveton. Advancing some distance it came upon an open plain where it took position on the extreme left of the Union line, and pushed immediately out through a piece of wood. A rebel battery which had been posted on an elevation about a half mile to the left and a little to the rear of the line of the division, now opened fire upon it. With a view of getting upon the enemy's right flank, the division was immediately faced about and marched a short distance to the rear, remaining in no single position any length of time, but making a demonstration first at one point and then at another, constantly under the enemy's fire, but not firing a single shot in return. Late in the afternoon an attack was made on the right by General King and at the same time a demonstration was made on the left by General Reynolds. Moving forward through the wood, across the cornfield in front, under a galling fire from the battery occupying a high position only a few hundred yards distant, the Reserves reached the base of the elevation upon which the rebel force was stationed. This position was so completely under the hill that the rebels could scarcely depress their guns sufficiently to affect the lines of the Reserves. The Sixth advanced up a ravine to the right flank of the battery, with orders to capture it if possible. After reconnoitering the position and becoming satisfied that the battery, which was supported by a heavy infantry force, could not be taken, the fact was reported to General Reynolds, who speedily withdrew the division to the rear, and afterwards to the same grounds occupied the evening before. During the night the position of the division was very imprudently disclosed by the kindling of fires in the rear, for the purpose of making coffee; seeing which, the rebels opened fire from one of their batteries, which became very annoying. Singularly enough one of the first shots fired struck one of the men who had been its cause and carried away his arm.

On the morning of the 30th, the sun rose cloudless, and everything was quiet and calm upon that field soon to be made the scene of carnage and death. Troops began to move early, preparatory to the day's work. The Reserves marched to the left of the Warrenton pike, near Groveton, where the Sixth was ordered to the support of Cooper's Rifled Battery of the First Pennsylvania Artillery. In the meantime the skirmishers proceeded on past Groveton, and met the rebel skirmishers in the woods beyond. The regiment was then moved to the left and forward to a position slightly in the rear of the advanced line of skirmishers, covering the left flank of the division. This position was held until relieved by the advance of Porter's Corps, when the division was marched to the rear about two hundred yards, and massed on the top of a hill from which the operations of Porter's troops were plainly visible. Steadily the enemy was compelled to retire, until reinforced, when Porter was driven back with loss. The Reserve Division was ordered to form across their line of retreat, behind which they might rally and re-form. The First and Second Brigades had scarcely moved from their position, when the enemy appeared immediately to the left, and the Third Brigade, of which the Sixth was a part, was compelled to resist its advance. Gallantly did it perform its duty, but was obliged to retire before superior force. At this time General Reynolds was ordered to take position to the right of the Henry house, on the hill south of the Warrenton pike, a short distance from its junction with the Manassas road. The artillery was formed on the brow of the hill, and the division drawn up in column of brigade for its support. A brisk artillery duel lasted for some time, when the enemy in well dressed lines started forward, evidently intent on securing the road which lay between the contending forces. Immediately the word "forward" was given, and the Reserves swept down the hill with headlong impetuosity, reaching the bank at the upper side of the road, as the enemy was approaching the fence on the lower, and sprang down the bank into the road before them. The rebels, dismayed at the rapidity and success of the movement, turned and fled in confusion, under a terrific fire from the charging column. Thus was the enemy repulsed and an important position retained. In this charge the flag of the Sixth was shot from the staff while in the hands of Major Madill. It was instantly taken by the gallant Reynolds, who, holding it aloft, dashed along the line, the wind catching it about his noble form. The sight inspired the men to deeds of greater valor, and for an instant they paused in the midst of battle and gave a tremendous and soul-stirring cheer for their commander. Returning again to the hill, after resting an hour, night coming on, the division marched toward Centreville and bivouacked at Cub Run. The loss in this sanguinary battle, extending through three days, was six killed, thirty wounded and eight missing.

On the 31st it moved to Centreville, where, for the first time since the 24th, full and adequate rations were issued. The regiment was placed on picket near Cub Run, and remained through the following day. At 5 p. m. of September 1st, it was relieved and followed the division to Fairfax Court House, rejoining it at nine. The march was resumed on the following morning, the command passing through Annandale and Bailey's Cross Roads, to Hunter's Chapel, where it encamped for the night. Subsequently it removed to Munson's Hill.

On the evening of the 6th of September the regiment marched with the division across Long Bridge, through Washington, Leesboro', Poplar Springs and New Market, and shortly after noon on the 13th encamped on the west bank of the Monocacy creek. The following morning it moved via Frederick City and Middletown (Md.) to South Mountain, where the enemy was posted in large force, and took position in column of companies on the extreme right of the army. The line of battle advanced a considerable distance toward the summit, the enemy being compelled to fall back upon its supports. An attempt was made at this point by the Sixth to dash up the mountain side, with a view of getting on his flank. The movement was, however, discovered and the rebel lines again yielded without affording the regiment an opportunity to open fire. It then moved forward to a piece of woods near cleared land, on which the enemy hotly contested its advance. The time for earnest work had now come. The top of the mountain was only a few hundred yards distant, and when reached, would end the battle on that part of the field. Night was fast approaching and the battle raged furiously for many miles to the left. Five companies of the Sixth were ordered to seize and hold the knob of the mountain immediately in front. They marched from the wood, passed the enemy's flank and firing into it one volley made straight for the mountain top. When within one hundred yards they received the fire of the enemy protected by a ledge of rocks which capped the summit. The numbers of the enemy were largely in excess of this attacking force, but the men of the Sixth, who had been restrained in the earlier part of the battle, dashed like steeds released from the curb, against the very muzzles of their guns. The enemy, staggered by the impetuosity of the charge, yielded the first ledge of rocks and retreated to the second, from behind which he delivered a most galling fire, causing the advance to reel under the shock and threatening its annihilation. The rebel line to the left, which had been passed by these companies, had in the meantime been compelled to yield to the persistent hammering of the other regiments of the Reserves. The cheers of the brigade were distinctly heard by both, when the rebels broke in spirit by the severity of their losses and the determined front presented by the Reserves, fled down the mountain side. These five companies had performed an important service and driven before them in confusion the Eighth Alabama Regiment. The loss was twelve men killed, two officers and thirty-nine men wounded.

Remaining on the mountain until daylight, it having been ascertained that the enemy had retreated, the regiment with the brigade marched to Keedysville and encamped for the night near a mill on Antietam creek. On the morning of the 16th a general forward movement was made, the Sixth moving with the brigade across the creek where the enemy's line was found posted to resist further advance. The Bucktails were ordered forward as skirmishers, with the Sixth Regiment in support. Emerging from a wood the Bucktails soon became hotly engaged and the Sixth rushed to their assistance. The two regiments gained the contested ground, but it being already dark and no disposition to advance being manifest, the fire slackened and the lines were established for the night, the Sixth occupying the edge of the wood next to the cornfield. The night was very dark and the men slept on their arms ready at a moment's notice to repel an attack. The gray dawn at last appeared, and every man nerved himself for the conflict. The death-like stillness was at length broken, and the enemy advanced under cover of the corn. The caution was given to "fire low," and the sharp report of musketry soon marked the commencement of this fierce battle. The position was held, notwithstanding the persistent efforts of the enemy to advance, until the troops which had been pressed forward into the cornfield were compelled to retire, when the enemy gained the wood and subjected the Sixth to a flank as well as front fire. The line to the right having yielded, several of the rebel batteries concentrated their fire on the wood, which after unsuccessful attempts to clear it was abandoned, and, for the first time since the opening of the contest, firing ceased. Moving to the right, the division took a position in support of artillery, where it remained the balance of the day unengaged but subjected to the artillery fire of the enemy. In this engagement the regiment was much protected by the woods, yet sustained an aggregate loss of one hundred and thirty-two.

Resting on the battlefield during the following day, in which General Lee silently withdrew his forces, on the 19th it marched to the banks of the Potomac near Sharpsburg, where it remained until the 26th of October. During this period much attention was given to the discipline of the regiment, and it left camp one of the best drilled of the division, which reputation it maintained ever after. It marched via Berlin and Hamilton, crossing the Potomac on the 29th to Warrenton, where it arrived on the 6th of November and went into camp on the ground occupied by the Reserves a few days previous to the second battle of Bull Run. The camp at Warrenton was broken on the 11th and the march resumed through Fayetteville, Bealton Station, Morrisville, Grove Church, Hartwood and Stafford Court House, to Brooks' Station on the Acquia Creek and Fredericksburg Railroad, where a very comfortable camp was formed.

The movements preliminary to the battle of Fredericksburg began December 8th, when the Sixth with the brigade marched from Brooks' Station and reached the hills on the north side of the Rappahannock, overlooking Fredericksburg on the 11th. On the morning of the 12th it crossed the river on a pontoon bridge about three miles below the city. A line of battle was formed at right angles with the river, the left of the brigade resting upon it. This position was held until daybreak of the 13th, when the pickets became engaged, and the brigade, the Sixth in advance, crossing a small stream under a dense fog marched through a cornfield to the Bowling Green road where the line was re-formed. The regiment advanced as skirmishers and drove the enemy from the crest of the hill and from their shelter behind fences and the railroad embankment. The battle now raged furiously. The enemy's second line proved a formidable obstacle, but soon yielded to the impetuosity of the Reserves. Moving along up hill, followed closely by the brigade, it reached a road running along the brow of the hill near which a third line was encountered and a terrific fight ensued, ending in the discomfiture of the rebels. The regiment had now lost one-third of its entire number, the brigade had suffered heavily and Colonel Sinclair had been borne from the field wounded, when the enemy was detected moving through the woods to the right in large numbers. At the same time a terrific fire of musketry was opened on the left of the brigade. The line began to waver and no supporting troops being at hand it finally yielded, and the regiment with the brigade fell back over the same ground on which it had advanced. In this battle, of the three hundred men who went into action, ten were killed, ninety-two wounded and nineteen missing. Moving to the opposite side of the river on the 20th, the regiment went into camp near Belle Plain.

After having participated in the celebrated "mud march" it returned to its old camp and remained there until the 7th of February, 1863, when it was ordered to Alexandria to join the Twenty-second Corps. It did guard and picket duty until the 27th of March and then moved to Fairfax Station, where it remained until the 25th of June, when it moved to join the Army of the Potomac and participate in the memorable Gettysburg campaign. Marching via Dranesville, Edwards Ferry and Frederick, the regiment joined the army on the 28th, and was again assigned to the Fifth Corps. Continuing the march through Uniontown and Hanover, it reached Gettysburg at 2 o'clock p. m. of July 2nd, and made a charge from Little Round Top with but small loss. Remaining in front during the night, on the morning of the 3rd skirmishing commenced, which continued through the entire day. Towards evening another charge was made, capturing a number of prisoners, recapturing one gun and five caissons, and relieving a large number of Union prisoners. In this encounter the Sixth remained on the skirmish line until 2 p. m. of the 4th, when it was relieved and bivouacked on Little Round Top. It sustained a loss of two men killed, a lieutenant and twenty-one men wounded.

Pursuing the retreating rebels to Falling Waters, constantly skirmishing on the way, it encamped on the 14th, after having captured some prisoners near Sharpsburg, when it was ascertained that the rebel army had escaped across the river. Marching and an occasional skirmish and reconnaissance occupied the time until August 18th, when the regiment arrived at Rappahannock Station and remained until the 15th of September, when it left for Culpeper Court House, which it reached on the 16th and went into camp two miles beyond the town, where it remained until October 10th. Returning it recrossed the river on the 12th and encountered the enemy at Bristoe Station on the 15th, having three men wounded by his shells. On the 19th it crossed Bull Run and bivouacked on the old battleground. The march was continued on the next day through New Baltimore to Auburn, and from thence, on the 7th of November, to Rappahannock Station, crossing the river on the 8th and on the 10th taking possession of the rebel barracks, where it remained until the 24th. It again crossed the river on the 26th at Wykoff's Ford, and moving out on the road towards Gordonsville met the enemy at New Hope Church. The Sixth was deployed as skirmishers and sent forward to the support of the cavalry, which was now engaged. Two charges of the rebels were repulsed by the left wing of the regiment. Its loss was two killed and four wounded.

On the 5th of December the regiment went into winter quarters near Kettle Run, where it was engaged during the winter on guard duty. Preparations had been carefully made for the spring campaign, and breaking camp on the 29th of April it marched to near Culpeper, and on the 4th of May crossed the river at Germania Ford, halting at the Wilderness Tavern. On the following day the Wilderness campaign opened. It was actively engaged on the 5th, 6th and 7th, contesting with great gallantry every inch of ground. On the 7th Captain Allen, of company G, was wounded. At Spottsylvania, on the 8th, it was engaged in heavy fighting nearly the entire day, and on the 9th moved to the right of the line and built rifle-pits. On the 10th it made two unsuccessful charges upon the enemy's works, and again on the 12th. The loss during these engagements was thirteen killed, sixty-four wounded and nine missing. Constantly upon the skirmish and picket line, the Sixth met the enemy on every field with unflinching courage. On the 22nd it captured ninety men of Hill's Corps. At length the final day of its service arrived, and with it the crowning success of the Reserves at Bethesda Church. The regiment was deployed as skirmishers and had gained the Mechanicsville road, near the church, when it was attacked by an overwhelming force and compelled to retire with considerable loss. It then threw up a rifle-pit, upon which the enemy impetuously charged. Retaining its fire until the approaching foe was near, it poured forth a volley which inflicted most terrible slaughter. Although but about one hundred and fifty strong, the Sixth captured one hundred tnd two prisoners and buried seventy-two dead rebels in its immediate front. Two officers of the Sixth were wounded and nineteen men captured.

After three years of service in the camp and on the march, from its initial victory at Dranesville to its final brilliant success at Bethesda Church, sharing always the privations and hardships of the Army of the Potomac as well as the glory which clusters around its name, the regiment on the 1st of June started for Pennsylvania, where with the Reserves it was enthusiastically received, arrived at the State capital on the 6th and on the 14th was mustered out of service.

ROLL OF COMPANY G, THIRTY-FIFTH REGIMENT (SIXTH RESERVES, THREE YEARS' SERVICE).

Captains.

*Jacob Rehrer, April 22, 1861; discharged on surgeon's certificate, November 10, 1862.

Charles Allen, April 18, 1861; promoted from first lieutenant to captain, April 3, 1863; brevet major, March 13, 1865; wounded at Fred-

*Dead.

192 CHRONICLES OF MIDDLETOWN.

ericksburg, Dec. 13, 1862, and Wilderness, May 7, 1864; mustered out with company, June 11, 1864.

First Lieutenant.

*B. F. Ashenfelter, April 18, 1861; promoted from second lieutenant, April 3, 1863; brevet captain, March 13, 1863; mustered out with company, June 11, 1864.

Second Lieutenants.

*John Yentzer, April, 1861; resigned Nov. 15, 1861.
John McWilliams, April 18, 1861; promoted from first sergeant to second lieutenant, April 3, 1863; mustered out with company, June 11, 1864.

First Sergeants.

Joseph B. Rife, April 22, 1861; discharged Aug. 5, 1861, to accept promotion as second lieutenant, 6th U. S. Infantry.
George W. Horn, July 24, 1861; killed in action, May 9, 1864; buried in Wilderness burial ground.

Sergeants.

John R. Stoner, June 5, 1861; promoted to sergeant, April 1, 1862; mustered out with company, June 11, 1864.
Wall. W. Johnson, July 22, 1861; promoted to sergeant, April 11, 1863; mustered out with company, June 11, 1864.
B. R. Hayhurst, April 22, 1861; mustered out with company, June 11, 1864.
John A. Bonner, April 18, 1861; discharged on surgeon's certificate, March 23, 1863.
*James H. Stanley, April 18, 1861; transferred to 191st Regt., P. V., May 31, 1864; veteran.

Corporals.

George W. Gray, April 22, 1861; wounded at North Anna, May 23, 1864; absent at muster out.
Joseph H. Peters, April 19, 1861; mustered out with company, June 11, 1864.
George W. Cole, April 20, 1861; transferred to 191st Regt., P. V., May 31, 1864; veteran.
John D. Books, April 18, 1861; transferred to 191st Regt., P. V., May 31, 1864; veteran.
Lorenzo Horn, April 18, 1861; transferred to 191st Regt., P. V., May 31, 1864; veteran.
Thomas H. Abbott, April 19, 1861; promoted to sergeant-major, April 11, 1863.

*Dead.

Union Hose House.

CHRONICLES OF MIDDLETOWN. 193

William Fitting, April 22, 1861; killed at Fredericksburg, Dec. 13, 1862.

Jacob Shapley, January 1, 1864; not on muster-out roll; veteran.

Samuel Sides, Dec. 22, 1863; not on muster-out roll; veteran.

Calvin McClung, Dec. 22, 1863; not on muster-out roll; veteran.

Privates.

Alleman, Benj. F., April 18, 1861; discharged on surgeon's certificate, Oct. 29, 1862.

Baskins, George W., May 3, 1861; mustered out with company, June 11, 1864.

Bishop, Jacob, May 3, 1861; mustered out with company, June 11, 1864.

Berst, Levi, July 15, 1861; mustered out with company, June 11, 1864.

Breckbill, Pierce, April 18, 1861; mustered out with company, June 11, 1864.

Bear, Henry A., April 18, 1861; transferred to 191st Regt., P. V., May 31, 1864; veteran.

Barnes, Simon, April 18, 1861; transferred to 191st Regt., P. V., May 31, 1864; veteran.

*Bomberger, Michael, Sept. 5, 1861; transferred to 191st Regt., P. V., May 31, 1864; veteran.

Burg, William, May 1, 1861; died at Tenallytown, Aug. 5, 1861.

Bailey, Joseph, April 18, 1861; killed at Antietam, Sept. 18, 1862.

Curry, William M., July 15, 1861; mustered out with company, June 11, 1864.

*Chub, John, April 18, 1861; mustered out with company, June 11, 1864.

Cole, Alonzo, April 18, 1861; transferred from Veteran Reserve Corps; mustered out with company, June 11, 1864.

Camp, Simon C., April 18, 1861; mustered out with company, June 11, 1864.

Conroy, William, April 18, 1861; mustered out with company, June 11, 1864.

*Cain, William, April 19, 1861; discharged on surgeon's certificate, Dec. 27, 1861.

*Church, Geo. H., April 18, 1861; discharged March 20, 1863, for wounds received in action.

Cover, John, July 15, 1861; discharged Feb. 15, 1863, for wounds received in action.

Cornwell, Charles, April 22, 1861.

Depu, James F., April 18, 1862; absent, in hospital at muster out.

Dewalt, John, April 20, 1861; transferred to 191st Regt., P. V., May 31, 1864; veteran.

---

*Dead.

13

Dailey, Patrick, April 25, 1861; discharged on surgeon's certificate, Aug. 2, 1861.

Embick, Jacob A., April 20, 1861; mustered out with company, June 11, 1864.

Eichelberger, George, April 20, 1861; transferred to 191st Regt. P. V., May 31, 1864; veteran.

Etter, John C., April 18, 1861; discharged on surgeon's certificate, Dec. 11, 1863.

Eichelberger, H., Feb. 22, 1864; killed at Bethesda Church, May 30, 1864.

Elliott, Reuben, July 15, 1861.

Fish, Lewis, July 15, 1861; transferred to 191st Regt., P. V., May 31, 1864; veteran.

Fisher, Peter H., April 28, 1861.

*Giverren, Patrick, May 1, 1861; mustered out with company, June 11, 1864.

Gosline, James D., July 22, 1861; absent, in hospital at muster out.

Graybill, Jacob, April 22, 1861; transferred to 191st Regt., P. V., May 31, 1864; veteran.

*Garrigan, James, April 23, 1861; discharged on surgeon's certificate, June, 1862.

*Gibbons, Jacob, May 1, 1861; discharged on surgeon's certificate, Oct. 8, 1862.

Goss, George W., Sept. 1, 1861; transferred to 191st Regt., P. V., May 31, 1864; veteran.

Gould, James S., Feb. 1, 1862; discharged on surgeon's certificate, Feb. 10, 1863.

Geist, James, May 1, 1861; died at Alexandria, Jan. 24, 1862; grave 700.

Hughes, Christian, April 20, 1861; mustered out with company, June 11, 1864.

Hemperly, Geo. L., April 22, 1861; mustered out with company, June 11, 1864.

Hain, Robert, April 22, 1861; mustered out with company, June 11, 1864.

Houser, Frederick M., July 10, 1861; transferred to 191st Regt., P. V., May 31, 1864; veteran.

Henderson, Martin, April 22, 1861; died Dec. 14, 1862, of wounds received in action.

*Jury, Adam, Jan. 16, 1864; transferred to 191st Regt., P. V., May 31, 1864.

Kough, Henry A., April 22, 1861; discharged on surgeon's certificate, July 2, 1862.

Kohler, Charles, Feb. 4, 1864; transferred to 191st Regt., P. V., May 31, 1864.

---

*Dead.

CHRONICLES OF MIDDLETOWN. 195

*Linn, Jacob, April 18, 1861; mustered out with company, June 11, 1864.
*Lockard, John, May 1, 1861; transferred to 191st Regt., P. V., May 31, 1864; veteran.
Lemon, John, May 1, 1861; transferred to 191st Regt., P. V., May 31, 1864; veteran.
Leggore, William, Sept. 13, 1861; transferred to 191st Regt., P. V., May 31, 1864; veteran.
*Lloyd, John, March 7, 1864; transferred to 191st Regt., P. V., May 31, 1864.
Montgomery, John, April 20, 1861; transferred to 191st Regt., P. V., May 31, 1864; veteran.
Montgomery, William, April 20, 1861; transferred to 191st Regt., P. V., May 31, 1864; veteran.
Manly, Amos, April 18, 1861; transferred to 191st Regt., P. V., May 31, 1864; veteran.
Martin, Jacob G., April 19, 1861; transferred to 191st Regt., P. V., May 31, 1864; veteran.
Marquit, Andrew B., April 20, 1861; discharged on surgeon's certificate, date unknown.
Mushon, Francis, April 19, 1861; transferred to gunboat service, Feb. 10, 1862.
Murphy, Bernard, Aug. 29, 1862; killed at Antietam, Sept. 17, 1862.
*Orth, William H. H., April 19, 1861.
Peirce, Cyrus H., April 19, 1861; mustered out with company, June 11, 1864.
Peirce, George W., April 19, 1861; mustered out with company, June 11, 1864.
*Peters, John W., April 18, 1861; mustered out with company, June 11, 1864.
Powell, James, April 18, 1861; discharged on surgeon's certificate, May 16, 1863.
Peters, John M., July 1, 1861; killed at Antietam, Sept. 17, 1862.
Penneman, Robert, Sept. 1, 1861; killed at Gettysburg, July 3, 1863.
Quinsler, William, May 3, 1861; transferred to 191st Regt., P. V., May 31, 1864; veteran.
Rouse, Franklin, April 18, 1861; discharged on surgeon's certificate, May 13, 1862.
Reichenbach, Peter, Oct. 14, 1861; discharged on surgeon's certificate, Oct. 27, 1862.
Roburm, James, March 8, 1864; died May 9, 1864; buried in Military Asylum Cemetery.
Sullivan, Cornelius, April 18, 1861; wounded at Spottsylvania Court House, May 9, 1864; absent, in hospital at muster out.

---

*Dead.

Snavely, John D., July 15, 1861; wounded at Spottsylvania Court House, May 12, 1864; absent, in hospital at muster out.
Strauss, Aaron G., April 24, 1861; discharged Feb. 20, 1863, for wounds received in action.
Stores, Jonas F., July 22, 1861; discharged on surgeon's certificate, April 3, 1862.
Specht, Henry D., Nov. 28, 1861; transferred to 191st Regt., P. V., May 31, 1864; veteran.
Simmer, Charles, Sept. 13, 1861; dicharged on surgeon's certificate, Feb. 10, 1863.
Stehman, Henry C., April 20, 1861; discharged on surgeon's certificate, March 23, 1863.
Strickland, William, Feb. 2, 1864; transferred to 191st Regt., May 31, 1864.
Smith, Edgar, May 1, 1861; died, May 16, 1863.
Spencer, Lewis, May 10, 1861; killed at Spottsylvania Court House, May 12, 1864; buried in burial ground at Wilderness.
Smith, Daniel, Feb. 22, 1864; killed at Spottsylvania Court House, May 12, 1864; buried in burial ground at Wilderness.
Swigart, Aaron, April 19, 1861.
Swords, John, May 29, 1861; not on muster-out roll.
Townsend, W. Ford, May 1, 1861; commissioned second lieutenant, Dec. 4, 1861; not mustered; mustered out with company, June 11, 1864.
Vincent, Robert W., April 20, 1861; discharged on surgeon's certificate, Oct. 4, 1862.
Walborn, Frank R., April 20, 1861; discharged on surgeon's certificate, Dec. 24, 1862.
Weist, Daniel, April 20, 1861; died Dec. 14, 1862, of wounds received at Fredericksburg.
Wilson, Daniel, April 20, 1861.

XLI

EIGHTY-SEVENTH REGIMENT PENNSYLVANIA VOLUNTEERS (THREE YEARS' SERVICE).

Regimental organization completed Sept. 25, 1861. May 26, 1862, marched to Baltimore. June 23rd, ordered to New Creek, W. Va. In August ordered to Rowlesburg in pursuit of Imboden and Jenkins. September 12th returned to Clarksburg. October 20th went to Buckhannon; 31st, moved to Beverly; thence crossed Cheat and Allegheny Mountains to (November 12th) Franklin; thence returned to New

---
*Dead.
NOTE: These rolls contain the names of those who enlisted from here, and of those residents here, between 1861 and 1865, who enlisted elsewhere.

Creek. December 6th, to Petersburg; thence to Moorfield; thence, December 18th, in pursuit of Imboden, through Wardensville, Capon Springs and Strasburg, to Winchester, arriving on the 24th. In May, 1863, the regiment was ordered to Webster, on the B. & O. R. R., to look after straggling bands of rebels. On the 20th returned to Winchester. June 12th, on reconnoisance in direction of Strasburg, where it had an engagement with the enemy. Battle on 13th and 14th; retreated to Harper's Ferry; 16th crossed to Maryland Heights. July 1st, Maryland Heights evacuated; Eighty-seventh detailed to guard boats which carried quartermasters' stores to Georgetown, arrived on the 4th, and 7th joined the Army of the Potomac at Middletown (Md.). Participated in the engagement at Manassas Gap, July 23rd; at Bealton Station, October 26th; Kelly's Ford, November 7th; Brandy Station, November 8th; Locust Grove, November 27th, and at Mine Run, November 30th. Went into winter quarters at Brandy Station. Here one hundred and eighty of the men re-enlisted and were given a veteran furlough.

The Eighty-seventh bore a part in the battles of the Wilderness and Spottsylvania, but without serious loss. In the actions of the 1st and 3rd of June, 1864, at Cold Harbor, the regiment sustained a loss in killed and wounded of about one-third of its strength. With the corps it moved from Cold Harbor, crossing the Chickahominy to the James. It moved by boats from Wilcox Landing to Bermuda Hundred, where it remained three days with General Butler's command, then crossed the Appomattox and took position in front of Petersburg on the extreme left of the army. June 23rd, with part of the Sixth Corps, it moved upon the Weldon Railroad, tore up the track for a considerable distance, and had an engagement with the enemy. July 6th it moved with the division to Frederick. In the battle of the Monocacy it suffered a heavier loss than in any other battle during its entire term of service. September 19th it moved with the army under Sheridan against the enemy at Opequan. The Eighty-seventh lost in this engagement sixty in killed and wounded. In the action of the 22nd, at Fisher's Hill, the regiment lost one killed and one wounded.

September 23rd, its term of service having expired, it was ordered (with the exception of veterans and recruits) to York, and October 13th mustered out of service. The veterans and recruits were formed into a battalion of five companies. This battalion took part in the battle of Cedar Creek, October 19th. In March, 1865, five new companies were added to the battalion, making it a full regiment. April 2nd it participated in a charge upon the works before Petersburg, losing two officers and five men killed, and three officers and twenty-three men wounded. It was also engaged at Sailor's Creek on the 6th. Was finally mustered out at Alexandria on the 29th of June, 1865.

CHRONICLES OF MIDDLETOWN.

ROLL OF MIDDLETOWN VOLUNTEERS IN THE EIGHTY-SEVENTH REGIMENT.

Captain.

Solomon F. Cover, Co. I, March 16, 1865; 1 year; absent—sick at muster out.

First Lieutenant.

Caleb H. Rowe, Co. I, March 16, 1865; 1 year; resigned June 16, 1865.

Sergeants.

William Drabenstadt, Co. B, Sept. 14, 1861; 3 years; promoted from corporal, June 1, 1864; discharged Oct. 14, 1864—expiration of term.
John Burns, Co. I, Feb. 16, 1865; 1 year; mustered out with company, June 29, 1865.

Corporals.

*John A. Hiney, Co. B, Sept. 14, 1861; 3 years; absent—sick at expiration of term.
Lucas Shurer, Co. B, Sept. 14, 1861; 3 years; wounded June 23, 1864. Absent at expiration of term.

Privates.

*Bently, John, Co. B, Sept. 14, 1861; 3 years; died Oct. 19, 1861.
Crawford, William, Co. I, Feb. 15, 1865; 1 year; discharged by general order, June 16, 1865.
*Drabenstadt, Frank, Co. B, Feb. 15, 1861; 3 years; captured June 23, 1864; died at Andersonville.
Davis, John, Co. I, Feb. 16, 1865; 1 year; discharged on surgeon's certificate, May 16, 1865.
Eshinower, George, Co. I, March 11, 1865; 1 year; mustered out with company, June 29, 1865.
Fishburn, John L., Co. I, Feb. 20, 1865; 1 year; mustered out with company, June 29, 1865.
Fenzel, Francis, Co. I, March 14, 1865; 1 year; mustered out with company, June 29, 1865.
Forney, William, Co. I, March 14, 1865; 1 year; mustered out with company, June 29, 1865.
Green, John, Co. I, March 2, 1865; 1 year; mustered out with company, June 29, 1865.
Guistewite, John, Co. I, March 8, 1865; 1 year; mustered out with company, June 29, 1865.
Kendrick, James, Co. B, Sept. 14, 1861; 3 years; discharged Oct. 13, 1864—expiration of term.

---

*Dead.

*Lutz, Adam, Co. I, March 14, 1865; 1 year; died at Philadelphia, Pa., May 25, 1865.
Manning, Jacob, Co. I, March 9, 1865; 1 year; mustered out with company, June 29, 1865.
McCann, Jacob B., Co. I, Feb. 15, 1865; 1 year; mustered out with company, June 29, 1865.
McCann, M. W., Co. I, Feb. 15, 1865; 1 year; mustered out with company, June 29, 1865.
*Mattis, Silas, Co. B, Sept. 14, 1861; 3 years; absent—sick at expiration of term.
Mattis, Jesse, Co. I, Feb. 28, 1865; 1 year; mustered out with company, June 29, 1865.
*Myers, John, Co. B, Sept. 14, 1861; 3 years; discharged Oct. 13, 1864—expiration of term.
*Noll, John S., Co. I, March 11, 1865; 1 year; mustered out with company, June 29, 1865.
*Price, Thomas, Co. B, Sept. 14, 1861; 3 years; discharged on surgeon's certificate, May 3, 1863.
Ridley, Jacob, Co. I, Feb. 28, 1865; 1 year; absent—sick at muster out.
Roop, David, Co. I, March 7, 1865; 1 year; mustered out with company, June 29, 1865.
*Ritzel, John, Co. I, March 11, 1865; 1 year; killed at Petersburg, Va., April 2, 1865.
*Ruth, Henry D., Co. I, March 13, 1865; 1 year; died at City Point.
Sides Michael, Co. I, Feb. 21, 1865; 1 year; mustered out with company, June 29, 1865.
*Welker, Henry H., Co. I, Feb. 27, 1864; 1 year; died at Washington, D. C., April 6, 1865; buried in National Cemetery, Arlington, Va.

NINETY-SECOND PENNSYLVANIA, NINTH CAVALRY. (THREE YEARS' SERVICE.)

The Ninth Cavalry, first known as the Lochiel Cavalry, was organized August 29, 1861, and rendezvoused at Camp Cameron. November 20th it went by rail to Pittsburgh, and thence by boat to Louisville, Ky., where it went into camp on the opposite side of the Ohio river, at Jeffersonville, Ind. By January 10, 1862, the regiment had acquired such proficiency in drill that it was ordered to the front. On the advance of Generals Buell and Mitchell it was detailed to remain for the protection of Kentucky, and divided into three battalions. On the 5th of March the regiment was ordered into Tennessee. On the 4th of May the Third Battalion first met the enemy, under Morgan, at Lebanon, where with the Seventh Pennsylvania and the Third Kentucky Cavalry, it most signally defeated that daring partizan, capturing his second in command and 293 of his men, Morgan himself narrowly escaping capture by swim-

---
*Dead.

ming the Cumberland river. On the 14th of May the Third captured his rear guard at Spring Creek, and pushing on forced him into the Cumberland Mountains, where his command scattered over the various roads leading to Chattanooga. On the 3rd of June the Third advanced to Tompkinsville, Ky., and on the 6th defeated a largely superior force, under Colonel Hamilton, at Moore's Hill, losing in the engagement five killed and ten badly wounded. On July 9th, 1862, Morgan, with 2,000 men, advanced against Tompkinsville; there were but 200 men in the post to oppose him, and they, after maintaining an unequal contest for two hours, retired to Burksville, Ky. In this engagement, while the loss of the enemy was 57 killed and 140 wounded, the battalion lost but ten killed, fourteen wounded and nineteen taken prisoners. After the battle of Richmond, Ky., on the 30th, the regiment, in connection with the Ninth Kentucky Cavalry, covered the retreat of General Nelson to Louisville, fighting daily the enemy's advance. At Shelbyville it had a sharp encounter, defeating Jenkins, killing 27 of his men and capturing 44. Upon General Buell's arrival, in conjunction with the Second Michigan, it took the advance to Perryville, and by its boldness in pushing the enemy's rear brought on the sanguinary battle fought there, sustaining the fire of his infantry until relieved by General McCook's Corps. It then formed on the right of the line, and by its steadiness, foiled every attempt of the enemy's cavalry to turn its flank. In this action it had ten killed and twenty-seven wounded. In general orders, after the action, General Buell says: "The Ninth Pennsylvania Cavalry behaved most bravely, being at one time compelled to stand for three quarters of an hour under the concentrated fire of three batteries of the enemy's artillery, and only retired when ordered to do so." By this time the regiment was much weakened by hard service, and one-half the men were dismounted. It was therefore ordered to Louisville for fresh horses and equipments.

On the 22nd of December, in company with the Second Michigan, the regiment started on a raid upon the railroads communicating with the rebel capital. The command took to the deer paths of Pine, Cumberland and Clinch Mountains. These mountains are as cheerless, dark and savage as when Boone first saw them; at this point are one hundred miles wide, and can only be crossed by following the paths made by deer and Indians ages ago. It is difficult to form an adequate conception of the hardships the troops encountered on this march. January 1, 1863, it reached the Virginia and Tennessee Railroad at the Wautauga Bridge, and encountered a company of the enemy, under command of Gen. Humphrey Marshall, strongly entrenched. The place was carried by assault and the bridge burned. The captured prisoners were paroled and the command moved down the railroad to where it crosses the Holstein river. This bridge was defended by an entrenched force of 250 men. The works were stormed and the entire force taken prisoners. In this action the Ninth lost six killed and twenty wounded. The badly wounded were left with the paroled enemy. Leaving the Holstein

Bridge and destroying a mile long tressel work, the command commenced their return; by strategy, enterprise and rapidity of movement, it eluded a force of 8,000 of the enemy, under Marshall, and recrossed the Cumberland Mountains over the same paths by which it had advanced. The success of this raid, in the face of a greatly superior force, so chagrined the rebels, that Marshall was relieved of his command and never afterwards restored. The regiment reached Nicholasville, whence it had started, on the night of the 19th of January, with two-thirds of its men dismounted, the animals having been over one hundred miles without food. In this raid the Ninth lost thirty killed and one hundred wounded.

After a few days' rest the regiment marched to Louisville, was remounted, and proceeded thence by rail to Nashville. On the 2nd of February it went to Franklin, where, after a sharp skirmish, General Forrest's Brigade of the enemy was driven from the town. The regiment now formed the right wing of the army of the Cumberland; confronting it was the left wing of the enemy, a force of 12,000 cavalry, under General Van Dorn. For eighteen days the Ninth, aided by three hundred men from the Second Michigan Cavalry, confronted this strong rebel force, deceiving them as to their strength by frequent attacks upon their advanced positions. On the 4th of March Van Dorn advanced to storm the post, but a division of infantry having arrived on the night of the 3rd, the whole command advanced to meet him, and after a hotly contested engagement, lasting six hours, the enemy was driven back to his original position. In this action the regiment had twelve killed and fifty-one wounded. On the 5th the Ninth advanced and engaged the enemy, driving them from their position and holding the ground until the infantry formed and advanced to their relief. The action proved disastrous to the Union arms, and Colonel Colburn, with 3,800 infantry was captured; but the Ninth, under Colonel Jordan, fought their way back to Franklin, bringing off 220 prisoners, the entire artillery and baggage train of the army, and as many wounded as the ambulances could carry. For the heroic part borne by the regiment in this action, it was mentioned in special orders by General Rosecrans.

In the campaign against Bragg the Ninth took part, and with the First Brigade, First Division of the cavalry under General Stanley, led the advance of our army. It fought in the battles of Rover, Middletown and Shelbyville; at the latter place charging the left flank of the enemy, while the Seventh Pennsylvania charged the centre, and in a most stubborn hand-to-hand encounter captured nearly a thousand prisoners, with the enemy's battery, breaking up entirely his cavalry organization. In the action at Elk river it attacked the left flank of the enemy and forced him from his position. At Cowan, a few days later, it captured 200 of the rear guard of Bragg. A few days before the battle of Chickamauga it captured at Lafayette, Ga., a part of the advance guard of General Longstreet. At Chickamauga it held the right of our line, and after the defeat of Cook's Corps, closed on the right of General Thomas and defended his flank during the remainder of the battle. For its conduct in this encounter the regiment was commended by General Thomas in most flattering terms.

In the winter of 1863 and spring of 1864, it was in East Tennessee, and fought in the battles of Dandridge, New Market, Mossy Creek and Fair Garden, capturing at the latter place the artillery of the enemy. The regiment having re-enlisted, was given a furlough of thirty days, and returned to Pennsylvania early in April. In May, having recruited its thinned ranks, to twelve hundred men, it was again in the field at Louisville. While waiting at this place for arms and horses, Morgan made his last raid into Kentucky. The Ninth at once volunteered to defend the State capital. Colonel Jordan, seizing the horses necessary to mount his command, and arming his men with muskets, they marched to Frankfort by night, fifty-four miles, and held the place, compelling Morgan to fall back to Pound Gap, where he was badly defeated by a force of cavalry in his rear, under General Burbridge.

The regiment then marched to Nashville, thence to Chattanooga, arriving on the 2nd of September. It was immediately ordered in pursuit of the rebel General Wheeler, who had started on a raid into Middle Tennessee. On the 6th, at Reedyville, it defeated General Dibbrell's Brigade of Wheeler's command, taking 294 prisoners. On the 7th it went, with other cavalry, after the retreating enemy, and on the same day defeated Colonel Anderson of the rebel General William's Division. The pursuit was continued on the 8th and 9th, the enemy constantly avoiding an engagement, although of more than double the number of the Union force. At Sparta the rebels took to the mountains, and passed into East Tennessee. In acknowledgment of the conduct of the troops in this command, of which the Ninth Pennsylvania constituted two-thirds, complimentary orders were issued by General Van Cleve, at Murfreesboro; General Milroy, at Tullahoma, and General Steedman, at Chattanooga.

The regiment then joined General Sherman at Marietta, Ga., and on the 14th of November started with that great chieftain on his "March to the Sea." It was assigned to the First Brigade, Third Division of Cavalry, under General Kilpatrick, and led the advance of the right wing of the army. On the 16th it encountered General Wheeler's Cavalry, entrenched at Lovejoy's Station, on the Macon Railroad. By a gallant charge the Ninth drove the enemy from his works, capturing four guns and over 300 prisoners; these guns were retained by the regiment until the close of the war.

Early in December it skirmished heavily with the enemy's cavalry near Macon, pushing them within the defenses of the city. In conjunction with Woolcott's Brigade of the Fifteenth Corps, it fought the battle of Bear Creek, defeating Wheeler, but suffering a loss of ninety-five killed and wounded. Moving to the left flank of the army it demonstrated towards Augusta, then southeast towards Millen, one of the southern prison-pens. Here Wheeler made a night attack, and at

Waynesboro another. In both he was defeated. Finding that the Union prisoners had been removed from Millen, the command turned towards Louisville, Ga. At Buckhead Creek, Wheeler made a heavy attack upon the Ninth, hoping to cut it off from the rest of the column; by a bold charge the enemy was beaten off. In all these engagements Wheeler's Cavalry outnumbered that opposed to him. Two days later, in conjunction with infantry it defeated Wheeler again at Buckhead Church; the following morning he was attacked in a position where he had barricaded himself, and in twenty minutes was in full retreat. At Waynesboro he was again defeated. On this day the command faced towards Savannah, where it arrived with the whole army on December 21st.

After a month's delay the regiment again took the field, marching through Robertsville, Barnville and Blackville, S. C.; at the latter place it again defeated a portion of Wheeler's command. Three days later Wheeler, reinforced by Hampton's Division, attacked with their whole force, but were signally defeated. Without pausing the brigade moved towards Columbia; at Lexington defeated a portion of Wheeler's rearguard and at Blacksnake Station, on the Columbia and Charlotte Railroad defeated another force of the enemy. Crossing the Catawba it entered North Carolina, then crossed the Great Pedee river and occupied Rockingham. March 11th it reached Fayetteville. After a few days of rest it moved towards Goldsboro, and on the 16th, at Averysboro, was engaged from 6 a. m. to 2 p. m. with McLaw's Division of the rebel army, capturing a large number of prisoners. In the brigade every twelfth man was killed or wounded.

On the 17th the command marched towards Bentonville, on the left flank of the Twentieth Corps, and with it participated in the hotly contested battle of the 19th, assisting materially in securing a triumph. After refitting and resting near Goldsboro, the cavalry again took the field on the 9th of April. Marching day and night, by a circuitous route, it struck the head of Johnston's retreating columns, and after a sanguinary conflict compelled the enemy to change his course.

On the morning of the 13th it passed through Raleigh and encountered the enemy, under Wheeler and Hampton, in position on the Hillsboro road. In this engagement the Ninth bore the brunt of the action. The enemy fell back, hotly pursued by the cavalry for ten miles, to Morrisville, where he again made a stand. The line was quickly formed, the charge sounded, and the position carried, the enemy retreating in the wildest confusion over the plain, broken into fragments by the plunging fire of the artillery from the heights overlooking the valley. The columns being again formed, started in pursuit, when a flag of truce was discovered approaching. It was received by the Ninth, under which was delivered the letter of General Joseph E. Johnston, directed to General Sherman, asking for a meeting to determine the terms of surrender of the army under his command. This was the last fighting done, and the last guns fired in Sherman's command were from the battery of the Ninth Pennsylvania Cavalry. From Morrisville the command marched to Durham, and the escort to General Sherman when he proceeded to the Burnet House to meet General Johnston, and again upon the occasion of agreeing to the terms of surrender, was furnished by this regiment. After the surrender the command moved through Greenville to Lexington, where it remained until the 18th of July, when it was mustered out of service. Returning to Pennsylvania it was finally disbanded and the war-worn veterans retired to their homes and the peaceful avocations of life.

ROLL OF MIDDLETOWN VOLUNTEERS IN THE NINTH CAVALRY.

Captain.

*Thomas W. Jordan, Co. H, May 23, 1863; 3 years; promoted from second to first lieutenant, May 30th, 1864; wounded at Readyville, Tenn., Sept. 6, 1864; commissioned captain, June 16, 1865; not mustered; mustered out with company, July 18, 1865.

Second Lieutenant.

Jacob S. Wilson, Co. H., Oct. 29, 1861; 3 years; promoted to quartermaster sergeant Jan. 1, 1864; commissioned second lieutenant June 16, 1865; not mustered; mustered out with company July 18, 1865; veteran.

Sergeants.

James H. Harvey, Co. C, Oct. 11, 1861; 3 years; promoted to first sergeant May 20, 1865; mustered out with company July 18, 1865; veteran.

Jacob Wolfley, Co. C, Oct. 11, 1861; promoted to sergeant Jan. 1, 1864; mustered out with company July 18, 1865; veteran.

Bugler.

John C. Beachler, Co. I, Aug. 13, 1864; 1 year, discharged by general order May 29, 1865.

Privates.

Brestle, Henry C., Co. C, Oct. 11, 1861; 3 years; discharged Dec. 24, 1864, expiration of term.

*Books, Jacob R., Co. C, Oct. 11, 1861; 3 years; killed accidentally at Louisville, Ky., Sept. 9, 1862.

Bretz, William H., Co. C, May 9, 1864; 1 year; discharged by general order May 29, 1865.

Barnet, Augustus N., Co. C, Aug. 9, 1864; 1 year; discharged by general order May 29, 1865.

*Boyd, George E., Aug. 13, 1864; 1 year; discharged by general order May 29, 1865.

---

*Dead.

Beachler, Jacob, Co. K., Aug. 10, 1864; 1 year; discharged by general order May 29, 1865.
Brinser, Abraham F., Co. C, Aug. 12, 1864; 1 year; wounded at Averysboro, N. C., March 16, 1865; absent in hospital at muster out.
Brubaker, Thomas, Co. H., Aug. 16, 1864; 1 year; discharged by general order June 15, 1865.
Campbell, James P., Co. C, Oct. 29th, 1861; 3 years; captured at Tompkinsville, Ky., and paroled July 9, 1862; discharged Dec. 14, 1864 —expiration of term.
Clay, John H., Co. I, Aug. 9, 1864; 1 year; discharged by general order May 29, 1865.
*Cannon, Patrick G., Co. I, Aug. 10, 1864; 1 year; absent, sick, at muster out.
Campbell, James, Co. C, Aug. 31, 1864; 3 years; discharged by general order June 20, 1865.
Deibler, George, Co. C, Aug. 13, 1864; 1 year; discharged by general order May 29, 1865.
Earisman, Elias, Co. H, Aug. 15, 1864; 1 year; captured; paroled; discharged by general order June 18, 1865.
*Fisher, David N., Co. C, Aug. 12, 1864; 3 years; discharged by general order May 29, 1865.
Fortney, Allen B., Co. H, Aug. 29, 1864; 1 year; discharged by general order May 29, 1865.
*Genkes, Henry, Co. H, Aug. 25, 1864; 1 year; discharged by general order May 29, 1865.
Gutshall, John, Co. C, Aug. 13, 1864; 1 year; discharged by general order May 29, 1865.
Gutshall, George, Co. C, Aug. 9, 1864; 1 year; discharged by general order May 29, 1865.
*Gheistwhite, Robert, Co. C, Oct. 11, 1861; 3 years; discharged on surgeon's certificate, Jan. 5, 1865; veteran.
*Gheistwhite, John, Co. C, Oct. 11, 1861; 3 years; died at Louisville, Ky., Dec. 17, 1862; buried in National Cemetery, section B, range 8, grave 6.
Gruber, John B., Co. I, Aug. 16, 1864; 1 year; discharged by general order May 29, 1865.
Hickernell, Robert, Co. C, Aug. 8, 1864; 1 year; discharged by general order May 29, 1865, to date Oct. 26, 1864.
*Houser, Jacob R., Co. C, Aug. 12, 1864; 1 year; captured; died at Andersonville.
Hickernell, William H., Co. C, Sept. 6, 1864; 1 year; discharged by general order May 29, 1865, to date Oct. 26, 1864.
Irely, Samuel, Sr., Co. A, May 27, 1864; 3 years; mustered out with company July 18, 1865.

*Dead.

Irely, John, Co. G, May 30, 1864; 3 years; mustered out with company July 18, 1865.
Kellar, Jacob, Co. C, Oct. 11, 1861; 3 years; discharged Dec. 24, 1864—expiration of term.
Kline, William, Co. C, Aug. 9, 1864; 1 year; discharged by general order May 29, 1865.
Longenecker, I. K., Co. I, Aug. 10, 1864; 1 year; captured; paroled; discharged by general order May 29, 1865.
*Longenecker, Henry, Co. H, Aug. 15, 1864; 1 year; absent, in hospital, at muster out.
*Laughman, Daniel, Co. C, Aug 30, 1864; 1 year; discharged by general order May 29, 1865.
Lutz, John, Co. H, Aug. 30, 1864; 1 year; mustered out with company July 18, 1865.
Matthias, John, Co. C, May 30, 1864; 3 years; mustered out with company July 18, 1865.
Mansburger, Daniel, Co. E, Aug. 9, 1864; 1 year; discharged by general order May 29, 1865.
Miller, John, Co. I, Aug. 10, 1864; 1 year; discharged by general order May 29, 1865.
Miller, Henry, Co. I, Aug. 10, 1864; 1 year; discharged by general order May 29, 1865.
*McKinley, Jacob, Co. C, Aug. 12, 1864; 1 year; discharged by general order May 29, 1865.
Metler, Adam A., Co. H, Aug. 24, 1864; 1 year; discharged by general order May 29, 1865.
Miller, James D., Co. K, Aug. 15, 1864; 1 year; discharged by general order May 29, 1865.
*Neeter, John, Co. C, Sept. 10, 1864; 1 year; discharged by general order May 29, 1865.
Pike, Milton, Co. I, Aug. 10, 1864; 1 year; discharged by general order May 29, 1865.
Snyder, Samuel, Co. C, Aug. 9, 1864; 1 year; discharged by general order May 29, 1865.
Sheaffer, Jonathan, Co. C, Oct. 11, 1861; 3 years; captured at Tompkinsville, Ky., and paroled July 9, 1862; discharged Dec. 24, 1864 —expiration of term.
Sheaffer, Hamilton, Co. C, Oct. 11, 1861; 3 years; absent, in hospital, at muster out.
Stipe, Andrew J., Co. C, Aug. 9, 1864; 1 year; discharged by general order May 29, 1865.
Stipe, Washington, Co. H, Aug. 19, 1864; 1 year; discharged by general order May 29, 1865.
*Stipe, Jackson A., Co. H, Aug. 17, 1864; 1 year; discharged by general order June 7, 1865.

---

*Dead.

Snyder, John H., Co. C, Aug. 12, 1864; 1 year; discharged by general order May 29, 1865.
Sanders, Leander L., Co. H, Aug. 16, 1864; 1 year; discharged by general order May 29, 1865.
Stipe, G. W., Co. C, Oct. 11, 1861.
Snively, Charles H., Co. C, Sept. 6, 1864; discharged by General order May 29, 1865.
Trump, George W., Co. C, Oct. 11, 1861; 3 years; discharged on surgeon's certificate Dec. 4, 1862.
Uhlmer, Jacob, Co. E, Aug. 13, 1864; 1 year; discharged by general order May 29, 1865.
Whisler, John L., Co. C, Aug. 9, 1864; 1 year; discharged by general order May 29, 1865.
Willis, Henry, Co. E, Aug. 10, 1864; 1 year; discharged by general order May 29, 1865.
Willis, Isaiah, Aug. 10, 1864; 1 year; unassigned.

XLVII

NINETY-THIRD REGIMENT PENNSYLVANIA VOLUNTEERS.

Organized October, 1861. November 12th, went to Washington; December 2nd, to Fort Good Hope, Md.; January 22nd, 1862, to Tenallytown; 26th embarked for the Peninsula and until the 4th of May was posted at Warwick Court House, constructing rifle pits and forts along Warwick river. Suffered severely here from chills and fever. May the 4th, the regiment moved towards Williamsburg; on the 5th, in the battle of Williamsburg, its loss was six killed and twenty wounded; May 13th, on the Chickahominy. In the battle at Fair Oaks its loss was twenty-one killed, one hundred and eight wounded, and twenty-eight missing. A correspondent of the New York *Tribune*, writing of this battle, says: "Take the case of the Ninety-third Pennsylvania. This thoroughly trained body of troops fought, were driven back from position, but not broken; halted at word of command wheeled, fired, retreated, halted, loaded and fired again, and again, and came off the ground in perfect order, with their colors flying—a striking proof that the success of battles is in the discipline of the troops."

In the movement of the army from the Chickahominy to the James,

---

*Dead.
NOTE: These rolls contain the names of those who enlisted here; and of those residents here during the war who enlisted elsewhere.
NOTE: Some years after the close of the war the Ninth Cavalry formed a social organization. Their eighteenth annual reunion took place at Middletown, June 9, 1887. Seventy-one of the veterans attended. They held a business meeting in the room of Post 78, G. A. R.; a handsome flag was presented to them by Mrs. Colonel Reynolds; in the evening they had a convivial reception in the crowded Opera House, and concluded the day with a banquet in the Market House.

it acted as guard to the trains. At Malvern Hill the loss of the regiment was about twenty. On the evacuation of the Peninsula it moved by transport from Yorktown to Alexandria, thence to Chantilly, and was in the battle here of September 1st. On the opening of the Maryland campaign it moved to Harper's Ferry, making a reconnaissance as far as Sandy Hook. At the battle of Antietam it was held in reserve. In the battle of Fredericksburg, December 19, it was held in reserve. In the spring campaign, under Hooker, it was engaged in the Chancellorsville battle, its loss was six killed, forty-four wounded, and twenty-one missing. May 18, 1863, the regiment moved up the Rappahannock. The march to Pennsylvania now commenced, and on July 1st the regiment reached Manchester, Md.; at 9 a. m., on the 2nd, it crossed the State line. The men were worn out with fatigue, the day was excessively hot, and the roads dusty; but when the colors were unfurled, and the drums beaten, in token of their entrance upon the soil of their native State, they came to a quick step, with arms at a shift, and marched on gaily, singing, "Pennsylvania Again."

At 2 p. m. the regiment arrived at Rock Creek, just in rear of the line of battle at the Gettysburg cemetery. The Ninety-third was the first regiment of the Sixth Corps to get into action, and took twenty-five prisoners. Since 8 p. m. of the evening previous it had marched thirty-nine miles, fought three hours, and passed a sleepless night, without food. During the night of the 3rd it was engaged in burying the dead and bearing off the wounded. Its loss in this battle was eight killed, and twenty-one wounded. At the conclusion of this campaign it returned with the army to the neighborhood of Brandy Station and went into winter quarters in substantial log huts.

December 30th, it was detached, and, with the brigade, sent to Washington and thence to Harper's Ferry. Loaded upon open freight cars, without fire, the men suffered intensely from cold. The feet and hands of many were frozen, rendering amputation necessary in two cases, one of which proved fatal.

February 7th, 1864, two hundred and eighty-four of the men, upwards of three-fourths of the regiment, re-enlisted, and were given a veteran furlough. General Wheating gave a letter to Lieutenant Colonel Long, in which occurs this passage: "The great Keystone State has sent few regiments to the field who can return showing as handsome a record as the one you command."

On March 18th, 1864, the regiment, recruited to eight hundred strong, rejoined the brigade at Halltown, and soon afterwards returned to Brandy Station; May 4th, it set out for the Wilderness. In the engagements of the 5th and 6th, the regiment lost eighteen killed, and one hundred and forty-four wounded. The 7th was comparatively quiet, but on the 9th, 10th, and 11th, it was kept busy maneuvering, digging, and fighting. On the morning of the 12th it went into position at the right of the famous "Angle," advancing to within fifty yards of the rebel

Farmers' Bank.

works. The regiment here lost seventy-seven killed and wounded in the space of one hour. It participated in the fierce fighting of the army in its progress to the James, losing men almost daily; on the 18th of May having thirty killed and wounded. It crossed the Rapidan on the 4th of May, and entered the campaign with seven hundred and fifty men present for duty—as it marched from the trenches of Cold Harbor it had but three hundred and twenty-five of that number left in its ranks; fifteen officers and three hundred and ten men having been either killed or wounded, and ninety-five sick and sent to the rear; but nine men were captured, and these were wounded and left on the field. "From the 4th of May until the 12th of June," says a member of the command, "the Ninety-third marched three hundred and fifty miles, made twenty-six night marches, was fifteen days without regular rations, dug thirty rifle-pits, oftener at night than by day, and fought in eight distinct battles. During all this time there were but five days on which the regiment, or some part of it, was not under fire, and neither officers nor men ever took off their clothes, seldom their accoutrements, day or night. Clothes and shoes worn out were only replaced by those of dead men, and not until it arrived at James river, far from the presence of an enemy did the men enjoy the luxury of a bath."

June 15th the men arrived in front of Petersburg. Heavy skirmishing at once commenced and continued until the afternoon of the 18th, when they pushed close to the enemy's works on the Norfolk Railroad, entrenching, under a heavy fire, with their bayonets. One officer was here killed and five men wounded. It remained here until the 22nd under an almost constant fire. On the 22nd it supported the Third Division in an attack, losing thirteen killed and wounded. On the 29th it marched to the relief of General Wilson; after tearing up a portion of the Weldon Railroad it returned to camp.

On the 9th of July it was taken in crowded transports to Washington, then menaced by General Early. On the 17th there was a battle and Early was driven back and pursued across the Potomac. August 9th Sheridan assumed command in the Valley, and on the 27th, while under his command the Ninety-third had an engagement with the enemy. September 13th, it supported a battery on Opequan Creek, sustaining some loss. On the 19th, at Winchester, the regiment lost seven killed and forty wounded. At Fisher's Hill the loss was twenty-four killed and wounded; after pursuing the enemy up the Valley beyond Staunton the army returned to Cedar Creek. On the morning of October 19th the Ninety-third repelled several assaults of the enemy, but was finally outflanked and compelled to retire. The army was driven back four miles. General Sheridan arrived at two p. m. At three he rode along the line, saying, as he came to the Ninety-third, "We must sleep in our old camp to-night." The engagement was very severe, but the enemy finally gave way, and the rout was complete.

On October 28th, one hundred men whose term had expired were mustered out of the service. In November the regiment was ordered to Philadelphia where it remained until after the Presidential election, when it returned to Winchester. About the middle of December it moved to the lines in front of Petersburg. During the winter several hundred recruits were received, bringing its strength up to the minimum. On the 25th of March, 1865, in an attack on the enemy's works, the regiment lost fifteen killed and one hundred and thirty-six wounded. At four a. m. on April 2nd, with the rest of the brigade, the regiment charged the enemy's works, which were carried, the Ninety-third being the first to plant their colors on the ramparts. Their loss on this day was two killed and thirty wounded. During the night the enemy evacuated Petersburg. On the 6th the regiment participated in the battle of Sailor's Creek. On the 9th Lee surrendered.

The regiment returned by rail to Richmond, thence to Washington, and was there mustered out of service June 27th, 1865.

ROLL OF MIDDLETOWN VOLUNTEERS IN COMPANY I, NINETY-THIRD REGIMENT. (THREE YEARS' SERVICE.)

Captain.

*Daniel J. Boynton, Oct. 28, 1861; mustered out Sept. 24, 1864—expiration of term.

First Lieutenant.

Henry J. Waltz, Oct. 28, 1861; promoted to sergeant; to second lieutenant May 26, 1863; to first lieutenant January 1, 1864; mustered out Oct. 28, 1864—expiration of term.

Second Lieutenants.

Jacob S. Steese, Oct. 28, 1861; promoted from first sergeant July 22, 1862; resigned Jan. 5, 1863.

John H. Parthemer, Oct. 28, 1861; promoted to corporal Feb. 1, 1862; to sergeant Nov. 1, 1864; to second lieutenant Jan. 2, 1865; wounded at Petersburg, Va., March 25, 1865; mustered out with company June 27, 1865; veteran.

Alexander S. Black, Oct. 28, 1861; discharged July 22, 1862.

Sergeants.

Adam Bishop, Oct. 9, 1862; wounded at Opequan, Va., Sept. 19, 1864; promoted from private Jan. 2, 1865; mustered out with company June 27, 1865.

John S. Mackenson, Oct. 28, 1861; discharged on surgeon's certificate April 11, 1862.

*Dead.

CHRONICLES OF MIDDLETOWN. 211

Corporals.

*Elias Beidleman, Feb. 22, 1864; wounded at Wilderness, Va., May 5, 1864; promoted to corporal Jan 2, 1865; mustered out with company June 27, 1865.
*D. L. Hickernell, Feb. 29, 1864; promoted to corporal Jan. 2, 1865; mustered out with company June 27, 1865.
*Henry L. Light, Feb. 20, 1864; wounded at Wilderness, Va., May 5, 1864; promoted to corporal Jan. 2, 1865; mustered out with company June 27, 1865.
Daniel Parthemer, Oct. 28, 1861; discharged on surgeon's certificate Feb. 3, 1862.
George W. Stoner, Oct. 28, 1861; discharged on surgeon's certificate July 7, 1862.
William Condron, Oct. 28, 1861; wounded at Fair Oaks, Va., May 31, 1862; discharged on surgeon's certificate Sept. 30, 1862.
Harrison Earisman, Oct. 28, 1861; discharged on surgeon's certificate Feb. 17, 1863.
Martin P. Wetzel, Oct. 28, 1861; mustered out Nov. 11, to date Oct. 28, 1864—expiration of term.
*Henry Steel, Oct. 28, 1861; killed at Fair Oaks, Va., May 31, 1862.

Privates.

*Boot, John, Jr., Nov. 20, 1861; discharged on surgeon's certificate May 10, 1862.
Booser, Henry, Oct. 28, 1861; discharged on surgeon's certificate Jan. 13, 1863.
*Beck, William V., March 17, 1864; died May 14, of wounds received at Spottsylvania Court House, Va., May 12, 1864.
Bear, John, Oct. 28, 1861.
Core, Jacob, Oct. 28, 1861; wounded at Spottsylvania Court House, Va., May 12, 1864; absent at muster out; veteran.
Cassel, Hiram, Oct. 28, 1861; mustered out with company June 27, 1865; veteran.
Campbell, Simon, Oct. 28, 1861; discharged on surgeon's certificate Sept. 18, 1862.
Cole, John H., Oct. 28, 1861; transferred to United States navy June 20, 1864.
*Core, Benjamin. Oct. 28, 1861; died Feb. 28, 1862, at Tenallytown, D. C.
*Crawford, William A., March 11, 1864.
Day, John S., Feb. 29, 1864; wounded at Fisher's Hill, Va., Sept. 22, 1864; mustered out with company June 27, 1865.
Deabler, George, Oct. 28, 1861; discharged on surgeon's certificate July 9, 1862.

*Dead.

Embich, Frederick S., Oct. 28, 1861; mustered out with company June 27, 1865; veteran.
Earisman, Daniel, Oct. 28, 1861; discharged on surgeon's certificate Feb. 28, 1863.
Earisman, Absalom, Nov. 11, 1861; discharged Dec. 11, 1861.
Eves, Hiram C., Oct. 28, 1861; wounded at Fair Oaks, Va., May 31, 1862; mustered out Oct. 28, 1864—expiration of term.
*Geistwhite, Abram, March 16, 1862; dishonorably discharged March 24, 1865; veteran.
*Hunsberger, Daniel, Nov. 14, 1861; discharged on surgeon's certificate Nov. 7, 1862.
*Hawk, George W., Oct. 28, 1861; wounded at Fair Oaks, Va., May 31, 1862; discharged on surgeon's certificate Dec. 24th, 1862.
Keister, Francis, Oct. 28, 1861; not on muster-out roll.
*Light, Samuel, Oct. 28, 1861; died at Highspire, Dauphin county, Aug. 14, 1862.
Slecht, Jacob, Oct. 28, 1861; discharged on surgeon's certificate Feb. 21, 1863.
Simmers, Joseph, Oct. 28, 1861; discharged on surgeon's certificate Jan. 23, 1863.
Stipe, Andrew, Oct. 28, 1861.
Sipe, John, Oct. 28, 1861.
Sanders, Oleander, Oct. 28, 1861; not on muster-out roll.
*Stehman, Christian, Nov. 7, 1861.
*Whitman, John, Oct. 28, 1861; discharged on surgeon's certificate, Dec. 21, 1862.

XLVIII.

MIDDLETOWN VOLUNTEERS IN THE THIRTY-SIXTH REGIMENT—SEVENTH RESERVE. (THREE YEARS' SERVICE.)

Privates.

Campbell, James, Co. C, May 27, 1861; discharged on surgeon's certificate Aug. 18, 1863.
Gastwhite, Abraham, Co. C, May 27, 1861.
*Smith, Benjamin F., Co. C, May 27, 1861; died at Baltimore, Feb. 17, 1864.
The Seventh lost half its strength on the Chickahominy. After the "Seven Days' Fight" but two hundred men were left to answer roll-call, the killed, wounded and missing amounting to three hundred and one. At Fredericksburg it had six killed, seventy-two wounded, and twenty-two missing. The Reserves had by this time become so much

---
*Dead.
NOTE: These rolls contain the names of those who enlisted here; and of those residents here during the war, who enlisted elsewhere.

reduced by hard fighting that, early in 1863, they were transferred to the Department of Washington, where the Seventh remained on guard and provost duty until the spring of 1864.

FORTY-FIRST REGIMENT PENNSYLVANIA VOLUNTEERS—TWELFTH RESERVE. (THREE YEARS' SERVICE.)

This regiment was organized in June, 1861; August 10th it marched to Baltimore; August 20th it was attached to the Third Brigade; October 10th, marched to Virginia; December 20th was in the fight at Dranesville; May 6th, 1862, four men were captured by guerrillas; June 12th embarked at Belle Plain Landing to join McClellan on the Peninsula; debarked at White House on the 14th and marched to Dispatch Station; on the 18th marched to New Bridge on the Chickahominy; on the 19th, moved to Ellerson's Mill on Beaver Dam creek. From a hill in front of their camp they could see the spires of Richmond; here on the 26th, they were engaged with the enemy from three o'clock in the afternoon till nine o'clock at night; over one hundred rounds of ammunition per man was expended. Roger A. Pryor, of the rebel army, in his account of the "Seven Days' Fight," says: "Ellerson's Mill was defended with desperate obstinacy." At Gaines' Mill the regiment was for three hours exposed to a terrific fire, the loss was six killed and twenty-five wounded.

June 29th, an intensely hot day, it marched eighteen miles without food or water; that night it was ordered on picket. Colonel Taggart's report says: "The White Oak creek, which we crossed about noon, was a complete quagmire from the thousands of horses, teams and artillery which were passing, and water to drink was not to be had. Some of the men became almost delirious from thirst, and once, when I halted for a rest a few minutes, I discovered them drinking from a stagnant puddle in which was the carcass of a putrid horse. Poor fellows, I pitied them, but I could not permit this, and I promised them water at White Oak swamp, but as we arrived there we found it utterly unfit to drink. The disappointment was intense; but in the evening when we halted, and General McCall came up and told us there was plenty of good spring water in a rivulet close by, the joy of the men knew no bounds. Alas! little did they think that on that very spot, in less than twenty-four hours, many of them would pour out their life's blood, and the waters of that little brook be reddened by the vital current! Yet so it was."

On the 30th they were heavily engaged; the regiment lost six killed, thirty-six wounded, and twenty-three missing. At Malvern Hill the regiment was held in reserve; July 1st it moved to Harrison's Landing. The total loss of the regiment, in the Peninsula campaign, was thirteen killed, sixty wounded, and thirty-six missing. Much sickness occurred at Harrison's Landing, owing to the depression occasioned by repeated defeat, the unwholesome water and the miasmatic influences of the cli-

214   CHRONICLES OF MIDDLETOWN.

mate. From the Peninsula the Twelfth proceeded to Falmouth, and thence by a rapid and fatiguing march to join General Pope's army. July 29th, near Groveton, the regiment sustained considerable loss. On the 30th near the Henry House it had a severe engagement, holding its position against vastly superior numbers, until re-inforced; the loss was five killed and thirty-eight wounded. Near South Mountain its loss was six killed and nineteen wounded. August 16th and 17th, at Antietam, the regiment lost thirteen killed, forty-seven wounded and thirty-four taken prisoners.

In February, 1863, the regiment, now reduced to a mere skeleton, was ordered to the defences of Washington and attached to the Twenty-second Army Corps. In April it was ordered to Washington, where it performed provost duty for six weeks.

The Twelfth reached the battlefield of Gettysburg at ten a. m., on the 2nd of July. That night the Third Brigade took position on Round Top and built the stone wall connecting the summit of Round Top with Little Round Top. On October 14th the regiment was engaged at Bristoe Station; on November 19th at Rappahannock Station, and on the 26th at Mine Run. It went into winter quarters on the Orange and Alexandria Railroad.

May 4th, 1864, the spring campaign opened, and the Twelfth was hotly engaged during the three days in the Wilderness; on the 18th was in the fight at Spottsylvania Court House; on the 23rd at the North Anna River; and on the 30th at Bethesda Church; on this day the regiment's term of service expired. It returned to Pennsylvania, where it was enthusiastically received, and on the 11th of June was mustered out.

MIDDLETOWN VOLUNTEERS IN COMPANY G, FORTY-FIRST REGIMENT.

First Lieutenant.

George Huber, June 25, 1861; promoted to first lieutenant May 1, 1863; mustered out with company June 11, 1864.

Corporals.

*Daniel D. Bailey, June 25, 1861; died of wounds Oct. 8, 1862.

Hiram Kendig, July 11, 1861; discharged on surgeon's certificate May 21, 1862.

David Shirk, July 11, 1861; mustered out with company June 11, 1864.

Musician.

John S. Embick, June 19, 1861; discharged on surgeon's certificate March 20, 1864.

---
*Dead.

CHRONICLES OF MIDDLETOWN. 215

Privates.

Alexander, Washington, June 26, 1861; discharged on surgeon's certificate Feb. 20, 1863.
Breneman, Samuel, June 25, 1861; discharged on surgeon's certificate July 18, 1862.
Ingles, Frederick, Aug. 5, 1861.
*Mackinson, Edward, Aug. 3rd, 1861; mustered out with company June 11, 1864.
*Mentzberger, William, June 25, 1861; died Nov. 3, 1861; buried in Military Asylum Cemetery.
*Parson, Jeremiah, June 25th, 1861; transferred to 190th regiment P. V., May 31, 1864; veteran.
Shaefer, Augustus, June 25, 1861; mustered out with company June 11, 1864.
Simpson, Orlando, June 25, 1861; transferred to 190th regiment, P. V., May 31, 1864; veteran.
Stewart, Charles, July 26, 1861; discharged on surgeon's certificate Oct. 22, 1862.
Tennis, John, Aug. 3, 1861; mustered out with company June 11, 1864.

XLIX.

FORTY-THIRD REGIMENT PENNSYLVANIA VOLUNTEERS—FIRST ARTILLERY. (THREE YEARS' SERVICE.)

This regiment was organized in June, 1861; in August was ordered to Washington, where it was armed and equipped, and then moved to Camp Barry, east of the Capitol. Here the several batteries were assigned to different divisions and corps of the army, and were never again united as a regiment.

BATTERY A.

Battery A participated in the battle of Dranesville, December 20, 1861. At Beaver Dam it served with excellent effect. June 27th at Gaines' Mill, it was posted in an important position; being left without support and its ammunition becoming exhausted, it was captured by the enemy. It was re-organized and received new guns at Harrison's Landing. Participated in the battles of Bull Run, South Mountain and Antietam, maintaining its reputation for skill and bravery and leaving many of its men dead and wounded upon the different fields. At Fredericksburg, December 1st, it maintained its position under the concentrated fire of the enemy's batteries. Was attached to the army of the

---

*Dead.
NOTE: These rolls contain the names of those who enlisted here; and of those residents here during the war, who enlisted elsewhere.

James. Operated on the Black Water, at Deep Bottom, Fort Darling, Seven Pines and Petersburg. It entered Richmond with Weitzel's Corps on the day of that city's surrender, and was engaged in demolishing the rebel defences and removing their guns. After the completion of this duty in July, 1865, the battery turned in its guns at Richmond and marched to Pennsylvania, where, after a term of four years and four months' service, it was mustered out on the 25th.

BATTERY B.

The Middletown men joined this battery at Paoli Mills, near Kelly's Ford, Va., early in 1864. May 4th of that year the battery was in the engagements near the Lacy House; on the 9th it fired about forty rounds at the enemy beyond the Po river; on the 13th it was in position on the picket line; the two lines were very close, the men had little shelter, and it was only by working on their knees that they could load the guns. The battery was withdrawn and marched all night, joining the corps near Spottsylvania Court House; was immediately placed in position and engaged. On the 18th it was under the hottest fire that it encountered during the war. Here the rebels were treated to a little mortar practice by the gunners of Battery B. On the 21st this position was abandoned. On the 23rd, at Jericho Ford, the battery completely demolished a rebel battery that was annoying the Fifth Corps. On the 2nd of June it went into position at Cold Harbor. The new gunners did good execution, firing a greater number of rounds on the 2nd and 3rd than had been fired by the battery previously during that campaign. It arrived at Wilcox's Landing on the James, on the 15th, and in front of Petersburg on the evening of the 17th, and occupied several positions; on the 18th in front of Avery Court House, fired a number of rounds; on the 30th of July, when the fort in front of the Ninth Corps was blown up, it was in service. On the 18th, 19th, and 21st of August it was with General Warren's advance on the Weldon Railroad. December 21st it was relieved from duty on the front line and went into winter quarters about a mile in the rear. At different times during the winter it was on duty. When the enemy captured Forts Steadman and Haskell the left section kept a sharp fire on the forts in front. At midnight of April 1, 1865, all the batteries received orders to open fire; on the 2nd the firing was renewed, the gunners doing good execution. Two detachments of Battery B worked the guns in one of the enemy's batteries which had been captured; six hundred rounds left by the rebels were fired, besides a large number brought from the other line by the infantry. In the afternoon the rebels made an attempt to recapture the forts they had lost; deserted by the infantry Lieutenant Rice and his handful of men worked the guns with telling effect. The next day the battery was ordered to City Point. May 3rd it left for Washington, passing through Richmond. June 3rd the guns were turned in at Washington and the men went to Pennsylvania, where they were mustered out on the 9th.

BATTERY F.

Battery F was furnished in August, 1861, with horses, equipments and four smooth-bore pieces, and transferred to the camp of the Pennsylvania Reserve Corps at Tenallytown. September 12th it was ordered to join General Banks at Darnestown, Md., and was never afterwards connected with the regiment or the reserves. On October 8th, two steel-rifled ten-pounder Parrot guns were added to the battery. The Middletown men joined the company at its rendezvous at Chester, Pa., in February, 1864. On the 1st of March the battery returned to Virginia and took its place in the Second Corps. May 5th, 6th and 7th it was heavily engaged with the enemy in the wilderness. To add to the horrors of battle here the breastworks, which were composed of logs and rails, and the woods took fire, and many of the wounded perished in the flames. At Cold Harbor the battery was attached to the Eighteenth Corps, and was sharply engaged. On June 8th it returned to the Second Corps, having been in line of battle without relief for six days. On the 14th the battery was in position before Petersburg, and several hundred rounds were thrown into the city. On the 20th it was engaged on the Jerusalem Plank Road. From this time forward until the capture of Petersburg, the battery participated in all the movements of the corps, being constantly upon the front and engaged in the active operations of the siege. Upon the fall of the city, April 3, 1865, it was attached to the reserve artillery, and went into camp near City Point. Proceeding thence to Washington, where its guns and horses were turned over, it moved to Pennsylvania, where on the 9th of June, 1865, it was mustered out of service.

ROLL OF MIDDLETOWN VOLUNTEERS IN THE FIRST ARTILLERY.

Corporal.

*Franklin Houser, Battery F, Jan. 27, 1862; mustered out with battery June 9, 1865; veteran.

Privates.

*Ackerman, George W., Battery F, Feb. 6, 1864; mustered out with battery June 9, 1865.
Bretz, Thos J., Battery B, Feb. 11, 1864; mustered out with battery June 9, 1865.
Campbell, Alexander, Battery B, Feb. 6, 1864; mustered out with battery, June 9, 1865.
*Cox, John, Battery E, July 10, 1861; mustered out August 4, 1864 —expiration of term.
Campbell, Simon S., Battery F., Feb. 1, 1864; mustered out with battery June 9, 1865.

*Dead.

*Davis, Theophilus, Battery F, Feb. 2, 1864; mustered out with battery June 9, 1865.

Davis, Jacob, Battery B, February 8, 1864; mustered out with battery June 9, 1865; veteran.

Gottschall, William, Battery F, Feb. 6, 1864; mustered out with battery June 9, 1865.

Houser, John, Battery F, March 14, 1864; mustered out with battery June 9, 1865.

Jenkins, Henry S., Battery F, June 4, 1864; mustered out with battery June 9, 1865.

McGraw, Edward, Battery E, Feb. 2, 1864; mustered out with battery July 20, 1865.

*McKinley, Jacob, Battery A, August 1, 1861; mustered out July 12, 1864—expiration of term.

Pearson, William, Battery G, July 19, 1861, discharged by surgeon's certificate December 18, 1861.

Stewart, Michael, Battery B, February 2, 1864; mustered out with battery June 9, 1865.

*Swander, John, Battery B, Feb. 8, 1864; mustered out with battery June 9, 1865.

Shaffer, Lewis D., Battery A, May 29, 1861; mustered out May 28, 1864—expiration of term.

Weiting, Orlando L., Battery F, Jan. 4, 1864; mustered out with battery June 9, 1865. Went to West Point; commissioned first lieutenant, Twenty-third U. S. Inf.

L.

MIDDLETOWN VOLUNTEERS IN THE EIGHTIETH REGIMENT, PENNSYLVANIA VOLUNTEERS, SEVENTH CAVALRY. (THREE YEARS' SERVICE.)

Privates.

*Kore, Henry, Co. K, Feb. 3, 1864; mustered out with company Aug., 1865.

Poorman, Henry, Co. K, Feb. 8, 1864; mustered out with company Aug. 23, 1864.

Schock, Benjamin, Co. M, Feb. 8, 1864; discharged on surgeon's certificate March 20, 1865.

They were with Sherman, and in engagements, May 15, 1864, at Rome; 27th at Dallas and Villa Rica Road; June 9, at Big Shanty; 11th, at McAfee Cross Roads; 20th at Monday Creek; 27th at Kenesaw Mountain; July 18th in raid on A. & A. Railroad; 21st in raid on Covington; 28th at Flat Rock; August 1st at Atlanta; with Kilpat-

*Dead.
NOTE: These rolls contain the names of those who enlisted here; and of those residents here during the war, who enlisted elsewhere.

CHRONICLES OF MIDDLETOWN. 219

rick's raid; October 12th and 13th at Rome; at Lead's Cross Roads; at Nashville; at Plantersville; at Selma; and at Columbia.

MIDDLETOWN VOLUNTEERS IN COMPANY I, EIGHTY-THIRD REGIMENT, PENNSYLVANIA VOLUNTEERS. (THREE YEARS' SERVICE.)

Privates.

Campbell, Henry, Feb. 8, 1865; mustered out with company June 28, 1865.
Graft, Andrew, Feb. 8, 1865; mustered out with company June 28, 1865.
*Martin, James K. P., Feb. 8, 1865; discharged by general order June 27, 1865.
Phillips, William, Feb. 8, 1865; mustered out with company June 28, 1865.

This regiment was organized September 8, 1861. The Middletown men joined it at Hampton Station, Va., in the spring of 1865. They were in the engagements at Jones' Farm, White Oak Road, Gravelly Run, Five Forks, Southerland Station, Jettersville, and the pursuit to Appomattox Court House. The regiment was mustered out of service at Washington, and finally disbanded July 4, 1865.

MIDDLETOWN VOLUNTEERS IN COMPANY D, ONE HUNDRED AND FIRST REGIMENT PENNSYLVANIA VOLUNTEERS. (THREE YEARS' SERVICE.)

Corporals.

George Neiman, Feb. 21, 1861; mustered out with company June 25, 1865.
William H. Moore, March 10, 1865; mustered out with company June 25, 1865.
Richard F. Eppler, March 15, 1865; mustered out with company June 25, 1865.

Musicians.

Valentine Baumbach, March 7, 1865; mustered out with company June 25, 1865.
James P. Hipple, March 8, 1865; mustered out with company June 25, 1865.

Privates.

Countryman, Adam, March 1, 1865; mustered out with company June 25, 1865.
Copeland, Benjamin, Feb. 20, 1865; mustered out with company June 25, 1865.
Daugherty, James D., March 10, 1865; mustered out with company June 25, 1865.

---
*Dead.

James, David, March 13, 1865; mustered out with company June 25, 1865.

Kurtz, Levi W., Feb. 9, 1865; mustered out with company June 25, 1865.

Roop, Solomon, March 1, 1865; mustered out with company June 25, 1865.

Roop, Christian, March 1, 1865; mustered out with company June 25, 1865.

*Starr, William, Feb. 9, 1865; mustered out with company June 25, 1865.

Weirich, Jacob, March 10, 1865; mustered out with company June 25, 1865.

This regiment was organized in the fall of 1861. By the spring of 1865 it had been reduced to a skeleton. It was re-organized on Roanoke Island. In March of that year eight new companies (in one of which were the Middletown volunteers) were assigned to it; they were however never consolidated with the original companies, and on the 25th of June, 1865, the regiment was mustered out of service at Newbern, N. C.

MIDDLETOWN VOLUNTEERS IN THE ONE HUNDRED AND THIRTEENTH REGIMENT PENNSYLVANIA VOLUNTEERS, TWELFTH CAVALRY. (THREE YEARS' SERVICE.)

Sergeant.

John Core, Co. E, Feb. 23, 1864; mustered out with company, July 20, 1865; veteran.

Farrier.

*John Minsler, Co. E, Feb. 27, 1864; mustered out with company, July 20, 1865.

Private.

Winaugle, William F., Co. E, Feb. 3, 1864; mustered out with company, July 20, 1865.

They were in the campaign against Early in June, 1864; were in actions at Solomon's Gap, Pleasant Valley and Crampton's Gap; at Winchester on the 20th; at Kernstown on the 23rd; the loss of the Twelfth in this engagement was heavy; were with Sheridan in the Shenandoah Valley. In an engagement on the 21st of August they suffered loss. In December the regiment paroled the railroad from Harper's Ferry to Winchester, and here had frequent skirmishes; on the 22nd in battle at Harmony it had six killed and nineteen wounded. Their last skirmish was at Edinboro at the time of Lee's surrender.

---

*Dead.

CHRONICLES OF MIDDLETOWN. 221

MIDDLETOWN VOLUNTEERS IN THE ONE HUNDRED AND SEVENTEENTH REGIMENT PENNSYLVANIA VOLUNTEERS, THIRTEENTH CAVALRY. (THREE YEARS' SERVICE.)

Sergeant.

Benjamin F. Bretz, Co. F, Aug. 14, 1863; three years; promoted to corporal, March 1, 1865; mustered out with company, July 14, 1865.

Privates.

Coover, Adam G., Aug. 28, 1863; three years, mustered out with company, July 14, 1865.
Fortney, Christian, Co. I, Jan. 24, 1865; one year, mustered out with company, July 14, 1865.
Fratz, William H., Co. C, Aug. 14, 1863; three years, mustered out with company, July 14, 1865.
Gottshall, Daniel, Co. C, Aug. 12, 1863; three years, mustered out with company, July 14, 1865.
Hetrick, Daniel Co. C, Aug. 1, 1863; three years, mustered out with company, July 14, 1865.
Kough, H. A., Co. C, Aug. 7, 1863; three years, mustered out with company, July 14, 1865.
Miller, Frederick, Co. C, Aug. 12, 1863; three years, mustered out with company, July 14, 1865.
McBarron, H. H., Co. I, Jan. 24, 1865; one year, wounded at Raleigh, N. C., April 13, 1865; mustered out with company, July 14, 1865.

They participated in the cavalry engagement at Jefferson, October 12, 1863; here the regiment lost one hundred and sixty-three killed, wounded and prisoners; were engaged three days in the retreat to Centreville; participated in the severe fighting from the 5th to the 11th of May, 1864; in Sheridan's raid had engagements at Beaver Dam Station and Hawe's Shop; in the last affair the regiment lost ten killed and thirty-five wounded and missing; at Trevilian Station; June 24th at St. Mary's Church; in this action the Thirteenth lost three officers and thirty men, killed, wounded and missing; July 1st relieved Wilson; were engaged at Jerusalem Plank Road, Malvern Hill and Lee's Mills. At Coggins' Point one hundred and fifty of the regiment were captured; September 29th, in action at Wyeth farm, lost two officers and fifteen men; were engaged October 22nd at Boydton Plank Road; December 8th and 9th, at Hatcher's Run, it suffered severely. February 5th and 6th was fighting all of both days at Gravelly Run, and on the evening of the 6th at Dabney's mills. About the middle of February the Thirteenth went to North Carolina; had an engagement with Hampton's Cavalry; July 14th, returned to Raleigh, N. C.; on the 15th went by rail to City Point, Va., thence via Baltimore and Philadelphia to Camp Cadwallader, where it arrived on the 19th, and on the 27th was finally discharged.

NOTE: These notes contain the names of those who enlisted here; and of those residents here during the war, who enlisted elsewhere.

LI.

ONE HUNDRED AND TWENTY-SEVENTH REGIMENT PENNSYLVANIA VOLUNTEERS. (NINE MONTHS' SERVICE.)

This regiment, seven companies of which were recruited in Dauphin county, was organized August 16, 1862. Colonel William H. Jennings, Lt. Col. Henry C. Alleman, Major Jeremiah Rohrer. On the 17th the regiment, 969 strong, broke camp and proceeded to Washington. For ten days the One Hundred and Twenty-seventh, with other new regiments, were encamped on Arlington Heights. It was brigaded with the Twenty-fourth and Twenty-eighth New Jersey, and Twenty-seventh Connecticut, and on the 23rd assigned to duty in guarding Chain Bridge, where it remained until the opening of the winter.

At the beginning of December, upon the eve of Burnside's movement upon Fredericksburg, the regiment moved to Falmouth, where it arrived on the 9th, and was assigned to the Third Brigade of the Second Division, Second Corps. During the night of the 10th the engineers commenced laying pontoon bridges in front of the town, but before they were completed the workmen were driven away by the enemy's sharpshooters, concealed in houses along the water's edge. Defeated in his first essay, Burnside ordered up his heavy guns and opened upon the town. During the bombardment the regiment supported batteries, and when this failed of effect Burnside called for volunteers to cross in boats and drive out the rebel sharpshooters. A party from Hall's brigade was chosen, among whom were members of the One Hundred and Twenty-seventh, and leaping to the boats and pulling lustily in the face of a shower of bullets they succeeded in reaching the opposite shore. After a brief struggle the enemy was driven and the bridge was completed. Hall's brigade was the first to cross and immediately commenced skirmishing to clear the town. Concealed in houses and coverts, from which they could fire with impunity upon the advancing troops, the rebels clung to their shelter, and by their unerring aim caused grievous slaughter. Half of the town was thus skirmished through, the enemy leaving the houses from one side as the Union troops were entering at the other, when the brigade was ordered to halt and occupy the ground gained, and the columns of Sumner commenced crossing.

During the night of the 11th, Sergt. Solomon Cover and eleven Middletown men were captured and carried prisoners to Richmond. A fierce fire of artillery was opened upon the town on the following morning and the streets were torn by solid shot, but the brigade held manfully to its work. At a little after noon of the 13th, when repeated attempts to carry the heights in front of the town had failed, Owen's brigade, to which the One Hundred and Twenty-seventh was temporarly attached, was led to the assault. Moving out to the low, open ground to the left of the city, all the while under a fierce fire of artillery in front and a flank fire from a deflection in the hills to the right, Owen formed his men in line of battle, the One Hundred and Twenty-seventh on the left of the One Hundred and Sixth, and dashed forward to his desperate task. Braver hearts never beat than filled the bosoms of the men in that devoted line. Onward they went over the prostrate forms of the dead and the dying, and up to within seventy-five yards of the enemy's lines; but the storm of deadly missiles was here too terrible to breast, and they dropped prostrate upon the ground and commenced screening themselves behind the dead bodies of their fallen comrades, with which the whole plain was strewn. To raise a head was instant death. In this perilous position the regiment lay for hours, exposed to the pitiless fire of musketry and artillery, and until night had put an end to the contest. But out of that silence from the battle's crash and roar rose new sounds more appalling still; rose or fell, you knew not which, or whether from earth or air a strange ventriloquism of which you could not locate the source, a smothered moan that seemed to come from distances beyond reach of the natural sense, a wail so far and deep and wide, as if a thousand discords were flowing together into a keynote weird, unearthly, terrible to hear and bear, yet startling in its nearness; the writhing concord broken by cries for help, pierced by shrieks of paroxysm; some begging for a drop of water, some calling on God for pity, and some on friendly hands to finish what the enemy had so horribly begun; some with delirous, dreamy voices murmuring loved names, as if the dearest were bending over them; some gathering their last strength to fire a musket to call attention to them where they lay helpless and deserted; and underneath at the time, a deep bass note from closed lips too hopeless or too heroic to articulate their agony.

The regiment was relieved with the brigade during the night and returned to the town. At the conclusion of the battle it retired to its former camp beyond Falmouth. The loss in the engagement was very severe, being two hundred and fifty-seven killed and wounded.

The regiment was soon after settled in comfortable quarters, and was employed during the winter in picket and guard duty. On the 27th of April, at the opening of the Chancellorsville campaign, the Second Division, now commanded by General Gibbon, moved out to the front of Fredericksburg, and having laid a pontoon bridge, crossed on the 3rd of May. Gibbon was joined in the town by Sedgwick's Corps, which had crossed below, and during the night had moved up to the city. An assaulting column was formed and those frowning heights which had been so successfully defended by the enemy on the previous December, were now triumphantly carried, prisoners, small arms and guns falling into the hands of the victors. The enemy retreated towards Chancellorsville and was closely followed by Sedgwick as far as Salem Church, where Lee, having turned back from Hooker's front, fell upon and crushed Sedgwick's Corps, compelling it to withdraw to the left bank of the Rappahannock by Bank's Ford. In the meantime, Gibbon, who had been left to hold Fredericksburg, took position around the city, and commenced throwing up rifle-pits. With no barrier left to oppose him, the enemy pushed forward from his triumph over Sedgwick, and soon made his appearance in Gibbon's front, where sharp skirmishing ensued. His position was held until the morning of the 4th, when, under the cover of a dense fog, he recrossed the river. The loss of the regiment in the engagement was fifty-three killed and wounded. Lieut. Jacob R. Knisley was among the killed.

The nine months' term of service of the regiment expired on the 14th and in pursuance of orders it was relieved and returned to Camp Curtin, where, two days thereafter, it was mustered out of service. During its brief term of duty at the front, of a little more than five months, it was engaged in two pitched battles unsurpassed in severity, and lost an aggregate of four officers and eighteen men killed, fourteen men who died of wounds, sixteen who died of disease, thirty-eight who were discharged by reason of disability, eleven who were captured, ten officers and one hundred and twenty-two men who were wounded, and three officers who resigned.

ROLL OF COMPANY H, ONE HUNDRED AND TWENTY-SEVENTH REGIMENT, PENNSYLVANIA VOLUNTEERS. RECRUITED IN MIDDLETOWN.

Captains.

Jeremiah Rohrer, Aug. 14, 1862; promoted to major, Aug. 19, 1862.
*John K. Shott, Aug. 19, 1862; promoted from first lieutenant, Aug. 19, 1862; mustered out with company, May 29, 1863.

First Lieutenant.

Isaiah Willis, Aug. 14, 1862; promoted from second lieutenant, Aug. 19, 1862; mustered out with company, May 29, 1863.

Second Lieutenant.

*James R. Schreiner, Aug. 14, 1862; promoted from private, Aug. 19, 1862; mustered out with company, May 29, 1863.
*Jacob R. Knisley, Aug. 12th, 1862; promoted from first sergeant, March 7, 1863; died May 15th of wounds received at Chancellorsville, Va., May 3, 1863.

First Sergeants.

David Hyde, Aug. 12, 1862; promoted from sergeant, March 7, 1863; mustered out with company, May 29, 1863.

Sergeants.

Solomon Cover, Aug. 13, 1862; captured at Fredericksburg, Va., Dec. 11, 1862; mustered out with company, May 29, 1863.

*Dead.

Farmers' Bank.

Francis J. Rinehart, Aug. 12, 1862; wounded at Fredericksburg, Va., Dec. 11, 1862; promoted from private, March 7, 1863; mustered out with company, May 29th, 1863.

William E. Shaffer, Aug. 12, 1862; wounded at Fredericksburg, Va., Dec. 11, 1862; mustered out with company, May 29, 1863.

Caleb H. Roe, Aug. 12, 1862; promoted from private, Jan. 1, 1862; mustered out with company, May 29th, 1863.

Corporals.

Leander Sanders, Aug. 12, 1862; mustered out with company, May 29, 1863.

John P. Kleis, Aug. 12, 1862; mustered out with company, May 29, 1863.

Henry Willis, Aug. 12, 1862; wounded at Fredericksburg, Va., Dec. 13, 1862; mustered out with company, May 29, 1863.

John W. Klineline, Aug. 12, 1862; promoted to corporal, Nov. 1, 1862; mustered out with company, May 29, 1863.

Abraham F. Brinser, Aug. 12, 1862; promoted to corporal, Nov. 1, 1862; mustered out with company, May 29, 1863.

*David Fisher, Aug. 12, 1862; promoted to corporal Nov. 1, 1862; mustered out with company, May 29, 1863.

Robert C. Lowman, Aug. 12, 1862; promoted to corporal, Nov. 1, 1862; mustered out with company, May 29, 1863.

*James G. Davis, Aug. 12, 1862; discharged on surgeon's certificate, Feb. 6, 1863.

*Frank A. Shott, Aug. 12, 1862; died Nov. 10, 1862.

Musicians.

Henry Hipple, Aug. 12, 1862; mustered out with company, May 29, 1863.

Valentine Ruth, Aug. 12, 1862; mustered out with company, May 29, 1863.

Privates.

*Ackerman, Ansil, Aug. 12, 1862; mustered out with company, May 12, 1863.

Airgood, Paul, Aug. 13, 1862; mustered out with company, May 29, 1863.

*Atherton, Alonzo, Aug. 12, 1862; mustered out with company, May 29, 1863.

*Arnold, Jonas S., Aug. 12, 1862; died Dec. 22, 1862, of wounds received at Fredericksburg, Va., Dec. 13, 1862.

*Beck, William V., Aug. 12, 1862; mustered out with company, May 29, 1863.

---

*Dead.

Bancus, Henry, Aug. 12, 1862; captured at Fredericksburg, Va., Dec. 11, 1862; mustered out with company, May 29, 1863.
*Bretz, Elias Jacob, Aug. 12, 1862; captured at Fredericksburg, Va., Dec. 11, 1862; mustered out with company May 29, 1863.
Bretz, Benjamin F., Aug. 13, 1862; mustered out with company, May 29, 1863.
Brown, Andrew, Aug. 12, 1862; mustered out with company, May 29, 1863.
Bear, John, Aug. 13, 1862; mustered out with company, May 29, 1863.
Burns, John, Aug. 12, 1862; mustered out with company, May 29, 1863.
Branshoff, Henry, Aug. 12, 1862; mustered out with company, May 29, 1863.
Brandt, Benjamin, Aug. 13, 1862; mustered out with company, May 29, 1863.
Beachler, Jacob, Aug. 12, 1862; mustered out with company, May 29, 1863.
Brown, Henry, Aug. 13, 1862; mustered out with company, May 29, 1863.
Brinzer, John, Aug. 12, 1862; discharged on surgeon's certificate, Jan. 22, 1863.
*Bretz, Daniel, Aug. 13, 1862; died Dec. 31, 1862.
Campbell, Alexander, Aug. 12, 1862; mustered out with company, May 29, 1863.
*Cramer, John, Aug. 12, 1862; captured at Fredericksburg, Va., Dec. 11, 1862; mustered out with company, May 29, 1863.
Coble, Solomon, Aug. 12, 1862; mustered out with company, May 29, 1863.
Crick, Frank, Aug. 12, 1862; mustered out with company, May 29, 1863.
Campbell, David, Aug. 12, 1862; promoted to Q. M. Sergt. Dec. 1, 1862.
*Davis, Jacob, Aug. 12, 1862; mustered out with company, May 29, 1863.
*Davis, Theophilus, Aug. 12, 1862; mustered out with company, May 29, 1863.
*Detweiler, Jacob, Aug. 12, 1862; died at Washington, D. C., Nov. 16, 1862.
Epler, Richard, Aug. 13, 1862; mustered out with company, May 29, 1863.
Fratts, William H., Aug. 12, 1862; mustered out with company, May 29, 1863.
Fitzpatrick, Thomas, Aug. 13, 1862; captured at Fredericksburg, Va., Dec. 11, 1862; mustered out with company, May 29, 1863.

*Dead.

Hoover, Isaac W., Aug. 13, 1862; mustered out with company, May 29, 1863.
Hickernell, Robert, Aug. 12, 1862; captured at Fredericksburg, Va., December 11, 1862; mustered out with company, May 29, 1863.
*Hickerñell, David L., Aug. 13, 1862; mustered out with company, May 29, 1863.
*Houser, Jacob R., Aug. 12, 1862; mustered out with company, May 29, 1863.
Herold, Leonard, Aug. 12, 1862; mustered out with company, May 29, 1863.
Irely, Samuel, Aug. 12, 1862; mustered out with company, May 29, 1863.
Irely, John, Aug. 12, 1862; mustered out with company, May 29, 1863.
James, David, Aug. 12, 1862; mustered out with company, May 29, 1863.
Jenkins, Henry S., Aug. 12, 1862; captured at Fredericksburg, Va., Dec. 11, 1862; mustered out with company, May 29, 1863.
*Jones, James, Aug. 12, 1862; mustered out with company, May 29, 1863.
Koehler, Charles, Aug. 12, 1862; mustered out with company, May 29, 1863.
Keyser, Jacob, Aug. 12, 1862; mustered out with company, May 29, 1863.
*Lutz, William, Aug. 12, 1862; captured at Fredericksburg, Va., Dec. 11, 1862; mustered out with company, May 29, 1863.
*Laughman, Daniel, Aug. 12, 1862; discharged on surgeon's certificate, Dec. 30, 1862.
Miller, James, Sept. 16, 1862; mustered out with company, May 29, 1863.
Murphy, Robert, Aug. 12, 1862; mustered out with company, May 29, 1863.
*Manybeck, Amos, Aug. 12, 1862; discharged on surgeon's certificate, Oct. 16, 1862.
Miller, John, Aug. 12, 1862.
McBarron, William, Aug. 12, 1862; mustered out with company, May 29, 1863.
*McNeal, George, Aug. 12, 1862; mustered out with company, May 29, 1863.
*McBarron, John, Aug. 12, 1862; killed at Fredericksburg, Va., Dec. 13, 1862.
Null, Jacob S., Aug. 12, 1862; mustered out with company, May 29, 1863.
*Osman, John B., Aug. 12, 1862; died April 6, 1863.

*Dead.

Phillips, William, Aug. 12, 1862; mustered out with company, May 29, 1863.
Ruhl, Wilhelm, Aug. 12, 1862; mustered out with company, May 29, 1863.
Rehrer, Nicholas, Aug. 12, 1862; wounded at Fredericksburg, Va., Dec. 11, 1862; mustered out with company, May 29, 1863.
Rittersback, Jacob, Aug. 12, 1862; mustered out with company, May 29, 1863.
Ramsey, Charles J., Aug. 12, 1862; mustered out with company, May 29, 1863.
*Reed, John, Aug. 12, 1862; killed at Fredericksburg, Va., Dec. 13, 1862.
Schreiner, Henry J., Aug. 12, 1862; mustered out with company, May 29, 1863.
Stipe, Andrew J., Aug. 12, 1862; captured at Fredericksburg, Va., Dec. 11, 1862; mustered out with company, May 29, 1863.
Stipe, Andrew, Aug. 12, 1862; mustered out with company, May 29, 1863.
*Stipe, Jackson, Aug. 12, 1862; mustered out with company, May 29, 1863.
Sheetz, John H., Aug. 12, 1862; mustered out with company, May 29, 1863.
Shaffer, Isaac H., Aug. 12, 1862; mustered out with company, May 29, 1863.
*Snyder, Joseph H., Aug. 12, 1862; mustered out with company, May 29, 1863.
Snyder, Samuel, Aug. 12, 1862; mustered out with company, May 29, 1863.
Siple, William H., August 12, 1862; mustered out with company, May 29, 1863.
Snavely, John W., Aug. 12, 1862; mustered out with company, May 29, 1863.
*Swords, William, Aug. 12, 1862; wounded at Fredericksburg, Va., Dec. 13, 1862; mustered out with company, May 29, 1863.
*Singer, Philip, Aug. 12, 1862; mustered out with company, May 29, 1863.
Sebolt, John, Aug. 12, 1862; mustered out with company, May 29, 1863.
*Stipe, William, Aug. 12, 1862; wounded at Fredericksburg, Va., Dec. 13, 1862; discharged on surgeon's certificate, April 1, 1863.
Ulrich, Martin, Aug. 12, 1862; mustered out with company, May 29, 1863.
Ulrich, Solomon, Aug. 12, 1862; mustered out with company, May 29, 1863.

*Dead.

Wendling, John, Aug. 12, 1862; mustered out with company, May 29, 1863.
Whisler, John L., Aug. 12, 1862; mustered out with company, May 29, 1863.
Winters, David, Aug. 12, 1862; mustered out with company, May 29, 1863.
Young, Hiram, Aug. 12, 1862; mustered out with company, May 29, 1863.

LII.

MIDDLETOWN VOLUNTEERS IN THE ONE HUNDRED AND EIGHTY-SEVENTH REGIMENT, PENNSYLVANIA VOLUNTEERS.
(THREE YEARS' SERVICE.)

Musician.

Henry Hipple, Co. A, April 1, 1864; mustered out with company Aug. 3, 1865; veteran.

Privates.

Hipple, Benjamin, Co. H; May 7, 1864; mustered out with company, Aug. 3, 1865.
Irely, Samuel, Co. H., May 7, 1864; mustered out with company, Aug. 3, 1865.
McGinney, John, Co. H., May 7, 1864; mustered out with company, Aug. 3, 1865.

The regiment reached the army during the fighting at Cold Harbor; was under fire on the Chickahominy, June 7th, and on the 17th and 18th at Petersburg; it here lost one-tenth of its numbers, in killed and wounded, and won the special commendation of General Chamberlain; was again under fire on the 20th at Jerusalem Plank Road, and in engagements on the 18th and 19th of August, at Yellow House. September 22nd the regiment was ordered to Camp Cadwallader, near Philadelphia. It headed the Lincoln funeral procession from the Baltimore depot to Independence Hall; was left as guard of honor while the remains lay in state, and escorted them from Independence Hall to the New York depot when they were borne away. May 11th, 1865, it was detached for provost duty in different parts of the State and mustered out of service August 11, 1865.

MIDDLETOWN VOLUNTEERS IN COMPANY C, ONE HUNDRED AND NINETY-SECOND REGIMENT, PENNSYLVANIA VOLUNTEERS. (THREE YEARS' SERVICE.)

Privates.

Bankis, John, Feb. 9, 1865; mustered out with company, Aug. 24, 1865.

NOTE: These rolls contain the names of those who enlisted here; and of those residents here during the war, who enlisted elsewhere.

Bankis, Jacob, Feb. 10, 1865; mustered out with company, Aug. 24, 1865.
Brooks, Cyrus, Feb. 14, 1865; mustered out with company, Aug. 24, 1865.
Grafe, John, Feb. 9, 1865; mustered out with company, Aug. 24, 1865.
Hawk, George W., Feb. 10, 1865; mustered out with company, Aug. 24, 1865.
Lynch, John, Feb. 9, 1865; mustered out with company, Aug. 24, 1865.
Miller, Andrew, Feb. 9, 1865; mustered out with company, Aug. 24, 1865.
Ridley, Henry, Feb. 10, 1865; mustered out with company, Aug. 24, 1865.

The Twentieth Regiment, Pennsylvania Militia (1862) were reorganized and recruited in July, 1864, for one hundred days' service, as the One Hundred and Ninety-second Regiment of the line. Their term of service having expired the men were mustered out in November. One company re-enlisted to form part of a second regiment, still known as the One Hundred and Ninety-second. In the spring of 1865, nine new companies (in one of which were the Middletown men), were recruited and reported at Harper's Ferry. A regimental organization was effected in March. When the spring campaign opened the regiment moved up the valley to Staunton and Lexington; but few of the enemy were met, the fighting here being substantially at an end. It was, however, retained and engaged in various duties until the 24th of August, when it was mustered out of service.

MIDDLETOWN VOLUNTEERS IN THE ONE HUNDRED AND NINETY-FOURTH REGIMENT, PENNSYLVANIA VOLUNTEERS. (ONE HUNDRED DAYS' SERVICE.)

Captain.

George F. Ross, Co. D, July 18, 1864; mustered out with company, Nov. 6, 1864.

Sergeant.

Charles H. Snively, Co. D, July 18, 1864; transferred to 92nd Regiment, P. V., Sept. 6, 1864.

Privates.

*Atherton, Alonzo, Co. D, July 18, 1864; mustered out with company, Nov. 4, 1864.
Fortney, Christian, Co. D, July 18, 1864; mustered out with company, Nov. 6, 1864.

Hickernell, William H., Co. D, July 18, 1864; transferred to 92nd Regiment, P. V., Sept. 6, 1864.

Landis, Robert F., Co. E, July 18, 1864; mustered out with company, Nov. 6, 1864.

Marquart, Mahlon, Co. D, July 18, 1864; mustered out with company, Nov. 6, 1864.

Rife, John W., Co. D, July 18, 1864; mustered out with company, Nov. 6, 1864.

Stipe, Andrew J., Co. G, July 20, 1864; mustered out with company, Nov. 6, 1864.

This regiment was organized at Camp Curtin, July 22, 1864. On the day of its organization it moved to Baltimore, and went into camp at Mackin's Woods. September 1st it moved to Camp Carroll, one mile southwest of the city, on the line of the Baltimore & Ohio Railroad. Several of the companies were stationed in various parts of the city for provost duty. Details to serve as escorts and guards to rebel prisoners on their way to places of confinement, and for recruits destined for the front, were constantly made as long as the regiment remained in service. At the expiration of its term the scattered detachments were called in, and it proceeded to Pennsylvania, where on November 6th it was mustered out.

One Hundred and Nineteenth and One Hundred and Ninety-first Regiments, Pennsylvania Volunteers. (Three Years' Service.)

Upon the muster out of the service of the regiments composing the Reserve Corps, a large number of veterans re-enlisted. These, with recruits whose terms had not expired, were organized into two new regiments, known as the One Hundred and Ninetieth and the One Hundred and Ninety-first. Of the Middletown volunteers, those in the One Hundred and Ninetieth were from the Seventh Reserves; those in the One Hundred and Ninety-first from the Sixth. The last battle in which the Reserves participated was that of Bethesda Church, May 30, 1864. The two new regiments were organized in the field and at once pushed to the front. During the severe fighting at Cold Harbor they were subjected to a heavy artillery and musketry fire. At Charles City, on June 13th, they held at bay during the whole day a superior force of the enemy, and a number in both regiments were killed and wounded. At Petersburg, on the 17th, they captured the entire Thirty-ninth North Carolina Regiment and, though vigorously assailed, held their ground until relieved. Their loss was considerable. Until the morning of the 23rd, the brigade (190th and 191st Regts.) was kept on active duty, losing daily in killed and wounded. During the 24th and 25th, sharp-shooting was incessant on the picket line. On the 18th of August the brigade was ordered upon the skirmish line, and actively engaged without supports until 4 o'clock on the afternoon of the 19th, when it was completely surrounded and forced to surrender. The captives were hurried away to rebel prison-pens at Richmond, Salisbury† and Danville, and kept in confinement until near the time of Lee's surrender. A small detachment which had been ordered to the rear for provisions and ammunition escaped capture, and this, with men returning from furlough and detached duty, was reorganized under command of Colonel Pattee, and transferred to the Second Division, participating with it in the remaining hostile operations until the close of the year 1864. March 29, 1865, this detachment was engaged in skirmishing at Gravelly Run, and held its ground to the last, but was finally forced back, losing a number in prisoners; it re-formed further to the left and regained the ground lost in the morning. During the night it marched with the Fifth Corps to the relief of Sheridan at Five Forks, arriving within supporting distance on the morning of April 1st. Here the command was allowed some rest, of which it was sorely in need. At noon it was ordered forward, was as usual thrown on the skirmish line, and bravely advancing one hundred yards in front of the line of battle, led the way in that grand left-wheel around the rebel rear which crushed his entire force at one blow. When the last charge was made the skirmishers awaited the coming of the main Union line, when joining in, they advanced with the column and shared in the glorious triumph, bearing away guns and small arms, and crowds of captive officers and men. From the 2nd to the 9th the pursuit was pushed; on the morning of the 9th Colonel Pattee was summoned to the fort with his command. "At about noon on the 9th," says a member of the command, "we got the order, 'Bucktails to the front,' 'double-quick,' 'march!' and away we went, past our division, past the First Division, past the advance, out into an open space. 'Battalion into line,' 'deploy as skirmishers,' 'forward,' 'double-quick,' 'march!' rang along the lines. The order seems to ring in my ears now. Away we went, Sheridan's cavalry was just coming out as we went in. Soon we got sight of the rebels and they of us. We advanced double-quick, and they fell back double-quicker. They opened on us with a battery from the brow of a hill, first with shells, and as we got closer, with canister, and just as we were about charging on the battery—up over the brow of the hill in front came a horseman, then another, and another. The first bore a white flag. 'Cease firing!' 'cease firing!' was the order, and the rider passed down through our line. 'They've surrendered,' 'they've surrendered,' was repeated from man to man, until the whole army knew the glad tidings, and cheer after cheer rent the air. The glad hour for which we had been battling for four long years, had come." After the surrender the two regiments returned to the neighborhood of Washington, and went into camp, where, on the 28th of June, they were mustered out of service.

---

†The prison-pen at Salisbury was simply an open space containing about eight acres, enclosed by a high board fence. Cannon were placed at the corners of the enclosure to overawe the prisoners, and sentinels patrolled constantly around it on

MIDDLETOWN VOLUNTEERS IN THE ONE HUNDRED AND NINETIETH REGIMENT.

Privates.

*Parson, Jeremiah, Co. F., May 22, 1864; captured; died at Salisbury, N. C., Nov. 22, 1864; veteran.

*Simpson, Orlando M., Co. F., May 31, 1864; captured; died at Salisbury, N. C., Feb. 14, 1865; veteran.

MIDDLETOWN VOLUNTEERS IN THE ONE HUNDRED AND NINETY-FIRST REGIMENT.

First Sergeant.

*James H. Stanley, Co. F, May 31, 1864; prisoner from Aug. 19, 1864, to Feb. 28, 1865; discharged by general order, June 20, 1865; veteran.

Sergeant.

Lorenzo Horn, Co. F, May 31, 1864; promoted to sergeant, June 8, 1864; captured; mustered out with company, June 28, 1865; veteran.

Corporal.

John D. Books, Co. F, May 31, 1864; captured; mustered out with company, June 28, 1865; veteran.

Privates.

Bear, Henry A., Co. F, May 31st, 1864; deserted Aug. 11, 1864; returned March 20, 1865; mustered out with company, June 28, 1865; veteran.

*Bomberger, Michael, Co. F, May 31, 1864; mustered out with company, June 28, 1865; veteran.

Dewalt, John, Co. F, May 31, 1864; mustered out with company, June 28, 1865; veteran.

---

an elevated platform built outside. Although the country surrounding it was well wooded, the rebels refused to allow the prisoners to cut trees and build barracks for themselves, consequently they had no shelter except in such holes as they could dig in the ground with their pocket knives and tin cups. Their rations, at the best, were scanty, and sometimes they were for days together without any. There were about 10,000 prisoners in the enclosure. From exposure and lack of nourishment the mortality soon became fearful, and in January, 1865, reached fifty deaths per day; sickness in nine cases out of ten, meant death. After death, the bodies were stripped of all clothing, except undergarments—loaded in wagons like logs of wood—carried out and buried in trenches. Of the 514 prisoners captured from the two regiments, besides the large number unaccounted for, 144 are *known* to have perished in this hell, during the five months they were incarcerated there. After their release numbers of the living skeletons died before our lines were reached, and many immediately afterwards.

*Dead.

*Eichelberger, George, Co. F, May 31, 1864; mustered out with company, June 28, 1865; veteran.
Fish, Lewis, Co. F, May 31, 1864; mustered out with company, June 28, 1865; veteran.
*Houser, Frederick M., Co. F, May 31, 1864; captured; died at Salisbury, N. C., Oct. 22, 1864; veteran.
*Kohler, Charles, Co. F, Feb. 4, 1864; captured; died at Salisbury, N. C., Dec. 25, 1864.
Lockard, John, Co. F, May 31, 1864; mustered out with company, June 28, 1865; veteran.
Leggore, William, Co. F, May 31, 1864; captured; mustered out with company, June 28, 1865; veteran.
Lloyd, John H., Co. G, Dec. 11, 1862; not accounted for.
Montgomery, John, Co. F, May 31, 1864; absent with leave at muster out.
Montgomery, William, Co. F, May 31, 1864; prisoner from May 31, 1864 to Feb. 28, 1865; discharged by general order, June 1, 1865; veteran.
Martin, Jacob, Co. F, May 31, 1864; mustered out with company, June 28, 1865.

Two Hundredth Regiment, Pennsylvania Volunteers. (One Year's Service.)

This regiment organized at Camp Curtin, September 3, 1864. September 9th it was ordered to join the Army of the James, and was posted at Dutch Gap. November 23rd it was transferred to the Army of the Potomac, forming part of the First Brigade, Third Division, Ninth Corps, and was stationed near Fort Steadman. When on March 5, 1865, the rebels captured this fort and the batteries to the right and left, the Two Hundredth being the regiment nearest the fort, was ordered to oppose the advance of the enemy. Twice it was compelled to retire, but rallied and reformed, and other troops coming to its support, the entire line dashed resolutely forward. The triumph was complete; Fort Steadman was retaken with all its guns uninjured; the line lost was regained, and nearly three thousand prisoners captured. The loss of the regiment in this brief engagement was very severe, being fourteen killed and one hundred and nine wounded. Lieutenant Colonel McCall, who led the regiment, says in his official report: "The officers and men of my command all showed the greatest bravery. General Hartranft, commander of the division, in his official report, says: "The Two Hundredth Pennsylvania Volunteers deserves particular mention. This regiment was put to the severest test, and behaved with the greatest firmness and steadiness. The regiment made two stubborn attacks upon the enemy, and when compelled to retire it fell back in good order."

---
*Dead.

April 2nd, at 4 a. m., the division was massed and formed for assault, Lieutenant Colonel McCall leading the brigade and Major Rehrer the regiment. The Two Hundredth was held in reserve when the first dash was made, but was ordered to follow almost immediately, and was subjected to a destructive fire. Says Major Rehrer in his official report: "The officers and men in my regiment did, in this charge under a heavy fire from the enemy, behave with great gallantry and coolness, at no time showing the least sign of faltering or breaking. At this point of the enemy's works we came in possession of two batteries, each mounting three guns. I at once sent to the rear for the artillerists, who were accordingly furnished, and the captured guns turned upon the enemy. These works were held during the entire day by my regiment, and were all the time under a heavy fire of mixed artillery. Three desperate charges were made by the enemy in which they put forth every effort to recapture the forts, but they were each time repulsed speedily and with heavy loss. After darkness had set in, I was ordered to remove the abbatis and chevaux-de-frise formerly used by the enemy and now in our rear, round so as to confront and face the enemy, and I at the same time advanced one hundred men as a picket line. After this period no attempt was made by the enemy to retake the works, and by 10 p. m. firing began to be less rapid. At midnight no firing at all was done, except now and then a shot from a sharpshooter." At 4 on the following morning, the regiment, with the division, entered the city of Petersburg unopposed, the enemy having withdrawn during the night. The loss in this engagement was two killed, thirty-four wounded and three missing. Major Rehrer was among the wounded, but did not leave the field. The pursuit of the enemy was at once commenced, and continued until the 9th, when the rebel army surrendered.

The regiment went into camp at Nottoway Court House, where it remained until after the surrender of Johnston, when it marched to City Point, and thence proceeded by transport to Alexandria. Here it remained until the 30th of May, when the recruits were transferred to the Fifty-first Pennsylvania, and the rest of the regiment was mustered out of service.

MIDDLETOWN VOLUNTEERS IN THE TWO HUNDREDTH REGIMENT.

Major.

Jacob Rehrer, Sept. 2, 1864; promoted from private Co. C, Sept. 3, 1864; wounded at Petersburg, Va., April 2, 1865; to lieutenant colonel, April 2, 1865; mustered out with the regiment, May 30, 1865.

Captain.

George Huber, Co. G, Sept. 1, 1864; mustered out with company, May 30, 1865.

First Lieutenant.

John McWilliams, Co. G, Sept. 1, 1864; wounded at Fort Steadman, Va., March 25, 1865; brevet captain, April 2, 1865; mustered out with company, May 30, 1865.

Second Lieutenants.

David Campbell, Co. G, Sept. 1, 1864; mustered out with company, May 30, 1865.

John S. Mackinson, Co. B, Aug. 29, 1864; commissioned first lieutenant, March 31, 1865; not mustered; mustered out with company, May 30, 1865.

Sergeant.

Joseph A. Peters, Co. G, Aug. 31, 1864; wounded at Fort Steadman, Va., March 25, 1865; absent in hospital at muster out.

Privates.

Bailey, George H., Co. G, Aug. 16, 1864; mustered out with company, May 30, 1865.

Boner, John A., Co. G, Aug. 16, 1864; mustered out with company, May 30, 1865.

Brandt, Henry, Co. G, Aug. 16, 1864; mustered out with company, May 30, 1865.

*Chubb, John, Co. G, Aug. 30, 1864; mustered out with company, May 30, 1865.

*Davis, James G., Co. C, Aug. 31, 1864; mustered out with company, May 30, 1865.

Embich, Elijah S., Co. G, Aug. 18, 1864; mustered out with company, May 30, 1865.

Fry, Webster W., Co. G, Aug. 30, 1864; mustered out with company, May 30, 1865.

Hemperly, George L., Co. C, Aug. 30, 1864; mustered out with company, May 30, 1865.

Houser, Jacob, Co. G, Aug. 16, 1864; mustered out with company, May 30, 1865.

Hyde, David, Co. G, Aug. 16, 1864; mustered out with company, May 30, 1865.

*Jameson, John, Co. G, Aug. 16, 1864; mustered out with company, May 30, 1865.

*Linn, Jacob, Co. G, Aug. 23, 1864; mustered out with company, May 30, 1865.

*Pierce, George W., Jan. 20, 1865; unassigned.

*Seibert, George W., Co. G, Aug. 20, 1864; wounded at Fort Steadman, Va., March 25, 1865; absent in hospital at muster out.

*Dead.

Siders, John, Co. G, Aug. 16, 1864; mustered out with company, May 30, 1865.
Sipe, John F., Co. G, Aug. 16, 1864; mustered out with company, May 30, 1865.
*Sleeper, Joshua, Co. G, Sept. 7, 1864; wounded at Fort Steadman, Va., March 25, 1865; absent in hospital at muster out.
Snyder, John, Co. C, Sept. 4, 1864; mustered out with company, May 30, 1865.
*Wannemacher, John, Co. G, Aug. 16, 1864; wounded at Petersburg, Va., March 2, 1865; absent in hospital at muster out.
Young, Hiram, Co. G, Aug. 16, 1864; mustered out with company, May 30, 1865.

MIDDLETOWN VOLUNTEERS IN CO. G, TWO HUNDRED AND FIRST REGIMENT, PENNSYLVANIA VOLUNTEERS. (ONE YEAR'S SERVICE.)

Privates.

Beaverson, David, Aug. 19, 1864; mustered out with company, June 21, 1865.
Cain, George W., Aug. 16, 1864; mustered out with company, June 21, 1865.
Myers, Charles, Aug. 22, 1864; mustered out with company, June 21, 1865.
Milligan, Samuel, Aug. 19, 1864; mustered out with company, June 21, 1865.
Rodgers, Henry, Aug. 19, 1864; mustered out with company, June 21, 1865.
Strouse, Solomon, Aug. 16, 1864; mustered out with company, June 21, 1865.
Staeger, David C., Aug. 22, 1864; mustered out with company, June 21, 1865.
Staeger, William H., Aug. 24, 1864; mustered out with company, June 21, 1865.
Stees, Jacob S., Aug. 24, 1864; mustered out with company, June 21, 1865.

This regiment was recruited under the call of the President of July 18, 1864, for five hundred thousand men. Of the ten regiments required from Pennsylvania under this call, this was the first ready for duty. It organized at Camp Curtin, August 29th, and immediately proceeded to Chambersburg, where it went into camp of instruction. September 17th Companies F and G were ordered to Bloody Run. Shortly afterwards Company F was sent to McConnellsburg. During the fall and winter these two companies were employed in the disagreeable but arduous duties of arresting deserters, nearly five hundred being appre-

---

*Dead.

hended and sent to the front. May 24, 1865, Company G was ordered to Pittsburgh, where it was put upon provost duty, and its commander, Captain Ensminger, was made provost marshal. About the middle of June the scattered detachments assembled at Camp Curtin, where on the 21st the regiment was mustered out of service.

LIII.

MIDDLETOWN VOLUNTEERS IN THE TWENTY-SECOND UNITED STATES COLORED REGIMENT. (THREE YEARS' SERVICE.)

Sergeant.

Thomas H. Ayres, Co. E, Dec. 26, 1863; mustered out with company, Oct. 16, 1865.

Corporal.

*Eli Ayres, Co. E, Dec. 26, 1863; mustered out with company, Oct. 16, 1865.

Privates.

Henry, David, Co. G, Dec. 31, 1863; mustered out with company, Oct. 16, 1865.

Thornton, Robert, Co. G, Dec. 31, 1863; mustered out with company, Oct. 16, 1866.

This regiment organized at Camp William Penn in January, 1864; headed the charge at Petersburg, Va., June 15th, captured six of the seven guns taken by the division, and two of the four forts. Its loss in this engagement was eighteen killed, one hundred and forty-three wounded and one missing. In the assault at Chapin's Farm, September 29th, its loss was eleven killed, four wounded and eight missing. October 27th it led the charge of the column on the Williamsburg Road, and near the old Fair Oaks battleground was repulsed with a loss of over one hundred killed and wounded; April 3, 1865, was among the first of General Weitzel's troops to enter Richmond, and rendered important service in extinguishing the fires then raging in that city. It participated in the Lincoln obsequies, and was then sent to Eastern Maryland to assist in the capture of Booth and his co-conspirators. In May it was sent to Texas and assigned to duty upon the Rio Grande. It returned to Philadelphia in October and was mustered out of service.

*Dead.
NOTE: These rolls contain the names of those who enlisted here; and of those residents here during the war, who enlisted elsewhere.

MIDDLETOWN VOLUNTEERS IN THE TWENTY-FOURTH UNITED STATES COLORED REGIMENT. (THREE YEARS' SERVICE.)

Privates.

Bell, Preston, Co. D, Feb. 14, 1865; mustered out with company, Oct. 1, 1865.
*McClure, Walter, Co. H, March 3, 1865; died at Burkesville, Va., Sept. 13, 1865.
Thomas, Frederick, Co. B, Feb. 2, 1865; mustered out with company, Oct. 1, 1865.

This regiment organized at Camp William Penn, February 17, 1865; in May it proceeded to Washington and was placed in Camp Casey, opposite the city. June 1st the regiment was ordered to Point Lookout, Md., where it was employed in guarding rebel prisoners. In July it was ordered to Richmond, Va., and assigned to duty in the sub-district of Roanoke, with headquarters at Burkesville. Government supplies were distributed to the needy inhabitants, and the troops were employed in preserving order. In September the regiment was ordered to Richmond, and in October mustered out of service.

MIDDLETOWN VOLUNTEERS IN THE TWENTY-FIFTH UNITED STATES COLORED REGIMENT. (THREE YEARS' SERVICE.)

Privates.

*Bell, Franklin, Co. H, Feb. 2, 1864; mustered out with company, Dec. 6, 1865.
*Bouser, John, Co. I, Feb. 9, 1864; mustered out with company, Dec. 6, 1865.
*Bouser, George, Co. K, Feb. 10, 1864; died at Philadelphia, Pa., April 4, 1864.
*Thomas, Isaac, Co. H, May 7, 1865; discharged, to date Dec. 6, 1865.
Woodward, John, Co. G, Jan. 30, 1864; died at Philadelphia, Pa., March 2, 1864.

This regiment was organized at Camp William Penn in February, 1864. It was ordered to Indianola, Tex., and March 15th sailed for New Orleans on the steamer Suwanee. In a storm off Hatteras the steamer sprung a leak, the men were put to work with buckets, and managed to keep her afloat until, after thirty-six hours of hard work, she was brought into the harbor of Beaufort, N. C., where she was abandoned. The enemy was closely pressing the siege of Little Washington, in that State, and the Twenty-fifth was placed in the defenses until the emergency passed, when it was sent to New Orleans, where it ar-

*Dead.

rived May 1st. The regiment then went to Barrancas, Fla., where it was charged with garrison duty. During the spring and summer of 1865 the men suffered terribly from scurvy, about one hundred and fifty dying, and as many more being disabled for life. The mortality at one time amounted to from four to six daily. This was the result of want of proper food, but not until the disease had run its course were the appeals of its officers for supplies answered. The regiment remained on duty at the forts until December, when it was ordered to Philadelphia, and on the 6th at Camp Cadwallader was mustered out of service.

Speaking of the Twenty-fifth, Colonel Hitchcock says: "I desire to bear testimony to the *esprit de corps* and general efficiency of the organization as a regiment, to the competency and general good character of its officers, to the soldierly bearing, fidelity to duty and patriotism of its men. Having seen active service in the Army of the Potomac prior to my connection with the Twenty-fifth, I can speak with some degree of assurance."

MIDDLETOWN VOLUNTEERS IN COMPANY G, FIFTH MASSACHUSETTS CAVALRY. (COLORED.)

Sergeant.

William Harley.

Privates.

Samuel Harley, Alexander Hilton, William Lum, Benjamin Lum, Thomas G. Stanton, Samuel Thomas, George W. Washington.

They were enrolled February 27, 1864; went to Boston; were mustered in March 4, 1864; mustered out with company at Clarksville, Texas, October 31, 1865.

LIV.

MIDDLETOWN VOLUNTEERS IN OTHER REGIMENTS.

*Capt. B. F. Ashenfelter, Co. H, 201st Regiment, P. V., Aug. 28, 1864; one year; mustered out with company, June 21, 1865. (See 35th Regiment.)

Rush Bennett, 54th Regiment, Massachusetts Colored Infantry.
Henry Campbell, Co. K, Fourth U. S. Infantry.
*William Gillette, Co. K, Fourth U. S. Infantry.
Benjamin Campbell, 9th Regiment, New York Volunteers. (Hawkins' Zouaves.)
Philip C. Elberti, Co. A, 91st Regiment, P. V., Aug. 21, 1861; promoted to hospital steward, Dec. 4, 1861; transferred to United States service as hospital steward May 26, 1862; discharged May 26, 1865; expiration of term.

*Dead.

Middletown Reservoir, near Round Top.

George W. Farrington, seaman, U. S. steamer *Essex;* discharged by general order, Aug. 5, 1865.
Calvin Garret, Co. H, 195th Regiment, P. V., Feb. 27, 1865; discharged by general order, Jan. 31, 1866.
*Dr. James A. Lowe, assistant surgeon St. Joseph's Hospital, Philadelphia.
*Augustus Long, Battery I, 152nd Regiment, P. V. (Third Artillery); March 11, 1864; discharged by general order, July 5, 1865.
Alvan McNair, Co. D, 6th U. S. Cavalry, Aug. 31, 1861; three years; discharged Aug. 31, 1864; expiration of term.
Dr. George F. Mish, surgeon 5th P. M., Sept. 13, 1862; discharged Sept. 27, 1862; assistant surgeon 160th Regiment, P. V. (Anderson Cavalry), Oct. 4, 1862; Captured at Stone River, Dec. 29, 1862; ordered to attend Union prisoners during their passage from Chattanooga to Richmond, Va.; attended prisoners in Libby; released Feb. 1863; mustered out with regiment at Nashville, Tenn., June 21, 1865.
*Rev. John McCosker, chaplain 55th Regiment, P. V., Dec. 6, 1861; three years; died at Philadelphia, June 4, 1862.
John Poorman, Q. M. Serg't, 64th Regiment, P. V., Jan. 4, 1864; three years; promoted from private March 1, 1865; mustered out with company, July 1, 1865; veteran.
Capt. George F. Ross, 13th Regiment, Iowa Volunteers; appointed A. D. C. to General Crocker, Sixth Division Iowa Volunteers; wounded at second battle of Corinth. (See 194th Regiment, P. V.)
George W. Rodfong, Signal Corps, U. S. A., Feb. 18, 1864; three years; discharged by general order, Aug. 28, 1865.
*George Seibert, Co. I, 51st Regiment, P. V., Jan. 23, 1865; discharged by surgeon's certificate, July 27, 1865.
*Lieut. Frank R. Walborn, second lieutenant Co. K, 214th Regiment, P. V., March 25, 1865; one year; commissioned first lieutenant July 12, 1865; not mustered; mustered out with company, March 21, 1865; afterwards successively private in 6th U. S. Cavalry and first lieutenant in 31st U. S. Infantry. (See 35th Regiment, P. V.)

W. H. Embick, Co. A, 201st Regiment, P. V., one year's service, Aug. 18, 1864; mustered out with company, June 25, 1865.
Joseph H. Hoyer, Co. I, 2nd Regiment, P. V., 3 months' service, April 30, 1861; mustered out with company, July 26, 1861.
W. H. McBarron, Co. I, 201st Regiment, P. V., one year's service, Aug. 18, 1864; promoted to corporal, Aug. 24, 1864; mustered out with company, June 25, 1865.
Frederick Miller, Co. E, 117th Regiment (13th Cavalry), P. V., three years, Aug. 12, 1863; mustered out with company, July 14, 1865.

---

*Dead.
16

Jacob P. Shroy, Co. E, 117th Regiment (13th Cavalry), P. V., Aug. 8, 1863; died at Salisbury, N. C., Dec. 28, 1864.

Dr. Luther L. Rewalt, assistant surgeon, 25th Regiment, P. V., three months' service, April 18, 1861; mustered out with company, July 26, 1861; afterwards assistant surgeon 22nd Cavalry.

George G. Rakestraw, chaplain 201st Regiment, P. V., one year's service, Aug. 29, 1864; mustered out with regiment, June 21, 1865.

Captain George F. Ross, Co. G, 13th Regiment, Iowa Infantry, Oct. 28, 1861; wounded through bowels at battle of Corinth, Miss.; discharged by general order, April 28, 1863; assistant provost marshal 14th Pennsylvania district; captain Co. D, 194th Regiment, P. V., July 18, 1864; mustered out with company, April 6, 1864.

John C. Snyder, Co. E, 203rd Regiment, P. V., Sept. 6, 1864; promoted to corporal April 1st, 1865; mustered out with company, June 22, 1865.

Total number of Middletown volunteers (exclusive of re-enlistments and militia), 441.

The roll is completed. Middletown, a thriving place when Pittsburgh was a village, and Harrisburg not in existence; whose commerce once exceeded that of any other town on the Susquehanna; where it was once proposed to locate the county seat—the State Capitol—now exercises but small influence in State affairs and is rarely heard of outside her immediate neighborhood. Her sons fought in the early Indian wars of the Republic; battled for liberty in the Revolution, and at a later day, in a mightier struggle, maintained her ancient reputation for bravery and patriotism.

There she stands, with a record that few towns can equal—none surpass. With a population in 1860 of two thousand six hundred and sixty-seven souls (including Port Royal), and but about five hundred and thirty-four voters, she sent to the field in four years (excluding re-enlistments), four hundred and thirty-three men.

A quarter of a century has flown by since her volunteers, in the pride of their young manhood, left her homes, and went forth to battle for their country, and the war-worn veterans who survive, whose health and strength were sapped in the hardships of those weary campaigns, will, in a few years, join the comrades that shot, shell, starvation in rebel prison-pens and disease sent to their deaths earlier. But though no monument may ever be erected over them, long after the cowards who skulked and tories who sneered, are unremembered dust; long after the traitors who inaugurated the "Great Rebellion" have joined Iscariot, Arnold, Burr and their compeers in eternal infamy, the memory of the men who risked their lives to save that of their country will be enshrined in her heart, and their names remain inscribed in her annals.

> "Nor wreck, nor change, nor winter's blight,
> Nor Time's remorseless doom,
> Can dim one ray of holy light
> That gilds their glorious tomb."

[From correspondents in Tuscumbia, Ala., Artesian City, Dak. Ter. Philadelphia, and elsewhere, we have received the following additional information respecting Middletown men in the Union army. If our informants will read over the rolls already published they will find that the other names sent in have already been mentioned. Capt. Ross' record is re-printed because it is more definite than that first given.]

Quartermaster's Department, U. S. A. [During Early's raid the men in this department, numbering about eight hundred, were formed into a regiment to repel his attack. As Edward Allen, John B. Cole, George Rodfong, Sr., Levi Shaefer, Charles Allen and other Middletown men were in this regiment the following is of interest.]

QUARTERMASTER'S OFFICE (LINCOLN BRANCH), DEPOT OF WASHINGTON.

WASHINGTON, D. C., *March 3, 1866.*

This is to certify that George Rodfong, employed in the wheelwright shop of Q. M. Dept., Washington, D. C., was a member of Co. G, 1st Regiment, organized employes Q. M. Dept., and at the time of the rebel demonstration on Washington, in July, 1864, went into the rifle pits north of the city, in defense of the same; and that he further remained a member of said regiment, and did all the duties required of him as such, until the disbanding of the regiment on the 1st day of April, 1865.

CHAS. H. TOMKINS,
Bvt. Col. & Q. M. U. S. A., Col. 1st Regt. O. E. Q. M. D.
J. CALM,
Supt. U. S. Repair Shops & Major 1st Regt. O. E. Q. M. Dept.

LV.

MILITIA 1862.

After its triumph in the second battle of Bull Run, the rebel army hastened northward and commenced crossing the Potomac. The Reserve Corps which was originally organized for the State defense had been called to the succor of the hard-pressed army of McClellan upon the Peninsula, and was now upon the weary march, with ranks sadly thinned in the hard fought battles of Mechanicsville, Gaines' Mill, Charles City Cross-Roads and the second Bull Run, to again meet the foe, but powerless to avert the threatened danger. The result of the struggle on the plain of Manassas, was no sooner known, than the helpless condition of the State, which had been apparent from the first, became a subject of alarm.

On the 4th of September Governor Curtin issued a proclamation, call-

---

NOTE: These rolls contain the names of those who enlisted here, and of those residents here during the war, who enlisted elsewhere.

ing on the people to arm and prepare for defense. He recommended the immediate formation of companies and regiments throughout the Commonwealth, and for the purposes of drill and instruction, that after 3 p. m. of each day, all business houses be closed. On the 10th, the danger having become imminent, he issued a general order, calling on the able-bodied men to enroll immediately for the defense of the State, and to hold themselves in readiness to march upon an hour's notice; to select officers, to provide themselves with such arms as could be obtained, with sixty rounds of ammunition to the man, tendering arms to such as had none, and promising that they should be held for service, for such time only as the pressing exigency for State defense should continue. On the following day, acting under authority of the President of the United States, the Governor called for fifty thousand men, directing them to report by telegraph for orders to move, and adding that further calls would be made if necessary. The people everywhere fled to arms, and regiments and companies were forwarded as fast as they could be organized. Fifteen thousand men were concentrated in the neighborhood of Hagerstown and Boonsboro. Ten thousand more were in the vicinity of Greencastle and Chambersburg, and about twenty-five thousand were on their way or waiting for transportation to advance. Gen. John F. Reynolds, who was at the time commanding a corps in the Army of the Potomac, assumed command of the militia. On the 14th the head of the Army of the Potomac met the enemy at South Mountain and hurled him through its passes, and on the 16th and 17th a fierce battle was fought at Antietam, the enemy was defeated and retreated in confusion across the Potomac. The emergency having passed the militia regiments were mustered out and disbanded. With few exceptions they were not in actual conflict, but they nevertheless rendered most efficient service. They gave moral support to the Union army, and had that army been defeated they would have taken the place of the fallen. Called suddenly to the field from the walks of private life, with little opportunity for drill or discipline, they grasped their muskets, and by their prompt obedience to every order, showed their willingness—all unprepared as they were—to face an enemy before whom veterans had often quailed. The bloodless campaigns of the militia may be a subject for playful satire, but in the strong arms and sturdy hearts of the yeomanry of the land, who spring to arms at the moment of danger, and when that danger has passed, cheerfully lay them down again, rests a sure guarantee for the peace and security of the country.

In Middletown two companies answered the call; one was:

THE MIDDLETOWN GUARDS.

On the 10th of September this company formed and organized; left here on the 11th, reaching Chambersburg on the 12th. Says the Dauphin *Journal:* "A more courageous and enthusiastic set of men than this company represents never shouldered a musket, and although a number are quite young, their hearts are brimful of patriotism, and they are the right kind of boys to make the rebels howl." They were disbanded September 27th. (Some twenty of this company afterwards enlisted in volunteer regiments.)

Captain.
Enoch S. Yentzer.

First Lieutenant.
*Henry C. Raymond.

Second Lieutenant.
Joseph H. Landis.

First Sergeant.
*George H. Lenhart.

Sergeants.

Hiram H. Parson,
Franklin Smith,

*Nelson F. Wood,
George W. Ettele.

Corporals.

Joseph K. Oren,
Hamlet Murr,

John H. Shaeffer,
Simon S. Campbell.

Musician.
John R. Sonders.

Privates.

*Ackerman, Geo. W.,
*Antrim, Joseph H.,
*Arnold, James H.,
Brubaker, Henry M.,
*Beaverson, David,
Fishburn, John,
*Fencil, George,
Fortney, Christian,
Fry, Webster W.,
Griffey, John,
Hoffman, John,
Hickernell, Wm. H.,
Hipple, James,

Hawk, George W.,
Henry, Jacob,
Haggerty, John,
Irely, Samuel,
Irwin, George H.
Keller, John,
Lynch, John,
Leonard, David,
Moore, Matthew,
McGinnis, John,
*Norton, Patrick F.,
*Orth, Abraham L.,
Peters, Simon C.,

*Dead.

*Poorman, Andrew J.,
Rodfong, George W.,
Rife, John W.,
Smith, John,
*Starr, William D.,
Vincent, David,
Wentling, Orlando L.,
Winagle, Wm. F.,
Wilson, William I.,
*Wannemacher, John.

MIDDLETOWN CAVALRY.

Says the Dauphin *Journal* of Thursday, September 7, 1862: "This splendid and brave company, composed of our best and most enterprising citizens, left for Harrisburg on Monday afternoon (14th), and reported themselves at headquarters, but to their disappointment were not accepted. They were, however, ordered to return and hold themselves ready to move whenever needed. The following is a roll of the men who reported themselves, but there are a number of others who would have joined in, could they have procured horses."

Captain.
James Young.

First Lieutenant.
Henry J. Meily.

Second Lieutenant.
Jacob Landis.

Quartermaster.
John Raymond.

Cornet.
Henry Bumbach.

Privates.

Barnet, John J.
Books, Emanuel,
Brown, D. P.,
Balsbaugh, Solomon,
Croll, L. H.,
Croll, William A.,
Clark, Samuel H.,
Campbell, Joseph,
Christ, George, Jr.,
Earisman, Elias,

Eppler, John H.,
Etter, John,
Eshenauer, Christian,
Eves, Yetman,
Ebersole, Isaac M.,
*Fisher, E. H.,
Hendrickson, William D.,
Ginse, William,
Hinny, Henry,
Hake, Daniel J.,

*Dead.

Harry, Louis,
Jordan, Thomas,
Krumbine, J. S.,
Kauffman, B. S.,
Kauffman, H. B.,
*Kirlin, J. H.,
Laverty, J. D.,
Lame, Rev. J. S.,
Lamberton, W. H.,
*Landis, Solomon,
*Landis, Samuel,
*Martin, Wallace D.,
McClure, William F.,
McCreary, John,
Nisley, Jacob L.,

Nisley, Joseph H.,
Nisley, M. L.,
Peters, John,
*Rife, H. J.,
Strickler, Sol. N.,
Stiner, William,
Search, T. C.,
Swartz, Joseph W.,
Staub, John,
Teghtmeyer, D. W.,
Witherow, James P.,
Weistling, J. W.,
Weistling, B. J.,
Wilson, W. K.,
Yingst, John,
Zeiters, Solomon.

LVI.

1863.

The triumph of the rebel army at Fredericksburg, in December, 1862, and the still more signal success on the field of Chancellorsville, in the beginning of May, 1863, emboldened the rebel leader to again plan the invasion of the North. June 15th a brigade under General Jenkins entered Chambersburg, Pa. On the 16th the rebel General Ewell, with part of his corps, crossed the Potomac at Williamsport, Md. On the 24th and 25th the main body of the rebel army crossed the Potomac at Shepherdstown and Williamsport. The excitement in Pennsylvania was intense, and particularly in that portion of the State immediately menaced, in the Cumberland Valley and along the Susquehanna. Forts were thrown up at different points, and rifle pits were dug to command the fords on the river. Detachments of the rebels attacked the militia on the 28th at Columbia, when the bridge was burned to prevent them crossing the river, and at Carlisle, when the town was shelled. But by this time couriers had reached the scattered detachments of the rebel army, which was menaced by the Army of the Potomac, and recalled them to Gettysburg, where on the 1st, 2nd and 3rd of July a decisive battle was fought, in which the rebel army was beaten and compelled to return to Virginia.

MIDDLETOWN HOME GUARDS.

Most of the young and able-bodied men of Middletown, were, as the previously published rolls testify, in the army; but every remaining citi-

*Dead.

zen took up arms and organized themselves into "Home Guards." Two of the leading citizens, Henry Smith and Jacob Landis, went to the State Capitol and interviewed Governor Curtin. Two hundred and fifty muskets, and one thousand rounds of ammunition were secured from the State Arsenal, and three companies were organized.

List of names of Middletown Light Infantry, commanded by Captain B. W. Campbell:

First Lieutenant.
J. H. Landis.

Second Lieutenant.
D. W. Fisher.

First Sergeant.
R. C. Lauman.

Second Sergeant.
W. Siple.

Third Sergeant.
R. I. Young.

Privates.

W. N. Barron,
David James,
*Theophilus Davis,
*Joseph Antrim,
*Paul Airgood,
*R. H. Fairman,
C. F. Snyder,
L. W. May,
W. C. Barr,
*G. H. Irwin,
W. A. Snyder,
John Rife,
*O. L. Wieting,
*A. Atherton,
*A. E. Fairman,
*John Bair,
*David Hickernell,
*Siras Books,
*Daniel Gottshall,
Thos. McDevitt,

J. Fishburn,
John Beachler,
Alpheus Long,
J. H. Baker,
Alex Campbell,
Samuel Irely,
*Samuel Singer,
*Geo. Gottshall,
Valentine Ruth,
F. D. Ruth,
*Daniel Laughman,
Lewis D. Sheaffer,
Simon Peters,
Wm. Gottshall,
*Wm. Starr,
Henry Jenkins,
*Geo. W. Ackerman,
J. H. Schaeffer,
John Lynch,
James Hipple,

*Dead.

Robert Hickernell,
Val. Brumbach,
Jacob Davis,
*P. R. Singer,
Henry Schreiner,
Wm. Peters,
John Griffee,

Joseph Wilson,
J. R. Houser,
John Whisler,
Christian Flair,
Samuel Snyder,
H. Brandt,
Michael Brestle.

Of the second company, that commanded by Henry C. Raymond, I have no record.

The third numbered ninety men, whose muster roll is appended:

Captain.
John W. Klineline.

First Lieutenant.
Solomon Coover.

Second Lieutenant.
Caleb Roe.

First Sergeant.
H. C. Stehman.

Privates.

*Alleman, M. R.,
*Brestle, Michael,
Brestle, Joseph,
Books, Emanuel,
Barnet, T. T.,
Bachmoyer, John,
Baker, George,
Beane, V. B.,
Barnes, G. W.,
Bowers, Christian,
Campbell, Joseph,
Calor, J. K.,
Cobaugh, George A.,
Cobaugh, J. H.,
Croll, L. H.,
Croll, W. A.,
*Croll, G. L.,
Croll, J. A.,
Christ, George,

Davis, Gabriel,
Deckard, David,
Deckard, L. L.,
*Ehrehart, Rev. C. J.,
Ebersole, Abraham,
Ebersole, Isaac,
Ettele, G. W.,
*Etter, G. W.,
Eirely, John,
*Eshenauer, C.,
Fisher, Christian,
*Fisher, W. B.,
Gamble, John,
Gingerich, Elias,
Guise, William,
Hendrickson, W. D.,
Heinsling, John,
Henry, Will,
Heppich, John,

*Dead.

Hess, Jacob,
Hawn, Jacob,
Hill, William A.,
Hoffman, John,
Hummel, Levi,
Kendig, B. F.,
Kleindopf, William,
*Klink, Henry,
Krumbine, J. S.,
Lauman, G. A.,
Laverty, J. D.,
*Laverty, Rev. D. A. L.,
*Lauman, F. M.,
Lessing, D. P.,
*Long, Dr. R. P.,
*Long, Augustus,
Manning, Aaron,
Meily, H. J.,
*McCammon, E. G.,
McClure, William F.,
*Murphy, Robert,
Nisley, Jacob L.,
Nisley, Joseph H.,
Nisley, Martin L.,
*Irwin, Philip,

Noll, John,
*Nonamacher, J. W.,
*Peters, David,
Podlich, A.,
Rodfong, George,
Roop, David,
Roop, John,
Ross, John T.,
Reitzell, John Z.,
Selser, Samuel,
*Shadt, Philip,
Sinegar, Joseph,
Schurer, Frederick,
Shurger, John,
Strickler, Benjamin,
Strickler, G.,
Strickler, Solomon,
*Steinmetz, L. F.,
Teghtmoyer, J. L.,
Ulrich, John,
Weistling, B. J.,
*Weyl, Godfrey,
Yingst, John,
Yost, George.

The three companies guarded the river bank alternately, picketing and patrolling it from Middletown Ferry to below Buck Lock. The news of the victory at Gettysburg reached here on the evening of the 3rd of July, was received with the greatest joy, and the following day "The Fourth," was celebrated with unbounded enthusiasm.

LVII.

ORDERS.

FREE MASONS.

It was early in the settlement of this section of the country that the history of organized Free Masonry commences. Three years after the Declaration of Independence, and seven before the formation of the Grand Lodge of Philadelphia, to wit: in 1779, Perseverance Lodge, No. 21, A. Y. M., was organized in Lower Paxton township, Lancaster county.

NOTE: For assistance in compiling these chronicles I am greatly indebted to William H. Hickernell. For books and papers I am under obligations to Jacob L. Nisley, G. A. Lauman, Mrs. J. W. Stofer, Mrs. Maria McCord, John Fratts,

Prince Edwin Lodge.

In 1870 a meeting of Masonic brethren, members of different lodges, was held in Middletown, and after an interchange of opinion, it was resolved to make application to the Grand Lodge of Pennsylvania for a warrant for a new lodge. The subjoined paper was prepared and signed, as follows:

Middletown, Oct. 4, 1870.

We the undersigned Master Mastons, agree to withdraw from lodges of which we are now members, and join in the formation of a new lodge, to be located in Middletown, Dauphin county, Pa.:

Seymour Raymond,
George H. Lenhart,
Daniel J. Hake,
Charles H. Zigler,
George A. Cobaugh,
James J. Hubley,
John A. Witman,
Simon C. Peters,
George M. Zigler,
Ephraim B. Cobaugh,
Henry J. Rife,

Redsecker I. Young,
Joseph Campbell,
Joseph H. Nisley,
Delanson J. Young,
Hiram B. Draucker,
Jacob L. Nisley,
Thomas Montgomery,
James Young,
Henry Ettele,
Walter H. Kendig.

Those who signed made application to their respective lodges for certificates of withdrawal, which were granted. They then made application to the Grand Lodge of Pennsylvania, for a warrant of constitution, empowering them to meet as a regular lodge at Middletown, to be called "Prince Edwin Lodge," recommending Brothers Joseph H. Nisley for first W. M., Brother Seymour Raymond for first S. W., and Brother George H. Lenhart for first J. W.

At the annual meeting of the Grand Lodge in Philadelphia, December 27, A. D. 1870, the application was approved and the R. W. S. M., Robert E. Lamberton, designated Monday, March 27, A. D. 1871, as the time when the lodge should be constituted.

On the specified day Prince Edwin Lodge, No. 486, was solemnly consecrated and constituted by Robert A. Lamberton, R. W. G. M.; Samuel C. Perkins, R. W. D. G. M.; Alfred R. Potter, R. W. G. S. W.; Robert Clarke, R. W. G. J. W.; John Thompson, R. W. G. S., and a large number of other brethren.

---

and Jacob Rife, Jr. For valuable information I am indebted to Joseph A. Peters, Jacob Embich, Wm. Drabenstadt, John S. Fishburn, Jesse Mattis, Jacob Ridley, James Campbell, I. K. Longenecker, W. Stipe, David Snirk, Michael Stewart, Alex. Campbell, Hiram Parson, B. Shoch, V. Baumbach, H. Hippie, John L. Whisler, George H. Irwin, Jacob Landis and others.

[Each roll, being before published, was submitted to the survivors of the organization referred to. If any errors have occurred it is owing to the interest manifested by those who, after being solicited, failed to aid in making them correct.]

The officers installed were: Joseph H. Nisley, W. M.; Seymour Raymond, S. W.; George H. Lenhart, J. W.; James Young, T.; Walter Kendig, S.

ODD FELLOWS—TRIUNE LODGE, No. 307.

This lodge, so called because it was made up of members from three lodges, viz: Nos. 60, 70 and 160, was started March 20, 1848, and instituted a few weeks later. The charter members were:

R. C. Bates,
John S. Boyd,
C. W. Churchman,
Joshua Fackler,
John P. Farrington,
Frederick Fortney,
James Hipple,
Samuel Jenkins,

R. P. Long,
Charles McLain,
John Raymond,
John Ringland,
Mark Stauffer,
Thomas H. Totten,
George F. Witman,
James Young,

John Zimmerman.

Its first officers were: John P. Farrington, N. G.; Frederick Fortney, V. G.; John Ringland, S.; Thomas H. Totten, A. S.; John Raymond, T.

The first meetings were held in the hall over Augustus Shott's store, (southwest corner Union and Ann streets). In 1852 the lodge removed to "Rambler's Hall" (northeast corner Union and Railroad).

From various causes the membership dwindled away and the lodge finally ceased to exist. It was reorganized in January, 1868, and chartered February 15, 1868. The charter members were:

William Hinkle,
John Orendorf,
M. Orendorf,
Charles McLain,
Geo. F. Whitman,
Charles H. Ziegler,

M. G. Cryder,
D. W. Miller,
W. D. Starr,
John D. Peters,
David P. Lescure,
Geo. W. Farrington,

John. Lutz.

Its first officers were: Charles H. Ziegler, N. G.; M. G. Cryder, V. G.; G. W. Farrington, S.; John D. Peters, A. S.; Charles McLain, T.

In 1886 the lodge took into consideration the advisability of erecting a hall, and June 19th, a building committee was appointed. July 29th the lodge concluding to build, instructed the committee, consisting of seven members, viz: J. C. Lingle, A. J. Lerch, J. S. Keever, David A. Detweiler, Jacob S. Brandt, H. B. Campbell and Cyrus Stager, to commence operations on land owned by them at the northeast corner of Emaus and Catherine streets.

CHRONICLES OF MIDDLETOWN. 253

Tuesday, September 21, 1886, the cornerstone was laid. It contains a small lot of United States scrip currency; a copper tablet, inscribed with the names of the then President of the United States, Governor of Pennsylvania and acting officers of the lodge, and copies of the Middletown *Press* and *Journal*.

The building, a handsome three-story brick, mansard roofed edifice, costing $7,000 was (July 2, 1887) completed.

UNITED AMERICAN MECHANICS.

The Order of United American Mechanics, Middletown Council, No. 84, was organized May 22, 1848, by the judiciary committee of the State Council of Pennsylvania, viz:

Montgomery Carracher, Marietta, Pa.; Jacob S. Roath, Maytown, Pa.; A. H. Shott, Portsmouth, Pa. It met in Mrs. Meesy's frame building, on Main street, over the Nisley Brothers' hardware store. Its charter members were:

William De Witt,
Edmund S. Bargelt,
Elisha McCammon,
Henry D. Smith,
Daniel Funk,
Benjamin Eby,
William McClure,
Jacob Strouse,
Albert Kob,

James Ringland,
George Rodfong,
Hiram Pierce,
Le Rue Metzger,
William Starr,
Alfred Putt,
Jeremiah Rohrer,
Henry Lehman,
Abraham Rife.

This council, which at one time counted among its members nearly two hundred citizens of Middletown, dissolved about 1861.

Golden Centre Council, No. 193, O. U. A. M., was organized February 15, 1869, and met in Rambler's Hall. The charter members were:

Wm. H. Embick,
Abraham Rife,
John J. Rife,
William Forney,
Benjamin F. Bretz,
A. Fralich,
John Fishburn,

Reuben Snavely,
Ammon W. Beard,
Edmund Lerch,
George W. Ettele,
Geo. W. Eshenower,
John Heppich,
C. J. Ramsey,

John E. Haak.

This council dissolved in 1876.

JR. O. U. A. M.—MIDDLETOWN COUNCIL, No. 156.

This council was organized August 17, 1875. The charter members were:

C. N. Raymond,
J. H. Keever,
Jacob Dunkle,

Jos. Fishburn,
J. A. Ebersole,
Frank Winnagle,

Jos. Bollinger,
Jacob Earisman,
F. P. Bailey,
H. Diehm,
H. W. Schurtz,

Wm. Garreth,
John Gephart,
Frank Stipe,
W. Kurtz,
Thomas Embick,
George Mansberger.

Knights of Pythias—Middletown Lodge.

Middletown Lodge, No. 268, K. of P., was instituted October 5, 1870, with Jos. H. Nisley, J. H. Bletz, B. H. Benner, B. W. Sheaffer, W. F. McClure, H. C. Raymond, Geo. H. Koons, Augustus Rouch, Lewis Harry, W. T. Morehead, David W. Fisher, Frank Ziegler and Geo. M. Ziegler as charter members.

The first officers were: Jos. H. Nisley, V. P.; J. H. Bletz, W. C.; B. H. Benner, V. C.; B. W. Sheaffer, R. C.; W. F. McClure, F. S.; H. C. Raymond, B.; Geo. H. Koons, G.; Augustus Rouch, I. S.; Lewis Harry, O. S.

On the night of institution thirty-three additional members were initiated. The lodge started out with one of the finest sets of paraphernalia in the State, although there were, at the time, 268 lodges under the control of the "Grand Jurisdiction of Pennsylvania." It was free from debt and its progress during the first few years of its existence was satisfactory, but the financial depression existing all over the United States from 1873 to 1879, seriously affected it, and November 1, 1876, the lodge surrendered its charter and became extinct.

In the latter part of the year 1884, A. J. Lerch, John W. Klineline and J. W. Bletz, having secured the names of fifty-two members, applied for a new charter or the renewal of the old one. Their request was acceded to, and December 3rd of that year a new charter, retaining the old number of the lodge and containing the names of J. H. Bletz, P. C. Elberti, John W. Klineline, John Beachler, John H. Baker, A. J. Lerch, R. M. Zearing, E. Earisman, James Ralston, Eugene Walton, S. L. Yetter, D. C. Ulrich and Samuel Brandt as charter members, was granted. The lodge was reinstituted the same day, with the following officers: J. H. Bletz, P. C.; P. C. Elberti, C. C.; John W. Klineline, V. C.; John C. Beachler, M. at A.; A. J. Lerch, K. of R. and L.; R. M. Zearing, M. of F.; E. Earisman, M. of E.; James Ralston, I. G.; Eugene Walton, O. G.; trustees, S. L. Yetter, D. C. Ulrich, Samuel Brandt.

Ancient Order of Foresters—Court Ivy.

Court Ivy, No. 6797, A. O. F., was instituted in Middletown, April 30, 1881, by William J. Carr, D. H. C. R., assisted by George Taylor, Robert Benson and S. E. Richardson, all of whom were members of Court Equality, No. 6359, at McKeesport, Pa. The charter members were:

J. Senor Keever,
James Moore,
Donald McDonald,
Wm. Gallagher,
Scott Stevenson,
Robert Mitchell,
D. A. Hatz,
C. A. Ebersole,
George Graw,
H. J. Miller,
J. H. Keever,
George J. Robson,
Charles Fleming,
Jas. W. Bramwell,
John P. Siders,
C. W. Britwinder,
D. A. Detwiler,

S. S. Selser,
Geo. W. Fisher,
D. W. Smeltz,
John Wood,
Joseph Rigby,
J. Smith Keever,
M. Brestle,
Ed. S. Cobaugh,
S. L. Yetter,
J. W. Eshelman,
Samuel Singer,
Wm. H. Bradbury,
Henry Smith,
Christ. Hershey,
W. H. Beane,
F. E. Irwin,
H. H. Shellenberger.

IMPROVED ORDER OF RED MEN—RED WING TRIBE, No. 170,

was instituted in Middletown, April 11, 1872. It met at Rambler's Hall. Its first officers were: Prophet, P. C. Elberti; Sachem, Jacob Andrews; Senior Sagamore, Henry Anthony; Junior Sagamore, S. H. Milligan; Chief of Records, George H. McNeal; Keeper of Wampum, John H. Crown; Past Sachems, D. L. Stoud, P. C. Elberti. The charter members were:

F. A. Ziegler,
D. L. Stoud,
P. C. Elberti,
Jacob Andrews,
Geo. H. McNeal,
John H. Crown,
John L. Whisler,
John L. Sheetz,
Henry A. Anthony,
Nicholas Rehrer,

Daniel B. Snyder,
Reuben Snavely,
Henry Shetters,
John Irely,
S. H. Milligan,
B. F. Bretz,
Samuel Mateer,
A. W. Beard,
Jacob Schadt,
Jacob Brestle.

After an existence of over nine years the tribe finally disbanded, September 30, 1881.

ROYAL ARCANUM—SWATARA COUNCIL, No. 949,

was organized in Middletown, February 1, 1886. The charter members were:

A. S. Matheson,
Arthur King,
John Croll,
Edward Croll,
Leroy J. Wolfe,

J. H. Cobaugh,
S. S. Clair,
Elias Earisman,
Alvan McNair,
George S. Ettla,

W. L. Kauffman,   H. H. Shellenberger,
C. E. Pease,   J. H. Baker,
L. C. Keim,   J. W. Few.

Its first officers were: A. King, Regent; S. S. Clair, V. Regent; G. A. Lauman, Orator; W. L. Kauffman, Secretary; J. H. Cobaugh, Collector; Geo. D. Russell, Treasurer; Dr. C. E. Pease, P. Regent; J. Jos. Campbell, Guide; A. McNair, Warden; L. C. Keim, Sentry; J. Croll, Chaplain.

IMPROVED ORDER OF HEPTASOPHS—MIDDLETOWN CONCLAVE, No. 101, I. O. H.,

was organized in Middletown, June 6, 1885, with the following charter members:

W. H. Beane, M. D.,   E. S. Baker,
J. W. Rewalt,   L. C. Nisley,
C. W. Raymond,   A. S. Matheson,
Geo. S. Ettla,   Jas. H. Matheson,
Jacob R. Myers,   Martin Kendig,
H. H. Kline,   S. H. Ney,
C. A. Landis,   W. S. Fortney,
John A. Borland,   Leroy J. Wolfe,
John Hatz,   C. S. Roshon,
D. H. Bucher,   A. J. Lerch,
                Rev. Maris Graves.

The conclave disbanded June 22, 1887.

KNIGHTS OF THE GOLDEN EAGLE—SUSQUEHANNA CASTLE, No. 143.

The first preliminary meeting previous to organizing a castle in Middletown was held in Smith's Hall, October 20, 1886. A. J. Lerch was made chairman, C. A. Landis, secretary, and John H. Baker, treasurer. October 27th sixty new members were admitted, and November 3rd eighteen more. On the evening of November 10th forty-three of the members proceeded to Harrisburg and had the degrees conferred on them by Harmony Castle, No. 53, and November 17th the following charter officers were installed: P. C., W. M. Lauman; N. C., A. Lerch; V. C., J. Jos. Campbell; M. of R., C. A. Landis; C. of E., E. M. Raymond; K. of E., John H. Baker; S. H., John C. Buechler; H. P., F. B. Hampton; V. H., G. W. Bowman; W. B., R. F. Dasher; W. C., W. F. Arnold; Ens., E. S. Baker; Esq., Jas. R. Ralston; First G., W. S. Evans; Second G., H. Dietrich; Trustees, W. M. Lauman, H. L. Rehrer, J. H. Longsdorf; Representative to Grand Lodge, W. M. Lauman.

G. A. R.

The Grand Army of the Republic, an order whose ranks have no source of supply outside of the rapidly diminishing number of those who

Citizens' Bank.

fought side by side in the nation's struggle for existence, was founded by General Stevenson, of Illinois, assisted by a few companions who served with him.

POST NO. 78.

Post No. 78, G. A. R., was instituted at Middletown, August 26, 1867, by Gov. John W. Geary. The charter is signed by Louis Wagner, Grand Commander, and James Given, Assistant Adjutant General. The charter members were:

Jacob Rohrer,
David Shirk,
William H. Siple,
Joseph A. Peters,
James H. Stanley,
William H. Embick,
George L. Hemperly,

William D. Starr,
Jacob Keller,
Daniel J. Boynton,
Lewis Willson,
John H. Snyder,
John Hogendobler,
Samuel Snyder.

After an existence of two years the post disbanded in 1869.

WILLIAM STARR POST, NO. 78,

was reorganized by order of the Department Commander, by C. C. Hartline, May 28, 1877. The preliminary meeting was held under the trees on the lot where the new Lutheran Church now stands. The post was instituted in the Masonic Hall, on Ann street, June 22, 1877. The charter members were:

J. H. Stanley,
David A. Stephens,
William Hampton,
J. H. Wampshire,
John Houser,
William H. Spayd,
D. J. Boynton,

Jacob A. Embick,
J. K. Meanig,
Calvin Garrett,
George F. Mish,
John K. Weaver,
John S. Keever,
John L. Sheaffer.

The charter is signed by S. Irwin Given, Department Commander, and J. M. Vanderslice, Assistant Adjutant General.

LVIII.

MUSICAL ORGANIZATIONS.

THE MIDDLETOWN CORNET BAND.

This band was organized in 1855, as follows: Jeremiah Rohrer, Eb bugle; John Christ, Eb cornet; Valentine Dister (leader) Bb cornet; Henry Smith, Bb cornet; Joseph H. Nisley, alto; Henry J. Rife, tenor; John McMurtrie, trombone; John Landis, tuba bass; Reuben Miller, tuba; Charles Allen, tenor sax horn; Frank Peebles, also sax horn;

Abner Croll, bass sax horn; Thomas Humes, tenor drum; George Cobaugh, bass drum; Christian Fisher, cymbals. They met in Smith's Hall.

One incident connected with their history may be worth mention. They once proposed having a concert; it was to come off on a Monday night. Much to their disgust, a band from Harrisburg gave a performance on the Saturday preceding. By an appeal to local pride many of the town's people were induced to remain away from this rival exhibition, but those who did go, were enchanted with the skill of a certain youthful drummer, who accompanied the organization.

This rather disconcerted the Middletown band, who could offer no such attraction, but they resolved on securing his services themselves, and forthwith posted the town with bills, advertising, among other features, "The Infant Drummer." Unfortunately he could not be got. The boys were struck with consternation; it was too late to change the program; the town was excited over the reports of the performance of the aforesaid drummer, and a failure to produce him, would be attended with consequences too dire to contemplate. At the last moment a happy thought struck one of their number—a gleam of light shone o'er the troubled waves—he confided it to the others—it was a desperate expedient, but they adopted it.

Night arrived; Smith's Hall was filled to suffocation; even the stairways were thronged, all anxious to see the youthful prodigy of whom they had heard such glowing accounts. At the appointed hour the curtain rose and the band commenced to play. In front of them, standing on a big drygoods box (as his celebrated predecessor had been), wearing a diminutive cap and a soldier coat several sizes too small, with a drum strapped in front of him, on which (with imperturable countenance), he accompanied his fellows, stood the colossal form of our genial friend, Abner Croll.

The audience stared spellbound for an instant, and then as the gigantic absurdity of the affair struck them, burst into a hurricane of applause, hats were thrown up, handkerchiefs waved, and voices, canes, feet and hands made for several minutes a perfect pandemonium. It goes without saying, that Ab's expedient prevented a fiasco, and that the concert was a success.

This band, after an existence of eight years dissolved.

BAUMBACH'S BRASS BAND

was started in 1858. Its first members were:

Val. Baumbach,
Henry Baumbach,
Guido Baumbach (leader),
Reuben Miller,
Benj. Ashenfelter,
Felix B. Schraedley,

W. Wechter,
John C. Beachler,
George McCauley,
Jacob Landis,
George Horn,
John Embich,

James P. Hipple.

CHRONICLES OF MIDDLETOWN. 259

They applied for a charter October 24, 1868, and were incorporated December 3rd of that year, under the title of the "Original Harmonic Band of Middletown." The charter members were:

Wm. H. Duhling,
Stewart McCord,
F. B. Schraedley,
Guido Baumbach,
William Condran,
William Forney,

Nathaniel Baker,
John C. Beachler,
Adam Baumbach,
Jacob Embich,
Val. Baumbach,
James Hipple,

J. A. Peters.

In 1875 the title was changed to "Liberty Band," Valentine Baumbach (leader) Eb cornet; John Preston, solo Bb cornet; Elmer Shoop, Eb cornet; Henry Baumbach, first Bb cornet; Charles Baumbach, second Bb cornet; John Selser, third Bb cornet; Henry V. Baumbach, Eb clarionet; Guido Baumbach, solo Bb clarionet; William J. Tighe (musical director), first Bb clarionet; William Wallace, first Bb clarionet; John S. Gates, solo alto; Geary Mathias, first alto; John Hipple, second alto; Samuel Davis, third alto; John Leiby, trombone; R. W. Mowry, trombone; Frank Davis, first tenor; George Neiman, second tenor; John Hatfield, baritone; David Giberson, first bass; Scott Sides, second bass; Harry Draugher, bass drum; Perry Hipple, snare drum; John Stevenson, snare drum; Charles Houser, drum major.

The Junior Mechanics' Band

owes its inception to George Bowman. He, being a member of Middletown Council, Jr. O. U. A. M., fancied that there was enough musical talent in the council to start a band. April 5, 1884, he broached the idea to some of his friends, they embraced the suggestion with enthusiasm, and on the 11th of the month the band was organized.

Choral Association.

This organization, comprising about thirty members, was formed in 1874, and met in Smith's Hall, Abner Croll, leader; George L. Fisher, pianist. They gave several concerts, the last one at Smith's hall, in 1878. The society soon afterwards dissolved.

Gates' Orchestra

was formed in 1875. The members were: John L. Gates, first violin; Valentine Baumbach, second violin and clarionette; Guido Baumbach, bass viol; Henry Baumbach, trombone.

North Ward Band

met at Jacob Hatz's residence (southeast corner of Race and Main streets), July 4, 1876, and organized as follows: H. D. Dasher, President; W. A. Howdenshall, Vice-President; Henry Hatz, Treasurer;

CHRONICLES OF MIDDLETOWN.

Members.

John Aungst,
James Billet,
H. D. Dasher,
Samuel Davis,
George Eshenauer,
F. Eshenauer,
W. A. Howdenshall,
Henry Hatz,

John Hatz,
David Hatz,
John Keener,
Jacob Kleindopf,
Martin McNeal,
C. J. Sinnegar,
J. L. Sinnegar,
Samuel Selser.

They received and paid for their instruments, August 1, 1876. Their teacher was Felix B. Schraedley. They disbanded in 1879.

Colored Band.

This band was organized in 1882 by Samuel Stanton and Samuel Harley, with the following members:

S. Harley (leader),
William Harley, Sr.,
James Davis,
Louis Harley,
William Harley, Jr.,
Enos Banks,
Thomas Dorsey,

Jonathan Shultz,
George Stanton,
Christian Stanton,
Levi Contee,
Samuel Stanton,
James Moore,
James Clark,
John Only.

Lombardi Parlor Orchestra.

August 19th, 1885, a social club consisting of thirteen boys was formed, and styled the "Lombardi Club." On the 26th of November following, four of its members in connection with a few of their friends, formed the musical organization known as the Lombardi Parlor Orchestra. Its construction was: Miss Mame Landis, first violin; Miss Sue S. Campbell, first violin; Luther Nisley, first violin; Eugene Laverty, second violin; Edward L. Croll, flute; George S. Mish, flute; Christ. G. Nissley, cornet; Grant Shirk, trombone; Miss Rebecca Croll, Miss Jennie Laverty, accompanists.

The Arion Glee Club.

Instituted in 1884. The members were: I. O. Nissley, first tenor; William Keever, second tenor; A. H. Reider, first bass; George Klineline, second bass.

Polyhymnia.

January 26, 1886, a party of fifty-four young people met in the Presbyterian Church and organized as a musical association, with L. H. Park, leader; G. L. Fisher, pianist, and J. H. Baxtresser, business manager. A committee consisting of L. H. Park, I. O. Nissley and William Keever was appointed to select a place for holding meetings. February 8th, the High School building having been secured, the society, now numbering sixty-two, met there and at the suggestion of Professor Fisher adopted the name "Polyhymnia." May 7th, gave a concert at the Opera House. Receipts, $45.25. October 7th, after the summer vacation, the society reorganized with forty-six members.

January 6, 1887, J. H. Baxtresser resigned and A. H. Reider was elected in his stead.

February 4th, assisted by the Liberty Band, gave a concert in aid of workmen who lost tools at the destruction of the Middletown Car Works. Receipts, $148.50. May 13th, seventy members gave a concert in the Opera House to invited guests and adjourned for the summer.

ALMOND'S ORCHESTRA.

Started in 1886. Its members were: M. J. Almond (leader), first violin; Henry Baumbach, clarionette; W. T. Harley, second violin; Charles Neiman, first cornet; Charles Baumbach, second cornet; John Leiby, trombone; Guido Baumbach, bass viol.

LIX.

THE MIDDLETOWN CEMETERY

is at the northern extension of Union street, on the brow of a hill overlooking a wide extent of country. The corporation controlling it was chartered August, 1855, and until Portsmouth was consolidated with the borough, was known as the "Middletown Cemetery Association."

The petition for its establishment represents that the subscribers have associated themselves together and purchased eight acres of land in the vicinity of Middletown, for the purpose of converting the same into a cemetery, and desire that they may be incorporated under the title aforesaid, &c. The signers to the petition were:

Joseph Ross,
Archibald Wieting,
Daniel Kendig,
Brua Cameron,
J. Croll,
Philip Irwin,
James Young,
Raymond & Kendig,
Adolphus Fisher,
George Crist,

Philip Zimmerman,
George Rodfong,
Christian Fisher,
John Jos. Walborn,
Joshua Heppich,
John Landis,
John Monaghan,
Jacob L. Nisley,
E. J. Ramsey,
J. S. Watson,
John Care.

262   CHRONICLES OF MIDDLETOWN.

October 1st the association organized under their charter and elected Joseph Ross, president, and John S. Watson, George Crist, E. J. Ramsey, James Young and Adolphus Fisher, managers.

October 21st the cemetery was dedicated and a large concourse of people attended. A hymn, composed for the occasion, was sung, after which prayer was offered by Rev. Benjamin Sadtler; a chapter from the Bible was read by Rev. E. H. Thomas; Rev. J. Winebrenner delivered an address, and the ceremonies concluded with prayer by Rev. Valentine Gray.

The first interment (in April, 1855) was that of D. F. Boynton, a child of D. J. Boynton; the first adult (also in April) was James Ringland, a brother of Dr. John Ringland.

In the spring of 1886, James Young donated to the association a tract of land north of and adjoining the cemetery, containing about one and one-half acres.

At the left of the main entrance stands the neat building occupied by the superintendent. The grounds are surrounded by a high pale fence, are tastefully laid out, most of the lots being enclosed either by iron railings or stone curbs, and decorated with flowers and shrubbery. There are many handsome monuments and tombstones, and broad, smooth, neatly graveled walks and carriageways give access to every portion of the cemetery.

The officers of the association from its organization to 1887 have been:

Presidents—Joseph Ross, Dr. Mercer Brown, Adolphus Fisher, John Hendrickson, Joseph H. Nisley.

Secretaries—John Monaghan, Dr. John Ringland.

Treasurers—Daniel Kendig, D. W. Stehman, W. A. Croll.

Superintendents of Cemetery—Daniel Lehman, George Houser, John W. Parker, David L. Smith.

Included in the list of interments are those of many soldiers, some nineteen of whom were in the war of 1812, and one (Colonel Burd), served prior to the Revolution. There are many other soldiers' graves in the old forsaken burying grounds of the town. Men who fought in all the wars of the republic lie here; but most of their resting places being unmarked the location thereof is forgotten.

BANKS.

THE NATIONAL BANK OF MIDDLETOWN

was organized May 12, 1832, and was called the "Bank of Middletown." In 1864 it was changed into a National Bank. Its first president was Benjamin Jordan, who held this position from 1832 tilll 1841. He was succeeded by Dr. Mercer Brown, and he in turn, in 1854, by George Smuller. Mr. Smuller died in 1882, and J. Donald Cameron was chosen president, Seymour Raymond, vice-president, and Daniel W. Stehman,

CHRONICLES OF MIDDLETOWN. 263

cashier. Gen. Simon Cameron was cashier from 1832 to 1850, when his son, J. Donald Cameron (United States Senator), succeeded him. The first teller of the bank was John Croll, whose successor was John Monaghan, in 1856. Mr. Monaghan died in 1869, and was succeeded by Daniel W. Stehman, who held the office until he was elected cashier, and H. C. Stehman, teller. J. C. Bomberger, afterwards owner of the Mechanics' Bank, at Harrisburg, was some years earlier assistant teller in this bank. The bank finally closed its doors September 10, 1894.

THE FARMERS' BANK

was organized March 27, 1882, in Col. James Young's office on South Union street, with the following board of directors, viz: B. S. Peters, A. Dissinger, James Young, J. L. Longenecker, V. C. Coolbaugh, M. G. Keller and J. W. Rife. B. S. Peters was elected president, Lee H. Nissley, cashier, and A. H. Reider, teller. The bank was chartered April 12, 1882, with a capital stock of $50,000. The bank remained in this building until July 6, 1899, when, having purchased the building formerly occupied by the First National Bank, at the corner of Union and Emaus streets, they moved there. In July, 1894, A. H. Reider was elected cashier, and M. H. Gingerich, teller. The bank has had a successful and prosperous career, capital remaining the same, with surplus and individual profits at the present time (1905) of over $80,000. It was for many years the only bank in town.

THE CITIZENS' NATIONAL BANK.

Stockholders of the Citizens' National Bank met in the Young Men's Christian Association parlors on North Union street, April 26, 1905, and elected the following board of directors, viz: J. W. Rewalt, Dr. D. W. C. Laverty, W. R. Fisher, C. F. Beard, H. R. Saul, H. S. Roth, Josiah Foltz, C. M. Foltz and H. W. Bausman. The board organized May 2, 1905, by electing J. W. Rewalt, president; H. S. Roth, vice-president; Harry A. Bell, cashier, and Abraham Geyer, teller. It was chartered July 8, 1905, and immediately commenced the erection of a bank building on North Union street, north of the Philadelphia & Reading Railroad passenger station. Upon the completion of this edifice, November 1, 1905, the bank commenced business.

NEWSPAPERS.

The Middletown *Argus* was the first newspaper printed in town, and was established in 1834, by a Mr. Wilson. It was an independent and family journal. Mr. Wilson did the editorial work and his wife helped to set the type. The office was located on Main street, east of Pine street. It was discontinued in 1835.

The Middletown *Emporium* was established in 1850, by William Hemlock. It was printed as the corner of Pine and Main streets, and after being published for a year and a half, stopped.

The *Central Engine* was published here in 1851 and 1852, by H. S. Fisher, but the material was purchased and the paper merged into the *Swatara Gem*, in July 1853, by J. W. Stofer. This was a sheet of four pages and five columns to a page. In August, 1854, Mr. Stofer enlarged it to six columns and printed it on a sheet twenty-two by thirty-three inches. In August, 1856, he sold the paper and office to Benjamin Whitman, who retaining its size, changed its name to *The Dauphin Journal*. In September, 1856, a co-partnership was formed between Messrs. Whitman and Stofer and they continued to publish the paper jointly, enlarging and changing it to a quarto form. In January, 1857, Mr. Whitman retired, and J. W. Stofer became again the sole proprietor. In November, 1870, the paper was enlarged to seven columns, and printed on a sheet twenty-four by thirty-eight inches, the title being changed to the *Middletown Journal*. In 1885 it was purchased by A. L. Etter and a few weeks later was enlarged to a 30x44 sheet, being changed to an eight volume quarto. On December 1, 1890, Mr. Etter commenced the publication of a *Daily Journal* in addition to the weekly.

The Middletown *Press*, an eight-column newspaper of four pages, was established July 16, 1881, by J. R. Hoffer. Its editor was J. E. Hoffer. On March 28, 1882, the paper was sold to I. O. Nissley, who enlarged and still conducts it.

LX.

BIOGRAPHICAL.

COLONEL JAMES YOUNG.

One of the remarkable men connected with Middletown's history was Col. James Young, who was born at Swatara Hill, near Middletown, July 25, 1820, and died May 4, 1895.

His ancestors acted somewhat prominently in pre-Revolutionary times, and during that conflict. His father was born in Berks county, Pa., in 1781, and from 1820 to 1834 kept the stage house at Swatara Hill. In 1835 he took charge of the Washington House, corner of Union and Ann streets. James received a common school education and then helped his father in the hotel. The little money that he earned he saved until he had an opportunity to invest it. The first hundred dollars he made he purchased a horse and ran a hack between Middletown and Hummelstown. Soon after he was the owner of two horses and a hack, which he used in the transportation of passengers and freight between the points named.

After acquiring several hundred dollars he went to Dickinson College and applied for admission as a student, but finding that it would take much more than he possessed to graduate, he soon left and returned to his father.

At the age of nineteen he invested his savings in a canal boat, and took charge thereof, running for nearly a year between Hollidaysburg and Philadelphia. He then opened a lumber yard in town, to which he soon after added a coal yard.

About this time Gen. Simon Cameron* interested himself in him and made him a director in his bank. He remained in this capacity for over thirty years.

Seeing opportunities for profit in railroad building, which was then active, he took contracts for furnishing supplies to the Pennsylvania Railroad and did a large business. For eight successive years he furnished all the ties and wood used by that road between Harrisburg and Philadelphia. He also furnished the wood and ties for the Northern Central Railway for ten years, before and during the Civil War. When a second track was laid on the latter road he contracted for a portion of it and was engaged in it for years, having given up the lumber and coal business, in which he had been very successful.

In 1859, he purchased a valuable limestone quarry at Leaman Place, Lancaster county, and from it, for twenty-five years, supplied a large part of the stone for building the bridges and abutments of the Pennsylvania Railroad. This also yielded him a handsome revenue.

These are but a few of the enterprises in which Mr. Young engaged, until from the small sum which he had gained by his own efforts, he became the possessor of large wealth. He was emphatically one of the self-made men of this country, having been the architect of his own fortune.

In 1858 he purchased a farm of about two hundred acres, near Middletown. To this tract he kept adding, year after year, until his farming property exceeded fourteen hundred acres, exclusive of 400 acres of pasture land, known as the "Round Top."

His main farming tracts comprised land formerly occupied by thirteen farms, and agricultural experts deemed it one of the finest bodies of cultivated land in America.

He also paid great attention to the breeding of cattle, and his herd of Jersey cows was reported to be one of the finest known. Said one historian: "Perhaps nowhere in the United States are to be found a series

---

*Gen. Simon Cameron resided here for over twenty years, and here his son Donald, was born.

of farms which, for all that represents farming in the highest order, in every detail, equal those located near the borough of Middletown, Pa., and owned by Col. James Young, of that place."

Visitors from all over the country, from even the most remote States and Territories of the Union, Presidents of the United States, Governors of States and distinguished men from almost every walk of life, in this country, and from the nobility of Europe, were frequent and admiring observers. Among those who have visited these farms are the Duke of Sutherland, Gen. Simon Cameron, Major Luther Bent, of Steelton; Frank Thompson, First Vice-President of the Pennsylvania Railroad; Charles Pugh, General Manager, and a number of leading English stockholders in the same road; Hon. Salmon P. Chase, Chief Justice of the United States; Andrew Carnegie, Henry G. Phipps and Edward G. Bailey, members of the firm of Carnegie, Phipps & Co., of Pittsburg, Pa.; General U. S. Grant, James D. Allen and Eugene De Zellenkoff, English and Russian Commissioners to the Centennial Exposition; Mr. Congosto, Consul from Spain; Mr. Coleman, editor of the London *Field*. (These last four gentlemen, some instructed by their governments, others voluntarily, wrote on their return home, elaborate articles describing these farms, the high standard attained and excellent management.) W. D. Garrison, of Litchfield, England; Maj. Gen. W. S. Hancock, Joseph R. Greatorex, William H. Cheetham, Arthur W. Hutton (the latter three from England), delegates to the world's convention of stenographers; the Supreme Judges of Pennsylvania, and many others too numerous to mention, who were surprised to find them under the management of a man who had received no educational advantages, who was a novice in the beginning, and nevertheless the high position he occupied as a farmer was remarkable. They could not understand how a man who was identified with several of the largest enterprises in the country, could at the same time find opportunity to build up a system of farm operations that was admired and appreciated by the leading people of the civilized world.

Colonel Young was President of the American Tube & Iron Company, a director in the Lochiel Rolling Mill Company, a director, for over thirty-three years, in the Harrisburg, Portsmouth, Mount Joy & Lancaster Railroad Company, director (and organizer) of the Farmers' Bank, Middletown; of the First National Bank, Steelton; Merchants' National Bank, Harrisburg; President of the Cameron Furnace Company, a stockholder in the Pennsylvania Steel Works, a director of the Lancaster City Electric Railroad, of the Harrisburg, Steelton & Middletown Electric Railroad, and a member of the State Board of Agriculture.

That he was a man of great executive ability is obvious. Stern and inflexible in guarding his business interests, he was, nevertheless, a man of generous heart and marked public spirit, freely aiding the really deserving, and never withholding liberal support to promising enterprises conducted by capable men.

www.ingramcontent.com/pod-product-compliance
Lightning Source LLC
Chambersburg PA
CBHW062001220426
43662CB00010B/1192